Acting

wcb Wm. C. Brown Co. Publishers
Dubuque, Iowa

Graphic Illustrations
Ellis M. Pryce-Jones

Contents

Acting training is serious work, not grim but serious. The authors of this book respect that seriousness which is to the great advantage of the readers. Because we are all actors of sorts, as revealed by J. Alfred Prufrock's famous line:

> There will be time, there will be time,
> To prepare a face to meet the faces that you meet; . . . .
>   T. S. Eliot

many uninformed people in this country look upon acting as a natural activity of all people, a gift with which all of us are blessed. The endless stories about girls with pretty faces and good-looking legs sitting in drug stores waiting to be discovered as Hollywood actresses add to our misconception of the actor's craft. So does the fact that personalities famous for their skills in politics or sports can move right into films as full-fledged actors when they have never been trained in that profession. These violations of the art of acting, this insult to the actor's craft, make the training of actors in this country all the more difficult. Although we honor and respect the training necessary to develop athletes and dancers, we do not honor the same need for actors. Somehow we deny the seriousness of the actor's profession. Happily, this book attempts to counter such an attitude.

One of the most significant principles practiced in the training of actors is that "imagination is in the choice." That principle means that an actor must consider a host of options or alternatives from which he selects the most appropriate as the proper behavior for the character he is portraying. His job is to think of the variety of possibilities, try them, and then with the director's help choose one way as the most suitable. The exercising of his imagination is not mystical, magical, or fantastic; it is a realistic solution to a realistic problem. The way an actor chooses to take a chair, pour wine from a bottle, walk across the room, laugh, stammer, and the like, all express the specific way he has chosen to characterize the role he is playing. These specific actor's choices from the available alternatives considered reflect the actor's imagination. Just as your life and mine is only as imaginative as the choices we have made, so an actor's portrayal is as imaginative as the choices he gives the character. The enemy to imagination is generalized behavior; the friend is in the specific and particular gesture.

By providing you with exercises and history, all of which are directed to help you be more specific, the authors of this book have tried to help you cultivate your imagination. Always emphasized is the need for you to be concrete rather than abstract. Such an orientation demands your familiarity with history, not only because of the variety of styles, but also because of your part in the thread of the narrative which is history. I once made the point (before the days of the women's liberation movement) that history is His Story, the story of Man, and studying it should be an exciting pursuit for anyone interested in the story of the human race. When I returned to my office a few hours after my lecture, I found a note left on my desk by one of my students:

Dear Mr. Stein:
History may be His Story, but mystery is My Story.

Acting is indeed part mystery, part history, and plenty of craft. To apply that craft to the profession is to collaborate with a playwright. In fact, a play has been defined by Granville-Barker as an act of collaboration between an actor and a playwright. Oddly enough, this book you are about to study is also an act of collaboration between an actor and a playwright and indeed provides you with a comprehensive introduction to the art of making a play. By their choices, the authors have exercised their imagination. Now it is up to you to exercise yours.

Howard Stein
Associate Dean
School of Drama
Yale University
New Haven, Connecticut

This book is designed to assist in the training of the beginning and developing actor at the college and university levels.

Acting: In Person and In Style approaches actor training through the concept of personalization. Personalization is a process whereby the actor discovers and explores in himself characteristics, qualities, and attributes which are legitimate dimensions of the role he is creating.

In addition to the concept of personalization, Part I discusses traditional acting techniques including relaxation, breathing, kinesics, concentration, sensory awareness, emotion, imagination, improvisation, voice, speech and language, character work in *scenes* from plays, auditioning, role analysis, rehearsal, and performance. Part II discusses theories and history of styles of acting, proceeding chronologically from fifth century B.C. Greece to the present. The book includes many practical exercises in acting.

Throughout, we have used the literary convention of *actor* to include both men and women. We regret the inconvenience this may cause women readers. However, not only does such usage simplify reading, but it also follows a traditional custom of theatre reference.

Other important features of Part II include prechapter quotations which establish the spirit of the style discussed in each chapter, an actor checklist for every style under consideration, recommended roles and scenes for practice and study, and suggested readings.

Appendix A gives detailed instructions for play analysis and Appendix B discusses important experimental theatre groups. Also provided are a glossary of theatre terms and an index.

Part II is dedicated to style and is intended for use only after completion of the work on beginning acting given in Part I. Style should be encountered only when an actor is advancing in development. The chapters on style combine vital theatre history, personalization, and the specifics of each style under study.

Assign:

① Preface
Intro
Chap 1
Chap 2: Anged 1-9:
&l 6: 1-4
7-8
See p. 13 for no' nos!

We are grateful to the following people who so generously gave of their time and professional ability in the completion of this book: Ellis M. Pryce-Jones, Howard Stein, Salem Ludwig, Jerome F. Snyder, Pat Crawford, Sharron Cope, Harriet Gray, and John Unruh.

Special thanks are extended to the following persons and publishers for granting permission to reprint from their copyrighted material: J. Gordon Green, Speech and Theatre Department, Northern Arizona University, Flagstaff, Arizona, audition material, "The Actor Auditions," *Southern Theatre* 16, no. 1, Fall 1972, and 16, no. 2, Winter 1973; Macmillan Publishing Company, Inc.; Harcourt Brace Jovanovich, Inc.; W. W. Norton & Company, Inc.; Harper & Row, Publishers/Simon & Schuster, Inc.; Simon & Schuster, Inc.; Random House, Inc.; University of Minnesota Press; The Bobbs-Merrill Co., Inc.; McCann & Geoghegan, Inc.; McGraw-Hill Book Company, Barry Ulanov, and Robert C. Roby; Viking Press, Inc.; Atheneum Publishers and Earl Graham; Grove Press, Inc.; M. B. Yeats, Miss Anne Yeats and Macmillan of London & Basingstoke; Methuen and Co., Ltd.; and very special thanks to a very special person, Karen Gilligan, our production editor.

Acknowledg-
ments

Inmate from *Marat/Sade*
by Peter Weiss.

Acting "is forever carving a statue of snow." So stated Lawrence Barrett, nineteenth-century American actor. It has also been said that the actor is at once the piano and the pianist. And They have said acting is being; acting is believing; acting is feeling; acting is doing; acting is becoming; acting is illusion; acting is technique; acting is instinct; acting is craft; acting is creative; acting is rehearsing; acting is game; and so on.

Traditionally and historically, acting has been associated with mimicry, exhibitionism, and imitation. The eighteenth-century French actor Francois-Joseph Talma declared that acting demanded "unusual sensitivity and extraordinary intelligence." Acting is based on the presentation of "emotion," which is defined as human feeling manifest as impulses toward open action. It follows that the actor must understand the working of the human personality and feeling. The key problem in acting is whether the actor should project the *illusion* of an emotion or genuinely feel that emotion. (Even if a role demands the portrayal of a mechanical robot, that robot will be imitating *human* behavior.) Men have always found it difficult to define acting because the appreciation of it is greater than the understanding of it. Despite that difficulty, theorists and practitioners of the art of acting can come to grips with certain skills, processes, and disciplines germaine to acting and performance.

What is the reply when the young aspiring actor asks, "What is acting?" Primarily, acting is a person behaving honestly, truthfully, economically, and comfortably in front of other people in a place used for theatrical presentation. Usually an actor performs a role written by a playwright; occasionally he performs improvisationally, that is, without a script. No matter what role or character the actor is called upon to create, or what activity he is asked to perform, his person and personality are on public view and frequently exhibit what is typically private behavior. Such work demands physical and vocal skill or craft, emotional stability, alert thinking, freedom of behavior, and confidence and trust in one's self and one's fellow actors.

One approach to the study of acting is to progress through theory and exercise work and to go rather quickly into what is popularly called "scene and role creation." Such an approach is designed to train the actor almost exclusively for the performance of roles written in a script by a playwright. While much of contemporary theatre is indeed of this nature, much of it is also improvisational. In improvisational theatre, a play script may evolve out of acting exercises. For example, Megan Terry's *Viet Rock* developed out of improvisational acting. It therefore follows that training in present-day theatre must be broader than it was in the past. Today, the actor must be capable of traditional performance of a written role as well as of improvisational stage behavior that can best be likened to modern dance or even gymnastics and acrobatics—at times with dialogue and at times without it. In improvisational theatre, the actor-performer also uses *himself* as a basis for creation of a performance. In both written and nonwritten theatre work, the task of the actor should be based upon economical, honest, and truthful use of himself and thereby eliminate much of the artificiality which pervades most acting.

The concept of personalization will be discussed again and again in this book and made specific in terms of its use in training, rehearsal, and performance.

Personalization has always been a feature of acting. Thespis, the acknowledged first actor of Greece in the sixth century B.C., undoubtedly used his entire person to the best of his ability in performing his roles. Dramatic theorists, actors, and directors have usually discussed the problem of how to utilize the actor's person in role creation and performance. Accordingly, it is necessary to review briefly the more important theories of acting to assist the actor in understanding personalization.

One of the earliest and most significant organized statements on the theory of acting was made by a nineteenth-century French theorist, Denis Diderot, in his essay *Paradox of Acting*. Diderot clarified the famous paradox of acting, namely, that in order to move an audience the actor must remain unmoved. From Thespis to present times, this paradox remains the central problem of acting. How much genuine feeling, if any, must an actor express to move an audience? Diderot knew that at times actors will feel and create believable emotion. However, he also knew that actors could not possibly sustain such creation over long periods of repeated performance. Inevitably, emotion would appear artificial. This fact lead Diderot to the realization that actors had to have training and certain skills to create the illusion of believable emotion. While Diderot did not provide a program of training for actors, we are indebted to him for one of the first clearly organized statements of the problem.

A nineteenth-century French teacher, Francois Delsarte, extended the influence of Diderot with respect to training and skills. Delsarte attempted to formulate laws of speech and gesture through diligent observation and study. Valuable and correct though some of his work was, it ultimately led to rigid and mechanical acting techniques.

Near the turn of the nineteenth century, the Russian actor and director Konstantin Stanislavski developed a thorough system of actor training. After Stanislavski's death, his protege, Yvegeny Vakhtangov, refined and completed the system. Stanislavski dedicated himself to the central problem of stimulating the actor's creativity. He based his system on lengthy and careful study of the actor's mind and emotion. He emphasized the use of observation, imagination, intuition, affective memory (sensory and emotional recall), combined with intensive vocal and physical study (these terms are defined in the Glossary). The concept of advanced psychology implicit in Stanislavski's work was heavily influenced by the French psychologist Theodule Ribot who in 1890 described the term *affective memory*.

The post-Stanislavski period has been marked by a variety of refinements of previous theories. Perhaps the most important contributions in this century have been made by Antonin Artaud, Bertolt Brecht, and Jerzy Grotowski. Artaud and Brecht were concerned with aesthetics. Grotowski is concerned with methods.

Artaud, a French actor and director, explained his theories in his essay "Theatre of Cruelty." Artaud believed that actors needed to develop an extreme use of gesture and sensory response in order to communicate psychologically with an audience rather than through words. He believed in assaulting the senses of his audiences through a variety of physical and emotive stage behavior, typified by violence and hysteria. Artaud labeled the actor "an athlete of the heart." He believed there was a kinetic or emotional relationship between the organic life of the actor and his audience. (Later, Grotowski was to refute this point by asserting that Artaud's aesthetics led to stereotyped or caricature acting.)

Brecht, a German playwright and director, was probably the most influential theorist since Stanislavski. He labeled his plays "epic realism" and published his acting theory under the title "Small Organum for the Theatre." The term *epic realism* relates to both his plays and his acting theory. *Epic* refers to the ancient narrative poem used by Homer. The epic play of Brecht is rambling and episodic in structure. It stresses narration and singing as well as dialogue. Brecht also attempted in his plays to de-emphasize emotional impact for the sake of the intellectual message. He believed in intermingling historic events and persons with modern events and persons. He called this technique "historification." Brecht's acting theories stressed the use of overt theatrical techniques to "alienate" or "make-strange" all dramatic activity, thereby reducing emotional impact upon the audience while increasing intellectual reaction. However, with certain characters in his plays Brecht was receptive to the kind of emotion advocated by Stanislavski. For example, the role of Mother Courage in the play of that name by Brecht demands acting which has an emotional effect upon the audience.

Finally, Grotowski, a contemporary Polish director, has made efforts to rediscover the elements of the actor's art. Grotowski rejected Stanislavski because he believed that the Russian permitted natural impulses to dominate the actor. Grotowski rejected Brecht because he thought Brecht was too concerned with the construction of the role for its intellectual impact. To Grotowski, the actor is merely a person working artistically in public with his body. In a sense, the actor publically offers himself to the audience. The Grotowski system involves years of physical, emotional, and vocal training and inordinate concentration for the total commitment necessary to achieve a state of "trance." The actor searches for signs which express the sound and movement impulses between dream and reality. Through these signs the actor develops a special system of psychoanalytic language of gesture. Grotowski's criticism of Artaud concerning acting that leads to stereotype is a criticism that can also be leveled at his work in the Polish Laboratory Theatre. Grotowski's theatre reveals little emotion and as a result has gained little public favor.

The theories just described will be referred to again and expanded in later sections of this book. All or any of these theories may be used with personalization to assist an actor in successful performance. It is our belief that no one system or theory is correct or advisable. Intelligent actors draw from all theories or any theory that assists them in role creation or performance. What works, works! However, personalization is always basic to the training discussed in this book.

What is "style"? *Style* is a frequently misunderstood and misused word in the theatre today. For example, it is a common mistake to call any non-realistic play or theatre experience "stylized." It is as though that one highly general term encompasses all possibilities and thereby all nonrealistic theatre activity is swept "by one broom into one basket."

The achievement of style in the theatre, particularly in the art of acting, requires specific analysis. For example, many actors do not know that Realism is as stylized as Romanticism or Expressionism. Realism is a distinct style of play requiring a distinct style of acting, just as does Expressionism or whatever.

No matter the style required, the initial and central problem of an actor is to use personalization to establish comfort and familiarity with his role or activity. Then he must communicate the intentions of the playwright as revealed by the action and characters of the script or the theatrical activity. Language, mood, emotions, thoughts, and physical activity are all parts of personalizing and communication.

In his important book *Theatre: The Rediscovery of Style*, Michel Saint-Denis discusses how *style* is rooted in the form and content of the play, in its language, and in its place in the past, that is, in its historical period. Saint-Denis emphasizes that each style has its own reality based on the totality of the script and its historic period. According to Saint-Denis, this is the same as saying "the style is the man himself." In other words, the style of the play is not determined merely by its language, or by the social conventions of the period, or by the design of the scenery. The *total* play in historic perspective creates its style, that is, its particular reality.

In its simplest and earliest definition, the word *style* comes from the Latin word *stilus,* a pointed instrument used by the ancients in writing on wax tablets. The stilus made an imprint, a definition, into the wax and left its expression in either design or words. This indentation made a distinct, original, and sometimes artistic impression. We loosely attribute style to a person who is an artist or who is artistic. In this sense, any person can be an artist who is said to have style, from the lady who wears her fox fur elegantly to a sculptor welding a metal collage. Style represents not only a personal stamp, but also a mode of perception by the artist. He chooses a recognizable pathway from his intention to his execution and synthesizes the form and material into a living emotional or intellectual experience which is particular to him. When a literary or dramatic artist can compel his language to conform to his mode of experience, his communication with the audience will be more precise and, therefore, comprehensible.

It is true that a playwright sometimes manipulates his material to create his personal stamp or style. By degrees and by kind, he incorporates lifelike qualities into his characters. Within each play will be various departures from true-to-life representations.

There are two courses open to a playwright when he re-creates a particular reality in the theatre. If he chooses a representational technique, he brings a truthful image of life into the theatre which establishes and enhances the illusion of his reality. The actors appear to represent true life by being *oblivious* of the audience and interact only with each other. In representational drama, the audience is only permitted to "peek through an illusory fourth wall." The other avenue open to a playwright is to utilize the presentational technique which directs the actor to focus on the audience with *awareness* that it is there watching. This creates a different kind of reality, one which *includes* the audience within it.

Saint-Denis clarified that learning to act in any style means accepting the concept that an acting style is an organic outgrowth of a play. Style is the truth or essence of any particular play. Primarily, it is the author's particular view of truth or reality. Even a distorted nightmare depicted on stage is truth and reality to its author.

As Saint-Denis also explained, the style of a play is additionally a process which creatively reflects the mode of some particular era. The author mirrors the hopes, desires, and attitudes of the people living in his age. The playwright is motivated by current psychological, social, religious, and philosophical influences. He is further influenced by the architecture of the theatre, the climate and geography of the country, the technical means of production, the traditions of playwriting, the theories of acting, and the nature of the audiences who see his plays. When an audience is led to identify and accept the reality of the artistic statement, then the mode of presenting the truth of the author and his age becomes the dominant style of the period.

How can we delineate the truths of the past? Style is captured by presenting the author's reality in its own way, not by imposing our own or some other reality on it. Much of the truth of an age resides in the values, personal relationships, and insights into the human condition revealed by its literary and dramatic artists. Also, the prevailing mood, the aesthetic and sensory awareness, the scientific investigation, and the search for knowledge are expressed in an individualized manner by the playwright.

However, all the traditions of a particular age cannot be translated from generation to generation. We can only infuse acting with style by commanding our attention to the plays which in turn will lead us to the spirit of the author and his age. After all, the theatre is not life. The theatre represents life.

How can the actor arrive at an authentic appraisal of the playwright's personal stamp or style? In order for the actor to comfortably adopt the original style, he must first examine the dramatic form of a play, either tragedy or comedy, or their derivatives, melodrama, farce, tragicomedy, and other subforms. The reading of plays will help one develop an understanding of the basic classifications of the drama. In addition, study in play analysis can bring awareness of the basic essentials that relate form to the literal and metaphorical content of a play (see Francis Hodge for an in-depth study of play analysis, as well as James H. Clay and Daniel K. Krempel for a meta-

Hecuba, *The Trojan Women* by Euripides.

phorical approach to play analysis).[1] Play analysis (which is specifically a director's responsibility, but is invaluable also to an actor) involves study of a play's form, literal and metaphorical content, structure (e.g., plot, character, thought, dialogue, melody, and spectacle), and author's intention. Play analysis precedes style analysis, which is the final clarification of a play's particular reality and its means of expressing that reality (a detailed guide to play analysis is provided in Appendix A).

Acting: In Person and In Style begins at the logical point of departure in the training of the collegiate actor: with the actor's person. The initial step involves the actor's becoming comfortable with himself, or in his learning how to use relaxation as the first acting tool.

1. Francis Hodge, *Play Directing, Analysis, Communication and Style* (Englewood Cliffs, N. J.: Prentice-Hall, 1971); James H. Clay and Daniel K. Krempel, *Theatrical Image* (New York: McGraw-Hill Book Co., 1967).

Acting: I
In Person

1 Relaxation

The first step in an actor's training program in personalization or self-exploration involves the concept of relaxation. By relaxation we do not mean passivity; relaxation is rather a positive physical condition whereby an actor finds emotional, mental, and physical freedom.

When awake, we are in what is called a conscious state. This means that we are mentally active. Relaxation is invaluable to the conscious state because it can enhance perception, thinking, physical activity, and emotional stability.

Relaxation is also invaluable if we are to probe the subconscious. The level of mental operation not yet present in consciousness is called the subconscious. The subconscious state of mind may be likened to that which is

Actors relaxing prior to a performance of *A Midsummer Night's Dream* by William Shakespeare. Directed by Joan Snyder. Ed W. Clark High School, Las Vegas.

forgotten or lying dormant in an unopened memory bank. While the actor is constantly functioning in a conscious state, he is frequently called upon to probe the subconscious. Probing the subconscious means to activate forgotten or suppressed experiences into remembered events. Relaxation is also invaluable to this process.

Exercises for Relaxing

People relax in different ways. Some people relax by reading; others, by playing golf, tennis, or handball. Actors use a variety of relaxing methods as warm-up and preparation for both rehearsal and performance. Some of these methods are group activities, while others are private, individual exercises. For example, a favorite group method of relaxation for actors is to stand in a circle and execute basic calisthenics. Simplistic vocal drills are also used in this situation. At times actors sit in a circle and play concentration and word games. Occasionally, they stand or sit in a circle and hold hands or put their arms around one another's waists. They hum or sing together or merely relax in silence with the trusting comfort of group harmony sustaining their relaxation. Individually, relaxation is often managed by reclining or even dozing prior to rehearsal or performance call. Some actors, on the other hand, like to "run" lines with another actor as preparatory relaxation. Still others enjoy jogging around a spacious area. Meditation of one kind or another is also practiced by actors as a form of rehearsal and performance relaxation. One to two minutes of silent relaxation just prior to entrance on stage is important for all actors. Eventually an actor must discover an individualized and effective way to relax. However, there are certain theatre exercises which are especially designed to assist everyone in the process of relaxing.

Exercise 1   Step 1   Body Alignment

How to relax? Recline on a firm surface, preferably on a clear floor. After you have reclined, it is absolutely imperative that you do not speak. Silence is the beginning factor in relaxing the mind and body. The next task is to remove general thought processes, which is difficult. When awake one has a natural tendency toward chaotic thinking. As you recline, begin by focusing on one thing and one thing only. For example, concentrate upon your right big toe. Ideally, move your thoughts from one part of your body to the next, lingering on each to concentrate on that part. In other words, a focused single thought can get the mind as relaxed and generally free of thinking as is possible; to go beyond this is to fall asleep and thereby destroy the purpose of actor relaxation which is positive and relatively energized. Your heels should be touching the floor, with the remainder of the foot at ease upon your heels. Rest the calves of your legs on the floor without strain or tension; your thighs should be in similar repose. The buttocks should be comfortable, not drawn or tense in any way. The two spinal curves of your neck and the small of your back should be aligned, meaning basically

Body alignment

straight with the lower half of your torso. The back of your head and the back of your body should rest comfortably without strain or control, thus permitting the abdominal muscles to relax naturally. Your shoulders should be slightly rounded and not pressed against the floor; your arms should be at your sides, resting naturally on the floor or surface and not crossed or in any way reclining upon your body. Your hands should rest lightly upon the surface or floor, probably with the fingers naturally curled under a bit because stretching or extending the fingers tends to create some tension for most people.

The self-exploration or personalization system of acting begins with the simple reclining exercise just described. The body functions best when muscle tension is released. Tension can be released either by suggestion (i.e., being asked or directed by someone to relax, which works for some people, but not for many), by conscious effort (i.e., willing it oneself, which is also difficult), or by manipulation (i.e., moving the area of tension such as wiggling a tense foot, which nearly always works). The common areas of tension are the base of the back of the head and the neck, the small of the back, the hands and shoulders, and the calf-to-foot area of the legs. Once muscles are relieved of tension, actors are free to explore each physical area of the body separately and make inroads into the subconscious where emotions lie dormant.

Exercise 1   Step 2   Body Exploration

Begin by doing Exercise 1, Step 1, again. Exploration of the body should begin at one end of the body and progress to the other. Start by concentrating on the tips of your toes. Wiggle them and become acutely aware of them. Next transfer your concentration to the soles of your feet, then to the heels, and on to the ankles, calves, knees, thighs, hips, buttocks, abdominal area, rib cage, chest, shoulders, biceps, elbows, forearms, wrists, hands, and fingers. Now shift to the rear of the body at the base of the spine, move up the back to the neck, and around to the jaw, mouth, nose, cheeks, ears, eyelids, eyebrows, forehead, and top of the cranium. Imagine you are rolling your body into the top of your head in the manner that a sardine or coffee can lid is removed by coiling a metal key around a binding metal tape. After a few seconds, mentally release your body or unroll it in your mind to its full length. This action should actually provide physical release or relaxation from the mental stimulus.

Exercise 1   Step 3   Relaxation and Breathing

Step 3 in relaxation involves organic breathing. *Organic* means that the entire body is systematically coordinated with breathing (a detailed exploration of breathing mechanics is given in chapter 7). If you have completed Steps 1 and 2, you should be automatically breathing organically. At this point the mind must make a final contribution by actually concentrating upon the breathing. You must think about the attempt to memorize how your breathing *feels*. Concentrate upon the movement of the body in the area of the diaphragm (see figure p. 51), abdomen, rib cage, and chest. Most breathing is flawed because of tension. Accordingly, since most beginning actors are overly tense, most breathing is incorrect and adversely affects speaking, movement, and emotion.

Now come to your feet, move around, and properly align your body posture in such a way that it perfectly duplicates your reclining position. Similarly, your memory and concentration must re-create the exact way you were breathing while lying down. At this point you are truly in the actor's basic position of positive relaxation.

While most actors prefer the reclining position for relaxation, others prefer a sitting position. Both ultimately lead to relaxation while standing.

Exercise 2   Relaxation and Sitting

Relaxation and sitting

Place a comfortable chair in an area free from other objects. Normal room illumination should prevail, with no strong light upon the chair. Ideally, the chair should have armrests and a firm back and seat. However, the back and seat should be minimally padded for basic comfort. Sit in the chair with your feet resting comfortably on the floor. Remove your shoes if this aids your comfort. Rest your elbows on the armrests. Your hands should dangle naturally off the front end of the armrests. Your head should recline backward until it comfortably rests on the top of the chair. Adjust your body position accordingly to become comfortable. Close your eyes and concentrate upon your breathing. Move and adjust areas of tension. Remain in this silent, comfortable position for a minimum of three minutes. To test your relaxation, another actor should approach you and lift each of your arms by the wrist and drop them, move your legs by wiggling the knees, and roll your head from side to side. Any resistance in these areas will indicate tension. When tension is discovered, adjust your body position to a more comfortable one and relax in silence, concentrating on your breathing for two or three more minutes. When you are totally relaxed, your body will be limp and mobile. Remember that true relaxation never leads to sleep.

Stage Fright, the Actor's Malady

Relaxation exercises are basic to overcoming the main malady or problem of the beginning actor. Acting necessitates speaking and behaving in front of other people, activities which usually create excessive nervous tension. The popular label for this tension is "stage fright."

Although the term *stage fright* refers to the fear that takes place when an individual is on stage, it is the same human process one has when soloing a plane, appearing for an interview, attending an important meeting, competing in sports, or embarking on a dangerous trip. Fear becomes harmful only when we become afraid of being afraid. We may fall into the trap of thinking normal behavior is abnormal; such thinking produces more energy than we need. Excess energy becomes inordinate tension and manifests itself through trembling legs, twitching knees, fidgety fingers, facial grimacing, shifting weight from leg to leg, aimless walking, and breathiness. All these events are signals that we are self-conscious, that is, are unusually aware of being watched and listened to. We become self-conscious because we are aware that someone is judging us. We think our appearance, manner, intelligence, emotions, and movement are threatened. The natural instinct is to become defensive. The automatic response action is to withdraw mentally and physically—to become guarded. The result is usually artificial behavior which, of course, deteriorates an actor's effectiveness and believability. Unnatural behavior is in direct opposition to personalization, which is based on comfort, naturalness, and believable behavior.

Fear is also harmful when we do not know why we are afraid. We should therefore ask: What in me is being threatened? Is the threat real? What can I do to deal with the threat? If we know what is being threatened and admit the fact, we may be better equipped to cope with the threat.

Stage fright in its wider sense is not unique to actors; it is common to public performers ranging from basketball players to musicians to well-established stage and screen personalities.

Perhaps the most surprising and hopeful thing to note here is that emotional tension or anxiety in study, rehearsal, or performance is not necessarily an unfavorable condition provided that it does not become excessive and create the conditions just described. Some tensions prepare the body for better physical and mental effort. The body recognizes the presence of an urgent situation and prepares itself accordingly. The adrenal gland pumps adrenaline into the system; when adrenaline reaches the muscles, vitality is restored and reaction time is enhanced. The body releases larger quantities of sugar into the bloodstream, giving it greater ability to cope with physical problems. Breathing quickens as more oxygen is absorbed, and carbon dioxide is expelled more rapidly. As the pulse rate also quickens, more blood arrives at the muscles, the heart, the brain, and the central nervous system. The blood and the excess oxygen combine to make the brain capable of thinking with greater clarity, perceptiveness, and quickness; the muscles are capable of performing greater physical effort; and, finally, the central nervous system is capable of reacting more quickly. These distinct physiological changes make the body perform at a higher level of alertness than under normal conditions. *Constructive* tension, then, can assist one emotionally.

Exercise 3 Relaxation and Stage Fright

Place two or three small objects in the middle of a large area. Included might be an apple, a set of keys, and a cup. Take a standing position. Align your body using Exercises 1 and 2 until you are relaxed. Concentrate upon your breathing. When you feel relaxed, shift your concentration to one of the objects and walk to it. Pick up the object and examine it thoroughly. Return the object to the floor and finish walking across the room. Repeat this exercise until you do it with full confidence and without any of the nervous tensions described in the discussion of stage fright.

Object-related, goal-oriented physical activity is a key factor in the elimination of stage fright. If Exercises 1 and 2 are mastered, Exercise 3 should be executed without producing fear, self-consciousness, or stage fright. If excessive tension is suffered doing Exercise 3, return to the first two exercises and practice them as a preparatory technique to all stage activity.

Relaxation is the heartbeat of acting. Master it now.

Suggested Readings

Alexander, F. Matthias. *The Resurrection of the Body.* Edited by Edward Maisel. New York: University Books, 1969.

Behenan, Kovoor T. *Yoga: A Scientific Evaluation.* New York: Dover Publications, 1937.

Bergler, Edmund. "On Acting and Stage Fright," *Psychiatric Quarterly Suppl.* 23 (1949): 313–19.

Clevenger, T., Jr. "A Synthesis of Experimental Research in Stage Fright." *Quarterly Journal of Speech* 45 (1959): 134–45.

Pavlov, I. P. *Conditioned Reflexes.* New York: Dover Publications, 1927.

the alet technique by
Wilfred Barlow

Kinesics— 2
Body Dynamics

A person relaxed is a body relaxed. An actor works best in a state in which his muscles are free of tension. In other words, an actor's energy must be under control. Chapter 1 guides the actor toward an understanding of how to relax—the initial step in personalization. A natural extension of that step involves working with the internal muscular energy, usually referred to as *kinesics*, or body dynamics.

Personalized Kinesics

Kinesics refers to internal muscular energy produced by what the body is doing. Begin kinesic work by performing a simple exercise.

Exercise 1   The Fist

Align your body in the standing position. Make a fist with one of your hands and then spread your fingers; the fingers, being extended, will energize by themselves. Now let the fingers move toward one another. Your muscular activity will flow easily. Try the exercise several times; you will feel the natural change from energy to lightness.

The fist

Kinesics sensitizes an actor to a specific flow of energy. By becoming aware of muscular activity, actors can be conscious of what is happening to their energy. In Exercise 1, activity of the fist and fingers is natural and immediate. Note that no thought or emotion colors the quality of action. Action is relatively pure. Emotional involvement, if it occurs at all, is instinctive—that is, occurs on its own. Repeat the fist exercise until you feel emotional involvement of any kind. At that point, immediately stop the exercise. It is important to keep the exercise in a pure state of mental awareness of muscular activity. Later you will learn how to combine kinetic activity with emotion.

The relaxation and fist exercises are designed to eliminate muscular tension. Breathing should be organically correct in order to free the actor to respond naturally to physical needs. Movements should be simple and unaffected; they should be naturally personalized, that is, honestly, truthfully, the actor's *person* or self. The body should perform as an unbroken unit or in what some acting teachers call *gestalt* (see Glossary).

The natural, undirected movement of the body must be shaped; that is, an actor must use body energies effectively. Movement must have some control or shape to it, in terms of both form and function. Relaxation will activate internal body movement in a natural and comfortable manner. A more difficult process is shaping or controlling external body movement.

The body performs a variety of natural external movements every moment of a waking day. For example, we stretch, yawn, shake, shrug, wiggle, fidget, and scratch; on a slightly more complicated level, we stand, sit, and walk or run. We also perform a variety of highly complex and individualized movements such as driving cars, lifting objects, and making things. The comfortable personalization of these everyday, every-moment movements becomes the initial task in shaping the dynamics of the body. Stretching, yawning, and shaking must be shaped or controlled truthfully before an actor can begin imitating activities demanded by a playwright, a director, or an artist-leader.

Begin by examining basic body movements on what might be called an average day.

Exercise 2   The Stretch

Assume the reclining position described in Exercise 1 in chapter 1 (p. 4). Follow the same procedures until you are in a relaxed state. Close your eyes for a few moments. When it seems suitable to do so, open your eyes as you do when you awaken on an average morning in your life. From this point on, the exercise will shape or control your external movements. Slowly stretch your right arm into the air, moving it past your ear and extending it to the floor behind you. Stretch the arm to the fullest possible extension. Repeat the same movement with your left arm. Now stretch both arms simultaneously above your head. Try to feel the elongated muscular pull in your arms. Begin to arch the small of your back in an upward motion, continuing to stretch to the point where the entire back is raised off the floor, with your shoulders touching the surface. Your neck will automatically leave the floor, as will part of your head. At the same time, be aware that your legs have a tendency to leave the floor. You should feel a slight pull in the muscles of your legs. Slowly lower your body to the floor. Once again, stretch your right arm over your head, but this time stretch your right leg as well, being careful not to let either the arm or the leg leave the surface of the floor. Repeat the same process with the left arm and leg. Now reverse the process: stretch your right arm and left leg and vice versa. Now stretch both arms and both legs simultaneously.

Lift your head and body slightly off the floor, rolling on to the right side. Arch your back by allowing both arms and legs to form something resembling a half-moon or half-arc. Hold for the count of five. Again relax to a fully reclining position on your back; repeat the exercise on the left side.

Now roll over on your stomach. Lift your right leg off the floor and stretch. Repeat the movements with the left leg. Lift your right arm; stretch; lift the left arm; stretch. Lift both arms and legs off the floor simultaneously and hold for the count of five. Repeat the exercise, but this time lift your head off the floor and hold for a count of five. Now recline and relax again.

A final and vital exercise in the fundamental personalization of kinesics and external body dynamics is the "cat" exercise, a standard indispensable exercise employed by many actors and most acting teachers.

Exercise 3   The Cat

Begin from the reclining stomach position of Exercise 2. Extend both your arms away from the body, forming a T (your head should be

The cat

turned on either the left or right side). Slowly bring your hands in and up to your body, palms flat on the floor, very near your underarms. At the same time, point your toes toward the floor. Begin to lift your body on to the weight of your arms and toes, arching your back and neck as much as possible. Bring your legs into your body by walking on the toes and balls of the feet toward your hands, arching your back to a greater and greater degree. When you feel that you cannot walk any farther, stop. Raise the right leg high into the air and lift your head up. Stretch and lower the leg. Walk your legs away or backward from your arms, decreasing the arch in your back. Let your body descend to the floor and relax. Slowly curl yourself into a ball, holding your body very tightly by clasping your hand and arms around your knees as you lie on your side. Release your body from the ball, stretching every muscle in your body including those tiny muscles in your face by forcing a large, artificial cat yawn. As you are releasing your body, try this yawn at least three times.

Exercise 4   The Shakeout

Recline on your back and slowly begin to shake your body; increase the intensity of the shaking until you can shake no further. Stand up and shake your body again. At the point at which the shaking is most vigorous, begin to bounce lightly into the air off the balls of the feet. Your first bounces should be easy and relaxed. Increase the height of the bounces until you feel you are tiring.

Exercise 5   The Swing and Hit

Stand for a moment in a relaxed position. Now swing your body from side to side and in half-circles, beginning with the arms and then the head, shoulders, upper torso, waist, hips, and legs. Try simultaneously swinging as much of your body as possible. Evolve this swinging exercise into a striking or hitting exercise with the arms, hands, and fists. Strike at space with all parts of your body. Hit the air with your arms, head, chest, legs, chin, ears, and so forth. When you have used every part of your body, collapse your entire body to the ground in a naturally shaped and comfortable fall.

The swing and hit

Exercise 6   Additional Body Kinesic Exercises

1. Come to your feet. Try to fill the space around you by stretching horizontally as far as you can. Trying to make yourself as wide as possible, stretch from side to side.

2. Try to make yourself as thin as possible. Concentrate on being narrow.

3. Try to make yourself as short as possible. Concentrate on decreasing your vertical height.

4. In an exercise which will slowly relax your entire body, make yourself very tall by stretching your arms toward the ceiling. Slowly

start to relax your body, beginning with the fingers, then the arms, neck, shoulders, chest, abdomen, and so on. Let your body fall forward in a hairpin manner until the upperpart is hanging limply. The only tension should be in the legs and thighs. Alternate between the stretching toward the ceiling and the hanging positions.

5. Sit on the floor with your legs crossed in front of you in a comfortable erect position and eliminate all tension. Fall forward at the waist in the manner of a rag doll, letting your head dangle as far down as possible. Alternate between sitting erect and falling forward.

6. Imagine you have a metal band around your chest. Attempt to stretch the band by means of vigorous expansion of the trunk of your body.

7. To achieve a new kinesic position, squat with the head dropped forward and the arms dangling between the knees. Your buttocks should not touch the floor.

8. Stand straight, with your legs together, and bend forward from the waist in a rag-doll position. Bounce slowly, trying to touch the palms of your hands on the floor. Be certain your head is inclining toward the chest.

9. Vigorously rotate your trunk from the waist upward.

10. Rotate the head slowly in a circular fashion, changing directions if you feel dizzy. This exercise should be performed very slowly, starting at your front, then side, back, other side, and front again. Be careful to keep the shoulders and the remainder of the body motionless.

11. In order to warm the balls of your feet, stand in an aligned body position. Jump eight small jumps with the heels together and the toes apart. Make sure that your heels touch the floor on every jump. Bend the knees as you land. Repeat the jumps with the feet apart. Combine the two steps so that you do sixteen jumps, alternating feet together, then apart.

12. Keep both legs straight throughout this exercise. Extend your right leg back, pointing the toes. Keep the back lifted as you lower the body. The back leg will come off the ground. Take four counts to do this. Keep the head in line with the rest of the body. Place your hands on the floor and try to lift the back leg higher. Keeping the back lifted, return to the starting position. Repeat the exercise using the other leg.

Diligent repetition of the exercises described in this chapter, based upon solid understanding of the reasons for doing them, can accomplish the initial step of personalization necessary for a beginning actor. Additionally, invent exercises to suit your particular needs. This work may encompass several weeks, and can help one master the invaluable process of relaxation and body control.

Space Awareness Exercises

Comfortably aware of internal and external energy, the actor should now examine his relationship with the space he occupies.

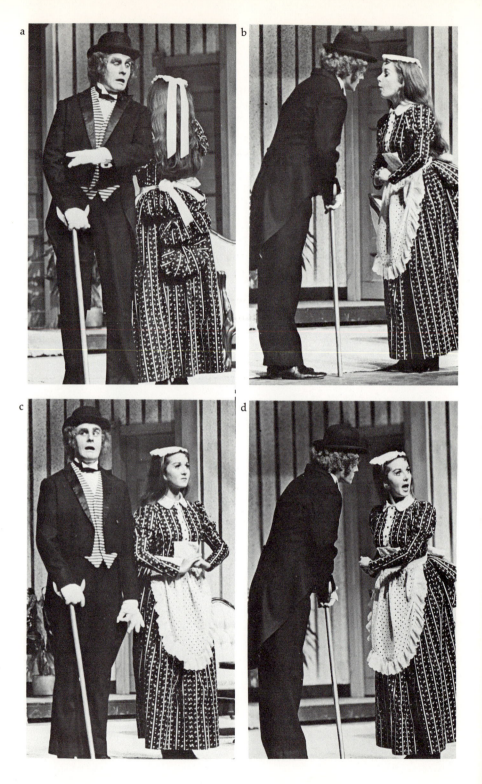

A sequence demonstrating: *a*, body discipline; *b*, facial expression; *c*, positioning; and *d*, timing. *A Flea in Her Ear* by George Feydeau. Directed by Jerry L. Crawford. Costumes by Pat Crawford. Scenery by Fredrick L. Olson. University of Nevada, Las Vegas.

If an actor is to become aware of the space he occupies, he must begin by again establishing a state of personal relaxation.

Exercise 7   Drifting

Sound (handwritten)

When you are relaxed, come to your feet and begin to walk slowly about the room. Concentrate initially on your breathing; as you walk, periodically check for undesirable tension in the arms, neck, and shoulders. Be certain your knees are flexing easily and naturally. Wiggle your third and fourth fingers on each hand, which will relax those areas. Remain silent; make no physical or visual contact with other persons. Permit your eyes to drift aimlessly to avoid running into people, but do not focus on anything or anyone. Keep your mind occupied with your breathing. As you move, your body is automatically molding your space by moving into it; that is, it is filling empty air with your mass, as well as making waves and abstract impressions in the air around you. In order to perceive your own energy and mass as it imprints itself upon space, first try to perceive the "space molding" that occurs from the impact of other people as they walk past you. Turn your mind from concentration upon your breathing to conscious search for the feeling of the waves in space from others walking by you. If you really concentrate, you can actually feel their energy in space as it strikes you.

Now shift your concentration to your own total energy and body. You should begin to feel or perceive your own space. A sense of lightness will ensue; every movement will take on new sensitivity. Your body will feel increasingly weightless, without mass. Instead of an awareness of walking, you will have a feeling of moving or floating, a distinctly different perception.

The first benefit reaped from self-perception in space is a sense of physical and mental freedom. The body will be instinctively more graceful and the mind unburdened. This exercise can eventuate beyond the classroom, rehearsal room, or stage into a perception of the variety of spaces one occupies in all everyday living experiences.

Exercise 8   Eye Contact

As you move with the awarenesses just described, begin to make eye contact for a few seconds with other people. It is vital to remain silent during this eye contact, but any other natural reaction such as smiling or nodding should be permitted. However, if you find these reactions distracting, and if they begin to create tensions or self-consciousness, eliminate eye contact and return to concentration upon your own space or breathing. Later, again try eye contact with others. Eventually, comfortable, relaxed eye contact should occur.

Visual contact with others expands one's perception to the energy and bodies of others. (Later this exercise will serve as the foundation for physical interaction. We will return to this factor when we discuss trust and related points in chapter 4.)

Exercise 9   Room Observation

After having established eye contact with other people in the room, turn your attention to the room itself and all inanimate objects within it. Observe the room carefully, but do not touch anything (touching objects comes later). Study each wall, window, door; note their location, shape, texture, color, and so on. Similarly, observe every object. Extend your perception into the atmosphere of the room. Does mood connotation emanate from contrasting light and dark patterns? Conclude the exercise with a group discussion of observations.

Note that all work to date has been accomplished without a role or character being involved. Your person has been sufficient. Personalization has carried us through work with relaxation and kinesics or body dynamics. The actor should now focus upon the technique of *concentration*. If mastery of the skills presented in chapters 1 and 2 have not been accomplished, it is advisable to repeat some of the previous exercises or to invent new exercises before advancing to the skills described in chapter 3.

Suggested Readings

Alexander, F. Matthais. *The Resurrection of the Body*. Edited by Edward Maisel. New York: University Books, 1969. Dell Publishing Co., 1971.

Birdwhistell, Ray L. *Introduction to Kinesics*. Washington, D. C.: Foreign Service Institute, 1952.

Birdwhistell, Ray L. *The Kinesic Level in the Investigation of the Emotions*. New York: International Universities Press, 1963.

Birdwhistell, Ray L. *Kinesics and Content: Essays on Body Motion Communication*. New York: Ballantine Books, 1972.

Cage, John. *Silence*. Middleton, Conn.: Wesleyan University Press, 1961.

Davis, Martha. *Understanding Body Movement: An Annotated Bibliography*. New York: Arno Press, 1972.

Feldenkrais, Moshe. *Awareness Through Movement: Health Exercises for Personal Growth*. New York: Harper & Row, 1972.

Grotowski, Jerzy. *Towards a Poor Theatre*. New York: Simon & Shuster, 1968.

Hall, Edward T. *The Silent Language*. Greenwich, Conn.: Fawcett World Library, 1959.

Hutchinson, Ann. *Labanation*. Boston: Little, Brown & Co., 1969.

King, Nancy. *Theatre Movement: The Actor and His Space*. New York: Drama Book Specialists/Publishers, 1971.

Knapp, Mark L. *Nonverbal Communication in Human Interaction*. New York: Holt, Rinehart & Winston, 1972.

Logan, Gene, and McKinney, Wayne C. *Kinesology*. Dubuque, Iowa: Wm. C. Brown Co., 1970.

Moore, Sonia. "The Method of Physical Action." *Tulane Drama Review*, Summer 1965, pp. 91–94.

Penrod, James. *Movement for the Performing Artist*. Palo Alto, Calif.: National Press Books, 1974.

Scheflen, A. E. "The Significance of Posture in Communication Systems."
 Psychiatry 27 (1964): 316–31.

"A Study of the Specificity of Meaning in Facial Expression." *Quarterly Journal of
 Speech,* October 1938, pp. 424–36.

Thornton, Samuel. *Laban's Theory of Movement.* Boston: Plays, Inc., 1971.

White, Edwin, and Battye, Marguerite. *Acting and Stage Movement.* New York:
 Arc Books, 1963.

Wolff, Charlotte. *A Psychology of Gesture.* Translated by Anne Tennant. 2nd ed.
 London: Methuen & Co., 1948.

3 Concentration

Aside from positive relaxation and kinesic discipline, concentration is probably the most important skill in the art of acting. *Concentration* is exclusive attention to what actors are doing, seeing, hearing, and feeling on stage. Concentration is also vital to offstage preparation and discipline. Concentration can be said to be the complete application of self to task.

Concentration is often the most abused technique of acting, in spite of the fact that it is the most important concept leading to interesting, dynamic, and believable performance on stage. Spencer Tracy once defined acting as simply learning lines and concentrating. Stanislavski placed great stress on concentration in referring to circles of attention for actors. By this he meant that actors must limit attention to separate parts of the stage established by objects. There are small, medium, and large circles of attention depending upon what the actor wants to include within his perimeter. An actor also has to learn to redirect attention from one circle to another. In beginning training, actors often have a tendency to let minor interruptions and random thoughts constantly break or disturb their concentration. They may hear airplanes flying over the building, voices out in the hall, and people talking in the theatre. An actor may find his mind wandering to thoughts of where he is going after class or rehearsal. Note the almost irresistible urge to look out at the audience, at the teacher, or at the director. Lack of eye contact is the clearest indication that actors are not concentrating. Concentration requires self-discipline and total dedication to the task.

An actor who is not concentrating has a tendency to *go up* with his lines, which means going blank or forgetting lines. Failure to concentrate

Photograph of a rehearsal in which intense concentration in a conflict situation between actresses is demonstrated.

leads to mistakes in blocking or movement patterns. It also leads to imprecise execution of stage business (*stage business* is defined as small, detailed actions of the body, often of the hands, such as handling a cane or smoking a cigarette). Above all, failure to concentrate on stage can result in an unmotivated and emotionally empty performance. It takes total concentration to focus the body energies and develop mental acuity to the point necessary to create believable emotion. Failure to concentrate offstage may cause an actor to miss an entrance or be late for it. Similarly, failure to concentrate offstage can result in distracting conversations that may disturb other performers who are on stage or about to enter.

Concentration to Enhance Personalization

Concentration is a skill which is best developed through rehearsal and performance experience as an actor. However, a beginning actor can gain immeasurable skill in concentration through execution of the following exercises. Remember that exercises are valuable only if faithfully repeated every day, just as a musician practices his instrument daily and a dancer exercises his body daily. Also note that these exercises are designed to enhance personalization. In other words, they are preparatory to acting in a role created by a playwright.

Exercise 1   Centers of Tension

Concentrate on and touch the following centers of tension in your body: the back of the neck, the sinus areas over the eyes, the small of the back, the calves of the leg, the soles of the feet, and the hands.

Exercise 2   Textures

Concentrate on the textures, materials, and objects worn on your body. With full concentration you can become aware of the differences in textures.

The mirror

Exercise 3   Mirror

Stand facing another actor. Designate one as leader and one as follower. Without touching, the leader performs slow and precise body movements, gestures, and facial expressions. The follower imitates every movement of the leader precisely. As the exercise develops, you will note that you and your colleague will blend into simultaneous activity if you are using full concentration. Change roles without breaking concentration.

Exercise 4   The Minefield

Imagine that the room or stage is a field hiding one active land mine buried beneath the surface of the ground. Crawl on your hands and knees over the field searching with full concentration for the hidden mine. Search until your concentration is broken with the futility of the search, or until you are certain you have located the mine.

Exercise 5   Listening

Stand or sit perfectly still. Close your eyes. Concentrate on identifying all sounds you hear. After three minutes, explain to your fellow actors exactly what sounds you heard.

Exercise 6   The Flower

Curl into a ball on the floor. Concentrate on being a particular kind of flower seed. When you feel motivated to do so, begin to grow until you reach full blossom. This activity is directly related to what Stanislavski called "focus of attention." In this instance, the focus relates your body to an object.

Exercise 7   The Circle

Sit in a circle with your fellow actors. One actor speaks a single word. The actor immediately to his left repeats the word aloud and adds another word from his natural association with the first word (for example, *green* followed by *grass*). The actor to the left of the second speaker repeats both words and adds a third. This process continues around the circle for as long as all words spoken aloud can be repeated by each actor. When an actor loses concentration and forgets a word, he must drop out of the circle. This exercise becomes an enjoyable game as it strengthens the power of concentration.

Concentration on Particulars

The following exercises will assist one in learning to focus full attention on particular tasks, both real and imaginary.

Exercise 8   Barefoot Walk

As you move, concentrate on imagining that you are walking barefoot on the following kinds of surfaces: wet grass, mud, hot sand, gravel, broken eggshells, waxed floor, and thick carpet.

Exercise 9   Weather

As you move, concentrate on imagining that you are walking in the following kinds of weather conditions: rain, snow, heat, hail, wind, sandstorm, tornado, blizzard, and hurricane.

Exercise 10   Small Object

Choose an object small enough to fit in your hand such as a comb. Concentrate on the object. Examine it thoroughly. Using concentration, be-

The flower, showing closed to full bloom (this exercise can be done from a rising position to an extended position).

come physically involved with the object and use it in four different ways. For example, rub it on your skin, touch it to your face, put it between your toes, and balance it on your head.

Exercise 11 Puppet

Begin this exercise by walking around the room with your own natural rhythm, letting your arms swing naturally. Gradually, concentrate on your arms and legs being stretched by strings pulled by the hands of a person above you (i.e., an imaginary puppeteer). React to the pulling of your arms and legs with puppetlike motions.

Exercise 12 Halving Your Body

Think of your body not as a total entity, but as a mass divided in half. For example, concentrate on the idea that your upper half is separate from your lower half, or that your right side is separate from your left side. Once you have divided your body in half, think of the two halves as opposing forces. For example, the upper half of your body is happy, and the lower half of your body is sad; or one eye is intelligent and the other eye is stupid. Move or react in a state of happiness, sadness, anger, and drunkenness.

Exercise 13 Separate Emotions in the Body

Choose an emotional reaction and focus it on one particular part of your body: for example, your head is laughing. Choose other parts of your body and create different emotional reactions. Now perform the exercise using two different parts of the body simultaneously responding to an emotional reaction: for example, your arms are bored and your toes are happy.

The following story demonstrates how powerful concentration can be as a fundamental acting technique.

It is told that when actor Sidney Poitier met Spencer Tracy for the first time on the movie set of *Guess Who's Coming to Dinner?* Poitier was not prepared for the intense concentration of Tracy. Entering the room in their first filmed scene together, Tracy looked up at Poitier and delivered a line with forceful concentration. Poitier froze and went *up* or blank, and had to take several moments to prepare an equal level of concentration in order to work comfortably in the scene with Tracy. Poitier later stated that he had never met an actor with such believable concentration as that of Tracy. The example to note from this story is that successful illusion of reality can best be accomplished through total concentration. Tracy's concentration was so complete that Poitier had to match it to do the scene successfully.

Good life habits become good stage habits. In daily life, practice full concentration on seeing, hearing, saying, and doing. Personalize on the stage; everyday living better equips us to exercise full concentration as actors.

Suggested Readings

Benedetti, Robert L. *The Actor at Work*. Englewood-Cliffs, N. J.: Prentice-Hall, 1970.
Boleslavsky, Richard. *Acting: The First Six Lessons*. New York: Theatre Arts Books, 1938.
McGaw, Charles. *Acting Is Believing*. New York: Holt, Rinehart & Winston, 1964.
Rockwood, Jerome. *The Craftsmen of Dionysus*. Chicago: Scott, Foresman & Co., 1966.

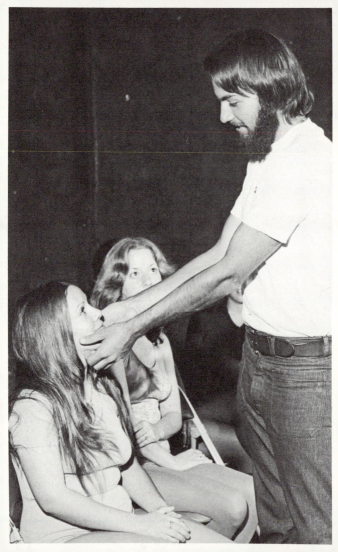

Another important aspect of personalization is working with the environment, with the sensory system, and with other actors.

The actor's environment is defined as his total working space and all external matter within that space. Therefore, the building, room or theatre, all scenic elements, and all objects including other people constitute the actor's environment. Actors should relate to and be familiar with their environment in order to humanize their acting. They relate to their environment through their senses. The five senses are seeing, touching, hearing, tasting, and smelling.

Sight Perception

The initial step in developing sensory awareness involves awareness of the room or theatre. Begin with visual perception. Normal vision implies that one sees clearly with or without glasses or contact lenses. It also implies that one is not color blind. However, the sense of sight involves more than looking at something clearly. To an actor, sight perception includes careful mental notation of what he sees. Actors should visually and mentally register what they see in their environment in order to relate to it better and to recall it later.

Exercise 1   Seeing Far and Near

Stand in a central location and visually examine every aspect of the room from the ceiling to the walls and all objects and people in it. Take all the time you need and register in your mind all that you see. Later, move about the room and visually examine everything at close proximity. Again register in your mind all that you see. Later, discuss your visual examination. Note what others saw that you did not see.

Touch Perception

When an actor becomes visually familiar with the room and its objects, he then begins the process of perception through the sense of touch. Touch perception involves physical contact of any part of the body against or upon any other matter. Touch implies tactile sensory awareness through physical contact. The mind helps interpret the sensory experience of touch.

Exercise 2   Room and Object Contact

Begin by touching walls, furniture, and objects with the fingers and hands. Initially, touch only the room proper and its inanimate objects. Do not touch other actors. Interpersonal touch comes at a later stage of development. Proceed slowly and methodically, attempting to elicit internal as well as external sensitivity as you touch things. After the initial response with the hands, close your eyes and repeat the process.

Now feel the objects with the side of the face, nose, chin, and so on. For example, the entire body should be pressed against a wall to gain total perception of it. Do not overlook any object in the room, using both open-eye and closed-eye touch perception. Your tactile response should clarify the difference in surfaces and textures of objects.

Exercise 3   Touch Recall

As another exercise in concentration and simple sensory recall, sit in a relaxed position, close your eyes, and vividly recall both visual and touch perception of the entire room and all its objects.

Exercise 4   Touching While Blindfolded

Move around the entire room with a blindfold over your eyes. Touch the room and objects again. Note the quantity and quality of information you have retained from the previous exercises. Without consciously doing so, you will discover that you have memorized the location, shape, and texture of many, if not all, the objects. During the blindfold-touch exercise in an acting class at the University of Nevada, Las Vegas, one of the actors spontaneously removed a small box from its place on a table and perched it on his head. Other blindfolded actors, having previously examined the box, returned for it and immediately perceived its absence. A slight furor resulted as the actors searched for the missing box with total sincerity and silent concentration. The experience demonstrates how conscious and complete touch perception can become for an actor.

Smell Perception

Smelling is perceiving through olfactory nerves to obtain the scent or odor of something. Smelling is strictly a sensory experience. It cannot reveal the shape or quality of things. Effective smelling is only possible when the nose, sinus, throat, and chest cavities are clear or free from congestion.

Exercise 5   Detecting Odor

At a designated time and day, each actor should bring a single object into the room with a particularly distinctive aroma or odor. The object must be concealed in a sack or bag (a plastic bag is best because it is relatively odorless). Blindfolds are once again used by everyone because sight remains the most predominant sensory experience available and, in this instance, you should restrict it. The sacks should be opened and placed in a line; thus, you will not have to touch objects in order to smell them. Move from sack to sack, smelling deeply and registering the smell in memory. When everyone has completed the exercise in silence, blindfolds should be removed and the smell of each object clarified and explored through discussion.

Taste Perception

Tasting is perceiving the flavor of something by touching with the tongue, utilizing the taste buds. Effective tasting is only possible when we are healthy, particularly without sinus problems, head congestion, or colds.

Exercise 6   Tasting

On a designated time and day, convert the sense-of-smell exercise (Exercise 5) into a sense-of-taste exercise, using a variety of fruits. Each actor must bring a minimum of three different kinds of fruit. The fruit should be arbitrarily exchanged. Taste the three pieces of fruit in sequence and register those tastes in your memory. When everyone has completed the exercise in silence, the taste of each object should be clarified and explored through discussion.

Hearing Perception

Hearing is perceiving sound through the ear mechanism. Effective hearing is possible only when the mechanism is in a healthy condition, unaffected by congestion or injury.

Exercise 7   Hearing

Everyone sit in a relaxed position. Either close your eyes or use a blindfold, whichever is most comfortable for you. Begin by trying to "listen" to silence (note that hearing is an automatic response, whereas listening requires mental concentration upon what you are hearing). Can you hear it? Your first perception will probably be that you cannot because your concentration will focus upon *any* sound. Do not resist listening to the sounds. Try to perceive precisely what is making the sounds and register them in memory. Occasionally you will note with delight that there are moments without sound and you will actually "hear" silence. After a comfortable duration of time, open your eyes and clarify and explore through discussion what you have heard.

Life Experience and Your Art

Having now completed exercises in sensory perception, you should be ready to turn to new exercises involving personalized observation and experiences related to sensory awareness. The sensory perception exercises extend an actor's creative development in relaxation, concentration, and observation. A common mistake made by some beginning actors is to leave all this work in the classroom, rehearsal studio, or theatre. Because of its personalization base, the art of acting cannot be professionally developed or maintained in a vacuum of time and place. Rather, the art of acting through personalization is another kind of life experience. It follows that the actor should extend the perceptions and awarenesses developed in the previous exercises into every waking moment. Initially extension must be practiced consciously whenever circumstances permit. Naturally, the details of occupation, family, and private life may not allow practicing these exercises frequently. However, if an actor insists upon some planned exercise work during his everyday life, eventually his subconscious perceptions may automatically continue without his being overtly aware of the fact. This is another way of saying that consciously and subconsciously an actor should be constantly intermingling his life experiences with the practice of his art. Like a sponge or a giant antenna, an actor should attract and select stimuli which will make him a richer person and his acting a richer art.

Exercise 8   Verbalizing Personalized Observation and Experience Concerning the Senses

After achieving a state of relaxation, select a vivid personal experience concerning one or more of your five senses and relate the story to your colleagues. Do not select an experience of unusual emotional intensity. Select an important but simple and comfortable experience rather than one which in any way might create tension or embarrassment for you. For example, you might relate the story of how at an important job interview you failed to hear a key question and you gave a strange response which lost you the job. As you relate your experience, you should recount it not only verbally, but also nonverbally. While some will be forgotten, any minor, comfortable feelings and sensations you experienced should be recalled and *may* even be re-created by movement or gesture if you tell the story well. Do not attempt to re-create such feelings and sensations, but do not suppress them if they are generated honestly. The value of this exercise lies in its extension of personal contribution to the art of acting. In other words, it contributes to honest self-revelation or a kind of unzipping of oneself. Provided that you avoid intense emotional recollection at this stage of development, you need not fear this exercise as being amateurish psychotherapy. While an aspect of psychology is always involved in acting, it is important to note that therapeutic benefit is incidental or subsidiary.

Exercise 9   Combining the Senses

Select a favorite and easily transported object which you consider a kind of extension of yourself in your environment. Take a relaxed position in front of your colleagues and show the object to them. As you do so, describe the object in detail, carefully noting how it feels, smells, sounds, looks, tastes, where you got it, when you got it, and generally what it means to you in terms of both utility and sentiment. Your honest comfort with this object should be demonstrated without any conscious effort. Once again, the exercise is valueless if you leave it in the realm of a classroom experience. You must take this exercise into your world of everyday existence. Become totally aware of all the objects you handle or engage. The result will be increased sensory awareness.

Actresses during re-
hearsal relating to objects
in their environment.

Sensory Awareness Through Interpersonal Contact

Finally, and perhaps most important, sensory awareness involves interaction with other people. In order to work with other people, we must trust them. However, before we can trust others, we must trust ourselves. Trust means possessing an honest confidence in ourselves and inspiring the same in others. The exercises previously encountered should have begun to increase self-trust. They should have increased awareness of self-trust and of the environment, emotions, senses, observations, and experiences. The actor should be more confident now of his sense of reality; that is, to use a psychological term, the actor should have a better grasp of personal identity. The personalization theory necessitates that the actor confront and accept his personality and life experiences, using his strengths confidently and coping with his weaknesses with equal confidence. It follows that the actor should now be ready to engage the personality, reality, and identity of other people.

Exercise 10   Engaging Other People with Trust

Begin by creating a state of relaxation. Walk about the room with awareness of yourself in space. When you are comfortable, permit eye contact with every person you pass; remain silent and walk slowly. Without forcing the action, begin to casually touch the other persons as you pass them, either on the hand, arm, or shoulder. Eventually, you may find a natural instinct to pause and hold on to a person's hand or arm for a moment. If this occurs, give in to the instinct provided that it is honest and comfortable for both of you (note that the latter is not an obligatory direction; if the instinct does not arise, do not force it). Those of you who do stop to linger a moment upon physical contact may also note the instinct to explore the other person's face visually. Follow that instinct if it occurs. Similarly, visual exploration may lead to a natural desire to touch the other person's face. Again, if both of you are honest, trusting, and comfortable, permit the facial touching. Progression to this point may take several hours of several days, depending upon the confidence and trust factors of the people involved. As trust grows, the touch exploration may extend to the hands and other parts of the body. (Exercise 10 is complete when you have accomplished physical contact with all other actors.)

Because our society is extraordinarily conscious of group therapy and Freudian psychology, the question arises as to how intimate touch perception will become in Exercise 10. The first answer to the question is obviously that it will be as extensive as trust and confidence permit. However, since there will be individuals capable of *total* body contact in this exercise, artistic discretion and public taste enter the picture. In other words, restrict touch perception at the point that it becomes private or sexually intimate. Later, if role creation in a play demands some kind of sexual physical contact, Exercise 10 can be reintroduced in a closed rehearsal under the supervision of a director or artist-leader. In no circumstances should this kind of work be permitted without that supervision because of the artistic necessities of craft and control involved. An objective and trained observer is needed to assist an actor in determining what works as art as opposed to what is merely self-indulgent. If for any reason Exercise 10 fails to accomplish trust through the sensory awareness of comfortable physical contact, use Exercise 11. However, this exercise should be directed and controlled by close supervision, if it is used at all, in order to restrict inordinate or embarrassing behavior.

Exercise 11   Specific Touching

Sit with your colleagues in a line of chairs and relax. The person at the left end of the line rises and faces the person next to him. Select some specific physical area of the person's *face, head,* or *hands* to touch and examine, basing your selection on the most natural instinct you have for touching that person in those areas. For example, you may have always wanted to touch a person's hair, chin, lips, or hands. This exercise will permit you to do so with comfort and trust. Proceed down the line of actors until you have made specific physical contact as just instructed with every person. As the first person performing the exercise moves past two or three people, the next person may rise and begin specific touching. Eventually all of you will be engaged in the activity. Comfortable and directed physical contact heightens sensory awareness and increases trust between actors. Exercise 11 is an effective preparation device for all theatrical performance work, as well as an invaluable training device in beginning acting.

Exercise 12 Touching People Without Seeing

Begin walking freely about the room again, but this time move very slowly with the eyes gently shut or blindfolded. The inevitable result of this movement will be gentle physical collisions with other people. To avoid injury, remember to move at a slow pace. Again, you must remain silent. Upon collision with another person, freeze. The point of mutual physical contact should be sustained as though you were glued together at that point. Resume movement together, moving cautiously enough to maintain the point of adhesion. Obviously, collisions will increase until a connected mass of human beings is created. Group movement will be increasingly cumbersome. For example, various levels of attachment will occur with some people moving on their knees, others on their hands and knees, and so on, depending upon whether the collision caused them to drop into such position. The value of this exercise lies in its extension of ensemble or group trust. When the entire group is connected, it forms into a circle with members on their feet, facing toward a mutual center with each arm locked around the small of the back and waist of the person on either side. With your eyes still closed, permit any natural instinct from the unit to sway from side to side. A rhythm will result. The instinct to make a small humming sound may arise in this "trust circle." To demonstrate the trust, follow any instinct to lean far backward or forward, provided that your weight or balance does not break the circle. You will find you are comfortably supported by the unit without danger or fear of falling or collapsing. When a harmonious unit is firmly established, open your eyes and continue any natural instincts toward swaying, weaving, leaning, humming, or even singing. Later at some point of comfortable silence, permit one member of the group to break from the circle and stand in the center as the circle reunites. The person in the center closes his or her eyes as the other members of the circle drop their arms to their sides. When you are the one in the center, and you feel the urge to totally trust the others, fall into space in any direction without fear of landing on the floor, knowing full well that members of the circle will catch you safely and return you to an upright position. After you have fallen comfortably several times, return to the circle while another member of the group replaces you. Continue the exercise until all of you have experienced the trust that accompanies falling without fear. While there may be tension early in this exercise among some members of the group concerning awkward or embarrassing physical contact, it will rapidly disappear with both the trust and fun involved in the falling action. This is particularly true because the contact, no matter where it is made, is extremely brief and

The trust circle

usually involves support from several people at the same time. (Incidentally, it should be obvious that good personal hygiene increases trust and confidence in group activity.)

Exercise 13   The Growth and Deterioration of Man

Extend your small catching circle into a very large one with plenty of space between one another to avoid collision in the following group exercise. Assume a human fetal position upon the floor and through your own pantomimic invention be "born" and "begin to grow." Let your growth progress into early infancy; move from reclining to crawling and then to standing and into toddling. Pass into childhood, adolescence, and young maturity. Continue through the "stages of Man" by physically moving around the stage until you reach middle age and, eventually, old age. Remain silent throughout this exercise, except for vocalization sounds such as crying, laughing, coughing, grunting, and so on. For example, to physicalize early childhood you might act out skipping rope and similar activities. For adolescence, you might imitate lighting a cigarette. For young adulthood, you might march as though in the army; at middle age, you might walk slower and do calisthenics with some difficulty, sit as though watching television, and so on. For old age, you might hobble on a cane or sit and stare blankly. This lengthy exercise should culminate in final deterioration leading to death. Throughout this exercise permit your instincts, confidence, and trust to carry you into any natural movement, physical interaction with others, and sound making. The exercise concludes in the position of the repose of death.

Personalization includes total sensory awareness of the self and the objects and people of one's personal environment. Hopefully, this awareness will increase with conscientious execution of the exercises given in this chapter.

Suggested Readings

Chekhov, Michael. *To the Actor on the Technique of Acting.* New York: Harper & Brothers, 1953.

Lewis, Howard R., and Streitfeld, Harold S. *Growth Games.* New York: Bantam Books, Inc., 1972.

McCaslin, Nellie. *Creative Dramatics in the Classroom.* 2nd ed. New York: David McKay Co., 1974.

Spolin, Viola. *Improvisation for the Theatre.* Evanston, Ill.: Northwestern University Press, 1963.

Ward, Winifred. *Playmaking with Children.* 2nd ed. New York: Appleton-Century-Crofts, 1957.

Way, Brian. *Development Through Drama.* London: Longmans, Green & Co. Ltd., 1969.

The Roots of Feeling: The Body and Emotion

Most people go to the theatre for an emotional experience. Whether they are conscious of it or not, they have a desire to witness and vicariously experience heightened emotional activity. People enjoy or find release from sharing emotions with others. Naturally, many people also go to the theatre for an intellectual experience. However, as Aristotle stated in the fifth century B.C., meaningful dramatic thought is emotionally based; that is, ideas and concepts usually follow emotional dramatic action rather than precede it. For example, the plays of a highly philosophical playwright such as George Bernard Shaw are effective on stage only when the author's ideas are projected from characters involved in emotional crisis. When his characters lecture, an audience does not become as involved.

Defining Emotion

Emotion is fundamentally feeling. For example, fear, anger, happiness, boredom, and grief are all emotions. When the mind enters into feeling or emotional experience, it usually suppresses, channels, or frustrates the feeling. Often, when emotional control is needed, it is the mind that brings control.

Emotions are primarily manifested in human beings in a physical way. Literally, *emotion* means "outward movement," which implies impulse toward open action. In everyday life, emotions cause the release of frustrations and anxieties in physical ways. If we are angry enough, we may throw something or hit something. If we are unhappy enough, we may shed tears and cry. If we are delighted by something or happy enough, we may laugh. All of these physical actions help clarify emotional conditions and hence increase perception of ourself.

In order for an emotion to be projected or even for an emotion to be experienced, some kind of internal physical response must be activated in the actor. On stage, emotion is best projected to and understood by the audience through *physical action*. More often than not, mental activity suppresses, dissipates, or controls emotion rather than generates it. This is precisely why people say to an angry person, "Sit down and think about this; be calm and get control of yourself." On stage, an actor says the line "I'm furious with you!" dozens of times without making the audience believe it if he relies only on the words and thought. The audience will only believe an actor is "furious" when his physical actions and vocal accompaniment so demonstrate. (The ramifications of vocal accompaniment are discussed in chapter 7.)

The relationship of emotion to physical response is clarified in a famous theory developed by William James and Fritz Lange near the turn of the nineteenth century. The basic point of the theory is that body activity and emotional activity are analogous. In other words, the activity of our muscles is emotional activity. Stanislavski and most modern theorists and practitioners of the art of acting are familiar with the James-Lange theory. In chapter 2 the exercises and discussion concerning body kinesics are directly related to this theory (i.e., emotional internal muscular activity creates external physical action).

To test the ability to transform emotion and internal muscular activity into external physical action perform the following exercises.

Exercise 1   Breathing Alone

Sit quietly and concentrate on your breathing; do not think about any emotions or experiences. Concentrate on the breath entering and leaving your lungs. Be aware of the shifting emotions which accompany your breathing.

Exercise 2   Breathing with a Partner

Sit on the floor and face a partner. Breathing is the only way you may shape the emotions communicated between you. (What happens to you as you explore this work? Will you stay in a human form? Do whatever is necessary to explore a full range of emotions as a result of breathing. You may vocalize sounds and noises, but no words.)

Emotion and Objects

Emotion is usually tied to physical activity, and most physical activity is usually tied to use of objects. Most of us instinctively relate to our environment to demonstrate or release emotion. For example, if we are furious, we usually hit a table or a wall or throw something; fury rarely stops with shouting.

When weeping, most of us lean or hold onto another person, a pillow, a handkerchief, or the sleeve of a garment.

When laughing, we slap our own leg, someone else's arm, and clap our hands together.

When afraid, we often clutch objects. The student sitting before a professor trying to explain why an assignment is not finished may fidget with a pencil, a coin, or a paper clip.

The study of emotion begins by personalizing. We live in a world of objects, most of which are inanimate. For example, we wear a wristwatch, shoes, clothing. We write with a pen and pencil. We drive an automobile and eat with utensils. The interesting philosophical or psychological question arises, Do any of these objects become an extension of you? An infant is totally comfortable without clothing until he is habitually forced to wear it. At a very young age, he learns that he must wear clothing in public to be socially acceptable. Early in life most children learn to attach themselves to a favorite object, usually a blanket, bottle, or toy. In our society, favorite objects of children include such things as Snoopy, Godzilla, King Kong, miniature trains, cars, airplanes, dolls, and baseball and football trading cards. (Take a moment to check your own fetish, that is, object of special devotion. Is it that guitar, that automobile, or that purse?) We instinctively develop personal ways of handling these objects. We store them in particular places and carry or wear them in special ways.

An actor is also inextricably tied to the objects of his environment, be it a stage setting, a classroom, or a rehearsal studio. If there is a table in that environment, he will relate to it even if he never touches it; he will do this by avoiding the table, which becomes a reverse aspect of relating to it.

Actors must carefully select objects to help demonstrate emotions on stage. Physical activity with objects can project the nature and degree of emotion more effectively than anything spoken. A playwright and a director automatically provide actors with many of these objects. (For example, a bouquet of roses should be used by Happy, Linda, and Biff in act 2 of *Death of a Salesman* by Arthur Miller.) However, the inventive actor provides additional objects to fully create character and emotion. If the performance is improvisational without a written script, objects and physical environment are even more important to the performer in the clarification and demonstration of emotion. In an improvisational theatre performance, a simple chair might provide several emotional possibilities. For example, as an obstacle to movement an actor may throw the chair aside with fury or exhilaration. The emotional point will be clearly made by the action with the object.

Actors are usually individualistic when selecting objects to demonstrate emotion; however, they should try to select things which are universally recognized as being related to an emotion and its physical manifestation. For example, the handkerchief is universally related to crying. For a comic or unusual object-emotion relationship, an actor might cry into a peculiar object such as a dishrag. Role and play analysis will assist in appropriate selection. (Role analysis is discussed further in chapter 10 and play analysis is discussed in Appendix A.)

For familiarity in handling objects related to emotions, perform the following exercises.

Exercise 3   Object Experience Story

Select an object directly related to an emotional situation you have experienced and bring it to class. Place the object in view of the class and describe it to them. Relate the emotional experience you had with the object. Without forcing it, permit yourself to re-create the emotion you experienced as you tell the story.

Exercise 4   Movement and Emotion

Walk around the room feeling relaxed and comfortable. Let your mind wander in free association with everything you see and hear. As you walk, permit your body movement to dictate or create an emotional response. This will happen automatically; it cannot be forced intellectually. If it is forced, it will be artificial. Whatever happens, permit to happen. If sounds, noises, or words result, permit them. The only caution is to avoid harming someone such as during a temper tantrum. (The caution or control factor is primarily the responsibility of the instructor who must intervene if necessary.) Later it might be interesting to discuss the root of the emotion and how it took shape.

Exercise 5   Contrasting Emotional Values

Imagine you are sneaking out of the house at midnight when your sister or brother discovers you and tries to stop you. Explore the emotional reactions of each person through physical activity and/or object-related activity.

Further note the possibilities of contrasting emotions in the activity. Repeat the exercise, deliberately selecting opposite emotional values.

Exercise 6   Ambivalence

Ambivalence is an emotional quality involved with desiring something and rejecting it at the same time: for example, a person on a strict diet loves ice cream and is offered a chocolate sundae. The emotional response is ambivalent; that is, the person is caught between equally desirable choices.

Select a recent personal experience in which you had ambivalent feelings about something. Re-create the situation on stage with the object.

Exercise 7   Fear of Height

Your instructor should lead the class to the top of a high building or structure such as to the top of a grid in a theatre. Note the nature of your emotional reactions the higher you get and the closer you get to the edge of the precipice. Be extremely careful not to fall or unnecessarily endanger life. When you have returned to the ground, note the additional emotional changes within you. Describe all the emotional activity you have undergone.

Exercise 8   Loss and Grief

Select an object that was a gift from someone now dead or gone out of your life forever. Bring the object to class and describe the person who gave you the object. Discuss their personality characteristics as well as the way they looked and behaved. Permit your emotions about the departed person to flow freely. The exercise should create a strong sense of personal loss and grief.

Exercise 9   Laughter

Everyone sit in a circle and remain silent. Let your eyes wander from person to person. Do not suppress any urge toward giddiness, giggling, or laughter. Do not force such responses, but permit them to flow freely if the natural urge strikes you. If you are so inclined to do so, join in the laughter. This exercise should permit infectious, spontaneous laughter, using other people as the object stimulus.

Exercise 10   Love

Bring a portrait or photograph of someone you love to class. Sit in a chair facing the class and look at the photograph awhile. Relate to the class why you love this person; describe what it is about the person that brings you happiness and love.

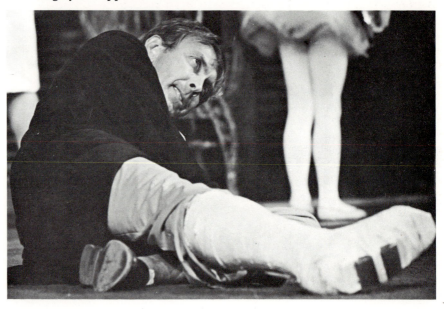

An actor demonstrating intense anger and pain after an exhausting struggle.

Dormant Emotion

Another important source of emotion remains to be explored—the emotion either forgotten or suppressed in the subconscious. Such emotion rests there in the fashion of a dormant volcano or seed. This store of emotion can perhaps be understood best through the metaphors of the volcano and the seed.

The earth holds several inactive or dormant volcanoes; that is, their active eruption has ceased. However, scientists have proved that deep within the recess of a volcano lies hot lava and potential explosive activity. Nature can provoke a dormant volcano into activity, or man can do it through use of explosives. Similarly, we may stand in the midst of a seemingly barren and dry desert, convinced that no plant or animal life exists there. A mere five-minute thundershower will stimulate seed and animal life to colorful and dynamic activity.

Dormant emotion resides within each of us at all times. Fears, rules, laws, mores, guilt, desires, and hosts of other conditions force us to terminate certain emotional experiences. We often try to forget them. For example, most people develop or learn the fear of death. If one is consistently conscious of the emotional fear of his own death or the death of loved ones, he might very well experience a nervous breakdown, go insane, or behave in unusual and possibly destructive ways. Consequently, most human beings confront the reality of death through religion on a conscious level or through unconscious suppression of mortality. Like the dormant volcano or desert seed, suppressed emotion lies deep within us and is a continually potential source of eruption. In everyday life, most people have no occasion to deliberately activate that potential. Most people are satisfied and happier keeping many emotions dormant. However, the actor in his work cannot afford that luxury. The personalization theory of acting utilizes dormant emotion, along with objects, as one of the primary sources, if not the primary source, of emotional stimuli. The longer we live, the more emotional experiences will be stored in our dormant "bank." If actors are to draw upon that bank, they may use what is commonly called *emotional recall*, or what Stanislavski called "affective memory." Stanislavski's concept focuses upon recalling emotion previously experienced. To do this, an actor must remember a specific experience vividly, attempting to recall what he did, said, and felt with as much of the original intensity as possible. The memory should create the desired emotion needed in an analogous situation in a play. The actor then uses the emotion of the life experience in the given circumstances of the play. The result can be very believable emotion on stage.

To illustrate the effectiveness of using dormant emotion, or affective memory experience, we cite an actual story of an actress performing the role of Irina in Anton Chekhov's play *The Three Sisters*. Near the end of the play, Irina's fiancé, Tusenbach, is killed in a duel with Solyony. Irina must receive the news of his death and cry. In early rehearsals the actress attempted the crying sequence strictly through use of mechanical technique. Upon hearing of the death, she took a handkerchief from her pocket, sat on a chair, collapsed her head upon her arms on the table, and shook physically, while emitting vocal sobs. The effect was not believable.

During the next week of rehearsals, the director assisted the actress with "affective memory." Through discussion, the director discovered that several years earlier the actress had lost her brother in a car accident. Her brother had been run over and killed in the street. The girl's memory of the death was vivid and painful. She was able to recall the experience intensely. Recalling this memory immediately prior to acting Irina's reaction to the death of her fiancé produced a very believable emotion, far more effective than the mechanical work of the previous week. The actress recalled the circumstances that occurred when she learned her brother had been killed. She sat down on a chair quietly and stared straight ahead. Tears slowly began to flow from her eyes. From affective memory, she created a believable emotion. The audience shared the experience, believed it, and was moved by it.

The following exercise will aid in the development of emotional recall. It is a very important exercise in preparation for later acting work in scenes and plays. However, if the exercise is unsuccessful, discretion should indicate postponing it until the actor has attained a more advanced state of development.

Exercise 11 Tapping Your Dormant Emotion

Begin by creating your own state of relaxation. When you are totally relaxed, come to a comfortable seated position on the floor or on a chair. Eliminate all body tension. The time necessary for you to relax and select an experience may be extensive, and may try the patience of other actors. Everyone must contribute to the aura of concentration and relaxation by maintaining silence. Development of art and craft necessitates this kind of discipline.

Select an important experience from your past in which you can vividly recall the circumstances of the experience. You may select experiences which occurred five to ten years ago. It is best to avoid selecting a recent experience (e.g., one year or less). The further away the experience, the more dormant is the emotion.

Once the experience is vividly recalled, describe it in detail for the class. Do not begin your description by explaining what emotions you experienced; rather, focus solely on the circumstances of the experience. In other words, vivid recollection will trigger the internal nervous and muscular systems necessary to activate dormant emotion. Consequently, as you recall and verbally explain what happened to you, it is highly probable that the original emotion will erupt or grow again. Do not be upset if this exercise is not immediately successful. It can be repeated or postponed to a later point of development. Emotional memory is a complex and difficult technique. Since the technique is rooted in the personalization factor, you may require several attempts at affective memory to succeed. Also, a coach, an instructor, or a director should be present to guide you in the event excessive emotion is released.

Exercise 11 takes time, patience, dedication, skill, and a climate of trust within the group. Above all, it takes a willing and cooperative actor. He must have the courage to explore highly personal experiences in public—experiences which have been heretofore suppressed in secrecy. The necessary aspect of "couch" psychology or group therapy must be accepted by all participants and naturally will be enhanced by the training and skill of the instructor. If an actor is not willing to explore dormant emotion in this way, by all means he should not try to do so. Also, the instructor or coach is free to use or not use Exercise 11. He may find someone trained in psychology to assist with the exercise.

Even successful completion of Exercise 11 will not *guarantee* continued skill with affective memory. However, introduction of the skill in the first year of training can permit an actor to extend his work with this complex process for two or more years. Hopefully the actor will personalize and refine the tool throughout his acting career.

Projecting Experience

Projecting experience is another valuable technique to use in the creation of believable emotion on stage. Projecting experience means mentally perceiving emotional experiences which will unquestionably or probably occur in the future. The best example of such experience is death. It is a fact of mortal existence as we know it that life will terminate in death. Therefore, when past experience is insufficient to create a believable emotion, projection of future experience may stimulate emotional response. For example, the actress discussed earlier in the role of Irina might not have had a past experience of death vivid enough to use as affective memory. She might then use the projected death of a loved one such as the death of her father to assist in the creation of grief.

Projecting experience implies use of imagination, an acting technique described in chapter 6. However, it should be noted that the projected death of a parent is not imagination; it is a fact. Death is not a fantasy. It is inevitable.

Exercise 12   Projecting Death

Relax in a chair on stage. Think of a living relative who is particularly close to you. For example, your father, mother, brother, or sister. Mentally project the death of the relative. Describe the circumstances of the death and funeral. (If your emotions become acute or excessive, stop the exercise.) Do not be alarmed by the seemingly maudlin or painful nature of this exercise. It is a proved and effective acting technique when handled maturely and efficiently.

While emotion is a physical or body activity, the nuances of its expression are greatly aided in the theatre by the ability to project the subtleties of one's personal emotional experiences.

Suggested Readings

Berne, Eric. *What Do You Say After You Say Hello: The Psychology of Human Destiny*. New York: Bantam Books, Inc., 1973.

Darwin, Charles. *The Expression of the Emotions in Man and Animals*. London: John Murray Publishers, 1872.

Davitz, Joel R., and Davitz, Lois Jean. "Nonverbal Vocal Communication of Feeling." *Journal of Communication* 11 (1961): 81–86.

Dittman, A. T. "Relationship Between Body Movements and Moods in Interviews." *Journal of Consulting Psychology* 26 (1962): 480.

Fast, Julius. *Body Language*. New York: Pocket Books, 1971.

Harris, Thomas A. *I'm OK—You're OK*. New York: Avon Books, 1969.

James, William. "What Is Emotion?" *Mind* 9 (1884): 188–204.

Koffa, K. *Principles of Gestalt Psychology*. New York: Harcourt, 1935.

Lange, Carl G., and James, William. *The Emotions*. Facsimile of 1922 ed. New York: Hafner Publishing Co., 1967.

Moore, Sonia. *The Stanislavski System*. New York: Viking Press, 1974.

Woodbury, Lael J. "The Externalization of Emotion." *Educational Theatre Journal*, October 1960, pp. 177–83.

Experiences, observations, and environment provide most of the emotional stimuli needed to perform effectively in the theatre. However, playwrights invariably create unusual and intense emotional situations requiring stimuli beyond these usual avenues. The most obvious example of this is found in *Oedipus Rex* by Sophocles. Probably no actor will be able to use specific, one-to-one personal experience, observation, or environment to create the correct emotional state of Oedipus when he discovers he has married his own mother and fathered children with her. The agony of despair and anguish in the man at the moment of that discovery usually requires use of imaginative stimuli.

Imagination

What is meant by *using imagination?* Imagination is the process of creating or inventing mental images or experiences. Everyone is born with a natural instinct for imagination, but relatively few people consciously develop the process as a skill. An actor must consciously work to cultivate imagination. Children are particularly adept at vividly imagining things. In some instances, children actually create imaginary playmates, brothers, and sisters. As we grow older, this process is referred to as *daydreaming*. Stanislavski said that an actor must learn to dream by use of his imagination. Dreaming for an actor must be directional; that is, it must have an artistic purpose to it. This distinguishes everyday imaginative dreaming from creative imagination for artistic purposes. For example, a young actress in an acting class

An actor beginning an improvisation.

(performing Exercise 1 given in this chapter) indulged in totally aimless, stream-of-consciousness fantasizing, without any direction to her story about an object. She and her listeners were only confused because of the lack of clarity and believability in her wandering story. Imagination must be channeled to a climatic conclusion in order to provide truth and believability in acting.

The rigors of formal education and increased maturity tend to stifle the daydreaming process. However, daydreaming is never totally eliminated because psychologists have proved that all people daydream or fantasize in highly imaginative ways during part of both waking and sleeping hours of each day. Escape and sexual fantasies are rampant among members of modern society. The task of the actor is to channel imaginative instinct into constructive actor training, role creation, and stage performance. How does the actor train this instinct?

Exercise 1   Imagination and an Object

Establish a personal state of relaxation, concentration, and correct breathing. When you have created this condition by application of selected exercises from chapter 1, accept a personal object from one of your colleagues such as a purse, ring, or watch. Examine it in great detail. It is crucial that the object be totally foreign to you, and if it is not, return it and accept another object from someone else. Let your creative imagination work upon the object. Imagine in specific detail where it came from originally. That is, where was it made and by whom? Imaginatively trace the object on its journey to the person you received it from and relate the story verbally to the other actors. Next, using your knowledge and observation of the person who gave it to you, no matter how limited that knowledge and observation may be, imagine a highly emotional experience involving the object and that person.

Exercise 2   Impromptu Imagination Work

Another exercise in rapid, spontaneous imagination work involves reacting immediately with verbal stories to impromptu (i.e., spontaneous or unrehearsed) questions or situations. For example, the following questions and situations may be used by the instructor or your colleagues to stimulate your imaginative response (it is crucial that you accept this exercise with total sincerity and believable involvement when you are either questioning or responding):

1. Your doctor informs you over the telephone that you have pernicious anemia and have less than three weeks to live. Describe how you will spend the next three weeks.

2. If you could be anyone in the world, past, present, or future, who would you be? What would you do?

3. You are awakened in the middle of the night by a totally unrecognizable sound in the next room. Describe the sound and what you do.

4. You receive an airmail special delivery letter postmarked from a foreign city. Describe the message in the letter.

5. On the day of your marriage, your mother tells you that your real father (who lives in another city) will not be able to walk down the aisle with you because he is in a federal penitentiary. How do you respond and what do you do?

6. You are about to be married when you learn your former husband, believed killed in the war, is alive and returning to you. How do you react and what do you do?

7. You are about to give birth to your first child when you learn your husband is having an affair with your best friend. How do you react and what do you do?

8. You are only one year away from retirement from a twenty-five-year job when your employer is forced to terminate you. How do you react and what do you do?

9. At the conclusion of a divorce, you learn that your two teen-age children wish to leave you and live with their father. How do you react and what do you do?

10. Recently married, you move happily into a new apartment, only to learn that your in-laws have rented the apartment below yours. How do you react and what do you do?

Freely using your imagination, invent or create similar questions and circumstances as additional exercises for you and your colleagues. Whenever possible, try to use highly emotional circumstances such as are found in dramatic literature.

Stanislavski once said, "Spectators come to the theater to hear the subtext. They can read the text at home." Stanislavski was referring to the meaning which lies behind the playwright's dialogue, that is, the subtext. He noted that imagination was a key factor in creating valid subtext for a role (subtext is discussed in detail in chapter 10). The preceding exercises can assist in stimulating and developing imaginative skills. Conscious use of imagination can make an actor more alert to the world around him, both on- and off-stage. Imagination can permit an actor to think on any theme or develop any idea. It can aid in understanding the past and future life of characters by providing details often omitted by the author. A trained imagination is precise and logical. It permits an actor to execute actions instinctively and naturally.

Imagination is particularly vital to the use of an important actor-training technique known as *improvisation*.

Improvisation

Improvisation is imagining and creating a very brief plot or story and implementing it with unplanned and unrehearsed dialogue. Usually two or more actors are involved. This technique is important to actors for three particular reasons: (1) as an aid in working with simple actions and characterizations and in evolving varied emotions, motivations, voice projection, and body movements; (2) in development of subtext; and (3) as a technique to implement the script and specific roles when some of the original spontaneity of character or environment is lost (points 2 and 3 are discussed in chapter 10). Plots for improvisation can be found in plays or created with original words and actions.

Improvisation obligates the actor to use imagination in the practical application of his skills. It provides a means to integrate the techniques of relaxation, kinesics, concentration, sensory awareness, and emotions. Improvisation permits maximum use of personalization in a flexible and individualized manner. Although the voice is used in improvisation, the intricacies of voice training for the stage are not necessary for successful improvisation work that stresses personalization. Use the voice as naturally and comfortably as possible in improvisation. The developing actor cannot be expected to think about too many things at one time. His energies should be concentrated on relaxed, physically free action and emotion.

Recently, improvisation has also evolved into total theatrical performance. The Living Theatre, the Open Theatre, and other groups have developed a distinct art form in which a script evolves or is created through rehearsal and performance rather than serving as a seminal point of departure. Playwrights such as Megan Terry and Jean-Claude van Itallie have published scripts *after* groups of actors have processed them through improvisation into a form permitting publication. These theatricals are guided by an artist-leader rather than by a director. This person often performs with the actors in addition to guiding their work. Julian Beck, Joseph Chaikin, and Jerzy Grotowski are leading examples of contemporary artist-leaders in the 1960s. Improvisational performances do not lend themselves to interpretation by performers outside the group because they are a special, improvised product of that group and are stamped with only one interpretation—the one each audience sees. Contemporary politics and social conditions are best suited to this work. Improvisational theatre is very much like a living newspaper. When a standard story such as a Greek myth or the Frankenstein fiction is used, it is reworked completely through improvisation.

How does an actor use improvisation as a beginning acting technique during his early training period? He selects a contemporary political or social topic of interest to him and his partner or group and answers the following questions. What kinds of people (usually stereotypes) are involved? Where does the action take place? What specific important actions are involved? Why was this topic selected? What point is to be made? (Each improvisation must have a goal or objective because achievement of the goal determines when the improvisation concludes.)

A minimum of discussion should be used. The questions should be answered without overintellectualizing the characterization, overplanning the story, or structuring the action meticulously. The improvisation should be put on its feet as soon as possible. Once it is in progress, aimless chatter should be avoided, and words should be used economically. Words should contribute only to the flow of action. The scene should be kept moving by having several possibilities of action in mind. Improvisation should not be used to entertain an audience, except in *special* performance circumstances. The actors should be sensitive to the feelings and changes in attitude of their partners. If choices are made, they should be performed naturally without contrivance.

Actors performing imaginative action. *A Flea in Her Ear* by George Feydeau. Directed by Jerry L. Crawford. Costumes by Pat Crawford. Scenery by Fredrick L. Olson. University of Nevada, Las Vegas.

Exercise 3   Group Improvisation

Create a topical and universal group improvisation. One of you acts as the president of the United States arriving for dinner at a "hippy commune." Perform the improvisation according to the suggestions just mentioned. The goal of the improvisation is met when the president is convinced that he should join the commune.

Exercise 4   The Revival Meeting

One of you is a fiery minister in a religious revival tent. Most of you are zealous believers. Create a revival meeting in which the goal is the conversion to religion of everyone in the room.

Exercise 5   The Audition

Two of you are roommates in New York City, struggling to become professional actresses. You have each auditioned for the same major role in a new play. One of you learns that you have been awarded the role. The goal of the improvisation is met when the other actress is told by her roommate who was cast.

Exercise 6   The Enlistment

Two of you are father and teenage son. The father wants the son to accept a scholarship at the local university. The son has secretly enlisted in the army. The goal of the improvisation is met when the son admits to the father what he has done.

Exercise 7   The Pregnancy

Two of you are a young married couple. You are poverty-stricken. The wife learns that she is pregnant, and knows they cannot afford to have the baby. The goal of the improvisation is met when the wife declares the pregnancy to her husband.

Create or invent other improvisations according to this format.

Imagination and improvisation enhance personalization during beginning work as an actor. These techniques provide further stimuli in the development of his skills.

Suggested Readings

Burger, Isabel B. *Creative Play Acting.* 2nd ed. New York: Ronald Press Co., 1966.

Hodgson, John, and Richards, Ernest. *Improvisation, Discovery and Creativity in Drama.* New York: Barnes & Noble, 1968.

McCaslin, Nellie. *Creative Dramatics in the Classroom.* 2nd ed. New York: David McKay Co., 1974.

Mearns, Hughes. *Creative Power: The Education of Youth in the Creative Arts.* New York: Dover Publications, 1958.

Mitchell, Roy. *Creative Theatre.* New York: Benjamin Blom, 1969.

Slade, Peter. *Experience of Spontaneity.* New York: Fernhill House, 1969.

Spolin, Viola. *Improvisation for the Theatre.* Evanston, Ill.: Northwestern University Press, 1963.

Ward, Winifred. *Playmaking with Children.* 2nd ed. New York: Appleton-Century-Crofts, 1957.

Way, Brian. *Development Through Drama.* London: Longmans, Green & Co., 1969.

The Actor's Voice, 7
Speech, and Language

Words and Meanings

Words are abstract symbols representing people, places, and things. While man is capable of some communication without words, verbal and written thoughts are our primary ways to communicate meaning.

Words are meaningless abstractions until our experiences define what the words represent. For example, when we hear or see the word *chair*, our mind automatically connects the object and the word. Experience has clarified that objects constructed with seats, backs, arms, and legs and used to sit upon are usually called chairs. However, isolated words provide no meaning past the identification or labeling of single objects, places, or things. Words placed together in sentences provide thought and more complex meaning because they form a context (or overall structure of the various parts). In the theatre, the playwright is predominately responsible for organizing words into meaningful context. Occasionally, in improvisational theatre, an actor is called upon to perform that task. It follows that an actor must be reasonably trained in reading skills and comprehension.

In order to speak well on the stage, an actor must develop certain mechanical vocal skills. These skills include breathing correctly; producing adequate sound; using pitch, range, tone, resonance, and timbre to create vocal quality; using inflection, intensity, rate or tempo, emphasis, pause, and rhythm to create vocal variety; using articulation, pronunciation, projection, phrasing, and context effectively—all to reinforce the words physically.

Breathing

As discussed in chapter 1, correct breathing is directly related to correct posture and relaxation. Breathing is necessary to the life process because oxygen removes waste products from the body, particularly carbon dioxide. Air is taken into the lungs and processed through the bloodstream. Inhalation and exhalation are the central factors involved in breathing. We are able to breathe through both the nose and the mouth. Air travels down the *trachea* or windpipe into the bronchial tubes and reaches the lungs. The size of the chest cavity enlarges, creating a partial vacuum. The air inhaled fills this vacuum and expands the lung sacs. An important muscle called the *diaphragm* located between the lower chest cavity and the upper abdominal cavity contracts due to the pressure of the air reaching the base of the windpipe. This muscular expansion forces the ribs up and out.

When air is exhaled, the abdominal muscles relax, the diaphragm flattens, and the ribs are pulled in. The process reduces the size of the chest cavity and compresses the lungs. As a result, air is driven out of the lungs, through the air tubes, past the *larnyx* (where sounds are produced), and out of the body through the nose and mouth (see diagram, p. 51).

Making Sound

In the upper part of the trachea or windpipe, there are two membranes called the *vocal cords*. These vocal cords are located behind the soft palate (the

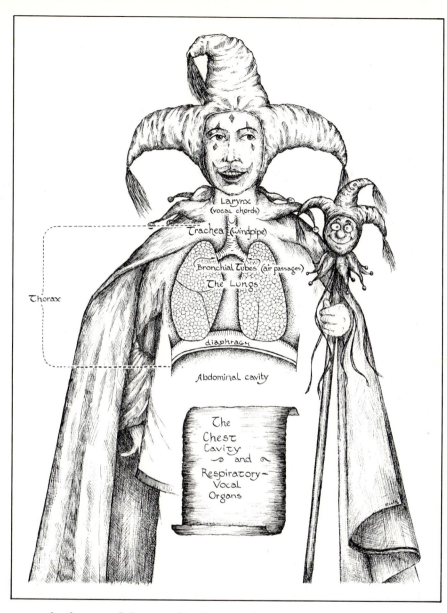

Larynx
(vocal chords)

Trachea (windpipe)

Bronchial Tubes (air passages)

The Lungs

Thorax

diaphragm

Abdominal cavity

The
Chest
Cavity
and
Respiratory-
Vocal
Organs

upper, back part of the mouth). The area housing the vocal cords is called
the *larynx* (the upper part of the trachea). These membranes serve as a
bridge for the breath stream as it flows in and out of the mouth. As breath
is taken in, the vocal cords spread apart and allow the passage of air. They
close during the act of swallowing. The space between the open membranes
is called the *glottis*.

When we decide to speak, the brain sends a message, or *nerve impulse*,
to the vocal membranes and causes them to close. Breath comes from the
lungs through the *bronchial tubes* and trachea into the larynx and builds up
pressure behind the closed vocal membranes. When the pressure is strong

enough, breath is emitted through the vocal cords and vibrates with rapid speed. The vibrating membranes send out waves which produce sound. The sound waves are located in and around the vocal membranes in the larynx. Hence, we may speak when we stop breathing, and we may breathe when we stop speaking.

Exercise 1   Diaphramatic Breathing—Correct Breathing

Stand in a relaxed position with good posture (i.e., posture which is a replica of your body position when you are reclining flat and relaxed on your back). Open your mouth and inhale deeply while holding the palms of your hands against your rib cage. You should feel your abdominal muscles expand your rib cage up and out. Hold your breath for a count of five and release it slowly through the mouth. You should feel your rib cage deflate (your diaphragm muscle will relax).

Exercise 1 can be extended by increasing the amount of air taken in; concurrently, the lung capacity will increase, which aids in breath retention. For example, large amounts of air in the lungs are needed for speaking verse, particularly Shakespearean iambic pentameter. Practice breath control and retention by timing the duration of breath exhalation in the diaphragmatic breathing exercise. The goal should be a minimum of sixty seconds of continual breath exhalation without having to take in new air. It follows that actors should not smoke and, of course, should keep the body in excellent physical condition.

Perform the following exercises for the development of good breathing:

Exercise 2   Breathing and Laughing

Since laughing promotes special breathing problems, begin by vocalizing a highly artificial laugh such as *ha-ha, ho-ho.* Check the action in your abdominal muscles. Your artificial laughter and that of others may lead you into group laughter. This is a desirable goal because then you can check the action of your breathing under honest conditions.

Exercise 3   The Alphabet

Practice projecting the alphabet. Repeat the exercise daily to increase the number of letters you can project without having to take in new breath. Then repeat the exercise calling and extending the sound of each letter as though trying to create an echo. Use all your breath on each letter. The effect will be tantamount to singing. (Incidentally, every actor should take singing lessons if at all possible, if only for breath development.)

Exercise 4   Question Responses

Select a partner at random and take turns asking important questions (for example: Are you married? Do you believe in God?) which require direct and simple answers, probably only yes or no. Notice that inhalation of breath is the first part of your responding action. Without forcing, try to increase the amount of inhalation with each response. This exercise can aid you in developing the habit of adequate inhalation of breath before you speak any unit of speech.

Exercise 5   Sounds

Practice breathing correctly as you project the following sounds:
1. *HAH   h-h-h-h!*
2. *HAY   a-a-a-a!*
3. *HEE   e-e-e-e!*
4. *HOO   o-o-o-o!*
5. *HI   i-i-i-i!*

Vocal Quality

Vocal quality refers to the way the voice sounds to the ear in terms of pleasantness or unpleasantness and includes consideration of pitch, range, tone, resonance, and timbre.

Pitch and Range

Pitch is how high or how low the voice sounds. Range is the distance measured in notes between the lowest and highest pitch of the comfortable speaking voice of an actor. An effective stage voice uses both high and low pitch, but probably modulates between the two much of the time. The potential range of most of us is as much as eight notes, but we tend to use only three or four notes.

Exercise 6   Pitch

Practice reading each of the following sentences with consistently high pitch and then with consistently low pitch. Finally, read the sentence aloud with modulated pitch between high and low, but slightly on the low end of the scale.

MACBETH   Tomorrow and tomorrow creeps in this petty pace from day to day.
Macbeth by William Shakespeare

BERNARDA   I have to let them feel the weight of my hand.
The House of Bernarda Alba by Federico García Lorca

BRICK   Wouldn't it be funny if that was true?
Cat on a Hot Tin Roof by Tennessee Williams

Exercise 7   Range

To increase the notes in your vocal range, practice the following:
1. Sing the traditional musical scale:
Do, re, mi, fa, sol, la, ti, do

2. Speak the following sentence aloud and correspond each note of the musical scale with a word in the sentence:

MACBETH   Life's but a walking shadow, a poor player.

Macbeth by William Shakespeare

Tone, Resonance, and Timbre

Tone refers to the quality of vocal sound and includes resonance and timbre which refer to a specific tone quality such as high, low, nasal, harsh, shrill, gutteral, and so on. Resonance is the proper amplification of tone. It relies upon the openness and flexible adjustment of the mouth and throat cavities. Resonance contributes to tone through the vibrating quality of the voice resulting from the proper use of the resonators (i.e., the throat cavity; the mouth, tongue, teeth; the nasal cavities; and the sinus cavities). If an actor wishes to improve his resonance, he may do so by practicing clear pronunciation, middle-register pitch, and clear projection of sound. Timbre reflects the peculiar or distinctive character of vocal tone—for example: squeaky, hoarse, mellow, and gravelly. A popular misconception holds that an actor must have a "pleasant, deep-sounding voice," or what used to be called a "radio voice." The correct conception is that any tone quality can provide an effective acting voice if it is clear, well projected, and understood. Unusual tone quality such as gutteral or shrill can be highly useable and advantageous on stage. Tonal quality is not as important as how the voice is used.

Exercise 8   Tone, Resonance, and Timbre

1. To develop your resonance and timbre, prepare to speak by opening the mouth and throat. Now close the lips and produce the sound \m\ as an easy hum at your medium-pitch level. Center the tone in your nasal cavities, but feel the vibrations at the front of the face and in the lips. Sustain your breath while making a sound. Repeat the exercise with the sounds \n\ and \ng\. Now combine \m\, \n\, and \ng\ with with vowel sounds. For example:

m-ah, m-o, m-u, m-a, m-e
n-ah, n-o, n-u, n-a, n-e
ng-ah, ng-o, ng-u, ng-a, ng-e

2. Intone a continuous series of vowels, changing smoothly and without break from one to the next: for example, \oo\ as in *ooze*, \o\ as in *ode*, \aw\ as in *all*, \o\ as in *odd*, \aw\ as in *alms*, \ow\ as in *ounce*, \a\ as in *add*. Control your breath during the sequence, opening the mouth freely to achieve maximum resonance.

3. Create an unusual vocal timbre such as nasality (e.g., force the sound into the nasal cavity). Speak several sentences from Exercise 7 aloud in nasal tone. Repeat the exercise without the nasality and note the difference between unpleasant and pleasant vocal timbre.

Vocal Variety

The ability to modulate or vary voice within a pleasant tone range creates a flexible vocal variety, as opposed to a monotone. A flexible voice creates vocal variety by effective use of inflection, intensity, rate or tempo, pause, and rhythm.

Inflection

Inflection is the rise and fall in pitch of the voice. Actors use inflection to shade feeling and meaning.

Exercise 9   Inflection

Practice reading the following sentences aloud providing a variety of inflections to shade feeling and meaning:

1. Were everyone for whom he did some loving service to bring a blossom to his grave he would sleep tonight beneath a wilderness of flowers.
   "At His Brother's Grave" by Robert Green Ingersoll
2. You shall not press down upon the brow of labor, this crown of thorns, you shall not crucify mankind upon a cross of gold.
   "Cross of Gold" by William Jennings Bryan
3. We have nothing to fear but fear itself.
   First Inaugural Address, Franklin Delano Roosevelt
4. Though passion may have strained, it must not break, our bonds of affection.
   First Inaugural Address, Abraham Lincoln

Intensity

The strength of feeling involved in the quality of speaking combined with manner determines the intensity of the voice. Intensity is the controlled vocal energy which reflects emotional tension.

Exercise 10   Intensity

Practice reading the following sentences with varying levels of tension and intensity generally applying increased or strong intensity:

1. The passage of these resolutions will show more clearly, more decisively, the deep indignation with which Boston regards this outrage.
   "Murder of Lovejoy" by Wendell Phillips
2. Crush the wretch. (Voltaire)
   "The Scholar in a Republic" by Wendell Phillips
3. Yesterday, December 7, 1941—a date which will live in infamy—the United States of America was suddenly and deliberately attacked by the Empire of Japan.
   "Declaration of War Against Japan," Franklin Delano Roosevelt
4. All they that take the sword shall perish with the sword.
   Matt. 26:52

Rate or Tempo

The speed with which one speaks determines rate or tempo.

Exercise 11   Rate or Tempo

Practice speaking the following sentences aloud with varied rate or tempo:

1. What are you going to do about that?

Anonymous

2. Wally whirled westward with a winning way.

Anonymous

3. [Speak] not as a Massachusetts man, nor as a Northern man, but as an American [man].

Seventh of March Speech, 1850, Daniel Webster

4. Their foot shall slide in due time.

Deut. 32: 35

5. They are as great heaps of light chaff before the whirlwind; or large quantities of large stubble before devouring flames.

"Sinners in the Hands of an Angry God" by Jonathan Edwards

Emphasis

Emphasis refers to the amount of stress, force, or vocal weight placed upon a particular word or words within a sentence to provide coloration and variety to the delivery. Proper use of emphasis greatly enhances meaning.

Exercise 12   Emphasis

Practice reading the following material aloud using different levels of emphasis on those words you consider important:

1. congratulations
   farewell
   good morning
   shut up
   come here
   never mind
   sensational
   terrible
   why not?
2. Let me pay the tribute which it is only just that I should pay to some of the men who have been, I believe, misunderstood in this business.

"For the League of Nations" by Woodrow Wilson

3. Yet, after all, it may be best, just in the happiest, sunniest hour of all the voyage, while eager winds are kissing every sail, to dash against the unseen rock, and in an instant hear the billows roar, a sunken ship.

"At His Brother's Grave" by Robert Green Ingersoll

4. Man thinking must not be subdued by his instruments. Books are for the scholar's idle times.

"The American Scholar" by Ralph Waldo Emerson

5. The actions and events of our childhood and youth are not matters of calmest observation. They lie like fair pictures in the air.

"The American Scholar" by Ralph Waldo Emerson

Pause

A brief suspension of the voice, or a hesitation in speech, is called a pause. We use pauses for emphasis, to divide thoughts, to permit a listener time to understand a point, to increase curiosity, and to breathe. In writing, commas, along with dashes, semicolons, and colons, denote the use of pauses. Periods usually indicate a full stop or a lengthy pause.

Exercise 13   Pause

Practice reading the following sentences aloud using appropriate pauses, indicated by punctuation or by your judgment or intuition:

1. We, too, have our religion and it is this: Help for the living—hope for the dead.

"At a Child's Grave" by Robert Green Ingersoll

2. The loved and loving brother, husband, father, friend died where manhood's morning almost touches noon, and while the shadows still were falling toward the west.

"At His Brother's Grave," by Robert Green Ingersoll

3. There was—there is—no gentler, stronger, manlier man.

"At His Brother's Grave" by Robert Green Ingersoll

4. With malice toward none, with charity for all, with firmness in the right as God gives us to see the right, let us strive on to finish the work we are in, to bind up the nation's wounds, to care for him who shall have borne the battle and for his widow and his orphan, to do all which may achieve and cherish a just and lasting peace among ourselves and with all nations.

Second Inaugural Address, Abraham Lincoln

Rhythm

The alteration of silence, sound, strength, and weakness in speech determines rhythm. Do not confuse rhythm with tempo or rate, which are parts of rhythm. Rhythm does not necessarily imply timing; it is rather a matter of accenting syllables. We create a rhythm when we speak as we combine pitch, range, inflection, intensity, rate, and pause.

Exercise 14   Rhythm

Practice reading the following material aloud, bringing your mind and emotions to bear in order to create a rhythm of speech:

1. O, what a noble mind is here o'erthrown!
   The courtier's, soldier's, scholar's, eye, tongue, sword;
   The expectency and rose of the fair state,
   The glass of fashion and the mould of form,
   The observed of all observers, quite, quite down!

   OPHELIA, in *Hamlet* by William Shakespeare

2. Help me do the job in this autumn of conflict and campaign; help me do the job in these years of darkness, of doubt and of crisis which stretch beyond the horizon of tonight's happy vision, and we will justify our glorious past and the loyalty of silent millions who look to us for compassion, for understanding and for honest purpose.

   Acceptance Speech, Adlai Stevenson

Articulation and Pronunciation

Articulation refers to the correct utterance of sounds, particularly the clear speaking of vowels and consonants. When people refer to speaking with good diction, they really mean using clear vocal articulation. Clear and accurate articulation leads to correct pronunciation of words. Pronunciation includes correct utterance of vowels and consonants with the proper accent on syllables. For example, the word *picture* is often mispronounced as the word *pitcher* \pich-er\ when the consonants *c* and *t* are not struck. Vowels are soft sounds such as \ā\, \ē\, \ī\, \ō\, and \ū\. Consonants are hard sounds such as \d\, \t\, \b\, and \k\. The best way to learn proper pronunciation is to examine the structure of a word in a dictionary and to hear it pronounced correctly. Also the study of phonetics will assist in learning how to pronounce words correctly.

Exercise 15   Articulation and Pronunciation

Practice proper articulation and pronunciation of the following words which are often poorly articulated or mispronounced:

probably	Tuesday
company	asked
athletic	decision
no	Grandma
tenth	zoology
get	fat
loose	can't
comparable	sure
library	potato
Wednesday	tongue
because	lend
just	throw
when	vehicle
what	Saturday
where	pitcher
can	homage
and	pseudo

that	statistics
often	egg
nose	Pete
guard	water
picture	lose
unanimity	February
tomato	root
preferable	pieced
photo	Washington
burial	orange

Also practice the following short sentences and brief phrase which likewise are frequently poorly articulated or mispronounced:

Have you eaten?
Didn't you?
ladies and gentlemen

A director coaches an actress in vocal projection and diction during rehearsal.

Projection

When he is dealing with spoken words, sentences, and thoughts, the foremost task of an actor is to speak loudly and clearly enough to make the audience both hear the words and understand the meaning behind the words of the playwright. The point also holds for nonscripted theatre activity if improvisational dialogue is involved. The most believable characterization work, the finest emotional creativity, and the most striking personality projection will not suffice if the entire audience cannot hear and understand an actor. Note the distinction between hearing and understanding. First of all, the voice must be heard; that is, the sound of the voice must be fully projected to everyone listening. Second, the audience must understand what it hears. For example, a strong, loud voice may carry sound to the back of a 2,000-seat auditorium, but if that sound is slurred or if words are pronounced incorrectly, the sound will be unintelligible. Effective vocal projection is directly related to good breathing as defined earlier in this chapter. Do not confuse projection with yelling or with speaking loudly. Even a *stage whisper* can be heard and understood at the rear of a large theatre if the actor is "projecting from the diaphragm," that is, using the entire breathing and vocal mechanism to project sound correctly. Projection is fundamental to acting and any kind of verbal performance. When an actor has difficulty with projection on stage, two specific techniques are recommended. First, practice speaking using a consistent tone. (Add vocal variety later, after the consistent tone is heard by listeners in all regions of the theatre or performance area.) Second, practice effective pronunciation and articulation. Use these two practice techniques without attempting characterization or emotion. Accordingly, mechanical skill and control of projected sounds, words, and sentences should improve.

Exercise 16   Projection

To improve your projection, practice speaking to a friend or teacher in a large auditorium or outside in a public place such as a park. Your friend or teacher should move from place to place as you practice conversing, reading, or reciting. Use a consistent tone with effective articulation and pronunciation. Resist the temptation to yell. Remember, projection is rarely a matter of loudness. It is rather a matter of sending the voice up and out clearly. Use any of the material given in the preceding exercises to practice projection. Be certain that your rate or tempo is not too rapid. In fact, an effective technique in projection includes deliberately slowing down at times.

Phrasing and Context

Phrasing is speaking two or more words which comprise a pattern of thought or a unit of sense. Playwrights provide material which actors use for phrasing. Improvisational performers phrase their own dialogue. Effective use of all the vocal skills learned in this chapter enhance an actor's individual phrasing. At times, the author's material is altered and meaning is shaded by the quality of vocal skills applied to the phrasing by the actor. Phrasing is inextricably linked to context.

Context refers to the possibilities of meaning for each word in each sentence and extends to the possibilities of meaning for each sentence within each paragraph (or speech) in a play. To discover context an actor must understand the placement of each speech within each scene and, in turn, within an entire play. Proper analysis of character, thought, and structure in a play will permit an actor to determine how best to phrase dialogue. For example, Hamlet's famous line "To be or not to be, that is the question . . ." has almost infinite possibilities for vocal phrasing. How actors phrase determines their interpretation. The line can be spoken flatly with no feeling or delivered as a question, superimposing new punctuation on it. Phrasing the line flatly without feeling connotes despair and suicide. Phrasing the line as a question connotes bewilderment concerning the nature of death as it relates to action. If the former contextual phrasing and interpretation are used, vocal work stresses slow rate, extensive use of pause, precise accents, and low, modulated, resonant tone to help evoke a somber mood. If the second contextual phrasing and interpretation are used, vocal work stresses rapid rate, infrequent use of pause, softer accents, and a higher, intensified, and less resonant tone to help evoke an excited but confused mood.

The importance of contextual understanding cannot be overemphasized if we are to apply effective phrasing and vocal technique in the theatre. The clearest and most pleasant speaking voice is rendered worthless if words and speeches are not placed into context.

Exercise 17   Phrasing and Context

1. Practice phrasing the following three words with as many different interpretations as possible:

   avalanche of hate

2. Now practice phrasing the three words within the context of a full sentence:

   What an avalanche of hate you've thrown on my heart.

3. Finally, practice phrasing the sentence within the context of a complete dramatic speech:

   BERNARDA   I saw the storm coming, but I didn't think it would burst so soon. Oh, what an avalanche of hate you've thrown on my heart. But I'm not old yet. I have five chains for you and this house my father built. So not even the weeds will know of my desolation.
   The House of Bernarda Alba by Federico García Lorca

Physical Reinforcement of the Verbal

Verbal communication with an audience may be clearly heard and understood and still not be interesting or dramatic. Most vocal work on stage requires visual and emotional reinforcement and accompanying physicalization to elevate it above the level of information. Word meanings are not always precise; even when they are, they may be mundane. How do actors refine meanings to make them precise and how do they make the mundane interesting? They can accomplish much of this by using physical reinforcement of speech. Such reinforcement can enhance meaning and provoke interest. Used discreetly and appropriately, physical hand gestures, facial gestures, and gestures from any part or all of the body can contribute immeasurably to vocal work on stage.

Adding physical activity to reinforce words can also help clarify imprecise meaning. For example, imagine that a young man is talking to his mother in the living room. He wants to use the family car. The mother is convinced by the argument and calls the father into the room. She glances up at her husband, turns smilingly to her son, and says, "We've decided you can have the car tonight." The father, observing that she is looking at the son when she speaks, glances confusedly around and asks, "Who's 'we'?" The mother points to the father with one hand and touches herself with the other hand. Anyone watching now knows who the "we" referred to a moment before is. On the stage, this type of physical clarification often makes words precise. Actors in plays are continually gesturing and pantomimically reinforcing language. An actor may have a line such as "He was this tall." Obviously the actor must pantomimically demonstrate how tall the man was if the line is to have any precise meaning. Also, actors must create something beyond cliché gesture in striving for ways to physicalize.

Physicalizing with the hands, the face, or any part or all of the body can rarely be directed by a playwright, a director, or an artist-leader. Physicalization is fundamentally an actor's responsibility. Physicalization can rarely be superimposed on an actor; it should come from within, from personal needs and motivations. Personalization is vital to individual physicalization. Later, personalization can be intermingled with the needs and motivations of a *character* if a script is involved. Of course, it is the responsibility of the director to help an actor see the possibilities for physicalization.

All physicalization must emanate from a center or primary energy source of an actor. That is, the right arm cannot just pop out from the shoulder on its own and do something. A unified activity must be operative. In physicalization a part always functions within a whole. Naturally, character and emotion are included in that whole. In other words, character, emotion, energy, mind, and body all combine to create appropriate, dramatic physical behavior that reinforces speech. (For example, the next time you have a strong emotional experience, recall exactly what you did physically immediately upon its conclusion. You may discover how emotion was vented through physical behavior as it reinforced what you said.)

Exercise 18   Physical Reinforcement of the Verbal

Memorize the following material and practice delivering it with a variety of appropriate physical activities including hand, face, and body gestures. Try to use physicalization to explicate meaning, clarify motivation, and reinforce emotion.

THE DEVIL   In the arts of peace Man is a bungler. I have seen his cotton factories and the like, with machinery that a greedy dog could have invented if it had wanted money instead of food. I know his clumsy typewriters and bungling locomotives and tedious bicycles: They are toys compared to the Maxim gun, the submarine torpedo boat. There is nothing in Man's industrial machinery but his greed and sloth: his heart is in his weapons. This marvellous force of Life of which you boast is a force of Death: Man measures his strength by his destructiveness.

"Don Juan in Hell" from *Man and Superman*
by George Bernard Shaw

Voice training in special *dialects* such as American Southern, Irish, French, German, Russian, Italian, and Oriental require concentrated, lengthy work which should be undertaken in specialized or advanced training. Excellent books and recorded material are available for this work (some sources are given in Suggested Readings at the end of the chapter).

Continued practice and extension of the exercises in this chapter should provide a sound basis for an effective speaking voice in the theatre. Serious students of acting practice vocal exercises daily as part of their habitual professional routine.

Suggested Readings

Andersch, Elizabeth; Staats, Lorin; and Bostrom, Robert. *Communication in Everyday Use*. 3rd ed. New York: Holt, Rinehart & Winston, 1969.

Blunt, Jerry. *Stage Dialects*. San Francisco: Chandler Publishing Co., 1967.

Brigance, William N., and Henderson, Florence. *A Drill Manual for Improvising Speech*. New York: J. B. Lippincott Co., 1939.

Buehler, E. Christian, and Linkugel, Wil. *Speech Communication*. New York: Harper & Row, 1969.

Chriest, Fred M. *Foreign Accent*. Englewood Cliffs, N. J.: Prentice-Hall, 1964.

Eisenson, Jon. *Voice and Diction*. 3d ed. New York: Macmillan Co., 1974.

Hall, E. T. *The Silent Language*. Garden City, N. Y.: Doubleday & Co., 1959.

Herman, Louis, and Lewis, Margaret. *Manual of Foreign Dialects*. New York: Theatre Arts Books, 1958.

Lee, Charlotte. *Oral Communication*. Boston: Houghton Mifflin Co., 1959.

Lessac, Arthur. *The Use and Training of the Human Voice*. New York: Drama Book Specialists/Publishers, 1967.

Machlin, Evangeline. *Speech for the Stage*. New York: Theatre Arts Books, 1970.

Mayer, Lyle V. *Fundamentals of Voice and Diction*. 3rd ed. Dubuque, Iowa: Wm. C. Brown Co., 1968.

Thompson, D. F., and Meltzer, L. "Communication of Emotional Intent by Facial Expression." *Journal of Abnormal and Social Psychology* 68 (1964): 129–35.

Tolch, Charles J. "The Problem of Language and Accuracy in Identification of Facial Expression." *Central States Speech Journal*, February 1963, pp. 12–16.

Turner, J. Clifford. Foreward by British actress Peggy Ashcroft. *Voice and Speech for the Theatre*. London: Isaac Pitman & Sons, 1950.

Vetter, Harold J. *Language Behavior and Communication*. Itasco, Ill.: F. E. Peacock Publishers, 1969.

Wise, Claude-Merten. *Applied Phonetics*. Englewood Cliffs, N. J.: Arc Books, 1963.

8 Character Work in Scenes from Plays

The exercise activity now graduates from work in basic acting techniques to work with the collaborative artist known as the playwright who provides the basis for the dramatic characterization. To create characterization an actor should analyze what the author has written using a detailed procedure known as *role analysis*. Role analysis is best applied to the creation of a complete role in a one-act or full-length play meant to be performed before an audience (role analysis is treated in detail in chapter 10). Work with a character in an extracted scene is less detailed because in class or studio experience one need use only five to ten minutes of the author's written role.

Four basic techniques suffice to create a character for an extracted scene: personalization, visualization, pantomimic dramatization, and character motivation. These techniques aid in creating a sufficiently believable character. A more important aspect of scene acting is to practice the acting skills learned to date such as movement, emotion, observation, imagination, use of past experiences, use of the senses, work with objects, improvisation, and vocalization. Acting in an extracted scene requires only moment-to-moment performance skill, with minimal reference to the entire role in the complete play. Full-scale role analysis is an intellectual process, entailing research and study as discussed in chapter 10. There is a time for an actor to be a thinker. However, in initial character work in scenes the actor should rely upon an intuitive factor and upon the exercise skills learned to this point, an appropriate step because he should learn to trust the moment-to-moment action of a scene. He should also learn to trust character relationships in brief scenes. Were an actor to do all the intellectual work involved in analysis of a complete role in preparation for a role in an extracted scene, that intellectual work would probably hinder rather than help—he might be thinking rather than doing. Later, with scene practice accomplished, an actor will be better equipped to do extensive intellectual work and apply it to a complete role without losing the intuitive physical and emotional effort necessary to effective acting. To put it another way: It is well to learn to walk before you run.

Personalization and Character in a Scene

Basic fundamentals again apply. Relaxation and effective breathing are paramount if an actor is to comfortably approach initial work with author characterization. Remember, for the most part the role will be the *person* of the actor. Character development based on role analysis of a complete play is virtually impossible in most five-to-ten-minute scenes. Accept this fact and utilize personalization with confidence and comfort. An exercise in personalization should assist an actor in preparing for character work in scenes.

Exercise 1   Human Contact from Personal Resources

Two actors create an improvisation in which neither actor is to speak without making physical contact with the other actor. Every time a new line of dialogue or new thought is introduced, a corresponding physical contact should be made by each actor. Only the actor who introduces the verbal line is to make the physical contact. Verbal sounds and noises do not necessitate physical contact.

This exercise automatically develops close communication between actors which is rooted almost totally in honest personality characteristics. It also provides a creative base for characterization because verbalizing requires some intellectual structuring related to instinctive physical activity. Mixing the verbal and the physical in this exercise increases dramatic tension onstage. This exercise relates personal activity to the rudiments of dramatic activity; that is, it relates the actor's *person* to the dramatic situation and conflict providing the roots of characterization.

Visualization and Character in a Scene

Visualization refers to a character's appearance including both his physical being and his dress. While an actor's person provides automatic visualization for much of his character in a scene, the playwright usually obligates an actor to add other visual elements to enhance basic characterization. For example, a character may be required to limp due to a physical deformity in one leg, as is true of Laura in Tennessee Williams' *The Glass Menagerie*. Similarly, a character such as Howard in Arthur Miller's *Death of a Salesman* may be obligated to wear a business suit.

An interesting use of visualization is for an actor to imaginatively relate himself and his role to the characteristics of an inanimate object. For example, he could observe the tall, clean lines of a Greek vase and incorporate such characteristics into his posture, movement, and activity. This technique is beneficial, for example, in portrayal of a king or other royal person or a statesman.

Similarly helpful is to select the characteristics of animal behavior in visualizing a character in a scene. Try to select an animal with characteristics analogous to the role under study. For example, the crude, snorting activity of a pig as it eats in a feedlot might provide visual characteristics for activity in a boorish eating scene.

In Exercise 2 the elements of visualization just described are combined to provide valuable preparatory training to character work in a scene. Remain flexible and imaginative throughout this exercise.

Exercise 2 Visualization

Recline on a firm surface and establish relaxation and effective breathing. Concentrate only on a specific animal image such as an elephant and its physical attributes and movement (be certain that you select an animal you are familiar with, one that will not require extensive research). When the animal image is vivid in your mind, rise to your feet and begin moving about in the manner of the animal you selected. Place emphasis on bone structure, rhythm of movement, and facial expressiveness. After a period of time, the instructor will ask you to stop your animal movement and take a relaxed standing position. Walk comfortably in your own manner; then subtly add key characteristics of your animal to your activity. Emphasize bone structure, rhythm, and facial expression again, but try to wed them to your own attributes, dropping out the more excessive imitative factors. You may also use noises or sounds made by the animal.

Later your instructor will announce your arrival at a specific place in the room or theatre to attend an auction of furniture and household goods. All of you are to be bidders at the auction. The auctioneer is imaginary. Each of you bids on an object with your private concept of

A static study of six distinct character types. The visualization of the five daughters and their mother reveals not only filial identity, but also individual characteristics. *The House of Bernarda Alba* by Federico García Lorca. Directed by Jerry L. Crawford. Costumes by Ellis M. Pryce-Jones. University of Nevada, Las Vegas. National Finalist Production, Kennedy Center for the Performing Arts, Washington, D. C., American College Theatre Festival, 1975.

what is being sold. You have the discretion of continuing the bidding, withdrawing from it, or concluding it with certainty that you have purchased the object. The vocal and physical work you have done with your animal should be apparent in your manner as you bid.

As you continue to bid, discard the animal characteristics and assume the characteristics of the object being sold. For example, if you are bidding for a short, squat cast-iron cooking pot, emulate similar physical characteristics as you bid.

Pantomimic Dramatization and Character in a Scene

Pantomime and *mime* are specialized kinds of theatre performances or exercises and are considered in their proper place in chapter 12, Commedia Dell'Arte. *Pantomimic dramatization,* as it is used here as a beginning acting technique in scene work in the class or studio, implies more than *pantomime,* which is action without words (what used to be called *dumb show*) and more even than *mime,* which is the imitating of scenes from life (usually as travesty or satire and usually without dialogue). *Pantomimic dramatization* is used here to refer to the process of discovering, creating, and using personalized physical action, or business, as it relates to objects. Effective pantomimic dramatization enriches, vitalizes, and adds distinction to the visual and physical impact of an actor and his role. The physical action may come from any part of the body or from all of it. For example, imagine an actress performing Blanche DuBois in Tennessee William's *A Streetcar Named Desire.* In a particular scene, Blanche breaks into sobbing hysteria following verbal and physical abuse from Mitch. Most young actresses have difficulty playing this scene believably. Pantomimic dramatization can greatly assist the effectiveness of acting this scene. Specifically, the actress could clutch a large pillow to her body, bury her face in it, and rock slowly from side to side. This clear visual action could be far more effective than artificial sounds of sobbing and violent screaming. The actress may not have to make a sound, or at best a muffled one into the pillow, to project the correct emotion.

Pantomimic dramatization requires an actor to use his imagination to determine what to do physically and visually while on stage. Exercise 3 assists an actor in learning how to arrive at that determination (pantomimic dramatization is used again in chapter 10 in developing role creation in a complete play).

Exercise 3   Pantomimic Dramatization

Select a role in one of the following scenes. Discover and create personalized physical action or business related to objects used in the scene. Write a list of all created action; then practice the scene and incorporate your pantomimic dramatization.

Elma and Grace   opening scene, Act I
 Bus Stop by William Inge

Laura and Jim   Scene viii
    The Glass Menagerie by Tennessee Williams
Willy and Linda   opening scene, Act II
    Death of a Salesman by Arthur Miller
Maggie and Brick   opening scene, Act I
    Cat on a Hot Tin Roof by Tennessee Williams
Biff and Happy   bedroom scene, Act I
    Death of a Salesman by Arthur Miller
Millie and Madge   opening scene, Act II
    Picnic by William Inge
Mel and Edna   beginning of Act II, Scene i
    Prisoner of Second Avenue by Neil Simon
George and Martha   opening scene, Act I
    Who's Afraid of Virginia Woolf? by Edward Albee

Motivation and Character in a Scene

The fourth element for successful acting in scenes is discovering or inventing valid motivations, or reasons, wants, needs, and desires, for everything done on the stage. The character should not seem to be arbitrary; that is, the audience should be able to recognize the purpose behind the behavior of the character. At times, the motivating factor will have occurred at some point in the play prior to the scene being performed. However, because it is generally not necessary to analyze the role in the complete play to perform effectively in a scene, the actor may have to invent appropriate motivation for some of the action. At other times, the motivation may be within the scene itself (incidentally, when a role in a complete play is analyzed, motivation is established in the same two ways: by situations provided in the script and by invented factors not readily apparent in the play). This procedure simplifies the acting task by restricting analysis to the perspective of an extracted scene.

Note: Instructors and actors who prefer a more extensive approach to role analysis in extracted scenes naturally are privileged to apply all of the procedures described in chapter 10 to this work in scene acting. For example, playing *opposite values* is an effective motivation and emotion technique to use in extracted scenes. If the script clearly calls for anger, as the emotion in place of it play love or happiness. In other words, determine the motivation and its related emotion and reverse the values. The purpose of this technique is to avoid rigidly setting a motivation and an emotion too early in rehearsal. The technique also permits further exploration of motivational and emotional values in a character prior to their final selection for performance. Beginning actors frequently become stymied in the middle of a rehearsal period and need fresh or revitalized motivation. Playing opposite values is both fun and a beneficial technique for revitalization. It is helpful in classroom and studio scene acting, as well as in regular production rehearsal of a complete play.

Exercise 4 gives assistance in preparation in discovery and invention of motivation for practice scene work.

Exercise 4   Motivation

The entire group takes a position onstage, standing or seated as they desire. The dramatic situation is that the group is locked in a room for an indefinite period of time and must pass the time waiting for release. No one may wait in total silence; as often as possible speaking must be included in the improvisational exercise. Your task is to find ways to pass the time without saying or doing things arbitrarily. In other words, all activity (both physical and verbal) must be truthfully and honestly motivated. Your instructor is to observe this improvisation carefully and may drop a person from the scene if that person appears to be "acting" or "performing without motivation." This exercise requires intense moment-to-moment concentration. The dramatic situation provides the possibility for motivational discovery. It also provides enormous possibility for invented motivation. The exercise concludes when the instructor has either removed everyone from the activity because of unmotivated work, or when the instructor announces that the waiting period has ended. (Note that this exercise also enhances work in believable and truthful stage activity.)

Selecting a Scene from a Play

Selecting an effective cutting from a play for scene practice is often a difficult task. Many scenes are available in published form in most bookstores (the Suggested Readings at the end of the chapter lists some of the popularly used scene books). If you use a library copy of a play as the acting script, do not mark in it. If a scene is extracted or cut from a play, make certain that it is at least five to ten minutes in length and that it is a manageable scene relatively complete within itself. Select a scene that seems to have interesting character work and emotional content within your current state of development (an instructor or coach can assist in assessing that development). Generally avoid intensely emotional scenes because an extracted form usually provides insufficient time to build much emotion. Select a character within your present basic age range and physical characteristics. Later in more advanced work it will be possible to select characters outside your age and physical type. It is also preferable to select a scene from a modern realistic play and to advance later to nonrealistic styles. Select a play from personal knowledge of dramatic literature; if your experience in this respect is limited, ask your instructor or coach for recommendations (sample scenes in realism are provided in chapter 16 and recommended characters and plays for scene playing are given at the end of all chapters on style).

When a scene has been selected, the actor is ready for his first rehearsal, which should be a simple, relaxed read-through of the scene with any other actor or actors involved. Read the role without any effort at characterization or emotion. Read it for information only. This reading familiarizes the actor with words, cues (see definition of terminology in this chapter), and other characters.

In the second rehearsal the scene or play is read again. This time the theory of personalization is put to work. The actor should use as much of his *person* as is naturally and honestly possible. At this reading actors can substitute personal names for character names, which greatly increases the personalization factor. A personal association should be managed for every line spoken. In other words, the actor tries to make the character "come to him." He remains free with the text which means he does not have to read letter-perfect. He establishes considerable eye contact with other actors. If possible, he eliminates the text altogether and improvises the dialogue to increase honesty with the other actor(s). (Avoid a solo monologue early in your actor training. The personal factor functions best in relationship with other people.) When they have difficulty sustaining eye contact, actors may use the scene and characters as totally flexible scenarios or outlines. An entirely new scene may be created if necessary so long as success with personalization is achieved. There will be plenty of time to return to the actual script. Eye contact can be increased by the actors sitting close to each other. The physical closeness also permits occasional natural touching. Actors should not suppress genuine behavior; rather, they should let happen whatever happens. For example, at this rehearsal actors frequently submit to the urge to laugh or giggle. They should do so without inhibition. Stricter discipline comes later. The goal is freedom, relaxation, and naturalness at this rehearsal.

Actors may continue the personalization process for as long a period of time as a situation will tolerate. If an actor is creating a scene for a class which is due to be performed within three weeks, a minimum of three-to-five personalization rehearsals are necessary (later, when a role for a full-length production rehearsing from four to six weeks or longer is created, it is good to use about two weeks of personalization rehearsal). Within the personalization period actors need make no *artificial* attempt at line memorization and, if the director permits, no attempt at fixed blocking (e.g., planned movement). When rehearsal returns to the playwright's script following personization work, lines and blocking should set rapidly and firmly. Appropriate motivation can also be found more easily. And most important, honest and believable emotion can be better stimulated. Further, interaction with other actors will generally be free of the artifice which accompanies so much of the traditional approach to rehearsals (e.g., immediate blocking and line memorization prior to character work).

During the personalization rehearsals, an actor learns to borrow freely from personal behavior, observation, and experience. Dustin Hoffman stated during the filming of the movie *Papillon*, "Anytime you can use real-life parallels in your acting, you use 'em." Also, personalization involves accepting the influence of the other actor's person. Hoffman continued, "Both of us [i.e., Steve McQueen and Hoffman] realized we needed each other's help and support. I can't really speak for him, but I believe he was thinking the same thing. In the movie one character is saying to another: 'You've got to help me or die; neither of us can do it all alone.' And for us actors the meaning is: We'd better help each other or we could die with this movie."[1]

While personalization is the free use of the self as far as is honestly and comfortably possible, and while it includes close interaction with other actors during the scene or play, it does not mean that actors must make intimate emotional commitment with fellow players. A friendly, cooperative manner is vital in acting, but in-depth offstage, personal involvement with colleagues usually creates obstacles to believable onstage work. Hoffman, who uses personalization so well as an actor, makes the latter point:

I always play it cool. I never get involved with anybody while I'm making a movie or doing a play. And I mean anybody. There's no question that you're bound to lose out if there are emotional commitments; people saying "Oh, let's not do it this way, let's do it this other way." People can use friendship as a lever to get you to alter what you believe in. So when I'm making a movie I don't socialize with the cast. I don't go to dinner with them. After the day's work is done I go home. I never met McQueen before the movie and I haven't seen him since. But suppose I'd just done a picture with a girl? I don't think you should go out and have an affair with a girl just because you're doing a love story with her. You know what? If you've been doing it in a hotel room, you aren't saving it for the camera, and on film your big love scene looks like a frozen fish dinner.[2]

In effect, Hoffman is saying in rather stark terms that personalization is not a license for undisciplined, self-indulgent behavior. It is a system of acting and an approach to role creation and performance.

Personalization will rarely take an actor completely through the creation of a role. At some point, he will be unable to produce or perform an emotion or action. Some kind of traditional acting technique is needed. Such techniques as observation, imagination, emotional-sensory recall (dormant emotion), pantomimic dramatization, and improvisation have all been discussed; any one or all of these techniques can be put to use as part of or an extension of personalization.

Standard Acting Terms

As rehearsals progress toward performance, knowledge of standard terms related to acting and the physical theatre become necessary. The following terminology and definitions are given here for the actor's convenience and assistance during rehearsal of characters in scenes. Note that some of the terms are defined further in the Glossary at the end of this book.

Acting Area

The traditional proscenium stage is generally divided as shown in the accompanying diagram.

1. Tom Donnelly, "Hoffman Makes His Minor 'Papillon' Role Major," *Las Vegas Review-Journal*, 9 January, 1974.
2. Donnelly, "Hoffman."

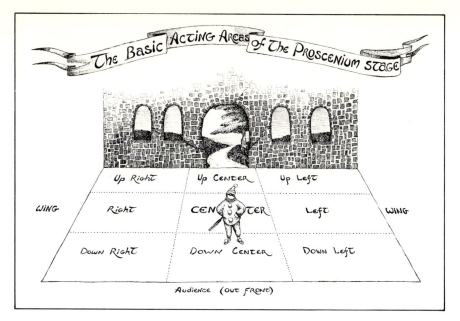

The traditional arena stage (central stage) is generally divided according to the accompanying diagram.

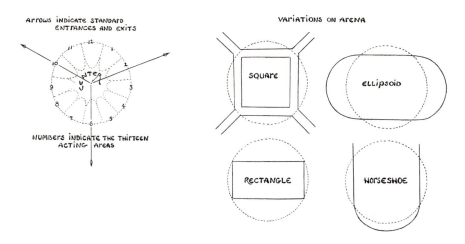

The basic acting areas of arena staging.

Acting Positions

Full-front   The actor faces the audience fully. This is a very strong position, but can be sustained for long periods of time only in nonrealistic plays and musicals.

Full-back   The actor stands with his full back to the audience. Used for special dramatic effect, the position is also very strong, but should generally be sustained only for brief periods of time.

One-quarter   The actor stands in a quarter turn away from the audience, usually facing another actor. This is a strong position, but less so than full-front. The position increases in strength when the actor makes the one-quarter turn toward the audience rather than away from it. This position can be sustained for the longest period of time in realistic plays.

Profile or one-half turn   The actor stands facing either right or left with his profile in view of the audience. Rarely a strong position, this stance is also used for comic effect.

Three-quarters   In this position the actor nearly turns his full back with less than one side of his head and a shoulder toward the audience. This is the weakest of the five basic acting positions.

Rehearsal Terms

Stage business   Small, detailed actions of the body (often the hands) such as drinking from a cup, lighting a cigar, mopping the brow, and so on.

Properties   Physical objects used on stage by the actor. The term is usually shortened to *props*. There are four classifications of props:

1. Hand props: Small objects which actors can carry or handle onstage such as books, drinking glasses, and the like.
2. Personal props: Items on the actor's person such as eyeglasses, jewelry, key chain, and the like.
3. Costume props: Costume accessories such as fans, gloves, handkerchiefs, and the like.
4. Stage props: Major objects related to the physical scene such as stools, pillows, lamps, furniture, and the like.
(The four classifications are interchangeable, depending on how the props are used.)

Ad lib   From the Latin *ad libitum* ("at pleasure"), the term applies to lines supplied by the actor when they are lacking in the script, but desired in the production (or lines invented when the actor has forgotten the memorized lines).

Aside   A line onstage directed to the audience which is not supposed to be heard by other characters.

Build   An increase in speed or volume in order to reach a climactic theatrical moment.

Cue   The last word or words of a speech or the end of an action which indicates the time for another actor to speak or move.

Drop   The drop in volume on the last word or words of a speech.

Pickup cue   A direction given to actors to avoid undesirable time lapses between lines or action.

Top   Delivery of a line or lines with more volume and intensity than the line preceding it or them.

Terms Related to Movement or Blocking

If personalization works correctly, little or no marking of the script in terms of movement or blocking will be necessary. However, blocking may be marked in the script at an early rehearsal. Following are some of the commonly used notations.

Terms for proscenium stage

    D   Downstage (forward; toward audience)
    U   Upstage (back; away from audience)
    L   Stage left (any area left of the actor as he faces the audience)
    R   Stage right (any area right of the actor as he faces the audience)
    C   Center stage (the approximate middle of the acting area)

(Variations should be self-evident. For example, *UL* indicates upstage left of the acting area.)

Terms for arena or central stage

    C   Center stage (the approximate middle of the acting area)
    Twelve o'clock   Arbitrarily established point of the acting area analogous to the number twelve on a clock (all other eleven acting areas are designated from that point according to the numbers on a clock).

Additional movement or blocking terms

    X   Cross (stage)
    XC   Cross center (stage)
    XDL Cross down left (stage)
    XDR Cross down right (stage)
    XUL, XUR, UDC, etc.

(A downward arrow ↓ may indicate "sit" and an upward arrow ↑ "rise.")

Short phrases can also be marked in the script, such as "close book," "slap him," and so on.

Example:

"O, woe is me—XDR

Fall   — T' have seen what I have seen, see what

↓ to Knees   I see!" ↑ Rise—run off DL

OPHELIA in *Hamlet* by William Shakespeare

Final Rehearsals and Performance of the Scene

Lines should be memorized at least one week prior to performance of the scene. By this time, stage properties and furniture necessary for performance of the scene should have been collected. These items should be kept to a minimum; it is not advisable to spend time and energy creating a believable scenic environment. In scene practice the audience accepts that the focus is upon the performer, with only essential scenic elements provided. These factors also hold true for costuming. What costuming is necessary can probably be provided from personal wardrobes. Also, basic properties and furniture are usually available as part of standard classroom or theatre rehearsal items. Occasionally, actors may have to provide these items as well. In many instances it is acceptable to use substitute facsimiles for properties. Normal room illumination or basic area lighting are sufficient for scenes. Actors in classes often must be content with general room illumination or what is called in the theatre "work lights" (meaning nonspecialized illumination). Generally, if music and sound effects are necessary or desired, actors must provide them by bringing a tape recorder or phonograph. Care must also be taken to provide adequate rehearsal time for the person who operates the equipment. As a general rule, stage makeup is not used for scene practice. Audiences for scene performances usually come from the class or acting company. Occasionally, friends, relatives, and other students and faculty or other theatre artists in the company are invited to view a scene performance.

After a scene is performed before an audience, standard practice is usually to have an informal critique or response from the instructor, director, or coach. Sometimes peers or colleague actors contribute to the response. Additionally, many instructors provide specific written evaluation of scene work.

Suggested Readings

Elkind, Samuel, ed. *32 Scenes for Acting Practice*. Glenview, Ill.: Scott, Foresman & Co., 1972.

Elkind, Samuel, ed. *30 Scenes for Acting Practice*. Glenview, Ill.: Scott, Foresman & Co., 1972.

Elkind, Samuel, ed. *28 Scenes for Acting Practice*. Glenview, Ill.: Scott, Foresman & Co., 1971.

Grumback, Jane, and Emerson, Robert, eds. *Actors Guide to Scenes*. New York: Drama Book Specialists/Publishers, 1973.

Grumback, Jane, and Emerson, Robert, eds. *Actors Guide to Monologues*. New York: Drama Book Specialists/Publishers, 1972.

Olfson, Lewy, ed. *50 Great Scenes for Student Actors*. New York: Bantam Books, Inc., 1970.

Robinson, Marion Parsons, ed. *Scenes for Women from the Plays of Shakespeare*. Boston, Mass.: Walter H. Baker Co., 1967.

Southern, Richard. *Proscenium and Sight Lines*. London: Faber & Faber, 1939.

Steffensen, James L., Jr., ed. *Great Scenes from World Theatre*. Vols. 1 and 2. New York: Avon Books, vol. 1, 1965, vol. 2, 1972.

At only one time does an actor find it relatively easy to gain a role or to become involved in a performance activity. This happens when he is given one of those opportunities in an acting class or a studio. There, he is simply assigned a part or is asked to participate in a related activity or he arbitrarily makes a selection. Thereafter, actors must compete. Competition is a necessary aspect of any acting career. As many actors as are available determine the range of selection possible for any given role or activity. There is always someone who can do the role as well as you; in some instances, better and more experienced people will challenge you. However, there are always people less capable of achievement than you. Be prepared to accept rejection or defeat and to return with resilience and renewed determination. Eugene O'Neill said that perseverance and good luck are the key factors to success in the theatre. When actors use phrases such as the big break and being in the right place at the right time, they are using catch phrases for good luck or good fortune. The shear volume of actors striving for achievement in the field automatically indicates that even high-quality talent will be overlooked in the scramble and competition for roles and jobs. Without question, no matter how good an actor is, he is also going to have to be lucky. Have no illusions about this fact. It is relatively true that "good contacts" are invaluable. Rarely, if ever, will such a contact *keep* an actor working, but that contact might increase his chances of getting the opportunity to work. The most classic misunderstood concept related to good contacts is the infamous myth of the casting couch. The connotation in that phrase is obvious, but generally incorrect. The so-called casting couch is neither necessary nor valid in terms of constant work in the theatre any more than in any other walk of life. The favors implied in such activities are no more valuable or invaluable than having a mutual friend establish a contact. An actor should never attempt to offer anything less than his skill, dedication, and experience as the selling features of himself as an actor. While an actor should take advantage of honest, ethical contacts to assist him in gaining work opportunities, he should never sacrifice his personal integrity.

The term *tryout* is generally used in the theatre to denote securing of a role by reading aloud from the script before a director, a producer, or an author. The term *audition* is generally used in the theatre to denote securing of a role by presenting prepared, memorized, and rehearsed material before a director, a producer, or an author. To simplify matters, throughout the following discussion *audition* will be used rather than *tryout*. Note however that the discussion applies to both terms.

How to Audition

We are indebted to Prof. J. Gordon Greene for making major contributions to the following material.

How does an actor best approach an audition? Since organization of auditions is a function of the director (and occasionally of the producer or

Call board

playwright), an actor participates as a performer. Following are some direct, basic suggestions for actors when they audition.

1. If you are auditioning for a written role, read the play in advance.

2. If you are auditioning for a specific part, practice key speeches for that role in advance. It is usually not necessary to memorize speeches unless audition directions call for it. What is desired is sufficient familiarization in order to permit glancing out at the audience occasionally.

3. Be extremely disciplined and courteous at auditions. Be punctual and be attentive to all directions and requests. Be totally silent except when you are asked to speak. Most directors become irritated by actors who stand or sit around chattering with other people at open auditions. It is also wise to avoid unnecessary commentary or discussion with the director, who is bound to be completely occupied. Any attempt at idle chatting is usually viewed as a device for gaining favor or special consideration. Be cooperative, but not aggressive.

4. If the audition is open, listen carefully to the competition as it may be beneficial to hear other interpretations. However, if you are particularly impressed by someone, it is generally best not to change your interpretation. Rather, use his work as stimulation to do an even better job with your audition. Do not imitate anyone else's work.

5. Avoid falling into the trap of self-criticism. If you strive for perfection, even one verbal error, for example, can lead to inordinate self-criticism and collapse of an entire audition. Reflection and self-evaluation should occur after the audition is completed. During the audition, remain flexible and good-natured no matter what happens.

6. How much emotion should an actor reveal at an audition? Again, personalization is the key to the answer. If the role and scene demand intense emotion, provide as much as your person can honestly project, but do not force emotion. Forcing inevitably leads to artificiality. Personal naturalness and comfort should be the guides. For example, it is said that Dustin Hoffman usually provides considerable, but natural and honest, emotion at an audition. However, once he has been cast, he reverts immediately to several weeks of relaxed, comfortable personalization during rehearsal. Remember that an audition is usually a heightened emotional experience. Unless the role calls for truly unusual emotional intensity, the audition situation may provide enough energy that you need not worry or think about creating emotion.

7. When casting is announced, be understanding and cheerful whether you are cast or not. It is juvenile and destructive to allow disappointment to affect progress for any length of time. The only thought an actor should have is what, where, and when is the next audition. It is particularly meaningless to second-guess casting decisions. To do so is to indulge in debilitating emo-

Pages 78 to 84 in this book were adapted from J. Gordon Greene, "The Actor Auditions," *Southern Theatre* 16, Fall 1972 and Winter 1973.

tionalism. It is the surest sign of unprofessionalism, and it invariably gains nothing but the possible disfavor of a director and your colleagues. Learn this lesson at the first unsuccessful audition.

Types of Auditions

Auditions will be either open or closed. In an open audition any interested person may participate. Traditionally, also at an open audition actors may watch other actors perform. In a closed audition the general public is usually excluded, and the audition privilege is limited to specific people and groups. Traditionally, at a closed audition actors may not watch other actors perform. In these auditions, actors are usually called at a specified time, and the length of the audition time is rigidly controlled.

Auditions are usually divided into two categories: specific and general. For example, at a specific audition, an actor might audition only for Hamlet, or only for Hamlet and Laertes. At a general audition the actor auditions for any role, and the director has the privilege of casting him in any role he wishes. Further, a general audition may be for membership in an acting company or group rather than for a specific role or play. For example, when auditioning for a summer stock group or repertory company, the actor may perform one or more short prepared audition pieces to demonstrate his general ability.

Selecting an Audition Piece

When an actor selects personal audition pieces, it is vital for him to select cuttings which best reveal the range of his *personal* acting abilities. Following are some direct suggestions to assist you in choosing selections from most classical and realistic plays:

1. Generally remain within your own basic age range and physical type. While everyone complains about type casting (see Glossary), the practice is used almost exclusively in the professional theatre and much more often than is admitted in educational theatre. How can you best function within the limitations of that concept? Above all, careful, critical understanding of yourself is essential. First, you know how old you are; your age range will generally not vary as a type beyond ten years on either side of your age, provided that you are at least twenty-six or twenty-seven years old (at eighteen years of age most actors cannot perform the role of an eight-year-old child). You also know your height, weight, and general physical characteristics. Painful though it may be, do not have illusions about yourself. For example, if you are not the correct age and physical type to perform Helen of Troy in *The Trojan Women*, do not audition for the role.

The most frequently used actor categories or types include the following:

> *Leading man*—age range from twenty-five to forty years; height from five feet ten inches to six feet two inches; relatively attractive; not overweight; pleasant voice; good posture.

Leading lady—age range from twenty-five to forty years; height from five feet four inches to five feet eight inches; relatively attractive; not overweight; pleasant voice; good posture.

Juvenile male—younger version of the leading man, except shorter; age range and appearance fifteen to twenty years.

Juvenile female (ingenue)—younger version of the leading lady; may be shorter; age range and appearance fifteen to twenty years.

Character men and character women—all shapes and sizes; age range and appearance usually forty years and beyond; vocal and physical eccentricities common.

2. Select characters with whom you can identify. It will strengthen your audition if you have some understanding and emotional identification with the character you are portraying. However, this does not mean that you must have experienced what the character has, nor does it mean that you must be a great deal like the character. You do need to have empathy or sympathy for the character because that will help you identify better.

3. Select modern realistic plays for audition unless there are specific directions to the contrary. The requirements for speech and movement of modern plays are usually more immediately comfortable to a young actor than are classical or nonrealistic styles of acting.

4. If your audition permits time for more than one selection, try to provide offerings with distinct rhythmic contrasts. In other words, if one piece is serious or tragic, the other should probably be light and comic.

5. It is preferable not to select a character for audition that demands a heavy vocal dialect or accent unless there are specific directions to the contrary. One reason for this is that it is difficult to do accents and dialects well and also to suit the concept of the people hearing you. Also, you do not want to risk having an accent or dialect misinterpreted as your own. Finally, because accents and dialects are largely a matter of mechanics, most directors will be more impressed by confident character work than with vocal techniques.

6. When you construct or cut a selection, it is best not to splice several different speeches together to make one excerpt. If another character is speaking to the character you are performing, that character's speeches can be eliminated. It is permissible to link your own character's speeches together as one excerpt. Avoid linking a speech from act 1 with a speech from act 3. Constructions like this are usually confusing, and transitions are difficult. In addition, the rhythm of the speech is sacrificed.

7. Extremely intense and climactic moments rarely make good audition selections unless the actor has sufficient time to build to those moments in a believable manner. An effective audition is usually complete within itself. When the requirement is to be extremely brief (e.g., two minutes is the usual time limitation), material should be selected for its unity and character nuances.

8. It is absolutely essential to time your selections carefully and finish within the time limitations. Discipline is vital. Excellent auditions have been ruined by self-indulgence.

Practical Suggestions

Here are important suggestions concerning how to dress for and how to conduct oneself at an audition.

1. You should generally dress for an audition in a comfortable, clean manner. The question arises, Should you dress appropriate to the attire of the character? The answer is in a reasonable way yes—with qualifications. Dress similarly to the attire of the character only for auditions for modern plays. If you are auditioning for the role of a truck driver, jeans, boots, and flannel shirt would be appropriate. If the role is a business woman, a tailored suit would be good. Obviously, if the role is selected from a historical play, you should not attempt to dress in period costume. In this instance, wear neat, but neutral clothing such as slacks and sweater (wear basic blue, gray, or brown colors). For women, a dress (or skirt and blouse) with simple lines and neutral colors is favored over slacks or jeans. While the latter are popular and acceptable, most directors need to see the legs of an actress because more plays require women to wear dresses than pants. Hair should be well groomed and kept out of the face of both men and women. Shoes and clothing should fit well and never hinder quiet, natural movement. Do not wear shoes with platform heels which adversely affect balance and movement. Also, unless necessary for a character type, do not wear tennis shoes or sandals. Shoes or boots are best for both men and women. Generally, it is important not to overdress and thereby have to compete against your own appearance. On the other hand, overly casual dress such as faded denims and sweat shirt is not desirable.

2. Be certain to establish your name clearly. Use the phrase "My name is. . . ." These first three nonessential words tune the listener into catching the important phrase, your name. If your name is unusual, spell it. If you have an audition number, announce it with your name.

3. Quickly determine the size of the room in which you are auditioning and adjust your vocal projection accordingly. If the listeners are at the rear of a large auditorium, you must amplify considerably. If they are only a few feet from you, do not blast them out of their seats. A cardinal rule is, If you err, do it slightly on the loud side.

4. Never apologize for your appearance or physical condition (such as a head cold). If you have a cold, it will be obvious and understood. Concentrate upon character. Do not fuss with yourself, the room, or the properties. Most auditions do not permit the use of props except for a chair. Remember personalization and do not push for artificial intensity. Use yourself to the best advantage no matter what character you are reading.

5. Repeat your name and number with warmth and sincerity before leaving the audition area. It is important to leave an impression of confidence.

An actress reading at a tryout-audition.

The Callback

Few actors are cast on the basis of one audition. Hopefully they are asked to return for a callback session. The callback may be for another reading or for a prepared performance, or it may be an interview (or all). The second reading or performance reveals more depth and usually more time is allotted. A callback generally permits an actor to discuss interpretation and other matters with the director—a distinct advantage over an open audition where the actor usually should not attempt discussion. Concerning the interview, answer all questions directly, economically, and honestly. Never lie or stretch the truth to gain an impression. Directors and producers are adept at spotting lies. They may believe that if an actor lies in an interview or on a résumé, he may lie or cheat at other things such as punctuality or reliability. If high school is your sole acting experience, so state and without apology. Finally, do not attempt to impress the interviewer by babbling on incessantly. Respect his time and simply offer him your photograph and a typed résumé of your acting experience. Never fail to thank the interviewer.

A recent sharp black-and-white photograph should be attached to the résumé. Eight-by-ten-inch prints are preferred. There are firms in large cities which produce one hundred such photographs for less than twenty dollars. Gloss-finish is preferred to mat-finish photographs because they reproduce better for publicity purposes. A single pose is preferred to a composite, a simple head shot is preferred to a full-length pose, and a natural, unretouched photo is favored over a glamour picture. A final caution concerning photographs: Never use ultradramatic poses because they connote amateurism. Use an informal unpretentious pose.

In acting, a cardinal rule is that a résumé never exceeds one page regardless of the length of experience. As roles accumulate, an actor becomes more selective as to which ones he lists. Learn to cite only representative roles and major credits and rarely more than fifteen or twenty. A half-dozen solid roles are more impressive than thirty small ones. The résumé should be neatly typed and easily read. List your name, full address, and phone number at the top. Next, list your height, weight, age, hair color, eye color, marital status, and all professional unions to which you belong. Under Training list schools, degrees, workshops, and well-known acting coaches under whom you have worked. Under the section labeled Acting Experience list the significant roles you have played, play titles, theatres, theatre locations, and directors if they are well known (list latest roles first). List television, radio, and film credits (if any) separately. Attach this eight-by-ten-inch résumé to the back of the photograph. Because putting together an effective résumé is expensive and time-consuming, leave extra room at the top for changes in address and phone number, plus empty space at the bottom to add recent credits and keep the résumé up-to-date.

An actor should never let the brief time allotted him for an audition mislead him into thinking that a director will not be able to recognize his ability. Ethel Barrymore once commented, "Well, if they've got any talent, you can tell it in a minute; and if they don't, it'll seem like an hour."

Obtaining a position in a performance group devoted to improvisation and work without script is usually made by personal application and interview. Good recommendations and contacts are invaluable here. Audition may or may not be used, depending upon the nature of the group. If you are interested in joining this kind of group, write to the group or preferably go directly in person.

Auditioning is a perennial affliction of the art of acting—exciting, tormenting, heartbreaking, and rewarding. Always vulnerable, always hopeful, the actor by necessity returns to audition again and again. Following the tenets of this chapter can at least provide an actor with confidence to meet the experience and can enhance his opportunity for success.

Sample résumé

Name

Actress

Address: Age Range:

Phone: Height:

Can also be reached: Weight:

                                                  Marital status:

                                                  Color of hair:

                                                  Color of eyes:

                                                  Member Actor's Equity:

Acting Experience
Stage

Juliet	*Romeo and Juliet* (UCLA)
Vibrata	*A Funny Thing Happened on the Way to the Forum* (UCLA)
Ellen Sewell	*The Night Thoreau Spent in Jail* (UCLA)

Television

Alison	*Look Back in Anger* (ABC TV)
Viola	*Twelfth Night* (ABC TV)
Nora	*Riders to the Sea* (NBC TV)
Ophelia	*Hamlet* (CBS TV)

Also roles in *The Happiest Girl in the World, The Hands of God, The Maids, The Serpent*

Other Experience

Lyceum Players, Longwood Garden Theatre
Hiram College Theatre
Ohio University Theatre
Temple University Theatre
University of Nevada, Las Vegas, Judy Bayley Summer Repertory Theatre

Professional Training

John Doe (in training at present)
Jane Smith (in training at present)
Bill Doe (mime)

Special Talents

Modern dance; tap (in training at present)
Dialects: Southern, Italian, Standard British, Irish
Fencing

Suggested Readings

Canfield, Curtis, *The Craft of Play Directing*. New York: Holt, Rinehart & Winston, 1963.

Cohen, Robert. *Acting Professionally*. Palo Alto, Calif.: National Press Books, 1972.

Dean, Alexander, and Carra, Lawrence. *Fundamentals of Play Direction*. 3d ed. New York: Holt, Rinehart & Winston, 1974.

Gallaway, Marian. *The Director in the Theatre*. New York: Macmillan Co., 1963.

Greene, J. Gordon. "The Actor Auditions." Part 1. *Southern Theatre* 16 (Fall 1972); Part 2. *Southern Theatre* 16 (Winter 1973).

Sievers, W. David; Stiver, Harry E., Jr.; and Kahan, Stanley. *Directing for the Theatre*. 3d ed. Dubuque, Iowa: Wm. C. Brown Co., 1974.

Welker, David. *Theatrical Direction: The Basic Techniques*. Boston: Allyn & Bacon, 1971.

Role Analysis
and Performance

Once an actor has auditioned and been cast, how does he begin role creation? And how does an actor utilize both personalization and traditional acting techniques (i.e., observation, imagination, improvisation, and so on) in rehearsal and performance?

Rehearsal

The initial rehearsals in most productions are devoted to *reading and play analysis, role analysis, production goals, organization, and discussion.* Except for role analysis, most of this material is handled by the director and his artistic staff. Although some directors provide written or verbal remarks on role analysis, many directors depend upon the actor to provide most of it. The following is an organized, precise, and practical approach to role analysis.

The Steps of Role Analysis

These steps have been refined through practical experience in actual productions.

1. *Read through the play for basic enjoyment and information.*

2. *Do some basic reading and research on the playwright.* Succinct biographical sketches can be found in *Current Biography* (H. W. Wilson Co.), a reference found in most libraries. If the author is not listed in that publication, look him up in the card file or in *Reader's Guide to Periodical Literature* (H. W. Wilson Co.). It is probably not necessary to read a complete biography of the playwright if one or more are available, although you may wish to do so for an in-depth study. It is true that the script itself is sufficient for an actor to perform a role well. However, it is also possible that some meaningful insights into the life and other works of an author may prove helpful to role creation. For example, knowing the relationship between Tennessee Williams and his sister and other family members might prove very beneficial to an actor playing Tom in *The Glass Menagerie*. Furthermore, knowledge of a playwright and his works expands your general knowledge of theatre.

3. *Do some basic study or research on the era in which the play was originally written and produced.* A play set in Atlanta, Georgia, in 1950 has an entirely different social milieu than a play set in the same city in 1970. The most immediate sources of material of this kind are standard history textbooks, periodicals, and newspapers.

4. *Read the play a second time focusing your attention on your role.* Try to locate any and all aspects of the role which you think are similar to your person, personality, and behavioral characteristics. Be certain that you take notes on these personalization discoveries in order to utilize them in the early part of your rehearsal period. Finding as many aspects of the role that are already like you decreases the chances for artificial or forced acting in the

crucial preliminary stages of rehearsal. Personalization is the key to early comfort, relaxation, and believability. This is part of the process loosely called "letting the role come to you rather than your pursuing it." The notes you take during your second reading begin your personalization work.

5. *The director or teacher usually provides the next step in role analysis, namely, play analysis.* Play analysis refers to the understanding of the form, structure, and literal and metaphorical content of a play. It includes a basic understanding of the play's type, style, subject issues, theme and intellectual content, exposition, point of attack, conflict, major dramatic question, protagonist or central character, antagonist or opposing force, deciding agent, struggle and complications, major crisis or turn, climax, outcome or denoument, and character drives (most of these terms are defined in the Glossary). While play analysis is basically the responsibility of the director, an actor can enhance his work greatly by knowing how the play is made and how it works in terms of performance. Play analysis is particularly important to an understanding of the emotional builds and peaks of your role. Therefore, if role analysis is not provided by a director or teacher, a thinking actor does well to analyze the play for himself. However, play analysis is a complex process and one which lies somewhat outside the province of basic acting techniques. A basic approach to play analysis is outlined in Appendix A of this book.

6. *Take a blue pencil or ball-point pen and underline all physical action performed by your character directly in your script.* Include action directed to you by "stage directions" as well as action clearly implied by dialogue (in which case, you need to make a marginal note of what action you think is implied by the dialogue). The question arises as to whether the actor should follow all stage directions printed in the script. Some directors follow these directions closely, although they may realize that all of the directions are not from the author. Most printed stage directions are from a master production script of a professional company. The actor has the same discretion as the director; he can completely ignore the directions in rehearsal and performance, he can follow them faithfully, or he can use some and disregard others. Whichever course *you* follow, it remains important to underline the directions in order to grasp the overall action pattern of your character as indicated by the author or other producers. Armed with this knowledge, you can better decide whether to retain or disregard the printed stage direction.

7. *Take a red pencil or ball-point pen and make a D to designate major character "discoveries" in the margin of your acting script.* A discovery is any knowledge you learn about the character ranging from such simple matters as "Frank is a black American male" to "Ellen suffers from guilt at having run away from home twenty years before the beginning of the play." Insert a red arrow connecting the letter *D* in the margin to the precise line or action which reveals the discovery. At times, you may wish to add a brief sentence or two beneath the *D* to clarify the nature of the discovery. In these instances, use phrases or simple sentences, not lengthy narrative.

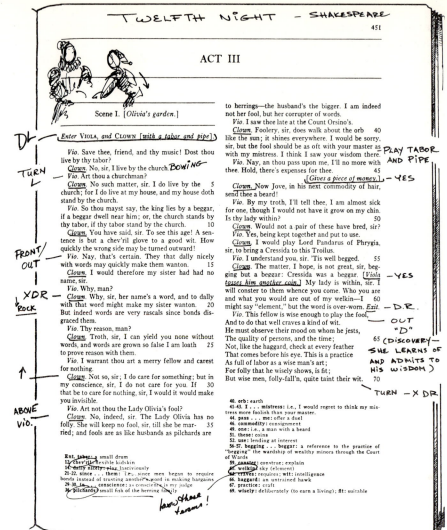

Marked script for CLOWN in *Twelfth Night* by William Shakespeare.

8. *Visualize your character carefully.* Begin with any description offered by the author either through stage directions or from dialogue. Complete the description with your own understanding of the character. Obviously, this description necessarily utilizes many of your own physical characteristics. After all, you are performing the role, and personalization dictates that the role is you to some extent. While makeup and costume alter this factor, your fundamental physical characteristics remain at the base of the visual aspects of your character. It is particularly important to note any physical abnormalities of your character such as a crippled arm, a humped back, and so on. Be aware of how your character wears his or her hair. Does your character wear glasses? Is your character bald? Does your character wear false teeth? Does your character have arthritis? Is your character hard-of-hearing?

Visualization includes careful understanding of how your character dresses; for example, is your character neat and well groomed or casual and slovenly? Is your character dressed in the latest style? Does your character favor certain colors? Know what kind of shoes your character wears because most movement will be affected by foot apparel. Also note what costume accessories your character uses such as jewelry, purses, handkerchiefs, hats, and so on. It is strongly recommended that you establish your visualization concretely by writing it out as a list.

Some actors complete character visualization by selecting an animal which in appearance, movement, or manner seems analogous to the role they are creating. For example, Marlon Brando used an ape as part of his visualization for the crude and savage role of Stanley Kowalski in Tennessee Williams' *A Streetcar Named Desire*. Select an animal analogous to your character and write out a description of the appearance, movement, and behavior characteristics of the animal, clarifying how those traits relate to your role. When you begin rehearsals, you may wish to consciously attempt some of the animal's movement and behavior to assist visualization.

9. *Study your role carefully in terms of emotional behavior and personality traits.* In other words, examine your role in terms of its psychological factors. For example, is your character generally quiet, demure, and retiring or loud, flamboyant, and extroverted? Note the basic emotions engaged in by your character: fear, love, hate, anger, pride, desire, jealousy, envy, and so on. Conclude by writing a personality description of your character as a list of phrases and simple sentences.

10. *Select someone from life well known to you; the person should be analogous to your role.* Do an observation study of this person. Try to select a relative or friend. Do not let the person know you are using him for observation. Note visual and psychological characteristics in detail. Write a description of the characteristics and behavior from your life study.

11. *Discover and specifically define the motivational spine of your character or what is often called the character's MF, that is, motivating force.* The motivating force should be stated as one complete sentence including the action verb *wants*; for example, "Willy wants Biff to love him again." Be certain that the statement is specific and involves other characters whenever possible. Conflict exists between two or more people more often than it exists between people and things or between people and themselves.

12. *Make a list of the major beats of action carried out in the play or scene by your character.* A *beat* is the distance from the beginning to the end of an intention. For example, a card game between two men on stage encompasses a beat. Changing from one subject under discussion in a play to a different subject also constitutes a beat. Your list of beats should be constructed sequentially from the beginning of a play or scene to the end of it.

13. *Based on your understanding of the printed text, write a creative imaginary biographical list of major subtext events in your character's life prior to the time of the play.* This list should begin with the specific date of

birth and astrological sign of your character, including a brief description of what the sign generally indicates. Knowing the significance of astrological signs is important to many people in contemporary society. However, if such knowledge is not of great significance to you, and the text does not indicate that it is significant to the character either, you may omit this point. Obtain your character's birth date by substracting the character's age from the year the play occurs; if the year of the play is not given, either use the present year or carefully select a year that seems sensible to the text. If your character's age is not given, use your own age *or* carefully select an age that seems sensible to the text. It is crucial that you restrict subtextual major life events to very important or traumatic events. Write these events as a list, not as a narrative. Do not let your imagination run wild and create subtext wholly out of keeping with your character and the play. *Subtext must always be justified by its relevancy to text.* If you have marked your textual discoveries well, noted your actions carefully, and thoroughly accomplished the textual work just described, you will rarely go astray in the process of creating *valid* subtext. For example, subtext might include such items as "had no formal education beyond second grade," "mother died when I was age thirteen," "went to work in coal mine at age fourteen," "father was an alcoholic," "fell in love for first time at age fifteen," "joined the army at age seventeen," and so on. Complete your subtext by creating a list of succinct subtext events related to text describing the major activities your character has undergone from the moment of rising from bed on the morning of act I to the exact moment you first enter the stage action.

14. *Create a brief list of subtext events for all offstage activity of your character following every exit made during the play,* concluding each offstage sequence at the moment your character enters the stage again.

15. *Create a brief list of major character idiosyncrasies, likes, and dislikes.* For example, "loves wine; hates meat; likes fish or fowl; suffers from insomnia; reads classical Spanish literature"; and so on.

16. *Maintain a rehearsal-and-performance log or diary concerning your work with your character.* No one but you and your instructor or director need ever read this log. The log should create a progressive and permanent record of your growth and development as well as of your disappointments and problems. Only experiences directly related to your role creation need be included. Note in the log all major events, changes, and experiences which affect your earlier role analysis.

17. *When the final performance of a scene or play is concluded, write a brief objective self-evaluation of final results of your work with the character in terms of role creation and execution of the part.*

Many directors use the second phase of rehearsals for *blocking the movement* of the characters. Often directors plan the blocking for the actor and dictate the movements at rehearsals. In these instances, you should mark all blocking in the script with a pencil, using the symbols learned in chapter 8 as a kind of shorthand. Later, as line memorization occurs and the script is no longer carried in rehearsal, the blocking patterns should also be memorized and become instinctive. However, some directors prefer to take a more flexible, organic approach to blocking. For a week or more such directors permit actors to move at will according to motivational instincts. Later, the director refines or polishes the movement. During either of these kinds of blocking rehearsals, it is advisable to use *personalization* for the sake of relaxation, comfort, and believability. In other words, an actor should not work immediately for characterization and emotion. Rather, he should use as much of his own person as possible in rehearsals to establish a comfortable base for later characterization work.

Following blocking and personalization rehearsals, most productions enter the period known as *work rehearsals*. These rehearsals are devoted to moment-by-moment coaching of actors by the director. Some directors use a technique known as *scene combing*. In these rehearsals a director permits actors to experiment in order to discover new values and character nuances. For example, a director may have an actor comb a scene by performing opposite values throughout; that is, when the script obviously calls for love, the actor performs hate; courage is displayed rather than fear; fear is used instead of courage. At times, directors have actors exchange roles in order to provide fresh insights into character. When they are working with a director who rigidly dictates all aspects of character development, an unwritten code of the theatre demands that actors oblige him. However, in these instances an actor has the right to question and discuss interpretation and, of course, to work privately (provided such work does not go directly against the intentions of the director). Remember that the theatre is a collaborative art, and in contemporary theatre the director usually has the final word on all aspects of production. Nonetheless, the wise director knows the actor is paramount in the production process because the actor communicates more directly with the audience than does any other theatre artist. Accordingly, a sensible director creates an environment which permits maximum actor creativity. During work rehearsals and scene-combing periods, both personalization and traditional techniques of role creation are used to advantage.

At what point does the actor turn to traditional techniques of role creation to complete what he is trying to accomplish with personalization? A skilled, understanding director can help you identify when to modify personalization and when to use traditional techniques. There are points of characterization which personalization cannot accomplish. In these instances, actors should turn to traditional techniques to handle a problem. These techniques range from use of makeup and costumes; to lighting; to properties; to physical mannerisms; to observation, imagination, and improvisation. However, great acting usually does not begin with those techniques. It begins with the richness of the person! Technique follows rather than leads. To demonstrate this point, we refer to a scene in the film *Bad Day At Black Rock*. Spencer Tracy exemplified the personalization theory of acting, whether the effort was conscious or unconscious. In this film, his portrayal of a crippled World War II veteran merged perfectly with his strong, stoic nature. However, the left arm of the character was deformed and useless; it rested continually against his side with the hand in a pocket, always unseen. Tracy had to manage complex physical activity including a major fight scene with only one arm. Personalization at this point was useless to Tracy who had, after all, two good arms. Any physical activity involving the arms required scrupulous technique. In similar fashion, Tracy's personality served well for the emotional demands of the character, with one exception. In a scene at the hotel counter, he had to explode in frustration at the young clerk who was refusing to help him escape from the town. The dialogue called for Tracy to say half of a sentence but not finish it due to his frustration. For whatever reason, the moment seemed unbelievable and forced to many viewers. Either Tracy or the director should have caught this moment. Since his personalization was insufficient, some other technique was needed, such as completing the sentence with invented dialogue or using a movement, property, or action to enhance believability.

Following work rehearsals, most directors utilize a number of *run-through rehearsals*. The director no longer stops the action for coaching. He devotes these rehearsals to continuity and rhythm. The actors polish their earlier work. The director takes notes which are relayed to the actors after rehearsals to aid their polishing.

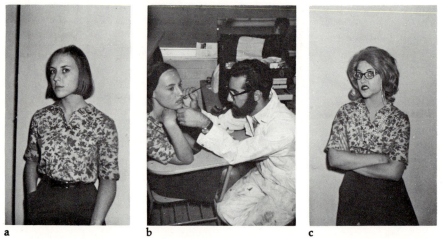

Series of photographs showing an actress: *a*, before makeup; *b*, makeup being applied; and *c*, after makeup has been applied.

a   b   c

Finally, *technical rehearsals* are used to implement scenery, lighting, properties, costumes, and makeup. These rehearsals culminate either in a preview performance before an invited audience or in the actual opening of the production before a paid audience. Some directors continue to give polishing notes or minor changes to actors during technical rehearsals and performances. In these instances, honor the desire to continue improvement. Other directors choose to completely "give a show over" to actors once performances have begun. Normally, the stage manager replaces the director as the production supervisor once performances begin.

Incidentally, in most college and university theatre an established custom following the final performance of a production is that all actors assist the technical crews in the *strike,* or dismantling and storing of all scenery, properties, and costumes.

Discipline: Working with a Director or Artist-Leader

Whether they are creating a role in a traditional theatre experience or creating a performance with an improvisational group, the key factor (beyond ability) required of actors by a director or artist-leader is discipline. What does the term imply? Implied are punctuality and reliability. It is an excellent idea to arrive consistently fifteen minutes prior to all rehearsal calls. This early arrival time should be used for preparation and warm-up. An athlete cannot compete in an activity without first warming up with calisthenics. An actor should not rehearse or perform without vocal and body exercises as a prelude to the rehearsal or performance. Warm-ups should be executed either as individual activity or as group activity. The latter frequently involves use of theatre games that focus on concentration and relaxation. Effective games include jumping imaginary rope in groups of four or five and playing catch with an imaginary ball. Word-repetition games whereby an actor says a word and each subsequent actor repeats that word and adds another, all the while repeating every word spoken before his turn, are effective also.

Reliability means consistent attendance at rehearsals. Legitimate illness and death in the family are probably the only valid excuses for missing a rehearsal. An actor should notify the stage manager or assistant director prior to the rehearsal of these circumstances. Reliability connotes dedication; in other words, it establishes an actor's reputation.

Discipline also establishes his rehearsal behavior. Poor discipline results in distracting chatter in the wings or auditorium, in missed cues or entrances, and absences from the theatre without the permission of the stage manager or assistant director. (Rarely should an actor bother the director or artist-leader by asking him for special consideration.)

An actor can best demonstrate good discipline at rehearsal by sitting quietly in the wings or auditorium, absorbing all activity. He can also accomplish good discipline by working with a colleague actor in the greenroom (i.e., actor waiting area) or other location in the theatre well away from the stage (provided that the stage manager or assistant director knows precisely where he is). Always plan economical use of offstage time at rehearsals because some directors fail to budget rehearsal time effectively.

Actors should never invite friends or relatives to a rehearsal or for a visit in the theatre (if someone is to meet you or pick you up, ask him to come to the greenroom or door of the theatre at a specific time and wait for you there).

Another important aspect of discipline is how well actors cooperate with the technical staff and crews. For example, be punctual for all costume measurements and fitting sessions. After their use, return all hand or personal properties to the proper person or replace them in the location established for such items. Have respect for and stay out of the way of the activity of stagehands and crew members. Be particularly respectful and pleasant to the costume dresser if the complexity of your changes merit your having a dresser. If potential dangers or problems are noticed or if irritations or complaints develop, do not brood about them or gossip about them with colleague actors. Discuss them politely and openly with the stage manager or assistant director. If either one believes the problem merits it, the director will be brought into the discussion. However, any onstage problem should be discussed immediately with the director at the moment it occurs or following rehearsal (again, never take petty matters to a fellow actor, expand such matters out of proportion, or create rifts and dissention). Theatre decorum provides a precise chain of command which should be rigorously followed. If an actor violates this decorum, creates dissention, or loses his temper, he gains the infamous label *prima donna*. Legitimate human behavior has its place in the theatre. If temper flares, let it, but end the episode quickly. There is no place in the theatre for holding a grudge or for self-indulgent behavior. (The precise chain of command for a particular production or performance is usually determined and announced by the director or artist-leader at the beginning of rehearsals.) Discipline is the heart of acting success because it demonstrates how to use one's ability for the benefit of group or ensemble harmony and achievement. Establish rigid, productive discipline in a constructive manner early in your training. Never deviate from a sense of discipline, especially when and if success and notoriety are achieved. Self-discipline is the mark of a professional artist.

Sustaining a Role or Performance

In educational theatre, actors will probably not encounter the problem of sustaining a role over a long period of time (unless they are fortunate enough to go on tour). However, performing in the professional theatre, repertory, and stock means sustaining an effective performance over several weeks, months, or even years. How does an actor sustain a fresh, spontaneous performance under such circumstances?

Improvisation is an effective technique to sustain role creation when spontaneity is lost. For example, an actress portraying Ophelia in a production of *Hamlet* was unable to create the appropriate emotion in the scene in which she explains Hamlet's mad appearance to Polonius. According to Shakespeare's script, the character Hamlet is not in the scene. To assist the actress with genuine visual and emotional recall, the director asked the actor playing Hamlet to *improvise* the unwritten scene with the actress playing Ophelia. The actor improvised all of Shakespeare's descriptions in carefully scored detail as the actress watched him and reacted to his improvisation. Later, the actress rehearsed the actual scene from the script with Polonius. Her description of Hamlet's appearance and behavior was charged with new emotional depth and believability.

Frequently, omitted or unwritten scenes in a play must be performed through rehearsal improvisation. It is an excellent technique and one that is all too infrequently used by actors and directors because it takes time and extra work. Insist on using the technique even if you must do it on your own, away from the theatre.

Other techniques for sustaining a role include spot rehearsals in which actors alter pantomimic dramatization, business, and movement.

Another interesting technique is to rehearse a problem scene by reversing roles with another actor. For example, two actresses playing Antigone and Ismene could exchange roles and a fresh viewpoint might result from the different interaction.

If a scene is difficult, again try the rehearsal technique of using animal mannerisms similar to those of your character (e.g., walk like an ape or strut like a peacock).

Still another technique is to rehearse the problem scene without dialogue relying strictly on pantomime or gibberish (i.e., nonsense sounds).

Playing opposite values is usually rewarding in revitalization of a role (see chapter 8).

It might also be effective to rehearse a scene in the dark with words only using no movement or business.

It is also a good idea to sit down with the play and read it again after performances have begun. Continuity will be increased and important factors may be caught which have been missed or for some reason have been eliminated (such as transitional words and specific stage directions).

Any type of fresh invention assists an actor in finding new life in a scene or moment gone dead.

As you conclude Part I of actor training, remember that there is no substitute for practice. All the theory in the world is useless if it is not applied. Merely reading this or any other book on acting is of little value if exercises are not practiced every day. An actor is no different from a muscian or dancer. There will never be time to practice—an actor must make the time if he is a serious student of acting. Katharine Hepburn has perhaps said it best:

A lot of hogwash is talked about acting. It's not all that fancy! When Nijinsky visited Chaplin on a set, Charlie was about to have a custard pie in his face and Nijinsky said, "The nuances! The miraculous timing!" And it's a lot of bunk. You laugh, you cry, you pick up a little bit, and then you're a working actor. It's a *craft!* You're out there desperately doing something you hope people will come and see. Nowadays directors, stars are constantly talking—pretentiously and a great deal more than they should—about their art. Talk, talk, talk, talk, *talk!* Spencer Tracy always said acting was "Learn your lines and get on with it," so does Larry Olivier, so does John Gielgud, and the great ones. . . . *Life's* what's important. Walking, houses, family. Birth and pain and joy—and then death. Acting's just waiting for a custard pie. That's all.[1]

In other words, there comes a time when intellectualizing and discussion must cease. Finally, acting is action—saying, listening, and doing! Acting is organic *reaction!*

1. Charles Higham, "Private and Proud and Hepburn," *New York Times,* 9 December, 1973.

Suggested Readings

Burton, Hal, ed. *Great Acting.* New York: Hill & Wang, 1967.

Cole, Toby, and Chinoy, Helen K., eds. *Actors on Acting.* New York: Crown Publishers, 1949.

Funke, Lewis, and Booth, John E. *Actors Talk About Acting: Fourteen Interviews with Stars of the Theatre.* New York: Random House, 1961.

Hodge, Francis. *Play Directing: Analysis, Communication, and Style.* Englewood Cliffs, N. J.: Prentice-Hall, 1971.

Lewes, George. *On Actors and the Art of Acting.* New York: Grove Press, 1957.

Marshall, Norman. *The Producer and the Play.* Rev. ed. London: Macdonald & Evans, 1962.

Matthews, Brander, ed. *Papers on Acting.* New York: Hill & Wang, 1958.

Osborn, Alex. *Achieving Characterization in Applied Imagination.* New York: Charles Scribner's Sons, 1963.

Redgrave, Michael. *The Actor's Ways and Means.* London: William Heinemann, 1953.

Stanislavsky, Konstantin. *Building a Character.* New York: Theatre Arts Books, 1936.

Strasberg, Lee. *Strasberg at the Actor's Studio.* Edited by Robert H. Hethmon. New York: Viking Press, 1965.

Strickland, F. Cowles. *The Technique of Acting.* New York: McGraw-Hill Book Co., 1956.

Styan, John Louis. *The Dramatic Experience.* London: Cambridge University Press, 1964.

Acting: II
In Style

11 Classical Antiquity

Restraint

Man's life is a day. What is he?
What is he not? A shadow in a dream
Is man: but when God sheds a brightness,
Shining light on earth
And life is sweet as honey.

Pindar
The Pythian Odes

Never man again may swear things shall
    be as they once were.

Archilochus
from *Ancient Gems in Modern Settings*

Pindar and Archilochus reflect the spirit of ancient Greece. Man was fated to be subservient to the gods, but in subservience he drew upon his free will and the sense of his own magnificence to create a civilization whose influence was to be with us always. Almost as though they knew this civilization would pass away, the ancient Greeks lived fully, and life was indeed "sweet as honey."

To Delphi by bus is a long, arduous ride through countryside that is at once beautiful, rocky, unfertile, and uninhabited. Sumptuous mountains stretch for miles around and sage covers the land. Although Delphi has many attractions, it is primarily the oracle that for centuries has drawn people to the shrine. After you have climbed from the road to the shrine, the Charioteer of Delphi is the first edifice to catch your eye. Another quarter-mile up the hill, the Temple of Athena and the Temple of Apollo stand blazingly in the afternoon sun. Weary tourists of every generation have walked the Sacred Way to face the oracle and ask for advice from Apollo. It strikes modern tourists that perhaps we, too, file past this once imposing monument seeking an answer to some impossible question. In ancient times, Delphi was Greece's central archive and seat of political intelligence and was the most sacred and powerful place in Greece. The oracle, as interpreted by the priests, wished to promote stability in government and religion. However, the priesthood strongly encouraged the orgiastic cult of Dionysus (the god of wine and fertility), who occupied the temple as alternate god in winter when Apollo was away.

Overview of Greek Tragedy

The origins of Greek drama are generally familiar, but extremely speculative. Few matters of scholarship are certain. Vase paintings, some extant

Greek mural design based on paintings on ancient Greek vases. Design by Larry Schumate, California State University, Sacramento.

plays, and writing fragments provide most of the available information. Greek drama probably evolved from the rites performed in honor of Dionysus by masked worshipers who danced and sang (e.g., Dithyrambs, or hymns to Dionysus) and worked themselves into a frenzy in order to lose their identity and merge with nature and gods. As drama slowly emerged from these ceremonies, it became more and more formalized. So, too, did the physical place evolve as a recognizable area for the presentation of drama. The very earliest *orchestra* or dancing place was probably a threshing floor worn smooth by oxen who trod grain upon it. Around the orchestra the *theatron* or seeing place developed where the spectators sat on the ground to watch the religious ceremonies. These earliest theatres were always built into a hillside to accommodate large numbers of people. Historical references are also made concerning the custom of having the actors change costumes in a tent or *skene* in a sacred wood nearby. As plays grew more complex, the actors were required to enter and leave the orchestra more quickly. Eventually a wooden skene, or scene house, containing dressing rooms and storage space was built directly behind the theatre for the actors. In time, painted set pieces were placed in front of this building to represent scenery. These became more and more intricate with the evolution of the *proskenion*, or central playing area, and the scene building itself became merely a background structure. Wooden and later stone seats were added to the hillside.

The first actor of record was Thespis, who was also a playwright and production manager or precursor of the director. We have evidence that Thespis performed in the first dramatic-religious festivals in Athens around 534 B.C. He probably wore different masks to represent different characters and was the sole actor in a tragedy. These early plays used a chorus or group of singer-dancers who sang odes between the actor's speeches or dialogue. The chorus served ultimately as character, narrator, participant, and ideal spectator. Only men were allowed to act in plays.

In tragedy, three great writers are noteworthy because of their exemplary work and their significant contributions to the development of dramatic art and theatre: Aeschylus (525–456 B.C.), Sophocles (496–406 B.C.), and Euripides (480–406 B.C.). In comedy, Aristophanes (ca. 448–ca. 380 B.C.) was probably the greatest Greek author of Old Comedy (meaning "early"). Later, another writer, Menander (ca. 342–292 B.C.), contributed significantly to the transition from Greek to Roman comedy.

Greek tragedy can be characterized as follows:

1. Use of a limited number of characters acted usually by one to three actors who changed masks to portray different roles. Most scholars agree that Aeschylus used a single actor in his plays; Sophocles, two actors; and Euripides, three or more.
2. Use of a singing-dancing chorus. It should be noted that Aeschylus emphasized the chorus in his plays and Euripides emphasized the actor, giving little attention to the chorus. Sophocles struck a balance of emphasis.

3. Use of iambic trimeter verse was used for dialogue and for choral odes.
4. Use of a superhuman hero in the plays of Aeschylus, usually a powerful mythological character whose will was continually subjugated to the higher impersonal power of the gods.
5. Use of refined, idealized characters with human problems (rather than religious themes) in the plays of Sophocles, centered on strong, forceful, vehement emotion with which the audience could easily identify.
6. Use of ordinary characters with everyday problems in which thought and emotion were unified in the plays of Euripides, providing the transition from old to new ideas and from religion-myth to human passion.
7. Use of sexual themes in the plays of Euripides to portray man's beginning struggle not with fate and the gods, but with society and his mind and emotions.

Beauty, truth, and grandeur were the objectives of the tragic writers. Greek verse is noble and poetic and stresses a measured cadence. Action is brief and straightforward and concentrates on a single point. Characters are present at any given time on the stage. The Greek authors carefully avoided indiscriminate realism or excessive violence in front of an audience; this action was performed offstage or told in the narrative (note the death of Ajax in Sophocle's *Ajax* and of Evadine in Euripides's *Suppliants*). Greek tragedy penetrates our feelings by its even flow of dialogue interspersed with passages of choral odes and subtle changes of metrical form enhanced by accurate vocal intonation.

Greek acting was characterized by the wearing of masks—large, serious masks for tragedy and somewhat more life-size but grotesque ones for com-

Scene from *Oedipus Rex* by Sophocles. Directed by Gerard Larson. Designed by Larry Schumate. California State University, Sacramento.

edy. Early in the development of Greek drama, simple slippers were used on the feet, and the actors may have also performed in bare feet. Later, thick wooden or cork shoes were worn. High shoes or boots called *cothurni* increased an actor's height to larger-than-life size. Long, flowing garments or short simple ones usually in brilliant colors, were used. The masks were also probably very colorful. Later, a high headdress was probably worn. (Highly simplified scenic equipment may have been available for performances, such as altars, statues, tombs, cranes, scenic prisms, and platforms.)

The exact style of acting in Greek tragedy remains uncertain. Scholars offer a number of theories from which we may determine the attributes of

Costume design for Poseidon in *The Trojan Women.*

a typical classical Greek actor. We do know that acting was considered a craft by the classical Greek philosopher Socrates. To Plato, his protégé and another great philosopher, acting was something that could not, and should not, be learned. The extant play texts reveal that acting in tragedy called for simple, direct action—clear, controlled, and orderly. Some realistic actions are suggested in the plays, such as running, weeping, and falling on the ground. Conventional action was often necessary, as in the choral passages where lyricism and dance are prevalant. While we know that actors had to play many characters within each play and that men took female roles, it may be that females acted minor comedy parts. Although we know that a

Poseidon in *The Trojan Women* by Euripides. Directed by Jerry L. Crawford. Costumes by Ellis M. Pryce-Jones. University of Navada, Las Vegas.

realistic or lifelike technique of acting was not employed totally by Greek tragic actors, performance of Greek plays today should not be devoid of identifiable human action. It is possible that actors created a sense of realism by discovering expressive and sympathetic characteristics and portrayed them in a somewhat idealized form. The total concept of characterization, then, was truthfulness in a somewhat larger-than-life impersonation.

Voice—Greek Tragedy

Acting techniques for the tragic Greek actor were very specialized due to the tremendous size of the physical theatre. The size can be calculated to be approximately the area of a football stadium and the number of spectators to range from 15,000 to 100,000. Acoustics in this bowl-shaped structure were good. Given a strong, resonant, clear voice, an actor probably did not exert excessive vocal effort. More than likely the emphasis was on vocal projection, not on increased volume. Perhaps actors were cautioned to deliver speeches with clear enunciation and heightened word emphasis. In effect, the impression created probably tended more toward a recitative or singing mode.

To perform Greek tragedy in present-day theatre, use strong vocal projection, heightened word emphasis, precise diction, and varied tonal qualities (singing a musical scale is an effective preparatory exercise for vocal work in Greek tragedy). Obviously you (and your director) should lessen or increase projection according to the size of the theatre. However, you should not de-emphasize the enunciative quality of Greek speech. You may encounter difficulty when working with Greek lyrical passages, especially in key emotional moments. When a long sentence is sustained, it is very difficult to maintain precise diction throughout the line. On the other hand, you also face the possibility of losing the emotional builds at the expense of achieving competence in projection and enunciation.

Exercise 1   The Voice—Greek Tragedy

1. Each actor sings a musical scale individually. Repeat the exercise as a choral group.
2. Practice speaking the following line individually as though chanting it in an echo chamber. Repeat the exercise singing the line. Finally, repeat the exercise and modify the recitative and sung experience into spoken delivery, but retain the larger-than-life quality of the first two deliveries. Repeat the exercise as a choral group.
    "Call no man fortunate that is dead. The dead are free from pain."
    Chorus, Sophocles
    Oedipus the King

Movement—Greek Tragedy

In keeping with the serious vocal tone of tragedy, the Greek actor had to carry himself with authority and confidence. Most of his movement was probably slow, majestic, and rhythmic. Movement must have been simplified and broadened to accompany the idealized characterization. Physical contact between actors was probably rare; more than likely the quality of restraint was accentuated by allowing great physical distance between characters. The long monologues in the plays would seem to indicate that body positions were mostly full-front, one-quarter, or profile. The manner of speaking was probably directed more toward the audience than toward other actors (i.e., presentational). Gestures must have been simple, large or even grand, flowing, and complete, emanating from the upper part of the body. They were probably conventionalized and immediately understood by audiences. It is unlikely that actors ever sat on the stage. It is also likely that simple hand props such as a staff, sceptre, or sword were carried. At times, certain characters such as a chorus of furies might have carried lighted torches. We can assume that the gods carried their emblems (e.g., a lion skin and club for Heracles).

A Greek tragedy given in today's theatre would probably utilize many of the original Greek conventions. Once again, depending on the size of the theatre, begin from the Greek concept of simple restraint. Generally perform slow, suggestive, rhythmic movements and gestures. The presentational mode of acting should probably dominate, but not to excess. However, a sensible balance between presentational and representational interpretation should be achieved; for example, when one actor turns to respond directly to the audience, the other actor should usually focus on the speaker. Individualized physical movements should be kept to a minimum. While you may move more onstage than your classical Greek counterpart, you must be extremely careful to sustain controlled physical presence. Modern adaptations of the Greek acting style rarely execute a purist concept of the original style. More often than not, you may be required to sit on occasion, carry more hand properties than the original Greek style, and interrelate with other actors more (e.g., touch, stand close, and so on).

It is not known in what exact style the chorus performed its dance functions. Here, too, a modern adaptation might be more flexible than suggested by the traditional Greek chorus. Since we have no record of choral dancing except descriptions that date back to the early religious ceremonies honoring the god Dionysus (e.g., dancing with animallike frenzy), the key to dance adaptation is probably to use controlled, dignified, stately movement with shifting rhythmic patterns.

It is difficult to speak about movements and gestures without again referring to the subject of masks and costumes since they directly affect an actor's physical projection. In the early development of Greek drama, masks may have been made of lightweight linen, wood, or cork. The mask was placed over the head of the actor and undoubtedly gave depth and clarity to facial expression and head movement. (The mask had an open mouth which a few historians say could have amplified the human voice; however, most recent scholarship does not support this view.) The mask indicated the essence of the character—tragic by an expression of physical or mental suffering and happy by a smile or contented look. In general, the mask showed the specific emotional state of the character. Sometimes, the actor changed masks as the character changed moods or as he changed roles. However, it would seem that the mask could be manipulated by the actor to create shadows which in turn gave an illusion of changing expression. Later in the development of Greek drama, most tragic characters wore a headdress or a wiglike structure called an *onkus* which was not unlike headdresses worn in everyday life. Together, the mask and the headdress probably restrained flexibility of head movement.

The body garment of the later Greek periods must have presented a problem of mobility. A long-sleeved, ankle-length, heavily embroidered tunic, or *chiton*, was worn by the major characters. According to scenes depicted on vase paintings, other characters wore native dress such as a short tunic, mourning clothes, or ragged garments, all designed to represent the daily clothes of ordinary Greek citizens. Indications are that the chorus wore clothing prescribed by age, sex, and national and social status. Although the clothing in later periods must have been somewhat restrictive due to length and heaviness, this in no way indicates that the actors were unable to move. In fact, costumes remained remarkably similar to the everyday dress of the citizens and did allow freedom of movement and speech and rapid change of roles, particularly during early development of Greek drama.

The modern actor need be concerned only with wearing a costume that does not inhibit freedom of movement. It would be a mistake to use a garment and its accompanying decor (e.g., headdress, boots) that would constrict you in any great way. The main concern is whether masks should be worn in a modern adaptation. It is our suggestion that masks be worn only when close fidelity to the original Greek is desired; generally we advise against use of masks in today's theatre. Instead, we suggest heightened, formalized makeup, applied to resemble remotely the look of a mask or half-mask.

Exercise 2　Movement—Greek Tragedy

1. All actors come to an aligned position on their feet, breathing comfortably in a relaxed state. Move through space in the manner of a slow-motion film or in the manner of moving through water or as a spaceman on another planet. Concentrate upon grace, rhythm, fluidity, and a sense of controlled restraint.

2. Repeat Exercise 1 using a modified tempo and permitting the slow motion to evolve into an acceptably believable or realistic tempo.

3. Practice various forms of stereotyped movement gestures which reflect emotional states, such as drawing one arm up slowly with the back of your hand in front of your eyes, your other hand protruding behind you, and your body bending backward to indicate grief. As a welcoming gesture, slowly extend both arms forward and upward with the palms up; the head should elevate somewhat, and the entire body should come to its full height. Freely invent other kinds of movement gestures.

Music—Greek Tragedy

It is important to understand the major emphasis placed on musical accompaniment in the original Greek plays. In the beginning, use of music was light, to underscore choral passages. Later, music became more prominent, and actors used a variety of instruments including the flute, whose tone was similar to that of a modern oboe or clarinet, and the lyre, a stringed instrument used for special effects. A flute player probably preceded the chorus into the orchestra, and played music as an accompaniment to underscore the emotions described in the choral passages. Occasionally, music might have been used during the episodes or acted segments. Music was extremely important in choral interludes because it made the singing and dancing more harmonious. Additionally, it aided in building choral passages to a climax.

Repeat Exercise 2 to the accompaniment of the extant musical fragments titled "Delphic Hymn" and "Epitph of Seikilos and Mandikiaw."[1] If this recording is not available in your school library, any recording utilizing flutes, drums, and string instruments played in a relatively slow tempo will do.

Character and Emotion—Greek Tragedy

Greek tragedy reveals the author's awareness of each character's underlying motives and justification for action and emotion, but not at the sacrifice of the lyric poetry of the verse.

The problems of a modern actor attempting to physicalize emotions in an ideal way, to maintain believability, and to achieve truthfulness in a Greek role are not insurmountable. Difficulty will arise if you overemphasize the physical aspects of style instead of maintaining a good balance of believable characterization grounded in the reality of the style. Examine the play for primary motivations and justifications, particularly those analogous or similar to yours in order to use personalization at the beginning of rehearsals; find the emotional builds within each scene; discover the intentions of the character as described by the playwright. At times you may encounter conflicting or paradoxical stylistic demands such as restrained versus heightened vocalization and movement. The solution is not to play one quality and eliminate the other. Modify both or adapt them to today's theatre, using both qualities in an appropriate mix of the restrained and the heightened. Role and play analyses will indicate to you when restraint should dominate the acting and when the acting should be heightened. For example, in the play *Oedipus* by Sophocles, the actor portraying Oedipus may effectively use restraint through modern, naturalistic emotion when Oedipus talks to his subjects about the plague early in the play. Oedipus is emotionally under control; he is a proud, majestic king whose voice and movement are characterized by precision and grace. Later in the play, when Oedipus discovers that ca-

1. RCA Victor Album *History of Music in Sound*, vol. 1, "Ancient and Oriental Music," LM 6057.

lamity is the result of his own actions, greatly heightened emotion, vocalization, and movement should be used, including rapid tempo, strong volume, expansive physicalization, and movement. Most Greek playwrights of tragedy wrote to idealize and to transcend the emotions of the ordinary Athenian citizens and to challenge them by exciting their pity for and fear of the character. To use both restrained and heightened emotion in a Greek tragedy requires careful analysis and intense concentration. You will need to adapt your emotion from so-called real-life emotion to the larger-than-life conception of the tragic writer.

Exercise 3   Character and Emotion—Greek Tragedy

Examine each of the following phrases which depicts a single idea and emotional disposition. Establish an immobile physical position which typifies the essence of the emotion or idea. The face and entire body should express the idea or feeling. Once this is successfully accomplished, place the physicalization and attitude into motion through simple walking, sitting, and gesturing. After this is accomplished, invent a complete sentence of dialogue expressing the idea or emotion you are depicting. Memorize the sentence, and as you physicalize and move, vocalize the sentence with different tempos and a variety of expressions ranging from classical restraint to naturalistic intensity.
1. Excessive pride
2. Incestuous passion
3. Obsessive revenge
4. Martyred sacrifice
5. Burial grief
6. Insane frenzy
7. Blind drunkenness

Overview of Satyr Comedy and Old Greek Comedy (Aristophanes)

As the Greek tragic playwrights acquired a following in the fifth century B.C., festival officials required them to present a satyr play when they competed in the festivals. A satyr play was a short comedy which usually burlesqued a Greek myth. This afterpiece utilized a chorus of satyrs whose function was to satirize the seriousness of tragic stories by parodying gods, heroes, tragic dances, actions, conventions of acting, costumes, and scenery. The satyrs wore a goatskin loincloth with a phallus (comic imitation of the male sexual organ) in the front and a horsetail in the rear. They wore tight flesh-colored garments which ridiculed tragic costumes. Some characters wore masks with fixed size and expression. In the earlier satyr plays, the masks were not large. Later masks covered the entire head and were decorated with hair, beards, and ornaments. The chorus usually wore identical masks representing animals; the actors wore masks with set human expressions. Characters who did not wear masks, primarily the satyrs, had a snub nose, dark unkempt hair, a beard, and pointed ears, or they were bald and wore horns on top of their head. All action concentrated on lewd pantomime and general buffoonery.

Today we have only one complete satyr play, *Cyclops* by Euripides. It is a parody of the serious story found in the *Odyssey*. A modern actor would rarely be asked to act in *Cyclops*. However, if you choose to perform a scene from the play, you might refer to the discussion of Greek comedy on pp. 110–112 of this book, paying special attention to the sections on the use of physical action.

Greek comedy was officially supported by the State beginning in 486 B.C. (it may have been part of the festival City Dionysia in 501 B.C.). The first professional comedians probably made their debut onstage around 455 B.C., displaying their buffoonery and comic jests. The chorus consisted of twenty-four members whose function was to perform music and dance.

Old Comedy as exemplified by the works of Aristophanes differed from tragedy principally in subject matter and in approach. The stories were concerned with contemporary matters of politics or art or with revealing corrupt public and private practices such as sustaining foreign war and the practice of pedantic sophistry. Well-known politicians, philosophers, and playwrights also received a fair share of notoriety in the plays. Usually institutions and public figures were satirized or held up to ridicule for their beliefs or practices. Plot was entirely the invention of the playwright, and unlimited license was the rule. Greek comic plays provided a balance between exaggeration and believability. Caricature was the prominent feature in character portrayal; however, roles of minor stature required closer fidelity to real life. These so-called low characters projected everyday emotional response. Hence, verisimilitude or fidelity to real life was vital in Greek comedy, although fantasy was occasionally intermingled (see *The Birds*, *The Frogs*, *The Wasps*, *The Clouds*, etc.).

Voice—Old Greek Comedy

Vocalization in Old Greek Comedy was undoubtedly much more lifelike than was vocalization in tragedy. Since the characters were often members of lower social status, everyday speech was necessary (the exception to this were characters such as gods and statesmen). Vocal variety, clarity of diction, and effective projection are standard techniques for successful vocalization of Old Greek Comedy. Occasionally, singing is required as well. Lyricism and rhythm are important in line delivery.

Exercise 4   Voice—Old Greek Comedy

1. Practice the following speech individually and then collectively, emphasizing vocal variety, clear diction, and effective projection.

Frogs   Brekekekex Koax Koax
        Brekekekex Koax Koax!

We are the swamp-children
Greeny and tiny,
Fluting our voices
As all in time we
Sing our Koax Koax
Koax Koax Koax

2. Repeat the exercise by singing it lyrically and rhythmically, both individually and collectively.

Movement—Old Greek Comedy

The movement in Old Greek Comedy was mimetic, large or bold, and expressive of a character type; expression undoubtedly developed from highly exaggerated wild-animal movements adapted from religious dances and victory celebrations. Emphasis was probably on kicking the buttocks, slapping the chest or thighs, leaping, high kicking, running, spinning like a top, and beating other actors. Some scholars think that three to five major characters in the play joined the chorus to perform pantomimic tricks and stage business with gusto and fast-paced rhythm. The movement must have depended on the performer executing a variety of skills. Athletic and disciplined, the actors probably reverted to extensive physical action and body contact, relying heavily on farcical and satiric invention and the interpolation of song, dance, and comic acrobatics.

Although comic costumes provided the actor with freer movement, they were not necessarily standard or prescribed. As seen on vase paintings, actors usually wore short, tight-fitting tunics (chitons) over flesh-colored tights to give the illusion of partial nakedness. Nudity and ridiculousness were further emphasized by attaching a phallus to the costumes of most male characters. As in the satyr plays, a mask was a common accoutrement

Scene from *Lysistrata* by Aristophanes. Directed by Jerry L. Crawford. Designed by Todd Dougall. University of Nevada, Las Vegas.

of the comic costume. However, masks were probably more specialized in function, depicting actual persons or representing animals, birds, insects, or exaggerated characteristics such as baldness, skinniness, and obesity.

When Greek comic acting is adapted for modern audiences, very little adjustment is needed. Personalization can again be used effectively in early rehearsals, particularly if you have an instinctive flair for comedy, timing, and laughter and a sense of humor. Major focus should be on the extensive use of physical action and body contact, with corresponding pantomimic business. This simply means to use as much burlesque or vaudeville activity as you can invent. Use music and dance, singing, and acrobatics to provide interpolation between dialogue as well as to punctuate comic lines. Play to the audience slightly more than to one another (e.g., presentational technique slightly dominates representational). Let movements and gestures be energetic, large, and rapid. Coordinate your movements with the satiric speeches to add stress and clarity to the thought. Respond to an emotion when it is appropriate, but do not indulge in the feeling, or tempo and pace will be sacrificed. Use costume to simulate nudity, and to provide an illusion of sexuality use a phallus, provided that it is used for comic exaggeration rather than as a sexual reality. Modern adaption probably calls for limited, or no, use of Greek comic masks. However, it would not be incorrect to use masks occasionally for minor characters, particularly when the playwright calls for a caricature or portrait effect (e.g., the creation of an animal face or the creation of a known individual such as Socrates in *The Clouds*). Most important, you must be physically able to handle the demands of Greek comedy. A high energy level helps provide the correct rhythm to the play; vocal variety, clear diction, and projection aid in crystallizing satirical points, and a relaxed, well-toned physical posture allows for body control and agility.

Exercise 5   Movement—Old Greek Comedy

> Repeat vocal Exercise 4, but this time concentrate on executing the following physical activities as you deliver the lines.
>   1. Somersaults
>   2. Cartwheels
>   3. High kicks
>   4. Handstands
>   5. Leapfrog
>   6. Pratfalls
>   7. Comic hitting, running, and animallike dancing
>   8. Juggling

Character and Emotion in Old Greek Comedy

Authors of comedy such as Aristophanes focused upon a single obsessive dimension of human character, utilizing it for stereotype or caricature (only occasionally did he create full-dimensional, believable human characters). Aristophanes also used animals, birds, and inanimate objects as character types to represent human beings. He mixed reality and fantasy and treated both in a satiric manner. Examples of his character types include the pompous statesman or philosopher (see Socrates in *The Clouds*), the frustrated lover (see Kinesias in *Lysistrata*), the vulnerable and effeminate god (see Dionysus in *The Frogs*), the comic bird (see Epops in *The Birds*), and the amusing slave or parasite (see Xanthius in *The Frogs*). The emotion depicted by these characters was frequently singular and obsessive. For example, Kinesias's sole interest was in sexual activity with his wife. Accordingly, character and emotion in Old Greek Comedy are much less complex to perform than in Greek tragedy. Emphasis must be on mechanical techniques, physicalization, voice, and movement as just described. However, personalization and a reality base should support all work with mechanics.

Exercise 6   Character and Emotion—Old Greek Comedy

Invent one comic emotional characteristic for each of the character types in the list that follows. Establish an immobile physical position which typifies the essence or idea. Your face and entire body should express the essence of the idea or feeling. Once this is successfully accomplished, place the physicalization and attitude into rapid motion through fast walking, sitting, gesturing, tumbling, hitting, and falling. After these movements are accomplished, invent a complete sentence of dialogue expressing the idea or emotion you are depicting. (For example, for pompous statesman, the sentence could be I am a great king.) Memorize the sentence and as you move, vocalize the sentence with different tempos and a variety of expressions, ranging from larger-than-life size to modern, naturalistic detail.

1. Pompous statesman
2. Braggart warrior
3. Passionate lover
4. Effeminate god
5. Comic bird
6. Comic frog
7. Comic wasp
8. Comic cloud
9. Comic slave
10. Comic poet

Transition—Roman and Medieval Drama

Greece attained its greatest influence during the fifth and fourth centuries B.C. Thereafter, military and economic difficulties eroded the power of Greece, while Rome became the dominant influence in the known world.

Roman Drama

Early Roman theatre utilized a crude form of improvised dialogue. Abusive and obscene, drama was given mostly at harvest and wedding celebrations. Favorite entertainment included chariot races, boxing contests, athletic games, and gladitorial contests in stadiumlike arenas. The dominate theatre form was the farce play. The farces were heavily influenced by Old Greek Comedy and the so-called Middle or New Comedy of Menander, written during the Hellenistic period of the fourth century. Menander reemphasized the ordinary characters and farce typical of Old Greek Comedy. By the middle of the second century B.C., Rome produced its first major playwrights, Plautus and Terence. Plautus wrote comic farces whose plot devices and low-life characters were of minimal dimension. The plays of Terence were more genteel, and their content was more educational in purpose. Available evidence indicates that the Romans produced comedies and few if any tragedies in their theatre. However, Seneca did write several tragedies based on Greek models. These tragedies, while probably never produced, had major influence on Renaissance playwrights hundreds of years later (this influence is discussed in chapter 12).

In serious Roman drama, Seneca's characters, modeled after their classical Greek counterparts, were deeply emotional.

In Roman comedy, the characters were one-dimensional stereotypes, particularly in the plays of Plautus. Plautine farces usually depicted characters of a single emotional bent. The plays of Terence contained a more lifelike human dimension and the characters were of a slightly more complex emotional level.

Since Roman dramas are rarely produced in the modern theatre, and because the style of acting in these dramas is so closely allied to the Greek style, this style of acting is merely summarized here.

Acting Roman Drama

Acting in serious Roman plays was probably closely allied to oratory. Actors probably declaimed to the audience, using little vocal variety. Evidence from Quintilian and Plutarch indicates that in oratory meaning and thought were stressed, rather than emotion and feeling.

In Roman comedy heightened vocal projection and close attention to comic patterns of speech are necessary. Increased emphasis on words and phrases will intensify the comic meaning.

Movement in serious Roman drama is best handled today by using the techniques explained in the Greek discussion of classical style, with some modification (i.e., less exaggeration in movement and gesture and less vocal size).

Roman comedy should probably be produced as originally presented—broad and lusty and with a large amount of physical contact between performers. Most of the material should be played directly to the audience (presentational). Again, dancing, tumbling, acrobatics, hitting, falling, running, and general slapstick behavior can be used effectively. Great emphasis should be placed on comic precision in the timing of business and dialogue. Many of the Old Greek comic properties such as clapboards, staffs, fans, money pouches, and so on should be used. As the guide to dress, use Roman period costumes. While masks were probably used in original Roman comedy, they are usually eliminated in present-day theatre and replaced with makeup. If you do use a mask, a half-mask might be appropriate.

Most of the acting style characteristic of Greek drama may be used (with modification) to perform Roman drama. The Roman theatre was important for vitality and entertainment, for perpetuating and adapting Greek drama, and for a heritage which Renaissance playwrights were to use so well.

Medieval Drama

The power of the Roman empire diminished by the sixth century A.D. Invasions by nomadic barbarians and the influence of the Christian Church splintered Roman power and dispersed popular entertainment and theatre activity. Popular theatre was forbidden during the so-called Dark Ages or Medieval Ages which ranged generally from the sixth century well into the tenth A.D. Ironically, the Church helped revive theatre activity by introducing exchanges of dialogue in the form of *tropes* or hymns into the mass between the priest and the choir. Later, actual scenery and costumes were used to help teach moral and religious lessons to the common people who were uneducated and easily influenced by dramatic display.

As the activity became increasingly secular and involved more participants, drama moved out of the church itself onto the church steps and into streets and courtyards. The mystery plays (Biblical stories), miracle plays (stories of saints and martyrs), and morality plays (stories with moral precepts) were produced on a simple platform. In England these kinds of plays were performed on pageant wagons which were drawn by horses through the streets, stopping to perform as a crowd formed. Trade merchants formed guilds which sponsored and produced these religious plays in England and on the Continent.

Eventually, secular, or nonreligious, material became more important than religious material in the plays. Native farce comedy began to dominate theatre activity and was a major development in the transition from the religious plays to the great theatre of the Renaissance. Interludes, another transitional dramatic form, were also performed and were particularly enjoyed by nobles and rich merchants. Interludes were often performed by minstrels or jongleurs (strolling players) who were skilled in singing, dancing, and storytelling. Medieval theatre produced few known playwrights. Authorship was generally anonymous.

Acting Medieval Drama

Several Medieval plays are still quite actable today. *Everyman* (anonymous), *The Second Shepherds' Play* (anonymous), *Pierre Patelin* (anonymous), *The Iron Pot* by Hans Sachs, and the short bible pieces of Hrosvitha the Nun, are among the most popular with audiences. If the limitations caused by negligible information on styles of Medieval acting are recognized, Medieval plays can be a valid acting vehicle if you begin by carefully defining your physical acting area. Since these plays were usually performed on a platform stage, adaptation of a Medieval play requires a similarly limited acting space. Generally, be careful not to perform on a large stage requiring a complicated set. Use smaller areas which limit movement and gesture. Rely essentially on strong, clear vocal work and stereotyped posture to project characterization. (Although characters are clearly and boldly drawn in Medieval plays, some subtle psychological traits, revealed primarily in monologues and isolated scenes, do exist.) Medieval drama should visualize a predominately lifelike quality. A study of the occupational characteristics prevalent during the Middle Ages will provide insight into details of everyday life. Since most of these plays emphasize religious allegories and everyday activities (e.g., a carpenter at work, a mason laying bricks, a cobbler making shoes, or a tailor sewing clothes), the modern actor needs to give his character sufficient stage business to develop believable characterization. The rare emotional scenes in these plays make a relatively brief but important contribution to the play's action. Perform these emotions with a direct and simple honesty, whether comic or tragic. Be sincere without belaboring the emotion.

The vocal and physical rhythm of the plays should be expressed in a steadily fluid manner. If the play is written in verse, speak with extra clarity and directness. When comedy appears in the play (e.g., a henpecked husband or a cowardly shepherd), convey the appropriate wide range of comic responses with exaggerated vocal detail and physical action. You must accept archaic conventions when they arise: for example, falling asleep instantly and awakening the next moment. React believably to the entrance of unusual characters such as angels or God in a scene. Be prepared to sing and move with ease. Maintain a realistic base when acting real-life characters by projecting commonplace details of human behavior.

Translators and Translations and Adaptations

The key to successful dramatic presentation of Greek, Roman, and most Medieval drama is to use a quality translation by an effective translator. Most plays, particularly verse plays, are performed best in their original language. Greek and Latin plays are particularly difficult to translate into effective English. As a general rule, a wise director, producer, and actor compare several translations of a particular play before deciding which translation should be performed. In this manner you can better judge what reads well, sounds believable, and would seem to interest modern audiences. Some authorities believe the more modern or recent the translation, the better will be the version. In some instances this may be true. However, some nineteenth-century translators remain the most widely used in the theatre today. Another reliable method of determining a good translation is to check which translations are most frequently published in dramatic anthologies.

An adaptation differs from a translation in that it goes beyond language translation into major textual changes. Greek drama, particularly comedy, is frequently adapted as well as translated. For example, there is a version of *Lysistrata* by Aristophanes which has been adapted to an American hillbilly environment. *The Frogs* by the same author has been presented as a 1920 vaudeville production, has been staged in the Yale University swimming pool, and has been played in a boxing ring at the University of Iowa. *The Bacchae* by Euripides has been staged in the manner of the American "hippy" movement of the 1960s. Selecting a translation or an adaptation is primarily the director's decision, but is of course of major importance to the actor. Your familiarity with different translations and adaptations will greatly assist your development in the art of acting.

Suggested Characters and Plays for Scene Work

Aeschylus

Agamemnon, Clytemnestra, Cassandra
  Agamemnon
Orestes, Electra, Clytemnestra
  The Eumenides

Sophocles

Oedipus, Jocasta, Tiresias, Messenger
  Oedipus Rex
Antigone, Creon, Ismene, Nurse, Messenger
  Antigone

Euripides

Medea, Jason
  Medea
Hecuba, Andromache, Cassandra, Helen, Menelaus, Talthybius
  The Trojan Women
Electra, Orestes
  Electra
Phaedre, Nurse, Hippolytus, Aphrodite, Artemis, Theseus
  Hippolytus
Dionysus, Cadmus, Tiresias, Pentheus, Agave
  The Bacchae
Cyclops, Odysseus
  Cyclops

Aristophanes

Dionysius, Xanthias, Aeschylus, Euripides
  The Frogs
Lysistrata, Myrinna, Kinesias
  Lysistrata
Epops, Peithetairos, and Euelpides
  The Birds

Additional Suggested Characters and Plays for Scene Work

Plautus

Menaechmus I, Menaechmus II, Cylindrus,
Erotium, Sponge
  The Twin Menaechmi

Euclio
> *The Pot of Gold*

Pyrgopolynices, Philocomasium
> *The Braggart Warrior*

Terence

Phormio, Phaedria, Pamphila
> *Phormio*

Micio, Aeschinus, Demea, Ctesipho, Pamphila
> *The Brothers*

Seneca

Atreus, Thyestes, the Ghost
> *Thyestes*

Anonymous

Abraham, Isaac
> *Abraham and Isaac*

Mak, Gyll
> *The Second Shepherd's Play*

Everyman, Good Deeds
> *Everyman*

Stevenson

Gammer Gurton, Diccon, Dame Chat
> *Gammer Gurton's Needle*

Anonymous

Pierre Patelin
> *Pierre Patelin*

Hrosvitha

Paphnutius, Thais
> *Paphnutius*

Sackville and Norton

Any role
> *Gorboduc*

Udall, Nicholas

Ralph Roister Doister, Dame Custance,
Mathewe Merygreeke
> *Ralph Roister Doister*

Actor Checklist   *Greek Tragedy*

Voice	Heightened word emphasis; precise diction; varied tone qualities; close to declamatory, rhetorical, oratorical, lyrical, or sung mode during the key emotional or lyrical moments.
Movement	Generally slow, suggestive, and rhythmic; rare use of sitting positions; rare use of physical contact with other characters; predominately presentational mode.

Gestures	Restrained, large, fluid, and complete; highly selective and mostly in the upper portion of the body.
Pantomimic Dramatization	Clear, appropriate, limited, and highly selective; rare use of hand props such as staffs, and emblems; use of full masks, half-masks, or makeup simulating a mask.
Character	Truthful, though somewhat larger than life; almost exclusively of high rank including gods.
Emotion	Complex and penetrating, particularly Sophocles and Euripides; clearly established and projected; somewhat larger than life; rooted in human psychology, particularly Euripides.
Ideas	Lofty, complex, clear; effectively theatricalized.
Language	Complex, clear, lyric, and rhythmic.
Mood and Atmosphere	Serious, restrained, lofty, passionate, and intense.
Pace and Tempo	Controlled, disciplined, rhythmic, and generally moderate to deliberate.
Special Techniques	Training in singing and dancing highly recommended, particularly for chorus members.

Actor Checklist *Old Greek Comedy*

Voice	Clear diction; projection with effective vocal variety.
Movement	Energetic, large, extensive physical contact with others; considerable use of sitting; balance of presentation and representational mode.
Gestures	Lifelike but expansive; detailed rather than selective; full use of the entire body.
Pantomimic Dramatization	Extensive interpolation of song, dance, and comedic acrobatics; wild-animal movements; adaptation of religious dances and victory antics, kicking, slapping, and so on; highly inventive use of half-mask or makeup.
Character	Exaggerated to level of caricature, particularly with chorus and minor characters; major characters somewhat closer fidelity to real life.
Emotion	Singular obsession; somewhat more complex in some major characters.
Ideas	Satiric; emphasized; clear.
Language	Mix of prose and verse; generally lifelike.
Mood and Atmosphere	Humorous; unrestrained; common; grotesque; fun.
Pace and Tempo	Rapid to moderate; exuberant.
Special Techniques	Singing, dancing, and acrobatic training highly recommended.

Suggested Readings

Allen, James T. *Greek Acting in the Fifth Century*. Berkeley: University of California Press, 1916.

Allen, James T. *The Greek Theatre of the Fifth Century before Christ*. Berkeley: University of California Press, 1920.

Allen, James T. *Stage Antiquities of the Greeks and Romans and Their Influence*. New York: Longmans, Green, 1927.

Aristotle. *Poetics*. Edited by A. Gudemen. Translated by Lane Cooper. Ithaca, N.Y.: Cornell University Press, 1928.

Arnott, Peter D. *Greek Scenic Conventions in the Fifth Century, B.C.* London: Oxford Clarendon Press, 1962.

Arnott, Peter. *An Introduction to Greek Theatre*. London: St. Martin's Press, 1956; Bloomington, Ind.: Indiana University Press, 1963.

Bates, William. *Euripides. A Student of Human Nature*. New York: A. S. Barnes & Co., 1961.

Bieber, Margarette. *The History of the Greek and Roman Theatre*. 2d ed. Princeton, N. J.: Princeton University Press, 1961.

Casson, Lionel, ed. *Masters of Ancient Comedy*. Translated by Lionel Casson. New York: Macmillan Co., 1960.

Chambers, E. K. *The Medieval Stage*. 2 vols. London: Oxford University Press, 1963.

Cornford, Francis M. *The Origin of Attic Comedy*. London: E. Arnold, 1914.

Corrigan, Robert W. *Roman Drama*. New York: Dell Publishing Co., 1966.

Craig, Hardin. *English Religious Drama of the Middle Ages*. London: Oxford University Press, 1955.

Duckworth, George E. *The Nature of Roman Comedy*. Princeton, N. J.: Princeton University Press, 1952.

Flickinger, R. C. *The Greek Theatre and Its Drama*. 6th ed. Chicago: University of Chicago Press, 1960.

Frank, Tenney. *The Status of Actors at Rome*. New York: Russell & Russell, 1933.

Gaster, Theodor. *Thespis; Ritual, Myth and Drama in the Ancient Near East*. New York: Abelard-Schuman Ltd., 1950.

Haigh, A. E. *The Tragic Drama of the Greeks*. New York, 1968.

Hamilton, Edith. *The Greek Way*, New York: W. W. Norton & Company, 1952.

Hamilton, Edith. *The Roman Way*. New York: W. W. Norton, 1932.

Kitto, H. D. F. *Greek Tragedy*. 2nd ed. London: Methuen & Co., Ltd., 1950.

Kitto, H. D. F. *The Greeks*. Baltimore: Penguin, 1964.

Meade, Anna McClymonds. "The Actor in the Middle Ages." Master's thesis, Columbia University, May 1927.

Murray, Gilbert. *Euripides and His Age*. New York: Holt, Rinehart and Winston, 1913.

Nicoll, Allardyce. *Masks, Mimes, and Miracles*. New York: Harcourt Brace Jovanovich, 1931.

Norwood, Gilbert. *Plautus and Terence*. New York: Cooper Square Publishers, 1932.

Norwood, Gilbert, ed. *Greek Comedy*. New York: Hill & Wang, 1963.

Pickard-Cambridge, A. W. *Dithyramb, Tragedy, and Comedy*. 2nd ed., rev. by T. B. L. Webster. London: Oxford University Press, 1962.

Salter, F. M. *Medieval Drama in Chester*. Canada: University of Toronto Press, 1955.

Segal, Erich W. *Roman Laughter: The Comedy of Plautus*. Boston: Harvard University Press, 1968.

Southern, Richard. *The Medieval Theatre in the Round*. London: Faber & Faber, Ltd., 1957.

Webster, T. B. L. *Greek Theatre Production*. London: Oxford University Press, 1956.

Young, Karl. *The Drama of the Medieval Church*. 2 vols. London: Oxford University Press, 1962.

Oedipus The King

by *Sophocles*

Translated by William Butler Yeats

Characters	Oedipus, King of Thebes Jocasta, his Queen (discovered later to be his mother)
Scene	The palace of King Oedipus.
Situation	Oedipus has promised his people to remove the plague from Thebes by discovering the cause of the affliction, not realizing it is himself (he has unknowingly killed his own father and married his own mother). Oedipus believes his brother-in-law, Creon, and the soothsayer, Tiresias, are plotting against him by accusing him of incest and patricide. Jocasta encounters Oedipus. Oedipus expresses his fears and Jocasta tries to reassure him.

JOCASTA   In the name of the Gods, King, what put you in this anger?

OEDIPUS   I will tell you; for I honour you more than these men do. The cause is Creon and his plots against me.

JOCASTA   Speak on, if you can tell clearly how this quarrel arose.

OEDIPUS   He says that I am guilty of the blood of Laius.

JOCASTA   On his own knowledge, or on hearsay?

OEDIPUS   He has made a rascal of a seer his mouthpiece.

JOCASTA   Do not fear that there is truth in what he says. Listen to me, and learn to your comfort that nothing born of woman can know what is to come. I will give you proof of that. An oracle came to Laius once, I will not say from Phoebus, but from his ministers, that he was doomed to die by the hand of his own child sprung from him and me. When his child was but three days old, Laius bound its feet together and had it thrown by sure hands upon a trackless mountain; and when Laius was murdered at the place where three highways meet, it was, or so at least the rumour says, by foreign robbers. So Apollo did not bring it about that the child should kill its father, nor did Laius die in the dreadful way he feared by his child's hand. Yet that was how the message of the seers mapped out the future. Pay no attention to such things. What the God would show he will need no help to show it, but bring it to light himself.

OEDIPUS   What restlessness of soul, lady, has come upon me since I heard you speak, what a tumult of the mind!

JOCASTA   What is this new anxiety? What has startled you?

OEDIPUS   You said that Laius was killed where three highways meet.

JOCASTA   Yes: that was the story.

OEDIPUS   And where is the place?

JOCASTA   In Phocis where the road divides branching off to Delphi and to Daulia.

OEDIPUS   And when did it happen? How many years ago?

JOCASTA   News was published in this town just before you came into power.

OEDIPUS   O Zeus! What have you planned to do unto me?

JOCASTA   He was tall; the silver had just come into his hair; and in shape not greatly unlike to you.

OEDIPUS   Unhappy that I am! It seems that I have laid a dreadful curse upon myself, and did not know it.

JOCASTA   What do you say? I tremble when I look on you, my King.

OEDIPUS   And I have a misgiving that the seer can see indeed. But I will know it all more clearly, if you tell me one thing more.

JOCASTA   Indeed, though I tremble I will answer whatever you ask.

OEDIPUS   Had he but a small troop with him; or did he travel like a great man with many followers?

JOCASTA   There were but five in all—one of them a herald; and there was one carriage with Laius in it.

OEDIPUS   Alas! It is now clear indeed. Who was it brought the news, lady?

JOCASTA   A servant—the one survivor.

OEDIPUS   Is he by chance in the house now?

JOCASTA   No; for when he found you reigning instead of Laius he besought me, his hand clasped in mine, to send him to the fields among the cattle that he might be far from the sight of this town; and I sent him. He was a worthy man for a slave and might have asked a bigger thing.

OEDIPUS   I would have him return to us without delay.

JOCASTA   Oedipus, it is easy. But why do you ask this?

OEDIPUS   I fear that I have said too much, and therefore I would question him.

JOCASTA   He shall come, but I too have a right to know what lies so heavy upon your heart, my King.

OEDIPUS   Yes: and it shall not be kept from you now that my fear has grown so heavy. Nobody is more to me than you, nobody has the same right to learn my good or evil luck. My father was Polybus of Corinth, my mother the Dorian Merope, and I was held the foremost man in all that town until a thing happened—a thing to startle a man, though not to make him angry as it made me. We were sitting at the table, and a man who had drunk too much cried out that I was not my father's son—and I, though angry, restrained my anger for that day; but the next day went to my father and my mother and questioned them. They were indignant at the taunt and that comforted me—and yet the man's words rankled, for they had spread a rumour through the town. Without consulting my father or my mother I went to Delphi, but Phoebus told me nothing of the things for which I came, but much of other things—things of sorrow and of terror: that I should live in incest with my mother, and beget a brood that men would shudder to look upon; that I should be my father's murderer. Hearing those words I fled out of Corinth, and from that day have but known where it lies when I have found its direction by the stars. I sought where I might escape those infamous things—the doom that was laid upon me. I came in my flight to that very spot where you tell me this king perished. Now, lady, I will tell you the truth. When I had come close up to those three roads, I came upon a herald, and a man like him you have described seated in a carriage. The man who held the reins and the old man himself would not give me room, but thought to force me from the path, and I struck the driver in my anger. The old man, seeing what I had done, waited till I was passing him and then struck me upon the head. I paid him back in full, for I knocked him out of the carriage with a blow of my stick. He rolled on his back, and after that I killed them all. If this stranger were indeed Laius, is there a more miserable man in the world than the man before you? Is there a man more hated of Heaven? No stranger, no citizen, may receive him into his house, not a soul may speak to him, and no mouth but my own mouth has laid this curse upon me. Am I not wretched? May I be swept from this world before I have endured this doom!

CHORUS   These things, O King, fill us with terror; yet hope till you speak with him that saw the deed, and have learnt all.

OEDIPUS   Till I have learnt all, I may hope. I await the man that is coming from the pastures.

JOCASTA   What is it that you hope to learn?

OEDIPUS   I will tell you. If his tale agrees with yours, then I am clear.

JOCASTA   What tale of mine?

OEDIPUS   He told you that Laius met his death from robbers; if he keeps to that tale now and speaks of several slayers, I am not the slayer. But if he says one lonely wayfarer, then beyond a doubt the scale dips to me.

JOCASTA   Be certain of this much at least, his first tale was of robbers. He cannot revoke that tale—the city heard it and not I alone. Yet, if he should somewhat change his story, King, at least he cannot make the murder of Laius square with prophecy; for Loxias plainly said of Laius that he would die by the hand of my child. That poor innocent did not kill him, for it died before him. Therefore from this out I would not, for all divination can do, so much as look to my right hand or left hand, or fear at all.

OEDIPUS   You have judged well; and yet for all that, send and bring this peasant to me.

JOCASTA   I will send without delay. I will do all that you would have of me—but let us come in to the house. *(They go into the house.)*

The Frogs

by *Aristophanes*

Translated by Dudley Fitts

Characters

Scene

Situation

Chorus of Frogs
Dionysos

Near the shore of a great river/lake separating the known world from the unknown world below. Dionysos is onstage, resting.

The God, Dionysos, caricatured as rather effeminate and ineffectual, is on his way to Hades to retrieve the poet Euripides from the dead and return him to earth to raise the level of tragedy being written in Athens. At the river/lake known as Styx, Dionysos encounters a chorus of frog creatures and engages in frivolity and crude conflict.

KOMMOS: CHORAL EPISODE

(*The* ACCESSORY CHORUS *of* FROGS *is heard, offstage.*)

FROGS   Brekekekéx koáx koáx
          Brekekekéx koáx koáx!
    We are the swamp-children
                        Greeny and tiny.
    Fluting our voices
               As all in time we
        Sing our koáx koáx
        Koáx koáx koáx
    For Dionysos
              Nysa-born
    On the Winey Festival
                    When the throng
    Lurches in through his temple gate,
    Every man as drunk as a hake.
        Brekekekéx koáx koáx
        Brekekekéx koáx koáx!
DIONYSOS   My arse is sore, koáx koáx.
FROGS   Brekekekéx koáx koáx.
DIONYSOS   And you don't give a damn, koáx.
FROGS   Brekekekéx koáx koáx.
DIONYSOS   Go jump in the lake, koáx, koáx!
    Let's have a different tune, koáx!
FROGS   Different? What a
                   Meddlesome fool!
    Pan and the Muses
             Love us, our whole
        Koáx koáx koáx
        Koáx koáx koáx

Draws down Apollo
                    Golden-lyred:
Ours are the marsh-reeds
                              God-inspired
That sing to his heavenly fingering
Their music with our own mingling
          Brekekekéx koáx koáx.
DIONYSOS   My hands are ablaze, my bottom's a wreck!
In a minute or two you'll hear it speak.
FROGS   Brekekekéx koáx koáx!
DIONYSOS   Silence, you lily-pad lyrists, koáx!
FROGS   No, we must sing. The
          Sunshine will bring the
              Glint to the pools,
                  The shimmer of reeds,
And when Zeus descends
      In rain on our heads
          We'll leap with our friends
              And pipe from our souls
                  Brekekekéx koáx koáx!
DIONYSOS   Brekekekéx koáx koáx!
Come, that's enough!
FROGS   We've hardly begun!
DIONYSOS   I suppose you think that rowing is fun?

(A furious increase in volume and tempo to the end of the chorus.)

FROGS   Brekekekéx koáx koáx!
DIONYSOS   Brekekekéx koáx koáx!
I wish you'd die!
FROGS   We'll swell up and cry
   Brekekekéx koáx koáx!
   Brekekekéx koáx koáx!
DIONYSOS   Brekekekéx koáx koáx!
I can beat you at that koáx koáx!
FROGS   The devil you can, koáx koáx!
DIONYSOS   I will, by God, if it takes all day!
          Brekekekéx koáx koáx!
Go and koáx yourselves away!
          KOAX KOAX *KOAX!* (*He breaks wind hugely; the* FROGS *are silent.*)
There! That settles your damned koáx!

Commedia Dell'Arte 12

Regeneration

The snow dissolv'd no more is seen,
The fields, and woods, behold, are green,
the changing year renews the plain,
the rivers know their banks again. . . .
Horace
in *A History of Latin Literature*

The poetic description by Horace of the regeneration of a Roman spring may well be applied to a theatrical regeneration that occurred several hundred years later in Italy and elsewhere on the Continent.

A major form of theatre and style of acting, *commedia dell'arte*, regenerated dramatic activity in the sixteenth century. More than a transitional activity, the *commedia dell'arte* became a unique actor-oriented form of theatre. The term *arte* was used to signify professional artists. Commedia performances were improvisational and performed by traveling companies of actors. These companies frequently consisted of members of a single family, such as the famous Gelosi company. The origin of the commedia may be traced to the Atellan farce of Rome or possibly to the plays of Plautus and Terence. Emerging into prominence around the sixteenth century, the influence of the commedia would be important for over two hundred years.

Overview of Commedia Dell'Arte

Commedia was a comedy of intrigue using stock characters, often masked, and largely improvised dialogue based on a brief scenario. (Serious dramatic activity was limited during these years, favored only in erudite court or noble theatres. Commedia was the theatre of the masses.)

Plays were topical, drawn from the immediate time and place. Commedia used considerable pantomime. Speeches were added as an accompaniment to gesture, movement, and stage business. The accent in commedia was on visual performance. Actors were given a standard plot. Memorized lines were used only when they coincided with specifically outlined action. Comic stage business called *lazzi* and comic verbal jokes called *burla* were interspersed throughout the story to provide bits of stage fun or tricky comic turns (e.g., an actor might pretend his hat was filled with cherries, daintily eat them, flick the pits into another actor's face, and remark, "a pit in the eye is worth two in the hand").

Commedia scenarios were refined and performed again and again until the last half of the eighteenth century. The most successful plots concerned love and intrigues, disguises and deception.

Commedia Dell'Arte masks. Designed by Jeff Rice, University of Nevada, Las Vegas.

During its peak years, from approximately 1550 to 1650, about ten or twelve famous commedia dell'arte troupes traveled the Continent. Seven or eight men and three or four women comprised each group. Together they generally formed two sets of lovers, a servant girl, a captain, two zanni (comics), and two old men. Handsome and well-educated young men and women portrayed "straight" roles, usually romantic in nature; these characters were fashionably dressed and not masked. Other characters such as Pantalone wore tight-fitting red vests, breeches, stockings, and a black, ankle-length matching coat. Pantolone was always depicted wearing a brown mask with a hook-nose and having unkempt hair and beard. Dottore's costume always consisted of a long academic gown and a cap. Over the years these costumes were adapted slightly to current trends. Harlequin often shaved his head and wore a comic hat with a black mask. He carried a slapstick or clapboard; originally he wore a suit of colorful diamond-shaped patches. Capitano wore a comic version of a military uniform with lots of green braid; he wore colorful plumes on his hat. Comic female characters

HARLEQUIN

Harlequin character in Commedia Dell'Arte.

Pantalone character in
Commedia Dell'Arte.

such as courtesans wore long, full-length dresses or skirts of current fashion; some were masked (further costume reference is provided by the illustrations and photographs in this chapter). Character roles required special physical traits to help define the older men such as Capitano, Pantalone, and Dottore. The servants or zanni (e.g., Arlecchino or Harlequin) needed to be physically agile and supple in order to project the ridiculous burlesque qualities of these clever comic characters.

Almost eight hundred commedia dell'arte scenarios exist in outline form today (a complete scenario is included at the close of this chapter). It is virtually impossible to obtain the actual quality of the commedia performance since we have little information concerning its execution. We know, however, that it took great physical skill and clown talent to act in commedia. Although this theatre developed without playwrights, its influence was felt throughout Europe and subsequently had tremendous impact on later actors and playwrights such as Molière (see chapter 14).

Voice

The key aspect of vocal training for commedia is mental acuity for line invention. In other words, it helps to be glib. However, your verbal invention must be relevant to the scenario or the contemporary situation under enactment. The essentials of good stage speech are vital to delivery. Clear articulation, effective projection, rapid tempo, and considerable vocal variety are most important. The presentational mode dominates, necessitating adroit comic timing and direct audience delivery. Establishing reliable verbal burle will greatly assist your ability to emphasize so-called punch lines of comedy.

Exercise 1   Vocal Dexterity and Mental Acuity

1. Recite individually the following comic tongue twisters aloud as rapidly and clearly as possible:

Red leather and mellow yellow make wet weather and jolly fellows.

Peter Piper picked a peck of pickled peppers; a peck of pickled peppers Peter Piper picked.

Following this format, invent and practice comic tongue twisters and punch lines.

2. Invent or recall and practice telling comic jokes aloud in under thirty seconds. Every actor must tell at least one joke (refrain from obscene or so-called dirty stories).

Movement

Without question, movement is the essence of successful acting in commedia. The style requires acrobatic ability, forceful, flexible and rapid activity, and occasionally gracefully executed dance movements. All of the farce activities of Old Greek and Roman Comedy again apply, with special emphasis on characteristic movements and gestures of stock characters. For example, Pantalone, the old, grumpy father, walks with a hunch using a cane. Capitano, the braggart soldier, struts about with his head held high using grand hand gestures, waving his plumed hat. Harlequin turns cartwheels and somersaults and dances about with great abandon.

Exercise 2   Movement

1. Invent and practice comic movement suitable to each of the following stock commedia characters:
   a. Pantalone, the old merchant, miser, or father
   b. Dottore, pedantic bore
   c. Capitano, braggart soldier
   d. Zanni (comic servant), Harlequin, Pulchinello, Brighella, Scaramouche, Scapin

e. Fontesca or Innamorata, comic maid

f. Young lovers

2. Execute a combination or series of acrobatic techniques ranging from tumbling to juggling.

3. To the accompaniment of rapid, high-spirited music (guitars, drums, and flutes are preferable), invent spontaneous and collective group dancing. In the event that music is not available, this exercise can be great fun by improvising the music with the aid of crude instruments such as washboards and metal pipes, bells, wooden sticks or shoes, humming through a piece of paper placed over a comb, and so on.

Character and Emotion

Commedia characters were one-dimensional stereotypes, usually possessive and obsessive, in the tradition of Old Greek and Roman Comedy. Commedia characters differ from their ancient counterparts in that their activity was more presentational. Except when performance was repetitive, dialogue and action for commedia characters were almost totally improvisational, and character types were refined and inflexible.

Commedia Dell'Arte production of *The Doctor in Spite of Himself* by Molière. Directed by Jerry L. Crawford. Designed by Pat Crawford. University of Nevada, Las Vegas.

Exercise 3   Character and Emotion

Utilizing the work in Exercises 1 and 2, create brief scenarios from the following situational ideas, identifying one stock character for each actor. When you have completed discussing the scenario, each actor performs the stock character he selected within the context of the scenario. Act the scenario as an improvised play, keeping the performance under five minutes.

1. A man refuses his daughter's hand in marriage to a young cobbler in favor of an old schoolmaster.

2. A long-lost twin is reunited with his brother who is identical in appearance.
3. An old miser is cheated out of his money by a clever servant.
4. A man masquerades as a doctor of medicine to gain access to the wife of an old merchant.
5. A soldier returns from the wars to discover his sweetheart has been forced into a marriage with an old attorney-at-law.

Transition—Tudor Drama

As the commedia developed and flourished in Italy and elsewhere on the Continent, Europe was prey to barbarism, sacrilege, and selfishness. Despondency was the prevalent mood. As early as the fourteenth century, the French poet Eustache Deschamps set the tone for the late Medieval period when he wrote:

Why is our life so cruel and dark
That men no longer speak to friend?
Why does evil so clearly mark
The monstrous government of Men?
Compare what is with what is past
And see how fraud and sorrow stand,
While law and justice fade so fast
That I know no longer where I am.
from The Horizon Book
of the Elizabethan World

The individual became engulfed in the tide of swelling institutional power. Man's life on earth lost meaning except as preparation for an afterlife.

Although Medieval institutions dominated, the spirit which sustained them eventually withered and died. The Holy Roman Empire was crumbling by 1400. Monarchs were subject to foreign invasions and international alliances. Throughout Europe, kingships were suffering paralysis. Economic, social, and political disasters seemed to be without end. Disease, death, suffering, and war took their toll on most of Europe. However, the picture of despair lessened somewhat in England with the presence of Henry VII, founder of the Tudor dynasty, who came to the throne in 1485.

Henry VII was part of the new breed of monarchs on the European continent. He worked to liberate royal government from ecclesiastical interference, enforced laws, promoted financial solvency, and achieved complete control over the nobility. The violent class turmoil in English life produced by the Wars of the Roses was beginning to settle into a less violent pattern of living in which middle-class gentleman gained predominance.

In drama, this transitional period produced a combination of Medieval-like Interludes performed by professional actors and classically inspired plays written at universities and Inns of Court performed by students. History was a popular subject, as were Bible stories rewritten in a romantic style. School drama was influenced by the plays of Plautus, Terence, and Seneca, all of which were read or performed in Latin. Original plays were written in both Latin and English, imitating the Roman or classical models. The most popular school plays were *Ralph Roister Doister* by Nicholas Udall and *Gammer Gurton's Needle* by Stevenson. The first known English tragedy was *Gorboduc* by Thomas Sackville and Thomas Norton. Other original native drama combined elements of classical learning (e.g., use of mythological figures) and English low comedy (e.g., use of farcical types). Even prior to Shakespeare's arrival in London, the theatre was under the influence of sophisticated playwriting. In his play *The Spanish Tragedy*, Thomas Kyd revealed the influence of Seneca by use of the revenge motif in combination with supernatural reference and suspenseful plot. (Shakespeare's *Hamlet*, written later, resembled Kyd's play closely.) Christopher Marlowe's contribution was to perfect blank verse as a medium for drama in his play's *Doctor Faustus, Edward II, Tamburlaine the Great,* and *The Jew of Malta.* John Lyly wrote prose comedies with themes from mythology which significantly developed comic playwriting beyond the crude farces of the Tudor period. All playwrights accented the chronological approach to action, emphasizing stage violence, a blend of serious and comic elements, poetic imagery, soliloquy, and short scenes.

Acting Tudor Drama

The Tudor acting style was both conventionalized and basically realistic or unconventional. The major convention was the performing of all female roles by young male actors. Considerable emphasis was placed on realistic contemporary life and manners, especially in the comedies. Actors arrived at an essential truthfulness of what we would term *human psychology*. That is, they created fundamentally convincing characters. However, there are exceptions to realistic character portrayal in these plays. There are roles in Tudor plays which call for a nonrealistic or highly exaggerated acting style, especially the farces in which a bizarre mixture of dramatic and comic elements appear (e.g., mixing serious mythology and low slapstick comedy).

An important outgrowth of Tudor drama in the development of theatrical art was the attention paid to costuming. Following the lead of society, dress for stage use also became quite exaggerated. Men's robes were larger, longer, and more elaborate than during early Medieval times. Young men often dressed in short formfitting tunics, pulled in with a belt. Hose and pointed shoes were worn. Sleeves were ballooned and gathered at the wrist; others were long enough to trail on the ground. Women's bodices also became more formfitting, with pinched waists, and skirts were fuller and heavier. Accordingly, acting style in plays was affected. Walking in a fourteenth-century skirt required extensive knee action. When a curtsy was executed, the front of the skirt was lifted to allow an actor to bend to the ground and rise gracefully. The skirt was held out and the head was inclined slightly to one side or slightly forward.

The men had difficulty executing movements due to their padded breeches. Walking and standing were cumbersome matters. However, men usually walked with a vigorous stride and displayed an athletic physique. Bowing usually occurred in the third ballet position, with toes and knees turned out, the rear knee bent, and the rear heel slightly off the ground; the forward leg was straight with the weight evenly distributed on both feet. Wearing clothes for the Tudor gentlemen was a pleasure. They were dedicated to showing off their legs and general attire.

Women, too, enjoyed elaborate display of clothing by keeping the torso straight and stiff, turning from the waist, and keeping the skirt in line with the shoulders. The head was poised to balance the headdress. The total physical effect of costuming, movement, bowing, and curtsying became a distinctive aspect of Tudor acting.

Late in the sixteenth century as the commedia dell'arte achieved prominence on the Continent, the limited but promising Tudor drama passed gradually into a new and distinct period in theatre activity and style—into the incomparable dramatic Renaissance of Elizabethan England—the age of William Shakespeare.

Suggested Characters and Plays for Scene Work

See any of the many extant commedia dell'arte scenarios. (Refer to Suggested Reading at the conclusion of this chapter for titles containing scenarios.)

Actor Checklist   *Commedia Dell'Arte*

Voice	Comic verbal invention and burle; clear articulation; effective projection; rapid tempo, considerable vocal variety.
Movement	Acrobatic ability; forceful, flexible, and rapid; occasional dance activity; balance of presentational and representational mode, with slight dominance of presentational.
Gestures	Stock character *lazzi;* considerable physical contact with others; lifelike but expansive; full use of entire body.
Pantomimic Dramatization	Extensive interpolation of song, dance, comedic acrobatics; highly inventive slapstick; use of full mask and half-mask on all characters except young lovers.
Character	Definitive types throughout; young lovers closest to real-life fidelity.
Emotion	Generally limited or one-dimensional; singular obsession.
Ideas	Satiric concerning local and contemporary references; generally light and fun-oriented; usually simple, love-triangle basis.
Language	Improvisational prose; generally memorized verse in songs.
Mood and Atmosphere	Humorous, unrestrained, common, grotesque, fun.

Pace and Tempo	Rapid to moderate; exuberant.
Special Techniques	Improvisational skill with dialogue and physical activity; singing, dancing, and acrobatic training highly recommended to relate comic stories.

Suggested Readings

Beaumont, Cyril V. *The History of Harlequin*. 1926. Reprint. New York: Benjamin Blom, 1967.

Disher, Maurice Wilson. *Clowns and Pantomimes*. New York: Benjamin Blom, 1968.

Du Charte, Pierre. *Commedia dell'Arte*. London: Peter Smith, 1965.

Du Charte, Pierre. *Italian Comedy*. New York: Dover Publications, 1965.

Lea, Kathleen M. *Italian Popular Comedy: A Study of the Commedia dell'Arte (1560–1620) with Special Reference to the English Stage*. 2 vols. 1924. Reprint. New York: Russell & Russell Publishers, 1962.

Oreglia, Giacomo. *The Commedia dell'Arte*. New York: Hill & Wang, 1968.

Salerno, Henry F., ed. and trans. *Scenarios of the Commedia dell'Arte Flaminio Scala's 11 Theatre Della Favole Rappresentative*. New York: New York University Press, 1967.

Sand, Maurice. *The History of the Harlequin*. 2 vols. 1915. Reprint. New York: Benjamin Blom, 1968.

Smith, Winifred. *The Commedia dell'Arte: A Study in Italian Popular Comedy*. New York: Benjamin Blom, 1965.

The Portrait
by *Flaminio Scala*

A Commedia dell'Arte Scenario

Translated from the French by Garrett H. Leverton

Vittoria	Flavio	*Characters*
Piombino	Pedrolino	
Pantalone	Arlecchino	
Gratiano	Captain Spavento	
Isabella	Lesbino, *later Silvia*	
Flaminia	A Rogue	
Oratio	Nobles and Civilians	

Parma.   *Place*

Midsixteenth Century.   *Time*

A troupe of actors were performing in Parma. According to the custom, the principal actress received many visitors, one of whom was a cavalier of the city named Oratio. During his visit the cavalier exhibited a locket in which was hidden the portrait of the very beautiful woman who had given him this locket. During the course of the conversation, the actress—Vittoria, by name—subtly removed the portrait from the locket before returning it, at the close of his visit. A few days later the husband of the beautiful woman came to see the actress. Vittoria, not knowing who he was, chanced to show him the portrait of his wife. The husband, Pantalone, was very much surprised, and at great length tried to persuade the actress to tell him the name of the man who had given her this portrait. Pantalone concealed the reason for his interest in the affair and returned to his home in a fury to inflict exemplary chastisement on his culpable wife. However, on arriving there, the wife gave so many good excuses in support of her innocence that she succeeded in appeasing his anger.

The persons concerned in working out this situation are the actress, Vittoria, and her comrade Piombino; the two old men Pantalone and Gratiano; their wives, Isabella and Flaminia; and the wives's lovers, Oratio and Flavio. Pedrolino is valet to Pantalone, and Arlecchino to Captain Spavento. A young Milanese girl, disguised as a page, comes under the name of Lesbino to offer her services to the Captain, whom she loves.

Act I, Scene i

After the quarrel between ISABELLA and PANTALONE, her husband, over the portrait which was last seen in the hands of VITTORIA, ISABELLA begins to doubt ORATIO's love for her. She orders PEDROLINO to go to ORATIO and to demand from him the portrait which she had given him some time previously.

Scene ii

CAPTAIN SPAVENTO tells ARLECCHINO how through being obliged to assist in the play, he has fallen in love with the actress, VITTORIA. ARLECCHINO tells him he is wasting time.

Scene iii

Later, the CAPTAIN consents to take LESBINO as his page, after asking him many foolish questions about his bravery and his military talents.

Scene iv

From her window, FLAMINIA calls to ARLECCHINO and asks him to carry a letter to a cavalier named FLAVIO, whom she will meet at the place where she conducts her rendezvous with gentlemen. ARLECCHINO takes the letter and promises to deliver it to the one to whom it is addressed. FLAMINIA gives him some money and withdraws. ARLECCHINO regards FLAMINIA's window knowingly.

Scene v

Doctor GRATIANO, the husband of FLAMINIA, seeing ARLECCHINO with a letter in his hand and gazing at his wife's window, becomes suspicious, and demands to know what he is doing there and for whom the letter is intended. ARLECCHINO replies that a man named FLAVIO gave it to him to deliver to a lady. The DOCTOR takes the letter and raps ARLECCHINO with his cane.

Scenes vi to x

PANTALONE comes between the DOCTOR and ARLECCHINO. FLAVIO presents himself. GRATIANO, furiously angry, returns the letter to him. FLAVIO receives it with profound humility. The others depart and FLAVIO reads the letter in which FLAMINIA begs him to frequent the theatre no longer.

Scene xi

When PEDROLINO asks the return of the portrait of ISABELLA, ORATIO explains that it is impossible to return it to him because the locket is being repaired at the jeweler's. PEDROLINO smiles and asks him how long it has been since he has gone to the theatre, questions him about all the actors, and finally about the SIGNORA VITTORIA.

Scene xii

At this moment ISABELLA arrives. She dissembles at first, then asks for the return of the portrait. But ORATIO repeats the same story he had already told PEDROLINO. She calls him a traitor and tells him she knows about his love for the actress to whom he has given her portrait. In her anger, she commands PEDROLINO to follow her and she leaves refusing to listen to ORATIO. ORATIO bemoans his ill luck and blames the presence of the actors as the reason for all his trouble. He is particularly discourteous in expressing his opinion of VITTORIA who has tricked him so deceitfully.

Scene xiii

The CAPTAIN, hearing what ORATIO says about the actors, and particularly VITTORIA, comes to their defense. He argues that the theatre is a noble diversion and that the SIGNORA VITTORIA is an honorable lady. ORATIO, furious, calls him a liar and reaches for his sword. At this the CAPTAIN asks ORATIO if he wishes to fight a duel with him. ORATIO replies that he is ready. Then the CAPTAIN says he goes to write a letter which will remove from ORATIO the responsibility for his death in case he is killed, and will prevent the officers of justice from regarding him as an adversary. He asks ORATIO to do the same for him. Then he departs. ARLECCHINO observes that his master has the appearance of wishing to escape the affair. Thus ends the first act.

Act II, Scene i

VITTORIA, richly dressed, with gold necklaces and pearl bracelets, with diamonds and rubies on her fingers, engages herself through PIOMBINO to the DUKE OF PARMA, recalling the many courtesies which she was constantly receiving from the Parmesan nobility.

Scenes ii to v

PEDROLINO praises his master PANTALONE to VITTORIA. PANTALONE appears but he does not dare to approach the actress because he sees his wife at the window. PEDROLINO persuades PANTALONE that the actress is in love with him. PANTALONE, flattered, expresses the intention of giving her a present.

Scene vi

While ORATIO recounts to his friend FLAVIO the unfortunate history of the portrait, ARLECCHINO brings him the CAPTAIN's letter of remission from blame. ORATIO strikes him with his fist and rushes off to the theatre.

Scenes vii to xii

FLAVIO and PEDROLINO, and then FLAMINIA attempt to reconcile ISABELLA and ORATIO. ISABELLA softens but she declares that ORATIO shall get nothing from her so long as he does not return the portrait, and she forbids him, moreover, to go, himself, to negotiate for its return. PEDROLINO informs them how the two old men, PANTALONE and GRATIANO, are paying attention to the actress.

Scene xiii

Now the DOCTOR arrives. PEDROLINO pretends to be arguing with FLAMINIA and is saying: "How do I know whether your husband goes to the theatre or not?" FLAMINIA, entering into the deception, pretends to be jealous of her husband. When she has withdrawn, PEDROLINO tells the DOCTOR of his visit to the SIGNORA VITTORIA and of how she is in love with the DOCTOR. GRATIANO is enchanted.

Scene xiv

PIOMBINO greets the DOCTOR in behalf of SIGNORA VITTORIA. He begs him to take to the actress a silver pitcher and vase which she needs for a play which she is going to present. The DOCTOR replies that he will send these by PEDROLINO. PIOMBINO assures him that the actress is in love with him, and that because of him, she rejects the attentions of all the gentlemen who call on her at home or at the theatre. The DOCTOR is overjoyed and promises a reward to PIOMBINO.

Scene xv

The CAPTAIN talks with his page, LESBINO, about the passion which the actress inspires in him. LESBINO tries to turn him away from this passion which he cannot make honorable. He asks him if he has never had another love. The CAPTAIN replies that he had been in love, in Milan, with a very beautiful young girl named SILVIA.

Scene xvi

ARLECCHINO interrupts his master to tell him that VITTORIA is waiting for him at a nearby jeweler's. LESBINO, desperate, seeks to persuade ARLECCHINO that he ought to kill him, LESBINO, because he has conceived the intention of killing his master. ARLECCHINO beats and injures the page. FLAMINIA and ISABELLA intervene.

Scene xvii

Suspecting that LESBINO is a woman in spite of her male attire, they take her to the residence of FLAMINIA. Thus ends the second act.

Act III, Scene i

VITTORIA and PIOMBINO go to dine at the house of a rich gentleman who gives them magnificent presents. They congratulate themselves because of the custom of making gifts to actors, a common custom in Italian cities and one which is seldom neglected by persons of distinguished rank. VITTORIA confesses that she laughs at all lovers who are not generous with her. PIOMBINO promises to provide well for her old age.

Scenes ii and iii

PANTALONE comes to call on VITTORIA. She thanks him for the presents he has brought to her and invites him to be present at the theatre for the opening of her play. PANTALONE promises to be there. Presently FLAVIO arrives and the actress detains him with engaging conversation.

Scene iv

But FLAMINIA sees them from her window. She is so angry that she goes out and slaps FLAVIO in the face and then returns to her house. FLAVIO, putting his hand to his smarting cheek, goes without saying a word. VITTORIA laughs heartily.

Scene v

PANTALONE who has been a witness to this *coup de théâtre* blames FLAMINIA for her effrontery. He congratulates himself that he has such a modest and well-bred wife. After these musings, he exchanges compliments with the actress. But ISABELLA appears.

Scene vi

She reproaches her husband for being gallant with other women while neglecting her. She lays all the facts before him and then adds that he does not deserve a wife like her. Finally, as her anger increases, she attacks him and puts him to flight. She turns to VITTORIA and tells her that if his honor does not prevent him from compromising himself with an actress, then he will have to be taught how to behave. ISABELLA then returns to her home. VITTORIA laughs and says that wherever one finds a troupe of actors, there also will be found married women with sour dispositions.

Scene vii

GRATIANO now arrives. "Behold, the other pigeon waiting to have his feathers plucked," says PIOMBINO. The actress flirts with the DOCTOR. PIOMBINO reminds him of the silver pitcher and vase which he has promised her. GRATIANO joyfully takes PEDROLINO with him in order to bring back these presents. The actors ridicule his stupidity.

Scene viii

ORATIO arrives and greets VITTORIA. He demands the portrait of ISABELLA. She replies, with a laugh, that she hasn't the slightest idea what he is talking about. Then she departs with PIOMBINO.

Scene ix

ISABELLA has seen ORATIO talking with the actress; she reproaches him for not keeping his promise. ARLECCHINO tells ORATIO that ISABELLA and FLAMINIA have taken his master's page away with them to their home, and are holding him there against his will. ISABELLA seizes the occasion to spite ORATIO and calls FLAMINIA, telling her to bring her new lover to the window. LESBINO appears and says to ISABELLA, "What do you wish of me, Signora?" ORATIO becomes enraged at the sight of this unknown person and withdraws, cursing ISABELLA.

Scene x

PANTALONE asks the reason for all this noise. ISABELLA says that ORATIO wished to take her page away from her. "And what do you want with this page?" PANTALONE asks angrily. Then ISABELLA tells the story of SILVIA, the Milanese girl. She then urges PANTALONE to go to the theatre, find the CAPTAIN and bring him back if possible. PANTALONE sees at once that this is the chance he himself needed in order to get to go to the theatre.

Scenes xi to xvii

The lovers begin to quarrel again. PEDROLINO observes that quarreling is a waste of time. Since their husbands are at the play which lasts for six hours, they could, therefore, use their time to much better advantage than quarreling. The lovers see the good sense in this remark and become reconciled. The valets try to decide on the best means to restore SILVIA to the CAPTAIN's good graces. The CAPTAIN appears.

Scene xviii

PEDROLINO tells the CAPTAIN that he will find VITTORIA at the home of PANTALONE. The CAPTAIN enters through the basement of the house where he comes upon SILVIA divested of her male attire.

Scene xix

The two valets, PEDROLINO and ARLECCHINO, are alone in the theatre. They sit on the floor and decide what they would say if the two old men were to return suddenly. At this moment in the scene there is some amusing pantomime. A rogue, carrying a lantern, sees the two valets. With many tears, he bemoans the fact that he has lost much money at cards. He does not have more than a dozen pieces of money left. The valets invite him to play with them. They play. The rogue wins the money and also the clothes of PEDROLINO and ARLECCHINO. He leaves them sitting on the floor in their shirts. The valets are very despondent.

Scene xx

A great tumult arises in the theatre. PANTALONE, GRATIANO and PIOMBINO rush in carrying VITTORIA. She begs them to protect her from the dangers of a brawl which has broken out because of her. These gentlemen brawlers—the *bravi*—pour in, their swords bared. They see VITTORIA, they seize her, and carry her out. PIOMBINO follows them with gestures of despair.

Scene xxi

PANTALONE and GRATIANO find themselves face to face with the valets who are clad only in their shirts. They ask them to explain what has happened. The valets invent an explanation and say that the crowd which just left the theatre, robbed them of their money and clothes. They add, philosphically, that although the theatre brings pleasure, it is also the source of numerous scandals. While they are indulging in these wise reflections, ISABELLA and FLAMINIA come in and ask their husbands why the play ended so soon.

Scene xxii

PANTALONE replies that a brawl interrupted it and that he has not seen the CAPTAIN. ISABELLA tells how they informed the CAPTAIN that he would find VITTORIA in the basement of their house, and that it is SILVIA instead of the actress who is waiting there for him. Fearing however, that the CAPTAIN, thus deceived might commit violence, they had asked ORATIO and FLAVIO to take the trouble to stay with them. PANTALONE and GRATIANO approve.

Scene xxiii

The CAPTAIN leaves the house swearing he has been betrayed. ORATIO and FLAVIO endeavor to calm him. PANTALONE and all the others intercede in behalf of SILVIA. The CAPTAIN listens. He admits that SILVIA is honorably born; that she is the daughter of a rich Milanese merchant; and that he loves her. This diabolical actress had so far bewitched him that he had forgotten poor SILVIA. But he returns to her and consents to marry her.

Scene xxiv

They bring in SILVIA and she learns that her lover returns her affection.

ISABELLA and FLAMINIA urge their husbands to stay away from the theatre, and instead to watch over their homes and the conduct of their wives. They reply that henceforth they will do as their wives ask. Everybody now goes to PANTALONE's home to celebrate the wedding of SILVIA and the CAPTAIN, and it is thus that the comedy of *The Portrait* ends.

Elizabethan and Shakespearean Style 13

Virtuosity

The Playgoers
In our assemblies at plays in London you shall see such heaving and shoving, such itching and shouldering, to sit by women —such care for their garments, that they be not trod on—such eyes to their laps that no chips light in them—such pillows to their backs that they take no hurt—such masking in their ears I know not what—such giving them pippins to pass the time—such playing at footsaunt without carts—such ticking, such toying, such smiling, such winking, and such manning them home when the sports are ended.

from *the schoole of abuse*
by Stephen Gosson

A goodly sport
Turner and Dun, two famous fencers, played their prizes this day at the Bankside, but Turner at last ran Dun so far in the brain at the eye that he fell down presently stone dead; a goodly sport in a Christian state, to see one man kill another!

from the diary of John Manningham,
a law student in Elizabethan England

Gosson's description of a spirited, flirtatious London theatre crowd reveals the new mood of the Renaissance. Man for the most part was happy to be alive and lived every moment with zest. Manningham's entry indicates the intriguing mix of barbaric sports and activities within a Christian state. In a single day, the average Londoner could go to church, see a criminal mutilated and hanged on the London Bridge, and see a poetic play by William Shakespeare.

Overview of the English Renaissance in Theatre

The English Renaissance in theatre was dominated by a single genius: William Shakespeare, the poet of London from the town of Stratford-on-Avon. Any study of drama in the age of the great Renaissance of learning and progress following the Medieval period must focus upon this great English poet and playwright.

Three fundamental ideas of the period must be kept in mind with this focus. (1) The concept of *ego*. The majesty of man must be exalted! His intellect and ability were believed unmatched among living creatures. (2) The concept of *individuality*. Nothing seemed beyond the vanity and confidence of any Renaissance artist. (3) The concept of *virtuosity*. Man had multiple capability and breadth of vision; art was a business and man practiced the art well.

Paul C. Harris, Jr., as Polonius in *Hamlet* by William Shakespeare. The design coming alive. Directed by Jerry L. Crawford. Costume and graphic designs by Ellis M. Pryce-Jones.

Shakespeare—The Man, The Theatre, The Art, The Acting

William Shakespeare, the dramatist, was melodic, free, and eratic in his verse. His plays possessed virtuosity. He was aware of space, of people—all kinds of people. With words, Shakespeare was capable of creating a "landscape." He was as brilliant, philosophical, and learned as any master musician of the Renaissance. In Shakespeare, genius and craft were welded in one incredible dramatist. He was the Michelangelo of playwrights.

Shakespeare wrote thirty-six plays within a short life span of fifty-two years (1564–1616). These plays and the Bible probably rank as the two richest sets of literary documents in the entire history of Western Man. Shakespeare accomplished all this having only what we would term an elementary school education, albeit equivalent to a modern secondary education.

How did it happen? How did such a man evolve? Why?

One must begin to find the answers in the Renaissance itself. When the Islam Turks (who lacked artistic interest) took Constantinople, the artists of the city escaped to Venice. There, a true revival of classical art and learning began. Thus, it was Italy, followed by England and Spain, that led the way out of the Middle Ages.

In England, Henry VIII built a strong Protestant nation which continued under Edward VI. Then, in 1558 the stingy but theatre-loving Queen Elizabeth I took the throne. Man became aware again of his "goodness," as well as of his "evil." Sir Francis Drake defeated "the invincible" Spanish Armada in 1588. England became a power and a glory, and her people developed a passion for their own history.

On the Continent in Spain and in Italy, similar impulses brought a flourishing of art, music, and drama led by writers such as Lopé de Vega, Calderon, and Niccolò Machiavelli. However, only England was able to produce a theatre genius of Shakespeare's magnitude.

As brief background, note that in fifteenth-century England actors were still considered vagabonds. However, by 1482 noblemen employed actors for local entertainment, and by 1572 actors were recognized legally when a statute requiring a license to act in plays was enacted. By 1574 all plays had to be approved for production by the Master of Revels. This form of control or censorship, which survived well into the twentieth century in England, provided both advantages for and limitations to the theatre.

Sponsorship of acting companies by noblemen in England increased, and the profession of acting was reborn, assisted greatly by the royal support of Queen Elizabeth who favored the activity. The strong Puritan element in England opposed the movement, but Elizabeth and the nobility triumphed, at least until well into the seventeenth century. Soon theatre was a prospering public concern. The great period of English Renaissance theatre dates from 1570 to 1620 (in 1642 the Puritans and the Commonwealth closed the theatres until the restoration of the throne to Charles II in 1660).

What were the key influences in the development of dramatic art in the Renaissance?

1. Schools and Universities. Formal educational institutions provided translations of Plautus, Terence, and Seneca. The English scholars wrote in imitation of these Roman classics and made a major contribution to dramatic activity.

2. The Inns of Court. Combined residences and training centers for lawyers developed, and there, too, classical drama was studied and imitated.

3. The heritage from English Medieval drama. Old farces, religious plays, and mixed forms of drama were studied. Portions of plays and techniques of writing were borrowed by Renaissance writers.

Certain key dramatists developed, all of whom had a decided influence on Shakespeare. Thomas Kyd, Christopher Marlowe, and John Lyly were all University Wits, or university scholar-artists, who wrote prior to Shakespeare. The youthful Shakespeare undoubtedly studied their work carefully and borrowed techniques, plots, and ideas. Later, literally dozens of fine playwrights developed to compete with Shakespeare, including such writers as Ben Jonson, Francis Beaumont and John Fletcher, John Webster, Thomas Dekker, and John Ford, among others. Marlowe, unusually adept at blank verse, and Jonson, skilled in comedy of humours (see Glossary), were particularly outstanding dramatists. However, for purposes of clarity and continuity a study of the acting style of the period should concentrate on Shakespeare, the foremost dramatist of the time and probably unrivaled among playwrights.

The structure of the Elizabethan theatre must be noted before we examine Shakespeare, his work, and the acting style necessary to performance of his plays. While evidence concerning these theatres is incomplete, and while scholarly disputes have resulted, it is generally accepted that two types of theatres flourished. One was the open-air public theatre (such as the famous Globe), and the other was the indoor private theatre (such as the Blackfriars). Actually, general audiences could enter both theatres for a fee, but the indoor winter or private theatres tended to be frequented mostly by nobility and royalty. The size of the more popular outdoor or public theatres varied, ranging in seating capacity from 2,000 to 3,000 patrons.

The theatres were enclosed in part by three tiers of roofed *galleries* which formed the outside of the structure. A large central area, popularly called the *yard* or *pit*, was unroofed. The least expensive ticket placed the customer in the pit where he stood to watch a play; by paying more, he could sit in one of the galleries. The *stage* itself was about four to six feet in height and thrust forward from one of the sides of the theatre (it is likely that the stage was portable or removable in most of the theatres, which permitted the theatres to be used for cruel sporting events such as bullbaiting and bearbaiting). The *roof* of the theatre was thatched with straw and wood; to the rear was an area similar to a small balcony called the *Heavens* where musicians sat and played instruments. It is fairly certain that one or more *trapdoors* were cut in the stage floor and that two large doors at the rear of the stage were used by actors to make entrances and exits. Probably a *pavillion* of some sort stood upon the rear center of the stage. The pavillion was more than likely hung with curtains which could be used to reveal new scenes of action in progress. It would seem that the theatre and stage just described permitted a rather continuous flow of dramatic action. There were probably no act or scene divisions in the playing of the scripts (most such divisions were added in later centuries by editors).

It is now believed that some minor scenery and stage machinery were utilized in Shakespearean, or Elizabethan, productions. Documented evidence exists of painted backdrops, rocks, trees, tables, and the like being kept at the theatre. Scenic effects resembled the freestanding three-dimensional units called mansions, popular during the Medieval period. However, they were probably more detailed than the sets used in Medieval drama. Elizabethans equipped their stage with such articles as trees, thrones, beds, scaffolds, barriers, prison bars, tombs, tents, caves, tables, and chairs. The large central area (the equivalent to the Medieval platea) could be localized. Set pieces were used when necessary or if they were available. Scenery was probably used when it suited the convenience of the actors, managers, and playwrights rather than to follow any principle of consistent scenic design. As knowledge of the court masques became public information, and royalty became increasingly interested in acting troupes, theatre owners paid more attention to scenic spectacle.

The costuming utilized contemporary Elizabethan street and court dress, with no or very limited attempt at historical accuracy. From 1558 to 1642 costumes were identical to Medieval and Renaissance dress. Attention was paid to correct dress according to rank and to fanciful garments worn by ghosts, fairies, and witches, and traditional kingly attire was copied for such characters as Henry VI, Falstaff, and Richard III. The Elizabethans spared no expense in executing their costumes. Garments were costly and elegant, combining satin, silver, silk, and lace. Color for costumes depended on propriety: foresters wore green, shepherds wore white, royalty wore purple, friars wore brown. In essence, the stage was a glass of fashion—the epitome of the art of wearing clothes.

An Elizabethan acting company was composed of ten to twenty members. The chief actor in Shakespeare's company was Richard Burbage, an accomplished tragedian. Will Kemp was the leading comic actor. Approximately ten members of the company were "hired" men. The latter included doorkeepers, musicians, stagehands, and box office personnel, all of whom were paid flat salaries or wages and did not share in profits. There were also three to five boy apprentice actors in the company who played all the female roles (not until the Restoration and the eighteenth century were actresses permitted on the stage). Productions were given at about three o'clock in the afternoon, and natural daylight illuminated the action. A volatile and noisy audience ate and drank during a performance and cheered or jeered their approval or disapproval. As the play ended at twilight, the highly diverse audience dispersed for a drink in a local public house or re-

a

Sequence of scenes from production of *Hamlet* by William Shakespeare. *a*, Hamlet meets the ghost of his father; *b*, encounter between Hamlet and Ophelia; *c*, Ophelia after she has gone mad; and *d*, the King, the Queen, and Laertes mourning the death of Ophelia. Directed by Jerry L. Crawford. Costumes by Ellis M. Pryce-Jones. Scenery by Fredrick L. Olson. University of Nevada, Las Vegas.

b

c

d

tired to dinner and conversation. At the end of each performance, the actors sang, danced, and performed comic action, even though the play may have been a tragedy. The theatrical custom was to end the performance on a light, happy note and to send the audience away in a good humor.[1]

Modern adaptation of the original style of Elizabethan acting will probably be minimal, as opposed to the extensive adaptation needed for Greek and Restoration acting styles. The following discussion of language, voice, gestures, movement, pantomimic business, character, emotion, and spectacle provides you with the necessary tools to perform in the acting style of the Elizabethan period, be it in tragedy or comedy.

Voice

In a letter to Mrs. Patrick Campbell, George Bernard Shaw advised the actress, "When you play Shakespeare, don't worry about the character but go for the music. It was by word-music that he expressed what he wanted to express, and if you get the music right, the whole thing will come right."[2] Shaw's advice is well taken. An understanding of the verse and poetry in Shakespeare's plays is the key to development of all other acting concepts —character, emotional quality, rhythm, gesture, and movement. In line with the theory of personalization, reducing verse to simple ideas gives you more confidence with your interpretive ability and thus enables you to approach the roots of Shakespeare's reality which is different from your own only in the manner of utterance and degree of intensity. You need to separate ideas clearly to give the proper shape to the verse, which will give the poetry a pervasive "music."

The most common problem a modern actor encounters with Shakespeare's plays is to achieve complete character portrayal while trying to speak the lines effectively. The audience must be stirred by the nuances of the poetry. What you must remember is that character and poetry are inseparable. A study of the details and nuances and structure of the lines will enable you to reveal and portray a character in depth.

Verse-speaking should be based on an understanding of the structure of the verse. To accomplish this task, you must study the organized relationship of words and sounds. During Shakespeare's time, school boys were taught to recognize figures of speech and pronounce them rhetorically with accompanying gestures. Recognition of metaphor is crucial in this task. You cannot circumvent the fact that Shakespearean poetry must be elevated somewhat above a conversational mode to achieve lyricism and beauty. Elevation is aided by permitting the presentational mode to dominate deliv-

1. For further, more detailed discussion of the physical properties of the Elizabethan theatre and audience, see C. Walter Hodges, *The Globe Restored*, 2d Ed. (London: Oxford University Press, 1968); Alois Nagler, *Shakespeare's Stage* (New Haven, Conn.: Yale University Press, 1958); Alfred Harbage, *Shakespeare's Audience* (New York: Columbia University Press, 1961).

2. Marowitz, Charles, *The Method as Means* (London: Herbert Jenkins, 1961), p. 77.

ery. You need not be confused by all this if you keep in mind the fact that unrhymed iambic pentameter or blank verse is the most malleable and adaptable of forms, open to variety and individuality of expression.

The verse is called *blank* because it allows both the speaker and the listener to anticipate rhymes when the rhythmical pattern is regular and the actor to emphasize sounds to reveal character and emotion.

An *iambus* is a foot of two syllables, a short or unaccented syllable followed by a long or accented syllable—brief, long, brief, long. The human heart, for example, beats in iambs, that is, in two recurring strokes—brief, long, brief, long. Breathing also occurs in iambic feet, outbreathing, inbreathing, with stress on the inbreathing because it takes longer and is consciously done, whereas outbreathing is automatic. Another analogy is the ticking sound of a metronome. The sound and movement of the metronome are measured. The rhythm never changes. The basic unit in a metronome is the *tick*. If you think of the basic unit of iambic pentameter as a *foot* (or two syllables) and establish that we must complete the utterance of those two syllables by the time it takes the bar of the metronome to tick from one side to the other, then you will be speaking in correct rhythm. If you stress or accent either of the two syllables, you will reveal ideas and feelings. Correct pronunciation will result. An example follows:

$$\acute{O}h, _1wh\breve{a}t—\acute{o}h, _2wh\breve{a}t—\acute{o}h, _3wh\breve{a}t—\acute{o}h, _4wh\breve{a}t—\acute{o}h, _5wh\breve{a}t$$

Note that the mark / indicates the short or nonstress syllable. The mark ⌣ is the long or accented syllable. If you speak comprehensibly, you are using meter and accent, or you are scanning the poetry.

When working with a line of five feet (or iambs), with accent on the second syllable of each foot, you should take from two-to-four seconds to speak. The formalized lines taken together are called iambic pentameter. Sometimes Shakespeare deviated from iambic pentameter in order to surprise or heighten a dramatic situation. For example:

$$Th\acute{o}ugh\ thi\breve{s}\ b\acute{e}\ m\breve{a}dn\acute{e}ss,\ y\breve{e}t\ th\acute{e}re\ \breve{is}\ method\ \acute{in}'t.$$

It is the task of the poet to decide the exact word or group of words to accent to express meaning or emotion. His designs are planned and carefully executed to produce intensity of expression.

Exercise 1   Iambic Pentameter

Read the following speech aloud with clear articulation and heightened projection, practicing correct iambic pentameter:

O, that this too too solid flesh
would melt,
Thaw, and resolve itself into a dew,
Or that the Everlasting had not fixed
His canon 'gainst self-slaughter. O
God, God,

> How weary, stale, flat, and unprofitable
> Seem to me all the uses of this world!
> > *Hamlet*   Act I, scene ii

Notice the repetitive, heavy sound of the words in expressing Hamlet's wish to leave a world which disgusts him. There is an effective repetition of the word *too* in the first line and of *God* in the fourth line. The heavy repetition dramatizes the emotion. The iambic pentameter is altered from time to time to keep the pattern from sounding monotonous and the delivery from sounding too austere.

Shakespearean language also reveals that clauses are frequently short. For example, Lady Macbeth says:

> The raven himself is hoarse
> That croaks the fatal entrance of Duncan
> Under my battlements.
> > *Macbeth*   Act I, scene v

Pauses are stronger or more imperative; for example, in the prose exchange between Hamlet and Rosencrantz and Guildenstern, Hamlet says:

> You were sent for, and there is a
> kind of confession in your looks, which
> your modesties have not craft enough to
> color. I know the good king and queen
> have sent for you.
> > *Hamlet*   Act II, scene ii

Transitions are abrupt; for example, the confrontation between Hamlet and Polonius in act 2, reveals such a transition:

> POLONIUS   My lord, I have news to tell you.
> HAMLET   My lord, I have news to tell you.
>   When Roscius was an actor in Rome—
> POLONIUS   The actors are come hither, my lord.
> HAMLET   Buzz, Buzz.
> POLONIUS   Upon my honor.
> HAMLET   Then came each actor on his ass—
> > *Hamlet*   Act II, scene ii

Questions and interjections abound; for example, in the same passage with Hamlet, Rosencrantz, and Guildenstern, Hamlet asks: "Were you not sent for? Is it your own inclining? Is it a free visitation?"

Imagery is frequently symbolic; for example, the rose is a symbol of youth and the lily is a symbol of purity. Shakespeare often used diverse images to illustrate a single idea. This quality increases the range of concepts and heightens the emotion (e.g., Hamlet's "To be or not to be" speech reveals a number of dramatic and diverse images).

Shakespeare often used the half-line in dialogue. A speaker ends his speech in the middle of a metrical line and another speaker takes the line up and completes it.

HORATIO   Friends to this ground.
MARCELLUS   And liegemen to the Dane.

You should note the atmosphere and mood of the scene in order to project the correct feeling of the lines. The illusion which the poet undertakes must be understood.

When speaking the verse, you should intone and stress the figures of speech to show the relationship of sound and meaning in the words. Learn to distinguish the words which are essential to expressing the individual figures of speech. You will use these figures to better express emotions and ideas. One of the most frequently encountered Shakespearean figures of speech is the "marching or climbing figure." In act 1 of *Richard III*, Richard says of the sickly king:

> He cannot live, I hope and must not die,
> Till George be packed with post horse up
> to heaven.
>> *Richard III*   Act I, scene i

At times you will see repetition of the same sound rather than a play upon different sounds. For example, in *Romeo and Juliet*, Romeo says to the Nurse:

> Where is she? and how doth she and what
> Says my concealed lady to our cancelled love?
>> *Romeo and Juliet*   Act I, scene iii

Puns are words which play upon multiple meanings. They were considered a vital part of Elizabethan word usage. Shakespeare's plays abound in puns (e.g., the dying Mercutio in *Romeo and Juliet* remarks to Romeo, "Ask for me tomorrow, and you shall find me a grave man").

Another peculiarity of Shakespearean language is the *conceit*. The Shakespearean conceit is a piece of extreme, unusual, and often witty poetic imagination.

For example, consider these lines from Romeo to Benvolio in *Romeo and Juliet* in which Romeo discusses the qualities of love:

> . . . O brawling love!   O loving hate!
> O any thing, of nothing first create!
> O heavy lightness! serious vanity!
> Mis-shapen chaos of well-seeming forms!
> Feather of lead, bright smoke, cold fire,
>   sick health!
> Still-waking sleep, that is not what it is!
>> *Romeo and Juliet*   Act I, scene i

These are conceits in which Shakespeare merely plays with opposites. Many of his conceits are shocking, melodramatic, and extreme and are usually rooted in the inner conflict of the character speaking the lines.

In his later and better plays, Shakespeare used conceits in an abstract way. In earlier plays, he merely listed apparent contradictions, while in *King*

Scene from *King Lear* by
William Shakespeare.
King Lear, Len Cariou;
the Fool, Nicolas Keprose.
The Guthrie Theatre,
Minneapolis, Minn.

154   Acting: In Style

Lear, for example, the Fool's speeches to Lear are used very precisely as commentary on Lear's weaknesses.

Awareness of the conceit device helps to better understand character and to better speak the tricky, ear-challenging, and thought-challenging conceits.

Shakespeare often joined contrasting ideas to make an expressive, compressed statement of equivalence or opposition (e.g., Hamlet's line, "A little more than kin and less than kind").

In all of the examples just given, meaning and emotion were integral to the structure of the pattern of sound. The most common sound pattern was *rhyme*, often used to end long speeches or scenes. Rhyme is created when the end sounds of lines correspond. (Other structures include *assonance*—likeness of sound in which the stressed vowel sounds are alike but the consonant sounds are unlike as in *main* and *came*; and *alliteration*—repetition of an initial sound, usually a consonant, in two or more words of a phrase as in "a fair field full of folk.")

·When studying the figures of speech in Shakespearean verse, you should discover words designed to simultaneously produce calculated and special emotional reactions. Claudius's soliloquy in *Hamlet* at the end of act 3 is a case in point. The lines depict the sound of rage:

> Oh, wretched state! O bosom black as death!
> O liméd soul, that struggling to be free
> art more engaged! Help, angels! make assay!
> > *Hamlet*   Act III, scene iii

Or note the sensual and romantic lines spoken by Juliet as she waits for Romeo:

> Lovers can see to do their amorous rites
> By their own beauties; or, if love be blind,
> It best agrees with night. Come, civil night,
> Thou sober-suited matron, all in black,
> And learn me how to lose a winning match,
> Played for a pair of stainless maidenhoods.
> Hood my unmanned blood bating in my cheeks,
> With thy black mantle till strange love grow bold.
> > *Romeo and Juliet*   Act III, scene ii

Shakespeare was a master at selecting *the* word and sound to express mood. A classic example is the witches scene in *Macbeth* where supernatural mystery is vividly duplicated:

> FIRST WITCH   When shall we three meet again?
>   In thunder, lighting, or in rain?
> SECOND WITCH   When the hurlyburly's done,
>   When the battle's lost and won.
> THIRD WITCH   That will be ere the set of sun.
> FIRST WITCH   Where the place?
> SECOND WITCH   Upon the heath.

THIRD WITCH	There to meet with Macbeth.
FIRST WITCH	I come, Graymalkin!
SECOND WITCH	Paddock calls.
THIRD WITCH	Anon!
ALL	Fair is foul, and foul is fair
	Hover through the fog and filthy air.

Macbeth Act I, scene i

The structure of Elizabethan language is fully realized when the pattern which emerges contains a rhythmic quality. The rhythm of a line is organic and is derived from the irregularity of the line. Each line usually has its own rhythm to give color, variety, and meaning. This rhythmic flow of sound is called *cadence* (do not confuse meter with rhythm; meter deals with feet and stresses, as in iambic pentameter). The rhythm of a line is punctuated by pauses called *caesura*. The pauses usually last the time it would take to speak ten syllables, which is indeed plenty of time to catch a breath.

Also note linguistic changes and modern alterations in word meaning as compared with the time of Shakespeare's time. It is important to study the original meaning of words (i.e., etymology—the additions and losses in vocabulary), semantics (i.e., alterations in meanings and associations of words), accidence and syntax (i.e., changes in inflection and construction of words to form phrases, clauses, and sentences), and phonological changes or equivalents.

A peculiar language situation developed during the Renaissance. Elizabethans loved to borrow phrases from foreign languages. Latin was favored by writers and served to enrich the English language. Latin words were either naturalized or added to the English language. Latin did not replace native words, but provided synonyms such as *wonder* and *admiration*, words derived from Latin. It follows that even a slight knowledge of Latin is a great advantage to the correct understanding of Elizabethan writers, especially when we consider that many Latin borrowings of the sixteenth century now have meanings different from the original. For example, the Latin sense of *apparent* no longer means visible or evident, and *intention* does not convey the idea of intentness. Some Latin forms such as the word *objectum* were later changed to conform to English spelling and accent.

French also supplied words and influenced changes in spelling. Commercial, religious, and architectural terms were adopted from the Spanish, Italian, and Dutch languages. Foreign influences on language provided unparalleled freedom of vocabulary and form. However, that freedom also produced confusion, and clarity and precision were often sacrificed. Nevertheless, the English language gained more than it lost by allowing in foreign importations. The number of compound words such as home-keeping wits was increased, and prefixes such as *dis-*, *re-*, and *en-* and suffixes such as *-ful*, *-less*, *-ness*, and *-hood* were introduced.

Perhaps the greatest problem encountered in the study of Shakespearean verse is not the deciphering of obsolete words, but the difficulty arising from the many times it is possible to get some idea of meaning, however imperfect it might be. It becomes a matter of missing exact shades of meaning and thereby misinterpreting the tone. The following Shakespearean words often differ from their present meaning:

a   he
ability   means, wealth
addition   title
admiration   wonder, careful, anxious
carry   manage
conceit   conception, idea
confusion   overthrow, ruin
fellow   equal
gear   matter, stuff, thing, business
humour   moisture, temperament, whine, caprice
modern   common, ordinary
moe   more
pregnant   resourceful, apt, inclined
prevent   anticipate, hinder

The foregoing analysis of Shakespearean verse and language in which the importance of relationships between words was clarified leads to a consideration of what is technically involved in speaking that verse and language. Once you have learned the details of emphasis, the technique usually becomes second nature. Do not aim solely at reproducing structural patterns because concentration on characterization will suffer. Elizabethan actors may not have had exact patterns or conventions for speaking on the stage, but they did adhere to general attitudes of speech. The actor needed a voice capable of tremendous range of tone and volume. The speaking style was partially influenced by the rhetoric of the Tudor period in that the Elizabethan actor was taught to heighten the simulation of emotion thus to move an audience. (An effective Elizabethan acting voice exhibits spontaneity and beauty of expression.) The speaking style was generally presentational. Verse necessitated a pattern of intonation which ran counter to the metrical pattern of stressed and unstressed syllables. The effect of the actor's delivery was musical, that is, well modulated. The voice was able to convey contrast among words, developing climaxes in tempo and rhythm. Thus, the vocal tone and emotional manner of the character were delineated more clearly. Emotion also played a part in producing the music of the line. Emotion gave color and life to the tones. (Be aware of which emotion is derived from a word or combination of words. An emotion may change just as the sense of a line changes.)

To perform Shakespeare's language you might do well to review Hamlet's advise to the players in act 3, scene 2. Hamlet warns the actors not to chant, whine, or elongate syllables: ". . . but if you mouth it, as many of our players do, I had as lief the town-crier spoke my lines." A fundamentally normal and controlled speaking voice is desired in delivery of Elizabethan prose. A natural vocal quality can best produce a melodic sound. We stated

Character from *The Tempest* by William Shakespeare. Directed by Orlin Corey. Designed by Irene Corey. Everyman Players.

earlier that verse should be heightened somewhat above the conversational mode. However, when the verse is less passionate and emotional, a more natural or conversational mode may be effectively used. It is sometimes difficult for a modern actor to believe in the concept of a natural (as opposed to a declamatory) style of speaking Shakespeare because of the fear that the music of the verse will suffer. If the structural organization of the language is correctly analyzed, the music of the verse can still be maintained with natural speaking. *Natural speaking* means to speak the verse with a sustained tone, giving diaphragmic support and clear, accurate articulation. For example, many people slur the letter *r* when speaking. The partial loss of *r* in modern English works to the detriment of acoustical richness and energy. Pitch and length of tone can change quickly and abruptly. Vary your pace according to the needs of the lines. Modern actors often have a tendency to overintellectualize word analysis when speaking Shakespeare by assigning *each word* a definite emotion and objective. A more accurate technique is to let the sense of the whole sentence decide the emphasis on any given word. Elevate or emphasize some words in each sentence and allow the lines to flow. Rarely pause under the pretext of thinking words out, as actors often do in modern naturalistic plays.

Exercise 2 Voice

Study the following speech by Prospero from *The Tempest*:

> You do look, my son, in a moved sort,
> As if you were dismayed. Be cheerful, sir.
> Our revels now are ended. These our actors,
> As I foretold you, were all spirits and
> Are melted into air, into thin air;
> And, like the baseless fabric of this vision,
> The cloud-capped towers, the gorgeous palaces,
> The solemn temples, the great globe itself,
> Yea, all which it inherit, shall dissolve,
> And, like this insubstantial pageant faded,
> Leave not a rack behind. We are such stuff
> As dreams are made on, and our little life
> Is rounded with a sleep. Sir, I am vexed.
> Bear with my weakness. My old brain is troubled.
> Be not disturbed with my infirmity.
> If you be pleased, retire into my cell
> And there repose. A turn or two I'll walk
> To still my beating mind.
> *The Tempest* Act IV, scene i

Practice the speech aloud:

  1. to establish the correct iambic pentameter rhythm.
  2. to focus upon correct pauses and transitions.
  3. to focus upon imagery, figures of speech, climbing figures, repetitions, conceits, and contrasting ideas.
  4. to focus upon emotion and mood (be certain to check an Old English dictionary or a Shakespearean glossary to determine exact meanings of words).
     In each of the foregoing exercise steps, utilize the best of the vocal characteristics learned in chapter 7.

Gesture and Movement

Elizabethan actors also used considerable gesture and movement to communicate what was being expressed in words. Gestures were occasionally conventional; they were undoubtedly also natural and precise, revealing the general disposition, humor, and state of mind of the character. The probable view among Elizabethan actors was that if a gesture was seen in daily life, its inclusion onstage was justified. For example, Richard Burbage, leading tragic actor in Shakespeare's company, probably noticed that Elizabethans frequently pointed a great deal with the forefinger; he undoubtedly used the gesture within a play if it was at all appropriate to the text and character. Perhaps this idea contrasts somewhat with the popular notion that in Shakespearean plays a heightened, elevated style of delivery necessitates use of conventional stereotyped gestures. A common misconception among many modern actors is to equate acting of Shakespearean drama with a system of external clichés. On the contrary, Shakespeare's characters exemplified truthful inner emotion, and action was suited to emotion and language. Elizabethans prided themselves on precise, explicit, heightened, and direct action that emanated from within an individual. Elizabethan stage acting surely demonstrated the same concept—expressing externally in a truthful manner what was felt inside.

As gestures acquired an appropriate, natural, though somewhat elevated appearance, so, too, did stage movements. Movements were characterized as full, fluid, and controlled. A consideration of the physical aspects of the Elizabethan stage and audience indicates the necessity to maximize all physical action. Since the acting areas were small and audiences were rowdy and loud, Elizabethan actors were trained in strong stage action such as fencing. The actor had to handle a heavy rapier in one hand and a dagger for parrying in the other. All fencing movements were highly calculated. Thrusting was accomplished at close quarters from the wrist and forearm and was usually aimed at the opponent's eye or below the ribs. In fencing, the actor had to achieve brutal reality to please the crowd. His training for theatrical fencing was highly rigorous and his physical coordination was excellent. Action was rapid and intensified.

The modern actor playing in an Elizabethan drama finds his stage movement immediately restricted simply because of the incredible weight of the costumes. It is commonly noted that Elizabethan clothes could "stand up by themselves." If we generalize the typical Elizabethan man as assertive, arrogant, and physically well toned, we create a picture of someone moving with confidence and vigor. However, he is attired in clothes that are difficult for us to wear. His doublet fits tightly to the body, the ruff fits stiffly around the neck, stockings reach to above the knee and are fastened up to the waistline by points or laces. Although physical action is startlingly limited within these confines, an actor must try to give the illusion of a rapid flow of movement. Continual practice in Elizabethan costume is the only solution for an actor who must be "swaggering and virile." Physical strength is further inhibited by the excessive padding under the garments which tends to throw modern actors completely off-balance.

Women also have their share of difficulty moving in costume. An immense amount of space is absorbed by the shape of the skirt (e.g., a bell-shaped skirt with a farthingale worn underneath, literally, a series of hoops which start at the waist and become progressively larger toward the ground). Moving through doors is awkward, approaching a chair and sitting in it pose problems, turning excessively is next to impossible, and hanging the arms at the sides is difficult. All stage movement must be taken in stride—no forced action or sudden moving. Women wear a long, tight bodice and tight *stomacher* (stiff front waist piece). They glide fluidly along the stage, holding the torso and head straight. (A wired ruff at the back of the head precludes excessive head movement; it also shields the face from the audience.) Hands can rest lightly on the top of the farthingale or strike a pose on top of each other, palms up, at the waist, or hands can be brought together at the waist with the thumbs on top and knuckles pointing down. Because of the stiff roll at the top of sleeves, underarms are held away from the body. Ladies usually carry a fan which is moved from the shoulder or from the wrist, depending on the cut of the costume. Fan movement usually involves the entire arm, not just the wrist, due to the tight-fitting sleeves.

The Elizabethan bow

Exercise 3   The Bow

Two types of bows and two types of curtsies should be learned to accommodate these important social customs used in most Elizabethan plays.

1. To execute a full or formal bow, stand with the feet astraddle in a normal standing position; withdraw either foot behind the other leg about 12 inches, turning the rear foot to form a 45-degree angle behind the other foot. The rear knee should now be bent. Remove the hat and drop that hand to one side or to the rear as you bend; turn the other hand palm forward to the person being addressed. Lower the head toward the chest, and bend the back forward slightly.

2. A less formal version of this bow is to simply remove the hat while bending the head and back slightly forward. The feet remain astraddle. This bow was used for respect to peers or for hurried recognition, while the full or formal bow was used to address noblemen or royalty.

The curtsy after the actress has risen from the floor.

Exercise 4   The Curtsy

1. To execute a full or formal curtsy, rest the hands on top of the farthingale or skirt. Withdraw one foot behind the other several inches; bend both knees, the head, and the back. If you are addressing a queen, your body might bend to the point where you are sitting on the rear foot with the head inclined forward to the floor and the arms outstretched. To curtsy to one's peers usually bend the knees only 6 to 12 inches with the head slightly inclined.

2. A less formal version of this curtsy can be accomplished by lowering the head slightly and bending both knees a few inches with the feet in a straddled position. This curtsy was used for making quick acknowledgments or for entering or leaving a room.

Exercise 5   Greetings

Practice the following greetings:

1. Greet another man with both arms extended while grasping one another simultaneously with both hands above the elbows or about the wrists.

2. Greet another woman by kissing her on the cheek as you meet.

3. One man extends his hand to a lady while walking by putting an arm forward at the elbow, palm down; the lady places her fingertips on top of his wrist or hand. As you walk by other couples, nod heads in informal greeting.

Following a course of movement in Elizabethan plays which is direct and decisive applies also to handling soliloquies (solo monologues) and asides (short addresses to the audience).

A popular opinion holds that an actor speaking a soliloquy must come downstage center to deliver his innermost thoughts directly to the audience. However, there is nothing sacred concerning the way an actor delivers a soliloquy. There is no special stage area where this intimate, intensive, and personal revelation must take place. Sometimes it may not be appropriate to address your character's thought to the audience at all, although the Elizabethan actor probably oriented much of his action in that manner. There are exceptions to the presentational directness of stage movements in every play including Elizabethan plays.

It is important to consider the appropriateness of the movement in the soliloquy and its effect on the character's emotions and thoughts. Modern lighting, for example, permits a soliloquy to be staged at any location onstage.

Exercise 6   The Soliloquy

Practice the following soliloquies by performing them at various stage locations, alternating direct presentation to the audience with self-reflective representational delivery. Invent your own movement and gestures.

The spirit that I have seen
May be the devil: and the devil hath power
To assume a pleasing shape; yea, and perhaps
Out of my weakness and my melancholy,
As he is very potent with such spirits,
Abuses me to damn me: I'll have grounds
more relative than this: the play's the thing
Wherein I'll catch the conscience of the King.

HAMLET *Hamlet* Act II, scene iii

How easy it is for the proper false
In women's waxen hearts to set their forms!
Alas, our frailty is the cause, not we!
For such as we are made of, such we be.
How will this fadge? My master loves her dearly;
And I (poor monster) fond as much on him;
And she (mistaken) seems to dote on me.

VIOLA *Twelfth Night* Act II, scene ii

The *aside* is an expression of thought spoken privately to the audience while other characters are present. Depending upon the circumstances in the play, the character may or may not move away from the other character or characters onstage. The actor delivering the aside may simply turn the body or face or change the voice. Asides can be spoken from all areas of the stage—from the rear to the front. An aside might be performed during action or other actors can *freeze* when the aside is delivered. It is not always believable to move away from other actors in an aside; however, the speaker usually remains relatively stationary.

Exercise 7 The Aside

Practice the following asides using the various methods of delivery just discussed. Invent any necessary movement or gesture.

HAMLET Let her not walk i' the sun: conception is a blessing: but not as your daughter may conceive. Friend, look to 't.

POLONIUS (*aside*) How say you by that? Still harping on my daughter . . .

HAMLET . . . for yourself, sir, should be old as I am, if like a crab you could go backward.

POLONIUS (*aside*) Though this be madness, yet there is method in 't. . . .

Hamlet Act II, scene ii

TOBY . . . Therefore draw for the supportance of his vow. He protests he will not hurt you.

VIOLA (*aside*) Pray God defend me! A little thing would make me tell them how much I lack of a man.

Twelfth Night Act III, scene iv

Elizabethan actors were highly selective concerning the use of panto-mimic business. Tragic plays did not require use of extensive and detailed stage business; conversely, comic plays tended toward use of highly inventive and extensive business. In tragedy, the Elizabethan audience loved to see an actor simulate running a sword through another actor's body or "tearing out his entrails." They cheered at the slight of hand. They wanted to see "real blood" (usually sheep's blood), which was put into a bladder with a hollow handle or slipped inside a white leather jerkin painted to look like human skin and punctured at the appropriate moment.

The play text itself will usually provide you with definite circumstances for stage business (e.g., knocking at a door, sword fighting, striking a bell, reading a book, holding a skull, holding a candle, etc.). Banquet scenes are frequently called for, as well as receptions, funerals, and *dumb shows*. Sometimes Shakespeare implied pantomimic business by mentioning the use of a book, dagger, or some other prop; at other times, more expansive physical action such as falling down was implied.

Note should be made concerning pantomimic dumb shows. These shows were performed in true commedia dell'arte style, using masks, appropriate costumes for stock characters, and detailed slapstick burlesque activities. Following the traditional Roman pantomime, no words were spoken. Movements were slow, precise, and exaggerated. For modern actors a dumb show should be truly improvisational. Later, the action can be set in order to perfect the precision of the pantomime.

Comedy permitted more flexibility in the use of stage properties and accessories; therefore, business was more inventive and detailed. Articles that a modern actor may utilize in comedy include handkerchiefs, keys, purses or notecases, letters, combs, and fans with mirrors hidden in them. Costume properties can also be considered material for stage business. For example, gloves sometimes concealed "poison." Comedy often called for disguise—for example, adding a hood or a hat or a mask to cover the head and face. It is characteristic in comic plays for actors to consider the circumstances of a situation and create appropriate pantomimic business to add interest and heighten the humor.

Exercise 8   Dumb Show

Read and study the following dumb show performed by the players in *Hamlet*, act 3, scene 2:

> Enter a King and a Queen very lovingly; the Queen embracing him.
> She kneels, and makes show of protestation unto him. He takes her up and
> declines his head upon her neck. He lays him down upon a bank of flowers.
> She, seeing him asleep, leaves him. Anon comes in a fellow, takes off his
> crown, kisses it, pours poison in the King's ears, and exits. The Queen
> returns, finds the King dead, and makes passionate action. The Poisoner,
> with some two or three Mutes, comes in again, seeming to lament with her.

The dead body is carried away. The Poisoner woos the Queen with gifts; she seems loath and unwilling awhile, but in the end accepts his love.

Exeunt

Form several casts of players and create the action called for in the dumb show. Improvise pantomimic dramatization as needed, including the use of any necessary props.

Character and Emotion

Shakespeare did not provide character description as many modern playwrights do. Nor did he provide many stage directions. It will be your and the director's responsibility to decide the quantity and quality of personality characteristics necessary for the development of character. Observe how the style of the speech affects the formality or informality of the person. You will often find that both qualities are fused. Although the formality does not necessarily mean a less natural performance, you must remain conscious of your character's emotions and actions. Again, the personalization technique permits you to rehearse the role first as if *you* were the character. The degree of realism will be determined by what the character says and how much he says. Natural acting orientated toward truthfully expressed emotion is essential to acting in an Elizabethan play, just as it has been in most plays throughout history.

Shakespeare's characters are extraordinarily well defined in the text and extremely varied and complex. The characters are multidimensional. The verse is an unusually sensitive gauge of the character's disposition and humour. Shakespeare's plays blend standardized fictional character types with well-known historical figures. Because Shakespeare's stories were usually based on existing stories or earlier plays, his characters retain a classical kind of clarity. A character comes from a definite place; he has traceable literary and historical progeny, fixed attitudes, indicative bearing, and pronounced temperament (e.g., think of Iago, Hamlet, Macbeth, and Falstaff). Shakespeare also utilized the Elizabethan society well by presenting the psychological and philosophical foundations prevalent in his milieu. Characters fit into a generic group whose behavior tends to conform to specific social classes. Shakespeare also differentiated characters within each class. For example, gentlewomen and ladies-in-waiting bore the signs of the upper class, yet they were given internal qualities and distinct characterization (e.g., Maria in *Twelfth Night* and Emilia in *Othello* may be portrayed as women of a certain social position in a particular social scheme and as highly individualized characters). Other generic types of characters were the messenger or servant and the clown. Their distinction lies in the particularized task required of them by the playwright. For example, these characters may affect the course of action (e.g., the Nurse in *Romeo and Juliet*); they may affect the plot (e.g., the Friar in *Romeo and Juliet*); they may sing (e.g., Feste in *Twelfth Night*); they may comment on character or situation (e.g., Reynaldo in *Hamlet*); they may plead or mock (e.g., the Fool in *Lear*).

Scene from *Romeo and Juliet* by William Shakespeare. Directed by Gerard Larson. Designed by Larry Schumate. California State University, Sacramento.

The difficulty encountered in delineating character development in any play need not concern you unnecessarily if the character's state of being is clear at the beginning of the play. Character development will come organically out of the whole play. Shakespeare was particularly careful to base character motivation on the broad desires that all men might experience. As with the Greeks, it was a belief of the Elizabethan society that affections or emotions *should* be controlled by reason. When passions rule, disaster follows. Men are motivated by specific ends and universal emotions—greed, love, hate, revenge, and jealousy. Reason remains powerless before the volatile and pervasive nature of emotion which can destroy the moral and political world.

Shakespeare defined his characters more by their emotion than by their reason. *How* the character speaks is often more important than what is said. Often the poetry seems to consume the character. Rhythmic and melodic recitation affect the emotions of the character and may be heightened by close physical proximity to the audience. It is through the verse that impressions of dignity, suffering, grandeur, and human significance are created. However, there is no need to portray Shakespearean emotion melodramatically or unconvincingly. The guide for today's actor is control and precision when handling Shakespearean emotion. Place your focus on the spoken word and the verbal display such as in soliloquies, orations, descriptions, repartee, and puns. Concentrate on emphasizing and elevating key words in sentences. Try not to "think the emotion out"; imagine the emotion of an actual person in a real situation. The outcome should result in contagious response of clear, disciplined, and appropriate emotion.

Exercise 9   Character and Emotion

Select a character from the list at the end of this chapter. Read the play and study the character with special focus on character development, character personality, and character emotion. Write a one-to-two-page paper in which you clarify what you learned from your study about the character and emotion. The paper should be read and discussed by your instructor and colleagues. Later you may wish to perform a representative scene to complete this exercise.

Dance and Music

It is a historical fact that most Elizabethan men were excellent dancers. In addition, some men, especially the nobility, were accomplished musicians. Elizabethan society was exceptionally conscious of the role that music and dance played in helping formulate the temperament of the times. Execution of dances was skillful and intricate. Dancing became a test of quick intelligence and physical agility. Men took the lead in creating a pattern of steps. There are many extant Elizabethan dances which can be performed either before a play, during intermission, or after a play. Performances traditionally ended with a dance called the jig. This was a violent, spectacular dance with many intricate steps. Actors executed exaggerated leaps called *caprioles* and violent lifts of one's partner high into the air called *voltes*. Other known dances were the Pavane (after the peacock's pride of bearing), the galliarde (a lively, nimble movement), and the alman or allemande (German or heavy type of movement with the feet).

The richness of the Elizabethan period was fully exemplified by its music. Nearly everyone sang and performed. Class distinctions ceased to exist when it came to music. The most popular kind of music was the madrigal, a song written with up to seven parts. There were drinking songs and solo love ballads. Unfortunately, most of Shakespeare's songs have to be adapted to modern music because the original melodies are lost. However, most scholars believe Shakespeare considered music to be supportive, not dominant, in his plays. Music was created for effect, to underscore some point, to add character dimension, or to introduce scenery and characters. Occasionally instruments were played by stage characters to add color. Musicians were used in dumb shows for entrances and exits of special (usually royal) characters, to underscore alliterative verse or repetition of phrases, and to intensify emotional effects. Mad or insane people also were associated with music, for example, Lear and Ophelia. Music was used for moments of fantasy (e.g., *The Tempest* and *A Midsummer Night's Dream*). In general, music was classified into three groups: fanfares, dances, and songs. The instruments varied greatly, but the main ones were the virginal, the lute, the viola da gamba, and the recorder. We are most familiar with the lute and the recorder. The lute was similar in shape to a bowl and was slung across the shoulders by brightly colored ribbons. The strings were plucked, and it was used primarily to accompany singing of love songs. The recorder, a thin-sounding instrument, has regained popularity in recent times. The virginal was played by the ladies who plucked the strings with quills to actuate the keyboard. The viol (viola da gamba) was a stringed instrument suitable for chamber music. Flageolets or penny whistles were also used to produce a sweet, melodic tone. The hautboy, a reed instrument, was rather shrill and harsh. Horns were used for hunting music; trumpets and drums were used as "alarums" and "flourishes" to announce royalty. Violins, cornets, flutes, hautboys, drums, and flutes were traditionally used in dumb shows. Instruments might be grouped by families, or small mixed combinations of three or four instruments with or without voices. The organ was used by itself primarily. It was a small instrument consisting of flute pipes and beating reeds which produced a harsh sound.

Learning to dance to Elizabethan music is a highly specialized technique which should not be undertaken in a single acting exercise. Extensive study and practice with a trained choreographer or director are required (study references are given in Suggested Readings at the end of this chapter).

Music and dance in Shakespeare's plays should always be considered in the light of how clearly and appropriately they support character, action, and mood and should rarely be used as spectacles in their own right. Music and dance are only supportive and must never dominate or destroy the power of what is inherently Shakespearean in terms of brilliant verse and characterization.

Suggested Characters and Plays for Scene Work

Shakespeare, William

Hamlet, Ophelia, Claudius, Gertrude, Polonius, Laertes,
Horatio, Ghost, First Gravedigger
    Hamlet
Othello, Desdemona, Iago, Emilia
    Othello
Romeo, Juliet, Mercutio, Nurse
    Romeo and Juliet
Anthony, Brutus, Cassius, Caesar, Calpurnia, Portia
    Julius Caesar
Richard III, Clarence, Lady Anne
    Richard III
Bottom, Puck
    A Midsummer Night's Dream
Shylock, Portia, Jessica
    The Merchant of Venice
Falstaff, Hotspur, Henry IV, Mistress Quickly
    Henry IV, Part I
Henry V, Katherine
    The Life of King Henry V
Rosalind, Jaques
    As You Like It
Malvolio, Feste, Sir Toby Belch, Sir Andrew Aguecheek,
Viola, Olivia, Maria, Duke Orsino
    Twelfth Night
Lear, Edmund, The Fool, Gloucester, Goneril, Regan, Cordelia
    King Lear
Macbeth, Banquo, Macduff, Lady Macbeth, The Witches
    Macbeth

Antony, Cleopatra
Antony and Cleopatra
Prospero, Caliban, Ariel
The Tempest

Jonson, Ben

Volpone, Mosca
Volpone
Morose, Epicoene
Epicoene
Jeremy, Subtle, Dol Common
Alchemist

Dekker, Thomas

Lacy, Rafe
The Shoemaker's Holiday

Webster, John

Duchess of Malfi, Bosola
The Duchess of Malfi

Marlowe, Christopher

Dr. Faustus, Mephistophilis, Wagner, Helen
Tragical History of Dr. Faustus
Barabas, Abigail, Ithamore
The Jew of Malta
King Edward the Second, Queen Isabella
Reign of Edward the Second

Actor Checklist   *Elizabethan and Shakespearean Style*

Voice	Clear articulation; well projected; varied; slightly elevated tone.
Movement	Full and fluid; appropriate to character; slightly elevated but natural and comfortable; highly selective for tragedy; free and spontaneous for comedy; presentational delivery generally used in soliloquy and aside; representational mode dominates slightly in both tragedy and comedy.
Gestures	Use of full body; clear, fluid, and appropriate; slightly elevated; highly selective in tragedy; flexible in comedy.
Pantomimic Dramatization	Clear, appropriate; use of hand and costume props, particularly in comedy; highly selective for tragedy; highly inventive for comedy.
Character	Truthful and believable; clear; empathic, if appropriate; appropriate dimension.
Emotion	Complex and multidimensional; clear; disciplined; rooted in human psychology.
Ideas	Complex and clear; rooted in Renaissance and Elizabethan social, philosophical, and theological thought; effectively theatricalized.

Language	Often unusual vocabuary; clear and understandable; iambic pentameter rhythmically intact with interpretative freedom permitted; correct pronounciation; lyrical and musical when intended.
Pace and Tempo	Varied; rhythmic; disciplined.
Special Techniques	Specialized dancing and singing depending on context; specialized musical instruments when required; language requires unusual vocal dexterity; unusual attention to movement in costume.

Suggested Readings

Adams, John C. *The Globe Playhouse: Its Design and Equipment.* 2d ed. New York: Barnes & Noble, 1961.

Adams, Joseph Q. *Shakespearean Playhouses: A History of English Theatres from the Beginnings to the Restoration.* Boston: Houghton Mifflin Company, 1917.

Beckerman, Bernard. *Shakespeare at the Globe, 1599–1609.* New York: Macmillan Co., 1962.

Campbell, Lily Bess. *Scenes and Machines on the English Stage during the Renaissance.* Cambridge: Harvard University Press, 1923.

Chambers, E. K. *The Elizabethan Stage.* 4 vols. London: Oxford University Press, 1923.

Chambers, E. K., and Williams, C. *A Short Life of Shakespeare.* London: Oxford, University Press, 1933.

Chute, Marchette. *Shakespeare of London.* New York: E. P. Dutton & Co., 1949.

Ellis-Fermor, Una. *The Jacobean Drama: An Interpretation.* 3d ed. London: Oxford University Press, 1953.

Farnham, Willard. *The Medieval Heritage of Elizabethan Tragedy.* New York: Barnes & Noble, 1936.

Granville-Barker, H., and Harrison, G. B. *A Companion to Shakespeare.* New York: Doubleday & Co., 1960.

Harbage, Alfred. *Shakespeare's Audience.* New York: Columbia University Press, 1961.

Hewitt, Barnard, ed. *The Renaissance Stage: Documents of Serlio, Sabbattini, and Furttenbach.* Coral Gables, Fla.: University of Miami Press, 1958.

Hodges, C. W. *The Globe Restored.* Rev. ed. New York: Coward, McCann & Geoghegan, 1968.

Joseph, Bertram. *Elizabethan Acting.* London: Oxford University Press, 1951.

Joseph, Bertram. *Acting Shakespeare.* New York: Theatre Arts Books, 1969.

Kernodle, George. *From Art to Theatre: Form and Convention in the Renaissance.* Chicago: University of Chicago Press, 1943.

Nagler, A. M. *Shakespeare's Stage.* New Haven, Conn.: Yale University Press, 1958.

"Shakespeare: An Annotated Bibliography," *Shakespeare Quarterly* (1924–19—). [*SQ* was originally called *The Shakespeare Association Bulletin.*] Annual bibliography of writings about Shakespeare.

Shakespeare Survey: An Annual Survey of Shakespearean Study and Production. Cambridge: Harvard University Press, 1948.

Smith, Irwin. *Shakespeare's Blackfriar's Playhouse.* New York: New York University Press, 1970.

Sprague, A. C. *Shakespearean Players and Performances*. Cambridge, Mass.: Harvard University Press, 1953.

Sprague, A. C. *Shakespeare and the Actors*. Cambridge, Mass.: Harvard University Press, 1945.

Thorndike, Ashley H. *Shakespeare's Theatre*. New York: Macmillan Co., 1960.

Webster, Margaret. *Shakespeare without Tears*. Greenwich, Conn.: Fawcett World Library, 1955.

Wickham, Glynne. *Early English Stages, 1300–1660*. 2 vols. New York: Columbia University Press, 1959–1962.

Hamlet
by *William Shakespeare*

from
Act III, scene i

HAMLET Prince of Denmark

Characters

OPHELIA daughter to Polonius, Lord Chamberlain of Denmark; beloved of
young Hamlet

Within the castle of Claudius, King of Denmark.

Scene

Hamlet, visited by the Ghost of his dead father, learns that his uncle Claudius
murdered his father. Walking within the castle, Hamlet contemplates the nature of
being, suicide, and death in a famous soliloquy. Encountering Ophelia, their love
revives for a few moments. However, suspecting her to be a pawn of her father
and the King, Hamlet violently denounces and rejects her.

Situation

(*Enter* HAMLET)

HAMLET   To be, or not to be, that is the question:
Whether 'tis nobler in the mind to suffer
The slings and arrows of outrageous fortune,
Or to take arms against a sea of troubles,
And by opposing end them. To die, to sleep—   60
No more; and by a sleep to say we end
The heartache, and the thousand natural shocks
That flesh is heir to. 'Tis a consumation
Devoutly to be wished—to die, to sleep—
To sleep, perchance to dream, ay there's the rub;   65
For in that sleep of death what dreams may come
When we have shuffled off this mortal coil
Must give us pause—there's the respect
That makes calamity of so long life.
For who would bear the whips and scorns of time,   70
Th' oppressor's wrong, the proud man's contumely,
The pangs of despised love, the law's delay,
The insolence of office, and the spurns
That patient merit of th' unworthy takes,
When he himself might his quietus make   75
With a bare bodkin? Who would fardels bear,
To grunt and sweat under a weary life,
But that the dread of something after death,
The undiscovered country, from whose bourn
No traveller returns, puzzles the will,   80
And makes us rather bear those ills we have
Than fly to others that we know not of?
Thus conscience does make cowards of us all;
And thus the native hue of resolution

65. *rub* obstacle (lit.,
obstruction encountered
by bowler's ball).
67. *coil* bustle, turmoil.

75. *quietus* settlement.
76. *bodkin* dagger;
fardels burdens.

79. *bourn* realm.

86. *pitch* height.

87. *regard* consideration.

Is sicklied o'er with the pale cast of thought,
And enterprises of great pitch and moment
With this regard their currents turn awry
And lose the name of action.—Soft you now,

89. *orisons* prayers.

The fair Ophelia.—Nymph, in thy orisons
Be all my sins remembered.

OPHELIA   Good my lord,   90
How does your honor for this many a day?

HAMLET   I humbly thank you, well.

OPHELIA   My lord, I have remembrances of yours
That I have longed long to re-deliver.
I pray you now receive them.

HAMLET   No, not I,   95
I never gave you aught.

OPHELIA   My honored lord, you know right well you did,
And with them words of so sweet breath composed
As made the things more rich. Their perfume lost,
Take these again, for to the noble mind   100
Rich gifts wax poor when givers prove unkind.
There, my lord.

103. *honest* chaste.

HAMLET   Ha, ha! are you honest?

OPHELIA   My lord?

HAMLET   Are you fair?   105

OPHELIA   What means your lordship?

HAMLET   That if you be honest and fair, your honesty should admit no
discourse to your beauty.

OPHELIA   Could beauty, my lord, have better commerce than with honesty?

HAMLET   Ay, truly, for the power of beauty will sooner transform honesty   110
from what it is to a bawd than the force of honesty can translate beauty
into his likeness. This was sometime a paradox, but now the time gives
it proof. I did love you once.

OPHELIA   Indeed, my lord, you made me believe so.

115. *inoculate* graft.

HAMLET   You should not have believed me, for virtue cannot so inoculate our   115
old stock but we shall relish of it. I loved you not.

OPHELIA   I was the more deceived.

HAMLET   Get thee to a nunnery. Why wouldst thou be a breeder of sinners?

119. *indifferent honest* moderately respectable.

I am myself indifferent honest, but yet I could accuse me of such things
that it were better my mother had not borne me: I am very proud,   120
revengeful, ambitious, with more offences at my beck than I have
thoughts to put them in, imagination to give them shape, or time to
act them in. What should such fellows as I do crawling between earth
and heaven? We are arrant knaves all; believe none of us. Go thy ways
to a nunnery. Where's your father?   125

OPHELIA   At home, my lord.

HAMLET   Let the doors be shut upon him, that he may play the fool
nowhere but in's own house. Farewell.

OPHELIA   O, help him, you sweet heavens!

HAMLET   If thou dost marry, I'll give thee this plague for thy dowry: be thou   130
as chaste as ice, as pure as snow, thou shalt not escape calumny. Get
thee to a nunnery, farewell. Or if thou wilt needs marry, marry a fool,

for wise men know well enough what monsters you make of them.
To a nunnery go, and quickly too. Farewell.

OPHELIA   Heavenly powers, restore him!   135

HAMLET   I have heard of your paintings well enough. God hath given you one
face, and you make yourselves another. You jig and amble, and you lisp;
you nickname God's creatures, and make your wantonness your
ignorance. Go to, I'll no more on't, it hath made me mad. I say we
will have no moe marriage. Those that are married already, all but   140
one, shall live. The rest shall keep as they are. To a nunnery, go. (Exit.)

OPHELIA   O, what a noble mind is here o'erthrown!
The courtier's, soldier's, scholar's, eye, tongue, sword,
Th' expectancy and rose of the fair state,
The glass of fashion and the mould of form,   145
Th' observed of all observers, quite quite down!
And I of ladies most deject and wretched,
That sucked the honey of his musicked vows,
Now see that noble and most sovereign reason
Like sweet bells jangled, out of time and harsh;   150
That unmatched form and feature of blown youth
Blasted with ecstasy. O, woe is me
T' have seen what I have seen, see what I see!

(END)

138–39. *make your wantonness your ignorance* excuse your wanton behavior with the plea that you don't know any better.

140. *moe* more.

144. *expectancy* hope.

145. *glass* mirror.

151. *blown* blooming.

152. *ecstasy* madness.

Twelfth Night

by *William Shakespeare*

from
Act III, scene i

Characters	Viola Clown (Feste)
Scene	In Olivia's garden.
Situation	The young maiden Viola, separated from her twin brother in a shipwreck, is dressed in disguise as a male. The Clown, servant to the beautiful Olivia, is leading Viola to a meeting with Olivia who has fallen in love with Viola, not knowing "he" is in fact a woman. The Clown and Viola engage in a typically Elizabethan exchange of wit.

(*Enter* VIOLA, *and* CLOWN [*with a tabor and pipe*].)

Ent. tabor: a small drum

VIOLA   Save thee, friend, and thy music! Dost thou live by thy tabor?

CLOWN   No, sir, I live by the church.

VIOLA   Art thou a churchman?

CLOWN   No such matter, sir. I do live by the church; for I do live at my house, and my house doth stand by the church.   5

VIOLA   So thou mayst say, the king lies by a beggar, if a beggar dwell near him; or, the church stands by thy tabor, if thy tabor stand by the church.

9. chev'ril: flexible kidskin

CLOWN   You have said, sir. To see this age! A sentence is but a chev'ril glove to a good wit. How quickly the wrong side may be turned outward!   10

12. dally nicely: play lasciviously

VIOLA   Nay, that's certain. They that dally nicely with words may quickly make them wanton.

CLOWN   I would therefore my sister had had no name, sir.

VIOLA   Why, man?   15

CLOWN   Why, sir, her name's a word, and to dally with that word might make my sister wanton. But indeed words are very rascals since bonds disgraced them.

17–18. since . . . them: i.e., since men began to require bonds instead of trusting another's word in making bargains

VIOLA   Thy reason, man?

CLOWN   Troth, sir, I can yield you none without words, and words are grown so false I am loath to prove reason with them.   20

VIOLA   I warrant thou art a merry fellow and carest for nothing.

23. in . . . conscience: as conscience is my judge

CLOWN   Not so, sir; I do care for something; but in my conscience, sir, I do not care for you. If that be to care for nothing, sir, I would it would make you invisible.   25

VIOLA   Art not thou the Lady Olivia's fool?

CLOWN   No, indeed, sir. The Lady Olivia has no folly. She will keep no fool, sir, till she be married; and fools are as like husbands as

29. pilchards: small fish of the herring family

pilchards are to herrings—the husband's the bigger. I am indeed not her fool, but her corrupter of words.   30

VIOLA I saw thee late at the Count Orsino's.

CLOWN Foolery, sir, does walk about the orb like the sun; it shines everywhere. I would be sorry, sir, but the fool should be as oft with your master as with my mistress. I think I saw your wisdom there.

VIOLA Nay, an thou pass upon me, I'll no more with thee. Hold, there's expenses for thee.   35

(Gives a piece of money.)

CLOWN Now Jove, in his next commodity of hair, send thee a beard!

VIOLA By my troth, I'll tell thee, I am almost sick for one, though I would not have it grow on my chin. Is thy lady within?

CLOWN Would not a pair of these have bred, sir?   40

VIOLA Yes, being kept together and put to use.

CLOWN I would play Lord Pandarus of Phrygia, sir, to bring a Cressida to this Troilus.

VIOLA I understand you, sir. 'Tis well begged.

CLOWN The matter, I hope, is not great, sir, begging but a beggar: 45
Cressida was a beggar. *(Viola tosses him another coin.)* My lady is within, sir. I will conster to them whence you come. Who you are and what you would are out of my welkin—I might say "element," but the word is over-worn. *Exit.*

VIOLA This fellow is wise enough to play the fool,   50
And to do that well craves a kind of wit.
He must observe their mood on whom he jests,
The quality of persons, and the time;
Not, like the haggard, check at every feather
That comes before his eye. This is a practice   55
As full of labor as a wise man's art;
For folly that he wisely shows, is fit;
But wise men, folly-fall'n, quite taint their wit.

(END)

32. *orb: earth*

33–34. *I . . . mistress:* i.e., I would regret to think my mistress more foolish than your master.

35. *pass . . . me:* offer a duel

37. *commodity:* consignment

38. *one:* i.e., a man with a beard

40. *these:* coins

41. *use:* lending at interest

45. *begging . . . beggar:* a reference to the practice of "begging" the wardship of wealthy minors through the Court of Wards

47. *conster:* construe; explain

48. *welkin:* sky (element)

51. *craves:* requires; *wit:* intelligence

54. *haggard:* an untrained hawk

55. *practice:* craft

57. *wisely:* deliberately (to earn a living); *fit:* suitable

14 Seventeenth-Century French Neoclassicism

Restraint Again

. . . Indeed, I think that it is much easier to soar with grand sentiments, to brave fortune in verse, to arraign destiny and reproach the Gods, than to broach ridicule in a fit manner, and to make the faults of all mankind seem pleasant on the stage. When you paint heroes you can do as you like.

> Dorante in *School for Wives* by Molière

. . . Aristotle laid down the rules of dramatic poetry, and Socrates, the wisest of the philosophers, did not disdain to speak of the tragedies of Euripides. We should like our works to be as solid and full of useful instruction as were those of antiquity. This might be a means to reconcile tragedy to a number of celebrated persons . . . who would undoubtedly cast a more favorable eye upon it [tragedy] if the dramatists endeavored to instruct as well as please their auditors, and so came nearer to the true end of all tragedy.

> Racine in Preface to *Phaedra*

Molière's delightful female character Dorante expresses the key problem confronting the comic playwright—how to reveal man's ridiculous nature, lower sentiments, and human faults in a humorous and, therefore, pleasant statement on a stage. Perhaps no comic playwright, with the possible exception of Aristophanes, Shakespeare, and Shaw, has succeeded in mastering this problem as well as the genius of the seventeenth-century French stage, Molière. Molière wrote a host of brilliant comedies with infinite dramatic variety. In tragedy, his chief counterpart, Jean Racine, in following the so-called new or Neoclassic bent, abandoned the flexible forms of Renaissance tragedy and returned to a restrained imitation of the ancient Greeks (refined through the influence of the Romans). Pierre Corneille in his plays also contributed to the reform of French tragedy, but the finest examples were those of Racine. The plays of Molière and Racine are the best for a modern actor to study when learning how to act seventeenth-century French Neoclassic drama.

Overview of French Neoclassicism (Seventeenth Century)

The period of French Neoclassicism (i.e., *New* Classicism) began in the third decade of the seventeenth century when Cardinal Richelieu became primate to King Louis XIV (the French often delete *Neo* from the name and refer only to French *Classicism*). During this period France was flush with a fierce nationalism which spilled into the cultural heritage of the nation. In 1630 under the guidance of Richelieu, a revolution in the arts was forged whose pattern of cultural development was modeled on the Italian Renaissance and derived primarily from the work of Castelvetro, a fifteenth-century Italian scholar. Neoclassic drama began with the study of classical Roman plays in the late fifteenth century and continued with the writing of Latin imitations of classical works in the early sixteenth century, and its influence spread to French drama after 1550. The principle of Neoclassicism was dramatization of abstract concepts. Plays were concerned with ideas and their effect on human beings—ideas such as honor and dishonor, sin and innocence, loyalty and treachery, will and necessity, respect and contempt, authority and servility. In Neoclassic plays, the concept of verisimilitude (likelife quality) was paramount in exemplifying generalized ideals. French playwrights wanted the audience to see the "appearance" of reality—a world perceived by the senses, a particularized world which the playwright allowed to be seen. The classical unities of time, place, and action were strictly supported. (The *unities* were attributed erroneously to Aristotle when actually they were misinterpretations of his writing by Italian Renaissance critics who studied Horace more than Aristotle.) Emphasis was on the universal aspects of character and situation. Character was synonymous with status, rank, and code of behavior. This concept of character became known as *decorum* or appropriateness of characterization. To Neoclassicists verisimilitude and decorum were essential to achieve complete universality in drama.

Neoclassic playwrights produced virile drama. Most plays were based on the models of Alexandre Hardy (ca. 1572–1632). Hardy was the innovator of the Alexandrine line, the basic verse used in Neoclassic drama (i.e., six iambic feet, with the caesure after the third foot). Romantic character dominated in his plays, whose trademark was a highly narrative elegiac style.

The first exponent of Neoclassic drama in France was Corneille (1604–1684). Corneille's use of simple characters and complex plots made him a highly popular playwright. *The Cid,* written in 1636, typified Corneille's use of a hero with an indomitable will. *The Cid* is perhaps most famous for having been the center of a controversy in the French Academy (formed in 1635 by Cardinal Richelieu to set cultural standards in France). Corneille's highly successful play was rejected by the Academy because it violated the unities. Subsequently, Corneille set out to write other plays which adhered to the Neoclassical rules of playwriting. However, they were singularly unimpressive as viable drama.

Jean Racine (1639–1673) was a much more impressive Neoclassic playwright. Racine's plays possessed a natural sense of order and good taste. He achieved the epitome of the Neoclassic style of tragedy in his plays—in effect, the Neoclassic form was truly an expression of his natural style of writing. His plays contained little external action. The drama resulted from internal psychological conflict centered on a single complex character. Racine de-emphasized the physical appearance of characters, emphasizing instead the psychological and moral states of the hero or heroine. Characters portrayed intense emotional depth which was manifested in great conflicts of passion and willpower (e.g., Phaedra). Human weakness and strength were exposed by simple dramatic passages. Departure from established decorum brought about the downfall of a character.

Comedy was very popular in France during the seventeenth century. True to the Neoclassic demands of the French Academy, Molière (1622–1673) wrote plays that conformed to the classical ideal of having five acts and adhering to the unities. His plays were usually set in a drawing room (rarely out-of-doors). Molière created dramatic action through the impact of events on character, which in turn reacted and created new events for counterimpact (i.e., *Tartuffe*). Molière drew his characters from all levels of society. Psychology was the mainspring of his plays, exposing humanized and vulnerable man in a weakened condition. Molière was essentially a satirist devoted to truth. He used satire to expose the pretentions of the world while attempting to bring about change. It is important to keep in mind that Molière was a great admirer of the commedia dell'arte (he toured with a commedia troupe as an actor). Many characters in Molière's comedies were based on commedia types (for example, Harpagon in *The Miser* is a Pantalone figure). Molière's farces also borrowed from Plautus and Terence and from Spanish and Italian sources. Although he wrote other types of plays such as ballets and tragedies, Molière's appeal has endured strictly because of his comedies.

Phaedra in *Phaedra*
by Racine.

Hume Cronyn as
Harpagon in *The Miser*
by Molière. Directed by
Douglas Campbell.
Designed by Tanya
Moiseiwitsch. The
Guthrie Theatre,
Minneapolis, Minn.

The major theatres of Paris included the Hotel de Bourgogne, the Theatre du Marais, and the Palais-Royal (first theatre in France to use a proscenium arch). Tennis courts were often converted into temporary theatres, with a simple platform for acting at one end of the court, while galleries and benches were placed on the sides and down the length of the court for spectators. The Hotel de Bourgogne was simply a long, narrow room with galleries on the sides and benches in front of a raised platform at one end. The Marais and Palais-Royal resembled the kind of theatres generally used today. The spectators sat on a sloping floor or in one of the three gal-

The Bourgeois Gentleman in *The Bourgeoise Gentleman* by Molière.

lery levels on the sides. Some people sat in the pit below the apron or upon the stage itself (thereby severely limiting the acting area). Scenic demands were simple, ranging from curtains and small three-dimensional units to painted representations of rooms, streets, and gardens. All scenic changes were executed in full view of the audience. Footlights as well as overhead lighting utilized candles and oil lamps. Poor lighting forced actors to play primarily downstage center. Movement was limited also by lighting and the spectators onstage.

Actors and actresses wore contemporary costumes except for well-known historic, fantastic, and allegorical characters. A variety of elaborateness prevailed in costuming, depending upon the character and the financial status of the acting troupe. Most characters wore long, full wigs. In a few plays the commedia influence resulted in the retention of masks by some characters. Costuming and contemporary dress were generally beautiful and elaborate, emphasizing lace, brocade, and other fineries (see illustrations and photographs in this chapter).

Voice—French Neoclassic Tragedy

The acting style in France during the seventeenth century was generally characterized as highly formal and conventionalized, with great emphasis on vocal recitation. The tradition for performing in plays by Corneille was that actors were to use grandiose recitation while standing rigidly in one place. On the other hand, for Racine's plays a less declamatory vocal delivery was necessary. Because Racine's characters explored the subconscious passions of the mind, the actor had to develop a new and fairly subtle naturalness in the voice. A trained voice is the key requirement for successful performance of Neoclassic French tragedy. The voice must vary with respect to passions and with differing parts of the classical oration; it also must vary with figures of rhetoric, unusual sentences, and unique words. Racine's art is a formal one contrived of human passion within strict linguistic limitations. In Alexandrine verse, recitation must achieve a balance of the rhymed couplet and the individual line. The line may or may not be broken in the middle by the caesure. The verse is "sculptured" to help compress passion into one major crisis. For example, Phaedra is a tormented woman trying to find a way to control her incestuous passion in act 4 as she speaks to Oenone:

Hypocrisy and incest breathe at once through all I do. My hands are ripe for murder. To spill the guiltless blood of innocence. Do I still live, a wretch, and dare to face the holy sun, from whom I have my being? My father's father was the king of gods; My race is spread through all the universe.—Where can I hide? In the dark realms of Pluto? But there my father holds the fatal urn.

Phaedra by Racine

Language is probably the most difficult problem in studying the acting style of Racine and Neoclassic French tragedy. The magnificent quality of his style with language can only be conveyed indirectly in English. Any translator of Racine begins by apologizing. Racine's language is considered to be the most nearly perfect example of purity of style of all French literature.

Alexandrine poetry was written in a twelve-syllable line of qualitative rather than quantitative verse, with a thirteenth unpronounced syllable permitted in a feminine line. The line was further divided into two hemistichs, with a caesura after the sixth syllable. Boileau-Despreaux, French dramatic critic, stated it this way for the actor:

Have an ear for cadence;
Always let your meaning, cutting off your words,
Halt at the hemistich, mark it with a stop.

There was also a requirement, extremely difficult to fulfill, that each line should terminate a logical sequence of thought with no carry-over to the next line. Such a carry-over, an *enjambement,* was considered a defect of style and a flaw in the writing. A kind of carry-over was allowed, in rare cases, for a special effect and was then called a *rejet.* A famous example of a successful *rejet* occurs in *Phaedra* in the scene between Phaedra and Hippolytus in the second act in which Phaedra makes five *rejets.* By use of this devise at precisely these points Racine called attention to the fact that Phaedra is distraught. She can no longer arrest her speech normally as a lady should. The five *rejets* which Racine used indicate to the audience that Phaedra is being carried away by her emotions.

The language of Neoclassic tragedy was aristocratic and removed from daily life. The poet spoke abstractly, with rarified elegance and great formality. Today this language is considered rather affected and is one of the difficulties in performing Neoclassic tragedy adequately for modern taste. A good English translation naturally accomplishes a great deal in making the verse palatable, but just as naturally also sacrifices much of the great beauty and meaning of the language in the process. However, awareness of the precision, beauty, and special effects as just described are a valuable part of an actor's training as he prepares to act Neoclassic tragedy.

Exercise 1   Voice—Neoclassic Tragedy

Practice the following selections aloud, emphasizing highly grandiose, declamatory delivery. Work to achieve balance of rhythm and rhyme. Try to achieve termination of thought in each line. Be highly selective in where you place emotion, inflection, and variety. Later repeat the exercise by modifying it to a level of what might be considered palatable or natural for contemporary audiences:

PHAEDRA   Although you hate me, I shall not
complain, My lord: for you have seen me
bent to harm you.
You could not read the tables of my heart.
I've taken care to invite your enmity,
And could not bear your presence where I
dwelt.
In public, and in private, your known foe,
I've wished the seas to part us, and even
forbidden
The mention of your name within my hearing.
But if one measures punishment by the offense,
If only hatred can attract your hate,
Never was woman who deserved more pity,
My lord, and less deserved your enmity.

HIPPOLYTUS   A mother jealous for her children's
rights
Seldom forgives her stepson. I know it,
madam.
Nagging suspicions are the commonest fruits
Of second marriage; and another wife
Would have disliked me just the same; and I
Might well have had to swallow greater wrongs.

Phaedra   by Racine

Movement—French Neoclassic Tragedy

All movement in Neoclassic tragedy is confined by the linguistic demands
of the playwright. That confinement requires that the actor achieve poetic
and precise command of gestures and movements highly elevated to a larger-
than-life level. The elevation should coincide with the formality of the
words. Movement should be characterized by elegance and gracefulness of
manner and bearing, reminiscent of the Classic Greek style. Modern actors
can benefit greatly from studying the paintings of such seventeenth-century
artists as Peter Rubens, Nicolas Poussin, and Charles Lebrun. These artists
depicted the dress and costumes of the time well and also captured gestures
and facial expressions which might be helpful. Movement was probably
very limited on the seventeenth-century French stage because of the poor
lighting, small acting area, and emphasis on language. The physical focus
was on the upper portion of the body, particularly the face, hands, and arms.
Naturally, in today's theatre more movement is employed in the staging.
However, emphasis remains on voice and character. Modern directors employ more use of sitting positions and handling of properties than in the
original style. Movement, sitting, and use of properties must be handled
discreetly; it is a mistake to use a great deal of realistic activity in a Neoclassic French tragedy. Similar to the seventeenth century, selective use of
hand and costume properties such as fans, handkerchiefs, staffs, canes, gob-
lets, capes, swords, and so on, is advisable today. Movement was generally
slow with rare physical contact with other characters. The presentational
mode dominated almost exclusively in the original style, but is, of course,
modified today.

Exercise 2   Movement—Neoclassic Tragedy

Perform the following action as a review of classical Greek movement
which relates closely to Neoclassic movement.

1. From an aligned position on your feet, breathe comfortably in a
relaxed state. Move through space in a slow-motion manner concentrating upon grace, rhythm, fluidity, and sense of controlled restraint.

2. Repeat the foregoing exercise in a modified tempo permitting the
slow motion to evolve into an acceptably believable or natural tempo.

Character and Emotion—French Neoclassic Tragedy

Except for the psychology of their emotion, characters in Racine's plays were not realistically conceived. They are contained in a condition of artistic purity. We see very little of their daily routine; they seem not to sleep, eat, or drink. They speak with an elevated and artificial (meaning "contrived by art") language. Their soliloquies are rational pieces of literature or rhetoric. However, close examination reveals shivering emotion beneath the reason. That emotion was based on valid human psychology having full, rich motivation. An intelligent approach to character and emotion in French Neoclassic tragedy is to establish a believable characterization beginning with the use of personalization. The personalization is best used in this style only for the sake of comfort in early rehearsals. While the language will dominate, the style works best in today's theatre with believable characterization. The language in itself will keep the character and emotion at a necessary larger-than-life level.

Exercise 3   Character and Emotion—Neoclassic Tragedy

Invent and perform a series of improvisations in pairs in which you explore the levels of human psychology concerning the following character and emotional states. Be certain that a goal or objective is established for each improvisation. For example, the goal of a *greed* improvisation might be: a wife discovers her husband has hidden a million dollar inheritance from her.

1. Greed
2. Ambition
3. Incestuous love
4. Pride
5. Jealousy
6. Grief
7. Hatred
8. Love

Voice—French Neoclassic Comedy

French Neoclassic comedy as exemplified by Molière was concerned with the manners and customs of the court and those persons who lived on the edge of the social life of the period. It was fashionable to be impious and licentious about serious subjects. Audiences probably enjoyed seeing their manners and customs mirrored. The focus of the acting style is on language, but due to the genius of Molière, equal focus comes to bear on character. Molière's plays conform to Neoclassic rules of structure and the unities; some of his plays were written in verse and others in prose. Rhythm and pace are crucial considerations when delivering Molière's comic lines.

His characters generally interacted rapidly. The vocal tempo is usually rapid and precise. Again it is necessary to check vocabulary carefully. Soliloquies and asides were frequently used. Unusually clear articulation, pronunciation, and projection are necessary to handle the rapid line delivery and varied language of Molière. Complex inflections and vocal variety are absolutely necessary in performing the language of Molière, who wrote primarily in Alexandrine couplets (some translators adapt his writing to prose at great damage to rhythm and lyricism).

Exercise 4   Voice—Neoclassic Comedy

Practice the following speeches for rapid delivery; comic repartee and inflection; clear articulation, pronunciation, projection; and variety. Perform entirely presentational; then modify and repeat the exercise with balanced use of representational and presentational modes.

> CLÉANTE   ... You agreed of late
> That young Valère might have your
> daughter's hand.
> ORGON   I did.
> CLÉANTE   You've not postponed it; is that true?
> ORGON   No doubt.
> CLÉANTE   The match no longer pleases you?
> ORGON   Who knows?
> CLÉANTE   D'you mean to go back on your word?
> ORGON   I won't say that.
> CLÉANTE   Has anything occurred
> Which might entitle you to break your pledge?
> ORGON   Perhaps.
>   *Tartuffe*   Act I, scene v, by Molière

> MARIANNE   Oh, you turn my blood to ice!
> Stop torturing me, and give me your advice.
> DORINE *(threatening to go)*   Your servant,
> Madam.
> MARIANNE   Dorine, I beg of you ...
> DORINE   No, you deserve it; this
> marriage must go through.
> MARIANNE   Dorine!
> DORINE   No.
> MARIANNE   Not Tartuffe! You know I think him ...
> DORINE   Tartuffe's your cup of tea,
> and you shall drink him.
> MARIANNE   I've always told you everything,
> and relied ...
> DORINE   No. You deserve to be tartuffified.
>   *Tartuffe*   Act III, scene iii, by Molière

Movement—French Neoclassic Comedy

Two points must be kept in mind when movement in Molière comedy is discussed. One, when heavy commedia dell'arte influence is obvious, commedia acting style should dominate; for example, *The Physician in Spite of Himself*, a farcical short play by Molière, is frequently performed in the commedia style (commedia style is discussed in chapter 12). Two, a unique, elaborate acting style is necessary in most of Molière's character comedies because they are rich in social satire. His character and social comedies were rooted in precise, inventive activity, and therefore movement should be selective and rapid in tempo. A highly theatrical, presentational mode should be used. For example, movement should focus on firm stride and erect standing position or posture (weight resting on the back foot with the front foot forward and to the side). Men walked with virility and used elaborate finger gestures. Gestures were broad and punctuated by use of fluid movements of the wrist and hand. Maids and servants bounced and pranced a great deal; central female characters generally glided in a highly elevated and charming manner. Clothing generally emphasized the figure.

Unlike Neoclassic tragedy, there was considerable stage movement, particularly in the plays influenced by commedia. Bowing and curtsying were used frequently. Pantomimic dramatization was inventive, emphasizing facial grimacing and extensive use of hand and costume properties. Hands were usually held high to reveal lace cuffs. Personal objects were handled with flourish: handkerchiefs were waved between the fingers; fans were fluttered at crucial moments of anxiety, discovery, or flirtation; half-masks were deployed at gala public affairs and out-of-doors; canes and staffs were swung about for emphasis or humor; and snuff was taken by most characters, male and female. Snuff was usually a mixture of tobacco and dried herbs or powders and occasionally drugs. Snuff was used to attract attention. Its use was a matter of great ceremony and social custom. On a practical level, taking snuff usually caused one to sneeze, thereby cleaning the nasal passages. It also had a slightly intoxicating and pleasant effect. Most people of upper society carried a small box of snuff with them. A snuffbox was taken from the waistcoat pocket, tapped at the top to make the particles fall to the bottom, and a pinch was taken with the thumb and second finger and either applied to the nose and inhaled or placed on the back of the hand and sniffed. The cuffs were then shaken or snapped at with a handkerchief to remove any clinging particles of snuff.

The male bow was slightly modified from that used in the Renaissance. A gentleman stepped back, bent one knee, and placed his right hand over his heart while bending slightly. Some men used a more elaborate bow by bending more deeply and sweeping their hats behind them. The female curtsy used the same variations as the Renaissance, and the use of fans and handkerchiefs made the curtsies more elaborate.

Soliloquies and asides were handled basically as they were in Elizabethan drama (see chapter 13).

Exercise 5   Movement—Neoclassic Comedy

1. Review all steps of Exercise 2 in chapter 12 on commedia movement.

2. Practice the modified bows and curtsies just described.
3. Study and practice the following:
   a. Take snuff according to the directions given in this chapter.
   b. Assume the male standing position with weight resting on the rear foot, the front foot forward and to the side. With arms extending slightly to the side, move rapidly about the stage with precision and elegance. If they are available, use walking staffs, canes, handkerchiefs, and costume properties. (Execute these movements with considerable male virility.)
   c. Assume an elegant and graceful female pose. The weight should be balanced on both feet with the arms and hands extended away from the body. Move gracefully and rapidly about the stage with precision and elegance. If they are available, use fans, handkerchiefs, and costume properties.

Character and Emotion—French Neoclassic Comedy

Stock characters prevail in the plays of Molière influenced by commedia. Your main concern will again be with singular obsession and usually one-dimensional personality characteristics.

The genius of Molière is exemplified in his great character creations in the social comedies such as *The Misanthrope, Tartuffe,* and *The Would-Be Gentleman.* The central characters in these plays are multidimensional, complex, and rooted in human psychology. The humanity of Molière's characters permit effective use of personalization in early rehearsals and in some instances beyond. Full-scale role analysis is necessary to create these characters. Molière's brilliant language in both prose and verse provides the key to character delineation. His characters have biographical background, clear attitudes, and temperament. They represented clear facets of society and current political, philosophic, and theological thought and ran the gamut of human feelings. Molière characters were highly motivated by clear emotional hungers and desires. Your approach to these roles must be serious and in no way mocking, detached, or superficial. The wit and comic situation tend to render the characters ludicrous and humorous, although a serious point of view underlies the comic facade. Create a complete human being; take the role seriously and reveal the various emotional desires which drive him such as greed, love, lust, avarice, and so on. If you play the role as though you or the character know you are humorous, you may destroy Molière's satire. The audience and other characters must recognize the ludicrous and comic element, but the actor and his character must not be aware of it. For example, Tartuffe in *Tartuffe* and Alceste in *The Misanthrope* are deadly earnest concerning their desires and problems. The situations Molière put them into, combined with his language and wit, turned the rich human characterizations into comedy. However, without detracting from foregoing points, it should be noted that Molière's characterizations were not totally natural. Behavior was altered; it was different from real life. It was magnified life.

Hume Cronyn as Harpagon and Zoe Caldwell as Frosine in *The Miser* by Molière. Directed by Douglas Campbell. Designed by Tanya Moiseiwitsch. The Guthrie Theatre, Minneapolis, Minn.

Exercise 6   Character and Emotion—Neoclassic Comedy

Select a character from the list of Molière plays provided at the end of this chapter. Read the play and study the character, with special focus on character background, development, personality, and emotional hungers. Carefully identify the obsessive aspects of the hunger which ultimately render the character ludicrous or comic. Write a brief paper in which you clarify your study. After the paper is read and discussed, perform a representative scene to complete this exercise.

Music—French Neoclassicism

Most of Molière's plays called for use of some music and dance. For example, a form of ballet interlude was required in *The School For Husbands*. In seventeenth-century France orchestral music was usually quite lavish, ranging from chamber groups to complete stringed orchestras. Viols, lutes, and organs were popular, along with wind instruments. Choral singing was also enjoyed.

While Racine and French Neoclassic tragedy are only occasionally performed today, Molière's comedies remain among the most popularly produced plays in the theatre. Effective translations are difficult to find because the elegant French language and meter suffer greatly when transposed into English. In recent years, poet Richard Wilbur has written highly acclaimed translations of Molière plays including *The Misanthrope* and *Tartuffe*.

French Neoclassic acting styles were influential on the Continent. Their influence was also seen in England with the restoration of the crown in 1660. However, as discussed in chapter 15, the glory of the French style was modified and uniquely adapted and altered by the artists of the Restoration.

Suggested Characters and Plays for Scene Work

Molière

Tartuffe, Orgon, Elmire
   Tartuffe
Alceste, Célimène
   The Misanthrope
Harpagon, Cléanté, Marianne
   The Miser
M. Jourdain, Cleante, Covielle
   The Would-Be Gentleman
Scapin, Octavio, Leander
   Scapin
Sganarelle, Isabella, Valère, Ariste
   The School for Husbands
Argon, Angelique
   The Imaginery Invalid
Arnolphe, Agnes, Horace, Oronte
   The School for Wives

Racine, Jean

Phaedra, Hippolytus, Oenone, Theseus
   Phaedra
Andromache, Hermoine
   Andromache

Corneille, Pierre

Chimene, Don Rodrique
   The Cid

Actor Checklist   *French Neoclassic Tragedy (Racine)*

Voice	Clear diction; oratorical, rhetorical, and declamatory; well projected; varied; highly elevated; smooth and polished delivery; generally restrained except for *rejet* moments.
Movement	Highly restrained; elevated; appropriate; graceful; coordinated with linguistic demands; highly selective; presentational mode dominates; slow-to-moderate tempo, but accelerated at emotional moments.
Gestures	Selective; elevated; restrained except when emotion overcomes reason as in the vocal *rejet*; focus on the upper part of the body; rare use of sitting position.

Pantomimic Dramatization	Clear; appropriate; elevated; restrained; use of hand and costume properties; selective.
Character	Psychological; believable and truthful; clear; empathic, if appropriate; full dimension in Racine; somewhat larger than life.
Emotion	Rooted in human psychology; well motivated; at times larger than life; controlled until moments of outburst.
Ideas	Exemplify Neoclassic mandates of verisimilitude and decorum; focus on reason over emotion.
Language	Lyrical; controlled Alexandrine verse; aristocratic, removed from daily life; abstract; elegant; formal; precise; beautiful.
Mood and Atmosphere	Correct and clear in terms of being supportive of character and action; no mix of comedy; pure in its seriousness.
Pace and Tempo	Moderate to slow except for moments of high emotion.
Special Techniques	Verse complexity requires great vocal dexterity.

Actor Checklist   *French Neoclassic Comedy (Molière)*

Voice	Exaggerated melodic patterns and inflections; rapid but clear; smooth and polished line delivery; precise diction, particularly in verse.
Movement	Elegant; elevated; graceful; controlled; well-executed use of bows, curtsies, asides, and soliloquies; balance of presentational and representational mode; generally rapid tempo.
Gestures	Hand, head, facial dominate; clear; elevated.
Pantomimic Dramatization	Clear and highly inventive; extensive use of period costumes and props such as fans, staffs, handkerchiefs, half-masks, snuff, and so on.
Character	Major characters are well motivated, multidimensional, complex, and rooted in human psychology; clear background, attitude, and temperament; representative social facet clear; serious actor involvement.
Emotion	Complex and multidimensional in major characters; clear; at times obsessive; rooted in human psychology.
Ideas	Clear; satiric; witty; to correct social injustices.
Language	Witty; rhythmic, brilliant vocabulary, and rich imagery; correct pronunciation; lyrical and musical when intended.
Mood and Atmosphere	Clear in terms of comic satire, farce or repartee and wit, as script demands; supportive of situation, action, character; generally comic with serious undertones.
Pace and Tempo	Generally rapid.

| Special Techniques | Wit and language demand unusual vocal dexterity; singing and dancing usually required of some characters; unusual attention to movement in costume. |
| For Commedia Influence | See chapter 12. |

Suggested Readings

Chapman, R. A. *The Spirit of Molière: An Interpretation.* Princeton, N. J.: Princeton University Press, 1940.

Fernandez, Ramon. *Molière: The Man Seen Through the Plays.* New York: Hill & Wang, 1958.

Hubert, Judd D. *Molière and the Comedy of Intellect.* Reprint of 1962 ed. New York: Russell & Russell, 1971.

Lancaster, H. C. *A History of French Dramatic Literature in the Seventeenth Century.* 9 vols. Reprint of 1942 ed. Staten Island, N. Y.: Gordian Press, 1966.

Palmer, John. *Molière.* New York: Brewer & Warren, 1930.

Tilley, A. A. *Molière.* Cambridge, Mass.: Harvard University Press, 1936.

Turnell, Martin. *The Classical Moment: Studies in Corneille, Molière, and Racine.* Reprint of 1948 ed. Westport, Conn.: Greenwood Press, 1971.

Vinaver, Eugene. *Racine and Poetic Tragedy.* Translated by P. M. Jones. Manchester: Manchester University Press, 1955.

Wilcox, John. *The Relation of Molière to Restoration Comedy.* New York: Benjamin Blom, 1964.

Wright, C. H. C. *French Classicism.* Cambridge, Mass.: Harvard University Press, 1920.

Phaedra

by Jean Racine

Translated from the French by Robert Henderson

from
Act II

Phaedra, wife of Theseus and stepmother to Hippolytus   *Characters*
Hippolytus, son of Theseus and Antiope (Queen of the Amazons)

In Traezen, a town of the Peloponnesus.   *Scene*

The goddess Aphrodite hates Phaedre and implants in her a guilty passion for   *Situation*
her stepson, Hippolytus. Thinking her husband, Theseus, is dead, Phaedre
confesses her love to Hippolytus who, reviled and shocked, rejects her.

PHAEDRA   They tell me that you leave us, hastily.
 I come to add my own tears to your sorrow,
 And I would plead my fears for my young son.
 He has no father, now; 'twill not be long
 Until the day that he will see my death,
 And even now, his youth is much imperiled
 By a thousand foes. You only can defend him.
 And in my inmost heart, remorse is stirring,—
 Yes, and fear, too, lest I have shut your ears
 Against his cries; I fear that your just anger
 May, before long, visit on him that hatred
 His mother earned.
HIPPOLYTUS   Madam, you need not fear.
 Such malice is not mine.
PHAEDRA   I should not blame you
 If you should hate me; I have injured you.
 So much you know;—you could not read my heart.
 Yes, I have tried to be your enemy,
 For the same land could never hold us both.
 In private and abroad I have declared it;—
 I was your enemy! I found no peace
 Till seas had parted us; and I forbade
 Even your name to be pronounced to me.
 And yet, if punishment be meted out
 Justly, by the offense;—if only hatred
 Deserves a hate, then never was there woman
 Deserved more pity, and less enmity.
HIPPOLYTUS   A mother who is jealous for her children
 Will seldom love the children of a mother
 Who came before her. Torments of suspicion
 Will often follow on a second marriage.
 Another would have felt that jealousy
 No less than you; perhaps more violently.
PHAEDRA   Ah, prince, but Heaven made me quite exempt
 From what is usual, and I can call

That Heaven as my witness! 'Tis not this—
No, quite another ill devours my heart!

HIPPOLYTUS   This is no time for self-reproaching, madam.
Perhaps your husband still beholds the light,
Perhaps he may be granted safe return
In answer to our prayers; his guarding god
Is Neptune, whom he never called in vain.

PHAEDRA   He who has seen the mansions of the dead
Returns not thence. Since Theseus has gone
Once to those gloomy shores, we need not hope,
For Heaven will not send him back again.
Prince, there is no release from Acheron;—
It is a greedy maw,—and yet I think
He lives and breathes in you,—and still I see him
Before me here; I seem to speak to him—
My heart—! Oh, I am mad! Do what I will,
I cannot hide my passion.

HIPPOLYTUS   Yes, I see
What strange things love will do, for Theseus, dead,
Seems present to your eyes, and in your soul
A constant flame is burning.

PHAEDRA   Ah, for Theseus
I languish and I long, but not, indeed,
As the Shades have seen him, as the fickle lover
Of a thousand forms, the one who fain would ravish
The bride of Pluto;—but one faithful, proud,
Even to slight disdain,—the charm of youth
That draws all hearts, even as the gods are painted,—
Or as yourself. He had your eyes, your manner,—
He spoke like you, and he could blush like you,
And when he came across the waves to Crete,
My childhood home, worthy to win the love
Of Minos' daughters,—what were you doing then?
Why did my father gather all these men,
The flower of Greece, and leave Hippolytus?
Oh, why were you too young to have embarked
On board the ship that brought your father there?
The monster would have perished at your hands,
Despite the windings of his vast retreat.
My sister would have armed you with the clue
To guide your steps, doubtful within the maze.—
But no—for Phaedra would have come before her,
And love would first have given me the thought,
And I it would have been, whose timely aid
Had taught you all the labyrinthine ways!
The care that such a dear life would have cost me!
No thread could satisfy my lover's fears.
I would have wished to lead the way myself,
And share the peril you were sure to face.
Yes, Phaedra would have walked the maze with you,—
With you come out in safety, or have perished!

HIPPOLYTUS Gods! What is this I hear? Have you forgotten
 That Theseus is my father and your husband?
PHAEDRA Why should you fancy I have lost remembrance
 And that I am regardless of my honor?
HIPPOLYTUS Forgive me, madam! With a blush I own
 That I mistook your words, quite innocent.
 For very shame I cannot see you longer—
 Now I will go—
PHAEDRA Ah, prince, you understood me,—
 Too well, indeed! For I had said enough.
 You could not well mistake. But do not think
 That in those moments when I love you most
 I do not feel my guilt. No easy yielding
 Has helped the poison that infects my mind.
 The sorry object of divine revenge,
 I am not half so hateful to your sight
 As to myself. The gods will bear me witness,—
 They who have lit this fire within my veins,—
 The gods who take their barbarous delight
 In leading some poor mortal heart astray!
 Nay, do you not remember, in the past,
 How I was not content to fly?—I drove you
 Out of the land, so that I might appear
 Most odious—and to resist you better
 I tried to make you hate me—and in vain!
 You hated more, and I loved not the less,
 While your misfortunes lent you newer charms.
 I have been drowned in tears and scorched by fire!
 Your own eyes might convince you of the truth
 If you could look at me, but for a moment!
 What do I say? You think this vile confession
 That I have made, is what I meant to say?
 I did not dare betray my son. For him
 I feared,—and came to beg you not to hate him.
 This was the purpose of a heart too full
 Of love for you to speak of aught besides.
 Take your revenge, and punish me my passion!
 Prove yourself worthy of your valiant father,
 And rid the world of an offensive monster!
 Does Theseus' widow dare to love his son?
 Monster indeed! Nay, let her not escape you!
 Here is my heart! Here is the place to strike!
 It is most eager to absolve itself!
 It leaps impatiently to meet your blow!—
 Strike deep! Or if, indeed, you find it shameful
 To drench your hand in such polluted blood,—
 If that be punishment too mild for you,—
 Too easy for your hate,—if not your arm,
 Then lend your sword to me.—Come! Give it now!—

(END)

The Misanthrope
by *Molière*

Act IV, scene iii   *Translated from the French by Henri Van Laun*

Characters   Célimène, a flirtatious lady of society
Alceste, the misanthrope, in love with Célimène

Scene   At Paris, in Célimène's house.

Situation   Alceste is bitter in his opposition to the superficial and hypocritical society of Paris; yet he loves Célimène, a clever and scheming lady of that very society. They meet in both love-play and conflict.

ALCESTE *(Aside)*   Grant, Heaven, that I may control my temper.

CÉLIMÈNE *(Aside)*   Ah! [*To* Alceste] What is all this trouble that I see you in, and what means those long-drawn sighs, and those black looks which you cast at me?

ALCESTE   That all the wickedness of which a heart is capable is not to be compared to your perfidy; that neither fate, hell, nor Heaven in its wrath, ever produced anything so wicked as you are.

CÉLIMÈNE   These are certainly pretty compliments, which I admire very much.

ALCESTE   Do not jest. This is no time for laughing. Blush rather, you have cause to do so; and I have undeniable proofs of your treachery. This is what the agitations of my mind prognosticated; it was not without cause that my love took alarm; by these frequent suspicions, which were hateful to you, I was trying to discover the misfortune which my eyes have beheld; and in spite of all your care and your skill in dissembling, my star foretold me what I had to fear. But do not imagine that I will bear unavenged this slight of being insulted. I know that we have no command over our inclinations, that love will everywhere spring up spontaneously, that there is no entering a heart by force, and that every soul is free to name its conqueror: I should thus have no reason to complain if you had spoken to me without dissembling, and rejected my advances from the very beginning; my heart would then have been justified in blaming fortune alone. But to see my love encouraged by a deceitful avowal on your part, is an action so treacherous and perfidious, that it cannot meet with too great a punishment; and I can allow my resentment to do anything. Yes, yes; after such an outrage, fear everything; I am no longer myself, I am mad with rage. My senses, struck by the deadly blow with which you kill me, are no longer governed by reason; I give way to the outbursts of a just wrath, and am no longer responsible for what I may do.

CÉLIMÈNE   Whence comes, I pray, such a passion? Speak! Have you lost your senses?

ALCESTE   Yes, yes, I lost them when, to my misfortune, I beheld you and thus took the poison which kills me, and when I thought to meet with some sincerity in those treacherous charms that bewitched me.

CÉLIMÈNE   Of what treachery have you to complain?

ALCESTE   Ah! how double-faced she is! how well she knows how to dissemble! But I am fully prepared with the means of driving her to extremities. Cast your eyes here and recognize your writing. This picked-up note is sufficient to confound you, and such proof cannot easily be refuted.

CÉLIMÈNE   And this is the cause of your perturbation of spirits?

ALCESTE   You do not blush on beholding this writing!

CÉLIMÈNE   And why should I blush?

ALCESTE   What! You add boldness to craft! Will you disown this note because it bears no name?

CÉLIMÈNE   Why should I disown it, since I wrote it.

ALCESTE   And you can look at it without becoming confused at the crime of which its style accuses you!

CÉLIMÈNE   You are, in truth, a very eccentric man.

ALCESTE   What! you thus out-brave this convincing proof! And the contents so full of tenderness for Oronte, need have nothing in them to outrage me, or to shame you?

CÉLIMÈNE   Oronte! Who told you that this letter is for him?

ALCESTE   The people who put it into my hands this day. But I will even suppose that it is for some one else. Has my heart any less cause to complain of yours? Will you, in fact, be less guilty towards me?

CÉLIMÈNE   But if it is a woman to whom this letter is addressed, how can it hurt you, or what is there culpable in it?

ALCESTE   Hem! The prevarication is ingenious, and the excuse excellent. I must own that I did not expect this turn; and nothing but that was wanting to convince me. Do you dare to have recourse to such palpable tricks? Do you think people entirely destitute of common sense? Come, let us see a little by what subterfuge, with what air, you will support so palpable a falsehood; and how you can apply to a woman every word of this note which evinces so much tenderness! Reconcile, if you can, to hide your deceit, what I am about to read. . . .

CÉLIMÈNE   It does not suit me to do so. I think it ridiculous that you should take so much upon yourself, and tell me to my face what you have the daring to say to me!

ALCESTE   No, no, without flying into a rage, take a little trouble to explain these terms.

CÉLIMÈNE   No, I shall do nothing of the kind, and it matters very little to me what you think upon the subject.

ALCESTE   I pray you, show me, and I shall be satisfied, if this letter can be explained as meant for a woman.

CÉLIMÈNE   Not at all. It is for Oronte; and I will have you believe it. I accept all his attentions gladly; I admire what he says, I like him, and I shall agree to whatever you please. Do as you like, and act as you think proper; let nothing hinder you and do not harass me any longer.

ALCESTE   *(Aside)*   Heavens! can anything more cruel be conceived, and was ever heart treated like mine? What! I am justly angry with her, I come to complain, and I am quarreled with instead! My grief and my suspicions are excited to the utmost, I am allowed to believe everything, she boasts of everything; and yet, my heart is still sufficiently mean not to be able to break the bonds that hold it fast, and not to arm itself with a generous contempt for the ungrateful object of which it is too much enamored. (*To* Célimène) Perfidious woman, you know well how to take advantage of my great weakness, and to employ for your own purpose that excessive, astonishing, and fatal love which your treacherous looks have inspired! Defend yourself at least from this crime that overwhelms me, and stop pretending to be guilty. Show me, if you can, that this letter is innocent; my affection will even consent to assist you. At any rate, endeavor to appear faithful, and I shall strive to believe you such.

CÉLIMÈNE   Bah, you are mad with your jealous frenzies, and do not deserve the love which I have for you. I should much like to know what could compel me to stoop for you to the baseness of dissembling; and why, if my heart were disposed towards another, I should not say so candidly. What! does the kind assurance of my sentiments towards you not defend me sufficiently against all your suspicions? Ought they to possess any weight at all with such a guarantee? Is it not insulting me even to listen to them? And since it is with the utmost difficulty that we can resolve to confess our love, since the strict honor of our sex, hostile to our passion, strongly opposes such a confession, ought a lover who sees such an obstacle overcome for his sake, doubt with impunity our avowal? And is he not greatly to blame in not assuring himself of the truth of that which is never said but after a severe struggle with oneself? Begone, such suspicions deserve my anger, and you are not worthy of being cared for. I am silly, and am vexed at my own simplicity in still preserving the least kindness for you. I ought to place my affections elsewhere, and give you a just cause for complaint.

ALCESTE   Ah! you traitress! mine is a strange infatuation for you; those tender expressions are, no doubt, meant only to deceive me. But it matters little, I must submit to my fate; my very soul is wrapt up in you; I will see to the bitter end how your heart will act towards me, and whether it will be black enough to deceive me.

CÉLIMÈNE   No, you do not love me as you ought to love.

ALCESTE   Indeed! Nothing is to be compared to my exceeding love; and, in its eagerness to show itself to the whole world, it goes even so far as to form wishes against you. Yes, I could wish that no one thought you handsome, that you were reduced to a miserable existence; that Heaven, at your birth, had bestowed upon you nothing; that you had no rank, no nobility, no wealth, so that I might openly proffer my heart, and thus make amends to you for the injustice of such a lot; and that, this very day, I might have the joy and the glory of seeing you owe everything to my love.

CÉLIMÈNE   This is wishing me well in a strange way! Heaven grant that you may never have occasion . . . But here comes Monsieur Dubois curiously decked out.

(*END*)

Restoration Comedy 15

Vitality

Our Galleries too, were finely us'd of late,
Where roosting Masques sat cackling for
    a Mate;
They came not to see Plays but act
    their own,
And had throng'd Audiences when we
    had none.
Our Plays it was impossible to hear,
Confound you, give your bawdy prating
    o're,
Or Zounds, I'le fling you'i' the Pit, you
    bawling Whore.
       Crowne   Epilogue to *Sir Courtly Nice*

Leaning over other ladies awhile to
whisper with the King, she rose out of the
box and went into the King's right hand,
between the King and the Duke of York;
which . . . put the King himself, as well
as every body else out of countenance. . . .
She did it only to show the world that
she is not out of favour yet, as was
believed.

       Samuel Pepys   *Diary*

Crowne's view of the boisterous and unruly theatre audiences of Restoration England typifies the excitement and vitality that characterized the revival of dramatic activity and the reopening of the theatres after their closing by the Puritans and Commonwealth government between 1642 and 1660. The accession to the throne of Charles II brought a fun-loving, woman-loving, theatre-loving king to power. Dramatic activity flourished again. As Pepys notes, the king was a frequent visitor to London theatres. He and his entourage played many of the same flirtatious games in the royal box as did the aristocratic populace in the galleries and pit. Elegant dandies and fops (effeminate males) sat upon the stage itself to exhibit their clothing and other fineries.

Restoration drama was noteworthy primarily for its comedies, although authors such as John Dryden, Thomas Otway, and others produced some interesting serious plays categorized Heroic Tragedy. Dryden's *The Conquest of Granada* was a notable example, although his tragedy about Antony and Cleopatra, *All for Love,* has proved more stageworthy. Excessively bombastic and written in rhymed heroic couplets, the tragedies are rarely if ever produced in the contemporary theatre. Were they to be produced, directors and actors could well utilize the acting style employed in seventeenth-century French Neoclassic tragedy.

Overview of Restoration Comedy

There are many similarities between theatre development in England and in France during the seventeenth and eighteenth centuries. Although the English Commonwealth under Cromwell suppressed plays and players from 1642 to 1660, theatre activity was not completely destroyed. Bandit actors and theatre managers provided a limited public with live "underground" entertainment. When Charles II was restored to the monarchy in 1660, the granting of theatre monopolies to William D'Avenant (Duke's Men) and Thomas Killigrew (King's Men) ensured competent management of plays, playwrights, actors, and theatres. Audiences attending the Restoration theatres (approximately 1660 to 1710) were predominately the aristocracy who demanded heroics in their tragedies and imitation of their own manners in their comedies.

Theatre structures in England were similar in style to the French theatres. Theatres were arranged in a semicircle ending in a gallery about midway in the auditorium. Most buildings provided a second gallery and a sloping pit with rows of seats arranged in a semicircle. The deep apron was backed by a raked stage whose depth from the front of the apron to the back wall was slightly less than half the total length of the building. The second Drury Lane theatre had two proscenium doors, one on either side of the apron with a box above each door (musicians usually sat in one of the boxes and spectators sat in the other box). In 1696, the apron was shortened by four feet and the downstage proscenium doors were converted into boxes. Additional benches were installed in the pit.

A feature of the French theatres not duplicated was the characteristic manner of moving scenery and producing scenic effect. On the Continent, scenery was moved by a pole-and-chariot system; in England a wing-and-backdrop system of sliding scenery was used. Grooves were inserted in the stage floor to receive the wing flats and shutters which formed the set. They were spaced to allow room between each set of scenes for placing furniture and assembling actors in a tableau. Sometimes scenes were cut out and set one behind the other to provide vistas and give the illusion of depth. Actors entered and exited through the proscenium doors. There was no act curtain; a front curtain was lowered and raised to begin and end the play. The audience never waited between scenes. The action was continuous due to the streamlined execution of scenery and the inclusion of songs and musical interludes between scenes.

Scenic demands for tragedies and comedies in seventeenth-century England were more elaborate than in France. Scenes were usually painted in perspective on wings, borders, and backdrops. However, the Neoclassic demand for universality was satisfied by the generality of the localized settings. As in France, few realistic set designs were needed for plays. The first move toward scenic realism came late in the eighteenth century (1771) when the scenic artist Phillip James De Loutherbourg was employed by the actor-manager David Garrick. Following the trend toward naturalism, Garrick removed all spectators from the stage (Voltaire accomplished the same thing in France).

The Restoration stage was generally poorly lit. Hooplike chandeliers obstructed the vision of the audience in the gallery seats. Oil lamps and candles were also used, and illumination was hazy. Later in the eighteenth century Garrick removed the chandeliers from the front of the proscenium

Scene from *The Country Wife* by William Wycherley. Directed by Roland L. Reed. Designed by Frank Mohler. Costumes by Erica Wertenberger. University of South Carolina.

and placed them in the upstage area, out of sight of the audience, which thus was given a clear view of the stage. Garrick was also able to illuminate the backstage area to heighten dramatic effects. In addition, he placed light behind the wings on a level with the actors, introduced lanterns and wall brackets as integral parts of the set, provided greater use of oil lamps, and used colored transparent silks to produce lighting effects in color.

Restoration comedy, or comedy of manners, was preeminent on the English stage from 1660 to approximately 1710. The English aristocracy were enthralled with the accurate imitation of their customs and manners mirrored on the stage. Restoration actors and actresses captured their audience with a flamboyant display of witty, bluntly sexual dialogue, boudoir intrigues, sensual innuendos, and rakish behavior. A narrow set of conventions entirely dominated Restoration comedy: constancy in love, especially in marriage, was a bore; sex should be tempting; love thrived on variety; genuine sexual feelings (e.g., sentimentalism) had no place on the stage. In play after play, characters clashed with other characters in situations selected to produce love entanglements and intrigues. Dorimant, a character in Etherege's *The Man of Mode,* summarized the Restoration philosophy: "Next to coming to a good understanding with a new mistress, I love a quarrel with an old one."

Country life was considered boring. The clergy and professional men were treated with indifference or condescension. The most popular Restoration playwrights of the comedy of manners were William Wycherley, George Etherege, William Congreve, Thomas Shadwell, and John Vanbrugh. These and many other comic authors proved once again that man was corruptible. The humor was in the satiric treatment of people who allowed themselves to be deceived or attempted to deceive others. Laughter was directed against the fop, the pretender at wit and sophistication, the old trying to be young, and the old man with a young and beautiful wife. For the most part, any standard of moral behavior was acceptable, but rewards and punishments were clearly meted out in accordance with the ability to achieve self-knowledge.

Prologues and epilogues were especially important in plays throughout the Restoration and well into the eighteenth century. Playwrights and actors-comedians continued the ancient stage tradition of introducing and concluding plays with special pieces, usually poetic, performed in a coarse, boisterous, hilarious manner.

The prevailing costume style was the contemporary dress of the late seventeenth and early eighteenth centuries. Every conceivable part of the human body was adorned. The actor wore a large-brimmed, plumed hat, a heavy periwig with curls over his forehead and down to his shoulders, a square-cut coat and a waistcoat hanging to the knees, wide, stiff cuffs and ruffles reaching to the knuckles, and ribbons on every available unmarked surface. The actress wore a gown with bell-shaped skirt and sleeves. A high mantilla and veil covered her head. Women were allowed to show their face, hands, and neck (and, of course, much of their bosom) when indoors.

However, when appearing outside, ladies wore large hooded cloaks. As the years passed, men's tights revealed more muscular contour of the legs. Women's dresses became more clinging and revealed more of the female body. Sumptuous costumes were worn by heroes and heroines. Eye patches were seen regularly. Both sexes wore excessive makeup, false noses, beards, mustaches, powder, rouge, pencil, lipstick, and beauty patches. Obviously, little attempt was made at facial expression; to do so meant risking a cracked face.

Voice

In Restoration comedy the focus was unquestionably on brilliant, brittle, witty language, usually in prose. The style of Restoration acting was characterized by harmonious fusion of heightened oratory and rapid repartee. Vocal tone was important to denote emotional quality. For example, a gay, soft, charming voice immediately denoted love to an audience; a sharp, sullen, severe voice denoted hate or anger; a full, flowing, brisk voice denoted joy. English actors deliberately imitated the Parisian aristocratic style of address with its rich heritage from Molière. Phrasing and precise pronunciation were anglicized and became the fashionable language of British upper society and aristocracy. Training in British schools included singing, dancing, posture, gesture, walking, and all the arts of deportment. Because of the spectators on the stage and the inadequate lighting, actors learned to use the downstage center portion of the apron area with proficiency and aplomb. Intricate vocal pauses and timing were developed. Vocal tempo was usually rapid. Articulation, pronunciation, and projection were clear and precise. Vocal asides and soliloquies (particularly in the prologues and epilogues) took on new dimension with the heightened presentational intimacy between performer and audience. Vocal inflection and variety were uniquely expansive. Vocal quality was totally contrived, that is, it was artificial. Decorous language was the heart of the acting style. In present-day theatre, Restoration comedy is every bit as challenging as the drama of ancient Greece and of Shakespeare, Racine, and Molière—at least in the vital structure of its language.

Exercise 1   Voice—Restoration Comedy

Practice the following verses individually and then collectively stressing a variety of vocal tones. Repeat the exercise stressing precise phrasing, clear articulation, pronunciation, and projection. Repeat the exercise stressing pauses, timing, and rapid tempo. Finally, repeat the exercise stressing expansive vocal inflection and variety.

King Charles, and who'll do him right now?
King Charles, and who's ripe for fight now?
Give a rouse: here's, in hell's despite now,
King Charles!

Who gave me the goods that went since?
Who raised me the house that sank once?
Who helped me to gold I spent since?
Who found me in wine you drank once?

    King Charles, and who'll do him right now?
    King Charles, and who's ripe for fight now?
    Give me a rouse: here's, in hell's despite now,
    King Charles!

To whom used by boy George quaff else,
By the old fool's side that begot him?
For whom did he cheer and laugh else,
While Noll's damned troopers shot him.

    King Charles, and who'll do him right now?
    King Charles, and who's ripe for fight now?
    Give me a rouse: here's, in hell's despite now,
    King Charles!

                  Anonymous English tune

Movement

As originally staged, Restoration comedies were almost entirely presentational. Major movement was concerned with entering through the proscenium doors and exiting through the doors later. Most of the action took place downstage center on the apron. When adapting Restoration comedy to the modern stage, you and your director should not confine your action exclusively to the apron. You should probably utilize the area behind the proscenium arch in addition to the forestage. Movement in Restoration comedy should be characterized by highly elevated, graceful patterns. All physical activity should be precise and inventive. A wide range of uniquely conventional gestures must be employed. For example, in the Restoration theatre an actor would point to his head to indicate reason and to his heart to indicate love or passion, raise his eyes or hands upward when evoking the gods, or extend his arms forward, palms out, to indicate horror or surprise. An elaborate system of facial grimacing, winking, and smiling was used both for humor and for intimate communication to the audience.

The *fop* was a very fashionable character and the butt of much sarcastic humor. Actors playing fops minced, strutted, and performed myriad flourishing hand and facial gestures. Outlandish posturing and posing were employed in a static presentational position. Actresses flirted continually over and behind fans, half-masks, and handkerchiefs.

Bows and curtsies in the seventeenth-century French manner were used throughout a play and were directed to other characters as well as to the audience. When one character passed another, they frequently performed the *en passant* which was a slight bow from the waist with one foot sweeping in an arc around the other foot without losing the pace of the walk.

Taking snuff, a very popular social custom enjoyed by both men and women of society, was frequently performed on the stage.

Taking snuff

A gentlemen always kissed a lady's hand when leaving her. Men always held their hands high and away from their body to emphasize their lace cuffs, handkerchiefs, and ornate walking sticks and canes. This was done in a masculine and virile manner, except by fops. Men also swaggered elegantly in high-heeled shoes and relished their expansive movement. While controlled, these movements were vital and zestful. The women balanced enormous and outlandish hats upon their head. Most women carried a muff which was used not only for warming the hands, but also as a place to hide objects such as love letters. The women walked in slightly curved, graceful patterns, their dresses held slightly off the floor in a delicate manner.

In modern adaptation of Restoration comedy, more extensive use of pantomimic dramatization is necessary than in the original plays. For example, more furniture is used. Use of the sitting position is fairly common although women find it difficult to manage because of the size of the long, full skirts. Similarly, hand properties are used more frequently today. Drinking tea is a common example of this kind of activity. Movement in Restoration comedy is perhaps the most decorous and theatricalized of any stage movement in the history of theatre and reflects an affected, artificial manner almost without modern parallel. The possible exception is the exaggerated, satirical presentation of cocktail parties and events of so-called high society (e.g., recall the Ascot racetrack scene from *My Fair Lady*).

Exercise 2   Movement—Restoration Comedy

1. Review and practice Exercise 5, chapter 14.
2. Organize and perform a group improvisation called "The President's Cocktail Party." Pantomime all activity in a highly exaggerated manner. Improvise dialogue and movement and overdo every action in

an extremely decorous but theatrical way. An actor and an actress should be designated host and hostess, while everyone else arrives and participates. The improvisation ends when the president of the United States departs.

3. Repeat Exercise 2 above in the manner of a Restoration high-society party. Employ all available Restoration properties and costumes or facsimiles. The improvisation ends with the departure of King Charles II.

Character and Emotion

Characters in Restoration comedy were notoriously one-dimensional, frequently caricatured by the implication in their name such as Snake, Lady Wishfort, Sir Fopling Flutter, Fainall, Lady Loveit, Sullen, Aimwell, Pinchwife, Manly, Horner, Lady Brute, Lady Fanciful, and so on. Characters were usually obsessed by a single emotional drive such as seduction, deception, gossip, greed, lust, and so on. A major distinction between characterization in Restoration comedy and French Neoclassic comedy is the actor's sense of involvement with a character. Whereas serious involvement is necessary for playing most of the major roles in Molière, in Restoration comedy performance will probably be more successful if a certain level of detached objectivity is retained. Even with personalization and subtextual role analysis, it is difficult to become involved with Restoration characters because of their lack of depth and subservience to plot situation and because of the mechanistic language. This is somewhat less true of the more intelligent Restoration characters such as Millamant and Mirabell in Congreve's *The Way of the World*. The question arises, How far do you take the sense of detachment or objectivity? Is everything an artificial mockery or put on? Actually, a highly affected, theatricalized performance which appears to be a kind of comment on itself can be very effective in staging Restoration comedy. However, a more discerning director or actor probably will not carry the detachment to that extent. In other words, the advice given for playing Molière's major characters may again be the best advice. Take your character and his emotional obsession or foible seriously enough for genuine human portrayal. Retain enough detachment to execute the role using the various stylistic mannerisms necessary to engage comic response. Characters were not defined realistically, but created according to conventional decorum. Despite this, Restoration comic characters do possess an element of believability and natural emotion. However, more often than not, characters built on principles, as they tend to be in Restoration comedy, rarely create a true illusion of reality. Audiences enjoy the dramatic vitality of extremely witty characters and laugh at the foolishness of those who would be witty but are not.

Although the aristocratic manners of the time were "realistically" portrayed on the Restoration stage, it is a mistake to interpret late seventeenth-century *realism* as the word is defined today. In other words, what was represented on the Restoration stage was a slight exaggeration of what happened in life (albeit in a small section of society). The wit, repartee, precision of language, and elegance of manners were realistic *in terms* of appearance before the Restoration audience. Bawdy, sensual situations were not new to English drama. The only innovative ingredient was the realism of sensuality given by the appearance of women onstage. The inclusion of women allowed the dramatist greater freedom to develop situations which had heretofore been denied him. Sex play was a favorite aristocratic pastime. The female was displayed onstage for provocation (e.g., witness the many examples in Restoration plays of partial exposure of a female bosom or of a girl wearing breeches disguised as a boy). These sexual conventions simply mirrored the practices of society. Frequently, court ladies dressed as boys in order to arrange a rendezvous with a lover. (Sexual flirtation was pursued just as vigorously in the auditorium among the spectators as onstage!)

Exercise 3   Character and Emotion—Restoration Comedy

Select a Restoration character from the list that follows and determine a singular emotional obsession appropriate to the implication in the name. Perform an improvised soliloquy in the manner of a Restoration prologue or epilogue in which you explain and pantomimically dramatize your emotional obsession, what you want, and how you are going to get it.

Sullen	Lord Plausible
Snake	Witwood
Lady Wishfort	Petulant
Scandal	Waitwell
Tattle	Foible
Mrs. Frail	Constant
Lady Pliant	Heartfree
Lady Fidget	Lady Fanciful
Mrs. Squeamish	Sir Novelty Fashion
Sparkish	Mr. Smirk
Pinchwife	Loveless
Horner	Sir Clumsey
Manly	Bull

Transition—Eighteenth-Century Sentimentalism and Nineteenth-Century Romanticism and Melodrama

The turn of the century (specifically, by 1710) saw the ushering in of sentimental treatment for both serious and comic material. By the beginning of the eighteenth century the number of people attending the theatre had increased (the population of Britain increased from six million in 1650 to ten million in 1800), and included many middle-class patrons. During the reign of Queen Anne (1702–1714) standards of decorum were higher. As interest in the court's activities lessened, middle-class self-awareness grew. No longer were theatre audiences predominately aristocratic. The purpose of sentimental drama was to show the middle classes the disparity between the real world and the ideal world. The sentimentalists believed that it was a part of Christian morality to see oneself as a moral paragon whose behavior was in many respects Christlike. Playwrights stressed the rewards of virtue and need for gentility. Great emphasis was placed on arousing sympathetic response to the misfortunes of others, and it was considered healthy to display emotion and to test one's virtues.

Scene from *The School for Scandal* by Sir Richard Sheridan. Directed by Al Muller. Designed by Rex Heuschkel. Costumes by Barbara Barretta. San Joaquin Delta College, Stockton, Calif.

Opposition to the Restoration high comedy of manners came first from the playwright Colley Cibber in his play *Love's Last Shift* (1696). Shortly thereafter, other playwrights adopted the sentimental theme. Although George Farquhar is considered a Restoration author, his plays *The Recruiting Officer* and *The Beaux' Stratagem* delineated high moral standards for the middle class. Sir Richard Steele's *The Conscious Lovers* aroused kindly laughter and tears, as did Richard Cumberland's *The West Indian*. Sir Richard Sheridan's *The Rivals* and *The School for Scandal* pointed out the distinction between true virtue and pious remarks and satirized human shortsightedness and frailty. In Oliver Goldsmith's *She Stoops to Conquer* deviations from morality were punished and traditional Christian values were upheld. George Lillo in *George Barnwell: The London Merchant* exalted the merchant class and presented a central character who was weak and pathetic and thus established the first bourgeois tragedy.[1]

New comic forms provided alternate entertainment during the eighteenth century: for example, the ballad opera, exemplified by John Gay in *The Beggar's Opera* in 1728. John Rich created pantomimes in which dancing and silent mimicry were performed to musical accompaniment. Burlesque was written by Henry Fielding (*Tom Thumb*). These forms of theatre entertainment required detailed scenery and special effects. They were highly popular with the middle classes and much admired for their dance and music.

The prologue acting piece reached its height of popularity in David Garrick. The epilogue was more strategically important than the prologue. It literally "saved" the play. The epilogue was usually assigned to an actress; the prologue, to an actor. Both pieces were accompanied by stage business, by noisy encounters of actors at the stage doors, and by a plea to judge the play by emotion and not by reason.

During the middle and late eighteenth century, periodic attempts at acting reform toward a more natural or lifelike style were made. A number of individual actors began to revolt against the traditions and conventions of acting styles. This emphasis on the individual artist coincided with other theatre developments. Newly constructed theatres such as the Haymarket used a smaller apron—a feature which in the earlier years of the Drury Lane, Covent Garden, and other theatres had severely limited the actors' freedom of movement. With Garrick's reforms in lighting, actors were moving away from the apron and behind the proscenium. Realistic details were more vivid in the upstage areas against a more naturalistic painted backdrop. When the spectators were finally removed from the stage, actors could give their characters a more realistic base, and thereby could pay more attention to the play than to the audience. Eighteenth-century dramatists began to write about middle-class characters who were undergoing personality change. Granted, the writing was strictly sentimental and stressed the rewards of virtuous behavior. The character traits, however, were grounded in reality. Unfortunately, playwrights detracted from realistic detail by emphasizing disguises, surprises, and generally superficial characters.

Except for the modifications just mentioned, throughout the eighteenth century emphasis was on rant or cadence in theatrical speech. Rant produces declamatory monotone. In a declamatory style, the actor runs on with little regard for accent or emphasis. Passion is revealed by turgid vocalization or effeminate whine.

Actors studied ancient orations, moral philosophy, and paintings of the period to learn manners and to delineate passion. The study of passion

1. It should be noted that Sheridan and Goldsmith attempted to break with sentimentalism and create brittle comedy in the Restoration style, but were only partly successful. Nonetheless, as examples of eighteenth-century comedy (sometimes called *baroque* or ornate) in the Restoration *tradition*, their work ranks high.

was highly scientific and systematized. Accompanying gestures were copied from prints and paintings; for example, the hands were never raised about the head unless for some extraordinary occasion, and a woman had to veil her face when expressing grief. As late as 1744, acting style was entrenched in exaggerated characterization, cadence, rant, and traditional convention.

However, in 1750, a change in theatrical speech somewhat supplanted cadence with natural speaking, and actors began creating specific characters. There was little sense of historical accuracy, but costumes were no longer based strictly on current fashion. Perhaps the most famous actor to discard contemporary dress was Charles Macklin who made history by wearing historically accurate costumes in his portrayal of Macbeth. Thereafter, most actors leaned toward realistic propriety in costuming.

In the Western world the nineteenth century was largely a century of revolution and turmoil. After a century of nature and reason, the nineteenth century, often called the Romantic Age, was an emotional, passionate time. The term *romance* implies emotional attractions, affairs of the heart, religious ideals, freedom, and strong emphasis on the needs of both the masses and the individual. This was the time of Napoleon and the French Revolution, a time in which the aristocracy was challenged by the middle and lower classes. It was as well a century of scientific innovation leading to the Industrial Revolution, to the evolutionary theories of Charles Darwin, and to the psychological insights of Sigmund Freud. In England, it was the era of the great Romantic poets such as Wordsworth, Coleridge, Byron, Shelley, and Keats; in Germany, of the poets and dramatists Johann von Goethe and Friedrich Schiller; in France, of the Romantic poet, novelist, and dramatist Victor Hugo.

Romanticism encouraged men to explore the unreal world of fantasy in juxtaposition to the world of natural phenomena. Men believed in religious transcendentalism, or the affinity of man and spirit and of man and nature. The Romantics believed in the autonomy of inspired genius, the necessity of releasing the imagination, the spontaneity of intuitive feeling, the freedom of artistic expression, and a vision of nature as part of a unified cosmos. Romantic idealism culminated in the notion of organic growth and development arising from an interest in the past, particularly in the Middle Ages. In Germany the Romantic movement was called *Sturm und Drang,* or Storm and Stress. Goethe wrote both Romantic and Neoclassic plays such as *Faustus* and *Iphigenia at Tauris.* Schiller wrote *William Tell* in the Romantic vein. Goethe is considered one of the precursors of what is now called the director in the theatre. In his theatre at Weimar Goethe succeeded in classifying many acting techniques.

The German playwright and critic Gotthold Lessing provided the foremost dramatic criticism of the period in his document *The Hamburg Dramaturgy.* Lessing attempted to modify the Romantic movement by advocating a return to Classicism. He examined Aristotle's *Poetics,* evaluated Shakespeare, and wrote a famous treatise on classic dramatic theory and criticism, *Laokoon.*

Movement Toward Realism

During the eighteenth and nineteenth centuries, acting style in German theatre continued to move toward naturalness. Actors became interested in techniques of role creation and in disciplined vocal and emotional work. Acting style was moving closer to Realism (discussed in chapter 16). Part of the transition toward Realism was accomplished by changes in the content and structure of plays. August von Kotzbue wrote the first melodramas, which were a combination of music and drama in the form of a three-act play accompanied by a musical score.

Finally, in mid-nineteenth century, theatre in Germany reached a new level of supremacy with the achievements of Richard Wagner and the Duke of Saxe-Meiningen. Wagner advocated either nonillusionary theatre or theatre devoted to dramatizing the ideal world. Conversely, Saxe-Meiningen aimed at producing lifelike pictorial illusions. Both of these men were among the first great directors. Saxe-Meiningen was instrumental in unifying theatrical production by using realistic costumes and sets and effective ensemble playing.

In France, Voltaire and Pierre de Marivaux led the way in theatre reform away from Neoclassicism toward Romanticism and ultimately to Realism. Late in the nineteenth century it was Denis Diderot, French encyclopedist, who above all argued against the limitations of Neoclassic drama. Diderot advocated reform in staging, in plays, and in acting and was instrumental in introducing the concept of the "fourth wall" in which the stage picture was filled with realistic detail and the audience peeked through an imaginary fourth wall to observe the action. His famous document *The Paradox of the Actor* was revolutionary in articulating a philosophy of acting based on minimizing the actor's emotional involvement. Diderot believed that the actor should feel nothing himself, but rather render the external signs of emotion in such a way as to convince the audience of the reality of the illusion (hence, the *paradox*)—an audience that is convinced it is seeing real emotion or feeling when in fact it is only the truthful *appearance* of reality. In an age when the acting style was still highly presentational and declamatory, Diderot's total insistence upon representational style brought adamant opposition from many critics and audiences. Diderot emphasized natural speech and pauses for thought and stressed use of lifelike gestures, pantomime, silence, and emotion. Diderot argued the revolutionary idea of conscious identification by the actor with his character through the use of imagination and impersonation. While little heed was paid at the time, Diderot's theories on acting were preparation for the turn-of-the-century movement toward realistic and naturalistic styles of acting.

Rene Pixérécourt did for melodrama in France what Kotzbue had done for melodrama in Germany (a melodrama is a serious play in which good and evil are clearly separated, characters are simple, action is full of suspense, a double ending rewards virtue and punishes evil, and plot and characterization are frequently reinforced by music and melody). Pixérécourt's melodramas paved the way for the rise of Romantic drama in France. In addition to Victor Hugo, Alexandre Dumas (père) and Alfred de Musset also wrote important Romantic plays. French Romanticism was ultimately modified toward Realism by the end of the nineteenth century. Great French actresses and actors contributed to the development of realistic acting during that century. Leaders of the group included Michel Baron, Adrienne Lecouvreur, Mlle. Clairon, and Françoise Talma. Françoise Delsarte also contributed to acting style by espousing a scientific system of gestures and vocal mechanics. The great actor Constant Coquelin exemplified this rigidly technical style of acting.

Eugène Scribe and Victorien Sardou contributed to the development of Realism (see chapter 16) in France by writing realistic plays which were tightly structured, or well made. The great playwright of early Realism, Henrik Ibsen, was greatly influenced by these plays.

Similarly in England the Romantic movement advanced toward realism. W. M. Macready, Charles Kean, and other actors were leaders in the development of increasingly realistic acting in the nineteenth century. They also introduced reforms in costuming, along with J. R. Planché, Madame Vestris, and C. J. Mathews. Madame Vestris also introduced the first realistic *box set* in England. The great English actors during these times included John Kemble, Mrs. Siddons, Edmund Kean, and Henry Irving.

Across the Atlantic Ocean, the new United States imitated English drama, but produced some excellent actors and men of the theatre such as Edwin Forrest, members of the Booth family (Edwin, Junius Brutus, and John Wilkes), and Augustin Daly.

Acting in Romantic Plays and Melodramas

Nineteenth-century Romantic plays and melodramas are rarely performed in the theatre today. In present-day presentation of a Romantic drama, the style of acting should emphasize intense emotional expression; rhythmic, melodic, poetic vocal delivery in a highly elevated manner; and sweeping, flowing movements and gestures. Center stage should be used predominately, and the focus should be on the presentational mode. The overall impression of style should be an elevated version of the Elizabethan acting style.

If you are cast in a nineteenth-century melodrama (not to be mistaken for the kidded or mocked comic melodramas of cabaret theatre), your style of acting should employ the tenets of Realism described in chapter 16—in other words, lifelike character creation, predominately representational mode (except for asides), detailed pantomimic business, and natural speech and movement.

What is known as the beginning of modern drama and modern styles of acting was initiated in the late nineteenth and early twentieth centuries. The foundation of all current acting styles commences with a study of Realism and Naturalism.

Scene from *Love for Love*
by William Congreve.
Directed by Peter Arnott.
Costumes by Pat Craw—
ford. The University
of Iowa.

Suggested Characters and Plays for Scene Work

Congreve, William

Millamant, Mirabell, Fainall, Mrs. Marwood
    The Way of the World
Valentine, Miss Prue, Sir Sampson Legend, Ben, Angelica
    Love for Love

Etherege, George

Dorimant, Bellinda, Lady Loveit, Sir Fopling Flutter
    The Man of Mode

Dryden, John

Antony, Cleopatra
  All for Love

Farquhar, George

Airwell, Archer, Bonniface, Cherry, Lady Bountiful, Dorinda, Sullen
  The Beaux' Stratagem

Wycherley, William

Marjorie Pinchwife, Horner
  The Country Wife
Manly, Olivia, Freeman, Widow Blackacre
  The Plain Dealer

Vanbrugh, John

Sir John Brute, Lady Brute, Lady Fanciful
  The Provok'd Wife

Gay, John

Macheath, Polly Peachum, Lucy Lockit
  The Beggar's Opera

Goldsmith, Oliver

Kate Hardcastle, Marlowe, Tony Lumpkin
  She Stoops to Conquer

Sheridan, Sir Richard

Sir Peter Teazle, Lady Teazle, Joseph Surface, Charles Surface, Maria, Lady Sneerwell
  The School for Scandal

Mrs. Malaprop, Lydia Languish, Captain Jack Absolute
  The Rivals

Additional Suggested Characters and Plays for Scene Work

Goethe, Johann Wolfgang von

Goetz, Bishop of Bamberg
  Goetz von Berlichingen
Doctor Faust, Mephistopheles, Margaret
  Faust Part I

Schiller, Friedrich

Mary Queen of Scots, Queen Elizabeth
  Mary Stuart
William Tell, Gessler
  William Tell

Hugo, Victor

Hernani, Dona Sol
  Hernani

Dumas (fils), Alexander

Marguerite Gautier, Armand Duval
  Camille

Rostand, Edmund

Cyrano de Bergerac, Roxanne, Christian
　　Cyrano de Bergerac

de Musset, Alfred

Camille, Perdican, Rosette
　　No Trifling with Love

Sardou, Victorien

Cyprienne, Des Prunelles, Adhemar
　　Let's Get a Divorce

Buchner, Georg

Danton, Robespierre
　　Danton's Death

Kotzebue, August

The Stranger
　　The Stranger

Actor Checklist　　*Restoration Comedy*

Voice	Exaggerated inflection; rapid but clear; smooth and polished line delivery; precise diction; clear articulation and projection.
Movement	Elevated; exaggerated; elegant when appropriate; controlled; well-executed use of bows, curtsies, and asides; predominately presentational; generally rapid tempo; highly artificial.
Gestures	Hand, head, facial dominate; clear; elevated; exaggerated, especially for fops.
Pantomimic Dramatization	Clear; inventive; selective; extensive and elaborate use of period props and costumes: female headgear, fans, staffs, handkerchiefs, half-masks, snuff, jewelry, makeup, and so on.
Character	Usually one-dimensional; extra dimension usually comes from intelligence and not from emotion; rooted in social mores, conduct, and foibles; representative social facet clear; actor involvement usually detached or objective.
Emotion	Usually single obsession; clear; nonsentimental; scheming and cynical.
Ideas	Clear; satiric; witty; cynical.
Language	Brittle; witty; rhythmic; brilliant vocabulary; correct pronunciation.
Mood and Atmosphere	Clear in terms of satire, repartee, and wit; supportive of usually cynical and flirtatious-sexual situation; little serious undertone.
Pace and Tempo	Generally rapid.
Special Techniques	Wit and language demand unusual vocal dexterity; unusual attention to movement in costume.

Suggested Readings

Bernbaum, Ernest. *The Drama of Sensibility: A Sketch of the History of Sentimental Comedy and Domestic Tragedy, 1696–1780.* Cambridge, Mass.: Harvard University Press, 1915.

Brown, J. R., and Harris, B. *Restoration Theatre.* New York: G. P. Putnam's Sons, 1967.

Campbell, Lily B. "A History of Costuming on the English Stage between 1660 and 1823." *University of Wisconsin Studies in Language and Literature* 2 (1918): 187–223.

Dobree, Bonamy. *Restoration Comedy, 1660–1720.* London: Oxford University Press, 1924.

Dobree, Bonamy. *Restoration Tragedy, 1660–1720.* London: Oxford University Press, 1929.

Fujimura, Thomas H. *Restoration Comedy of Wit.* Princeton, N. J.: Princeton University Press, 1952.

Furst, Lilian R. *Romanticism in Perspective.* New York: Humanities Press, 1969.

Hinshaw, N. W. "Graphic Sources for a Modern Approach to Acting Restoration Comedy." *Educational Theatre Journal,* May 1968, pp. 157–70.

Holland, Norman N. *The First Modern Comedies: The Significance of Etherege, Wycherley, and Congreve.* Cambridge, Mass.: Harvard University Press, 1959.

Joseph, Bertram. *The Tragic Actor.* New York: Theatre Arts Books, 1959.

Krutch, Joseph W. *Comedy and Conscience after the Restoration.* New York: Russell & Russell, 1949.

Lacey, Alexander. *Pixerecourt and the French Romantic Drama.* Toronto: University of Toronto Press, 1928.

Loftis, John, ed. *Restoration Drama, Modern Essays in Criticism.* London: Oxford University Press, 1966.

MacCollum, John I., Jr. *The Restoration Stage.* New York: Houghton Mifflin, Co., 1961.

Matthews, Brander. *French Dramatists of the Nineteenth Century.* 5th ed. New York: Benjamin Blom, 1968.

Matthews, Brander. *The Theatres of Paris.* London: Sampson, Low, Marston, Searle & Rivington, 1880.

Muir, Kenneth. *The Comedy of Manners.* London: Hutchinson University Library, 1970.

Nicoll, Allardyce. *History of English Drama, 1660–1900.* 6 vols. London: Cambridge University Press, 1955–1959.

Palmer, J. L. *The Comedy of Manners.* New York: Russell & Russell, 1962.

Reynolds, Ernest. *Early Victorian Drama (1830–1870).* New York: Benjamin Blom, 1965.

"The Romantic Movement: A Current Selective and Critical Bibliography." *English Literary History* (1937–49), Johns Hopkins Press; *Philological Quarterly* (1950–present), University of Iowa. Annual lists of publications.

Rowell, George. *The Victorian Theatre.* London: Oxford University Press, 1956.

Watson, Ernest B. *Sheridan to Robertson: A Study of the 19th Century London Stage.* Cambridge, Mass.: Harvard University Press, 1926.

The Country Wife
by William Wycherley

from
Act IV, scene iii

Lady Fidget
Horner
Mrs. Squeamish
Old Lady Squeamish
Sir Jasper
Quack
Pinchwife

Characters

Horner's lodging, London.

Scene

Horner passes himself off as a eunuch in London's elite society in order to gain easy access to the more enticing married women. In the famous "china" scene, he and Lady Fidget return from a bedroom escapade to engage with others in witty, sexual repartee.

Situation

(*Re-enter* LADY FIDGET *with a piece of china in her hand, and* HORNER *following.*)

LADY FIDGET   And I have been toiling and moiling for the prettiest piece of china, my dear.

HORNER   Nay, she has been too hard for me, do what I could.

MRS. SQUEAMISH   Oh, lord, I'll have some china too. Good Mr. Horner, don't think to give other people china and me none; come in with me too.

HORNER   Upon my honour, I have none left now.

MRS. SQUEAMISH   Nay, nay, I have known you deny your china before now, but you shan't put me off so. Come.

HORNER   This lady had the last there.

LADY FIDGET   Yes indeed, madam, to my certain knowledge, he has no more left.

MRS. SQUEAMISH   O, but it may be he may have some you could not find.

LADY FIDGET   What, d'ye think if he had had any left, I would not have had it too? for we women of quality never think we have china enough.

HORNER   Do not take it ill, I cannot make china for you all, but I will have a roll-waggon for you too, another time.

MRS. SQUEAMISH   Thank you, dear toad.

LADY FIDGET   What do you mean by that promise? (*Aside to* HORNER.)

HORNER   Alas, she has an innocent, literal understanding. (*Aside to* LADY FIDGET.)

LADY SQUEAMISH   Poor Mr. Horner! he has enough to do to please you all, I see.

HORNER   Ay, madam, you see how they use me.

LADY SQUEAMISH   Poor gentleman, I pity you.

HORNER   I thank you, madam: I could never find pity, but from such reverend ladies as you are; the young ones will never spare a man.

MRS. SQUEAMISH   Come, come, beast, and go dine with us; for we shall want a man at ombre after dinner.

HORNER   That's all their use of me, madam, you see.

MRS. SQUEAMISH   Come, sloven, I'll lead you, to be sure of you. (*Pulls him by the cravat.*)

LADY SQUEAMISH   Alas, poor man, how she tugs him! Kiss, kiss her; that's the
way to make such nice women quiet.

HORNER   No, madam, that remedy is worse than the torment; they know I dare
suffer anything rather than do it.

LADY SQUEAMISH   Prithee kiss her, and I'll give you her picture in little, that you
admired so last night; prithee do.

HORNER   Well, nothing but that could bribe me: I love a woman only in effigy,
and good painting as much as I hate them.—I'll do't, for I could adore the
devil well painted. (*Kisses* MRS. SQUEAMISH.)

MRS. SQUEAMISH   Foh, you filthy toad! nay, now I've done jesting.

LADY SQUEAMISH   Ha! ha! ha! I told you so.

MRS. SQUEAMISH   Foh! a kiss of his—

SIR JASPER   Has no more hurt in't than one of my spaniel's.

MRS. SQUEAMISH   Nor no more good neither.

QUACK   I will now believe anything he tells me. (*Aside*) (*Enter* PINCHWIFE.)

LADY FIDGET   O lord, here's a man! Sir Jasper, my mask, my mask! I would not
be seen here for the world.

SIR JASPER   What, not when I am with you?

LADY FIDGET   No, no, my honour—let's be gone.

MRS. SQUEAMISH   Oh grandmother, let's be gone; make haste, make haste, I know
not how he may censure us.

LADY FIDGET   Be found in the lodging of anything like a man!—Away.

(*Exeunt* SIR JASPER FIDGET, LADY FIDGET, OLD LADY SQUEAMISH, *and* MRS. SQUEAMISH.)

(*END*)

Realism and Naturalism 16

Selectivity and Photographic Detail

Zola descends into the cess-pool to take a bath, I to cleanse it.

Henrik Ibsen
from Vera Mowry Roberts, *On Stage*
A History of the Theatre.

Details are also the thing in the sphere of psychology. God preserve us from generalizations. Best of all, avoid depicting the hero's state of mind; you ought to try to make it clear from the hero's actions. It is not necessary to portray many active figures. The center of gravity should be two persons—he and she.

Anton Chekhov to his brother Alexander
from Ernest Simmons,
Introduction to Russian Realism.

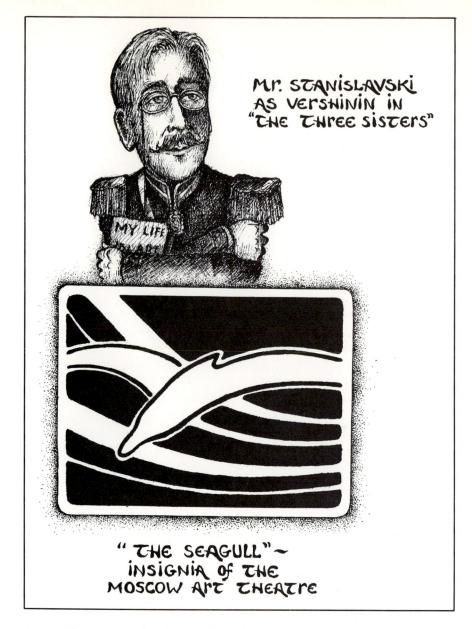

MR. STANISLAVSKI AS VERSHININ IN "THE THREE SISTERS"

"THE SEAGULL" – INSIGNIA OF THE MOSCOW ART THEATRE

As Chekhov revealed to his brother, the new dramatists at the turn of the century stressed mainly selective detail, not generalization—details whose origins were in human psychology and which emphasized the everyday reactions between men and women. Realists such as Henrik Ibsen carefully selected and arranged their material to create art which reflected social problems. Emile Zola, the French naturalist writer, went a step further into what might be described as scientific observation, revealing life in a seemingly indiscriminate, nonselective, photographic manner. At times this resulted in material which caught the "cesspool" or seamy side of life. No longer was drama restricted to artificial or contrived views of society and people.

The question arises, What were the distinctions between the plays of the realists (e.g., Ibsen) and of the naturalists (e.g., Chekhov and Zola)?

Read each of the following speeches aloud.[1] Compare them in terms of their lifelike qualities.

For eight years I've been waiting patiently; I knew, of course, that such things don't happen every day. Then, when this trouble came to me—I thought to myself: Now! Now the wonderful thing will happen! All the time Krogstad's letter was out there in the box, it never occurred to me for a single moment that you'd think of submitting to his conditions. I was absolutely convinced that you'd defy him—that you'd tell him to publish the thing to all the world; and that then—

Nora to Torvald   A Doll's House by Henrik Ibsen

Not only in two or three hundred years but in a million years life will be just the same; it does not change, it remains stationary, following its own laws which we have nothing to do with or which, anyway, we shall never find out. Migratory birds, cranes for instance, fly backwards and forwards and whatever ideas, great or small, stray through their minds, they will go on flying just the same without knowing where or why. They fly and will continue to fly, however philosophic they may become; and it doesn't matter how philosophical they are so long as they go on flying . . .

Tusenbach   The Three Sisters by Anton Chekhov

Scrutiny of the two speeches immediately reveals a measurable alliance between these lifelike speeches. The revolt against Romanticism and melodrama in the late nineteenth century produced two distinct literary trends throughout Europe: Realism and Naturalism. The new dramatic forms demanded more inquiry and observation of playwrights. Critics as well as audiences desired more controlled, true-to-life characterization. The foregoing examples of dialogue serve to illustrate the subtle differences between the two dominant dramatic movements of the late nineteenth century.

The most notable quality of Nora's speech to Torvald is its orderly arrangement of thought. It is selective in vocabulary and it flows with logical intent. The lines are believable and truthful for purposes of characterization; however, they are slightly heightened and intensified above normal conversational tone. Although the playwright carefully selected the vocal "pointing," his character is inwardly motivated. The style of the speech is *realistic*.

Tusenbach's speech is much closer to normal, reallife conversation. The emotional quality of his monologue causes immediate audience identification. Motivated thoughts and feelings are internalized, producing a truthful,

1. Nora's speech from *A Doll's House* by Henrik Ibsen. Translated by Eva LeGallienne. In *Landmarks in Modern Drama* edited by Charles Aughtry. Reprinted with permission of Random House, Inc., New York. Tusenbach's speech from *The Three Sisters* by Anton Chekhov. Translated by Constance Garnett. Reprinted with permission of Random House, Inc., New York.

believable quality. Incidental references are made as the logic flows in uneven and at times repetitive measures. In order to sustain his mood, an actor portraying Tusenbach may use silences and pauses as he speaks the lines. The style of the speech is *naturalistic*.

Overview of Realism

The movement toward Realism was allied with the origins of modern science Instead of being based on emotional or mystic explanations, late nineteenth century theatre was based on natural, rational explanation as evidenced and experienced through the five senses. The work of the philosopher August Comte (1798–1857) was a primary influence on realistic thought. His philosophy was based on "positivism" as the key to knowledge. Positivism was the examination of all apparent things, of all one could see. Evidence was based on precise observation and experimentation; events were understood in terms of cause and effect. When Charles Darwin published *On the Origin of the Species by Means of Natural Selection* in 1859, his advanced theories concerning the influence of heredity and environment on man's behavior gave tremendous impetus to the dramatic community. Man became one of many objects worthy of scientific study. The individual was part of an evolutionary movement whose hereditary traits and environmental conditions determine his existence and explain his character. The theory of evolution strengthened the theory of human progress—individual and collective improvement became inevitable.

The realists observed man and his environment primarily through the five senses. Playwrights consciously set out to abandon antiquated techniques such as formula plays, surface characterization, romantic subject matter, and scenic splendor in favor of duplication of contemporary life. Although realistic plays were well constructed, they were not overly predictable in terms of cause and effect. Characters were based on reallife, three-dimensional human beings. Plots were concerned with the problems of daily life —the environmental and social forces that encroached on man. Scenery mirrored contemporary environment in an attempt to express external realism. The playwright exercised careful selectivity and control in arranging events within a play. All action was motivated to achieve truth and believability in character portrayal. Although a character's actions were usually impelled by thoughts, feelings, and environmental conditions, realistic playwrights tended to emphasize outward action rather than inner psychology. Dialogue was significantly more conversational than, for example, the formal dialogue in plays by Scribe or Sardou. However, there was a tendency in realistic plays to heighten conversation at moments of high emotion.

Henrik Ibsen was the most representative playwright of the realistic school. A native of Norway, Ibsen gave Realism stature by writing plays with lifelike dialogue, settings, costumes, and stage business. However, the term must be qualified when it is applied to Ibsen. He never did copy reality in explicit detail. Because he was not interested in the raw material of life in the manner of a factual recorder, he became both a creative artist and a re-creative artist. His material was carefully selected and organized into a pattern of refinement, omission, and intensification.

Ibsen's themes suggest man's unending conflict between duty to himself and duty to others. His characters constantly try to achieve individual integrity. Although external action is somewhat static, his dialogue is tight, dynamic, and full of hints and allusions. Ibsen had a tremendous capacity for conveying the unspoken thought having emotional and mental undercurrents. In his realistic plays, Ibsen abandoned the aside and the soliloquy. Expository material was interwoven in cause-and-effect sequences.

Ibsen was flexible enough to explore many types of plays including historical-romantic studies (*The Pretenders*), poetic drama (*Peer Gynt*), realistic or thesis dramas (*A Doll's House, The Wild Duck, Ghosts, Hedda Gabler*), and symbolic plays (*The Master Builder*). His historic-romantic plays are militant in tone, inspired by his yearning for a better man and a better world. His poetic dramas are episodic, but impressive accounts of lofty ideals. Ibsen's realistic thesis or social-problem plays are perhaps most noteworthy for their convincing characters and dialogue, exciting and innovative social ideas, and realistic prose. His symbolic plays grope sensitively into mysticism. All of his plays blend art, morality, philosophy, and social considerations. Although Ibsen was basically a reformer and a fighter against the evils of society, his art has a warm feeling for life.

In England, the tenets of Ibsen's playwriting were emulated by Arthur Wing Pinero, Henry Arthur Jones, Sir James Barrie, John Galsworthy, and

Scene from *The Wild Duck* by Henrik Ibsen. Directed by Robert Loper. Designed by Wendell Cole. Stanford University.

George Bernard Shaw. Shaw fused paradox and satire effectively. He had a devastating wit aimed at shattering established beliefs and false ideals. Shaw was a master of clever, brilliant ideas. Although he sometimes made his characters a mouthpiece for his own ideas, Shaw created vital characters who discovered themselves during a crisis. The message in a Shavian play rests on character development. Some of Shaw's most famous plays include *Mrs. Warren's Profession, Arms and the Man, Candida, Man of Destiny,* and *Man and Superman* (a combination of Romanticism and Realism).

The impact of Ibsen's realism was not felt specifically nor purely in all countries at the same time or in the same manner. Since most dramatic work in Europe was in the Romantic tradition, playwrights varied in immediate acceptance of realistic techniques.

In Ireland, the first effective realistic dramas were the peasant dramas of Lady Gregory and the poet-playwright William Butler Yeats. In order to give Irish playwrights a "home," Lady Gregory and Yeats established the Abbey Theatre. Principal Abbey playwrights were John Millington Synge and, later, Sean O'Casey. The realism of Synge's modern dramas was infused with poetry shaped from Irish colloquial speech, Irish humor, and Celtic romanticism. Synge's realism was not inspired by that of Ibsen; it was unique because his poetic language was slightly elevated and the exhilaration of his characters was based firmly in the traditions of the Irish peasant class.

In Russia, Nikolai Gogol introduced Realism to the stage. Gogol's most famous play was a satire on provincial corruption called *The Inspector General.* Although his character delineation was somewhat exaggerated and grotesque, Gogol was notable for having ushered in Realism to Russian drama at a time when other European countries were still struggling with Romanticism and melodrama. Ivan Turgenev (*A Month in the Country*) explored psychological realism further by portraying ordinary men with humor and understanding (Turgenev was actually a precursor of Naturalism). Alexander Ostrovsky's plays (such as *The Thunderstorm*) depicted Russian middle-class life in considerable detail. However, most Russian playwrights of early realistic drama sacrificed subtle characterization for external realism.

Overview of Naturalism

In 1873, Emila Zola proposed the first naturalistic doctrine in the preface to his play *Thérèse Raquin.* In his treatise Zola stated his determination to base dramatic work on scientific methods of observation. Zola foresaw man formulating laws of human conduct based on observation, analysis, and classification of facts in a manner similar to that of scientists. *Naturalism* was a philosophical theory dating back to the sixteenth century which proliferated during the early nineteenth century. In Naturalism nature was considered the first principle in the universe, even above God. During the eighteenth century, Rousseau used the term *naturalism* to describe his concept of a "return to nature." In the eighteenth century advocates of the Age of Enlightenment also used the term as the basis for their spirit of inquiry. By the nineteenth century, Balzac, Flaubert, and the Goncourt brothers were already studying scientific methods. Zola's originality lay in the thoroughness of his scientific documentation and his choice of medical science as the inspiration for his literary work.

Zola's use of Naturalism was in rebellion against the stereotyped formula of morality and rhetoric fostered by the Romantic movement. In order to recapture truth in literature and drama, Zola attacked the conventions restricting the scope of the stage. He wanted to open the eyes of the public to the possibilities in new forms and new subjects. Zola prescribed lifelike scenery, costumes, and methods of acting. With the eye of a scientific observer, Zola wanted segments of life (*tranche de vie* or slice of life) to be represented onstage in exact duplication, as in a photograph. Scenery had to express the inner spirit of the play as well as the external details of its milieu. Action was simplified and lifelike. Characters were psychologically motivated and physiologically correct in appearance and manner. Environment was the primary influence on characters. Naturalistic plays did not present the logic of facts, sensations, or sentiments. For Zola, there was no difference between truth in the theatre and truth in life. Spectators were "invisible" to the actors. Although the public was invited to the theatre, they were required only to "peek through the fourth wall" to watch *life*, not a play. It was therefore proper for actors to stand with their backs to the audience and speak with slovenly diction. The correct attitude for naturalistic actors was to *live* the life of the character rather than to play the role. Zola strove to make the vocabulary of language different for each class. Since language had to fit the character and situation, crudity was appropriate in sordid scenes. The total effect of Zola's naturalism was to reproduce photographic detail on the stage.

Most naturalistic playwrights were preoccupied with human maladies. Among the foremost naturalistic playwrights (in addition to Zola) were Henri Becque (*The Vultures* and *La Parisienne*), Gerhart Hauptmann (*The Weavers*), Arthur Schnitzler (*Anatol* and *La Ronde*), August Strindberg (*Miss Julie* and *The Father*), Anton Chekhov (*The Seagull, The Three Sisters, The Cherry Orchard*, and *Uncle Vanya*), Maxim Gorky (*The Lower Depths*), and Sean O'Casey (*The Plough and the Stars* and *Juno and the Paycock*).

Dissatisfaction with nineteenth-century theatre produced a growth of individual writers, directors, and scenic and lighting designers (electricity was then in use) dedicated to eliminating abuses on the stage—namely, the commercial managerial system, the "staginess" of productions, and the histrionic style of acting with its emphasis on star roles. After 1875, playwrights demanded characterization from actors beyond their technical repertoire. Nineteenth-century acting in the declamatory style was so solidly entrenched in Europe that it inevitably fell to the director and the scenic and lighting designers to nourish the realistic and naturalistic movements. Director André Antoine, founder of the *Théâtre Libre* (Free Theatre) in Paris, was the practical, innovative leader of the naturalistic movement, and Gordon Craig, Aldoph Appia, and Vsevolold Meyerhold were the leaders of innovative scenic and lighting design.

Other new or little theatre movements occurred throughout Europe, paralleling Antoine's objectives (i.e., developing new writers and new acting styles). Otto Brahm's *Freie Buhne* in Germany, J. T. Grein's Independent Theatre in England, Lady Gregory's Abbey Theatre in Ireland, and, above all, Konstantin Stanislavski's Moscow Art Theatre in Russia gave impetus to theatrical experimentation and innovation. Stanislavski developed a system of acting techniques which became the foundation of all modern acting theory.

The evolution of realistic acting continued to vacillate between representational and presentational concepts until the emergence of Stanislavski and his partner Vladimir Nemirovich-Danchenko. Stanislavski's acting system was influenced by the work of the actor Mikhail Shchepkin. Shchepkin discovered that a natural speaking tone resulted in realistic characterization. Together with Gogol, Shchepkin urged actors to identify with the character being portrayed, to take on his identity, and to strive for truth and naturalness in speech and bodily movement. Character believability was further heightened by accurate study of the background of the role. It was Shchepkin who gave Stanislavski the motto for the Moscow Art Theatre: There are no small parts, only small actors. Although the playwrights Ostrovsky and Turgenev continued to develop the realistic style of acting, Stanislavski saw that even in the 1890s, realistic acting was still based on able elocution. During the last decade of the nineteenth century, Stanislavski and Danchenko were influenced by the work of the Duke of Saxe-Meiningen, an innovative German director who is often considered to be the first director in the theatre and notable for his emphasis on natural ensemble acting.

The policies of the Moscow Art Theatre, as described by Stanislavski (the artistic director) and Danchenko (the administrator), focused on the production of plays of distinction by both Russian playwrights and foreign writers and on the subordination of individual acting to the intention of the playwright. Careful attention to detail in scenic design and realistic characterization were prime considerations. A new rehearsal concept in which the cast studied plays in thorough detail, supervised by the director, was established. Rigid discipline was enforced throughout the rehearsal period.

Stanislavski's early efforts at theatre reform were directed against the style of acting noted for its shouting, rapid tempo, and exaggerated gestures and actions. Except for the few attempts at Realism mentioned earlier, theatrical productions prior to this time were notoriously contrived and stereotyped. Repertory offerings included light farcical plays whose only appeal was the Star in the lead role. Stanislavski's primary goals of reform were to discover a more realistic base for acting and to eliminate technical stage abuses. Early productions of the Moscow Art Theatre were more lifelike, perhaps even more realistic, than ordinary Realism—that is, superrealism or Naturalism. Stanislavski was dedicated to photographic duplication. Lighting and sound effects were essential to producing naturalistic sounds such as thunder, rain, wind, and ordinary sounds of daily life (e.g., birds singing, bells ringing, and dogs barking). Sound was used to reveal contrast or to heighten a significant moment. However, eventually scenic detail, three-dimensional settings, and external facts were overemphasized.

It was not until he worked on three plays by Maeterlinck (*The Blind, The Interior,* and *The Unbidden Guest*) that Stanislavski began to search for still newer forms of expression. Realizing that impressionist paintings and music usually produced fantastic and imaginative evocations of the mind and heart, he studied the works of modern painters, sculptors, and composers. This knowledge led Stanislavski to repudiate his former dependence on the scene designer. He realized that inner truth could not be achieved by the scenic atmosphere of a play. He made the key discovery that emotions and feelings come from the actor and his person.

The tenets of style encompassing Realism and Naturalism are contained within the techniques of acting described by Stanislavski.

In 1909, Stanislavski set down his refined principles of acting, and his acting system became the foundation for all realistic and naturalistic acting of the twentieth century. The most profound question probed by Stanislavski was, How can an actor achieve a creative mood which would favor inspiration?

Voice

Stanislavski did not neglect cultivation of the actor's external techniques. All his actors received vocal training for intonation, inflection, use of pause, and tempo-rhythm. Stanislavski believed that an actor should study singing in order to learn how to use the whole vocal scale. He treated the front of the actor's face as though it were a *masque* with resonators, and he stressed natural speaking using good breathing technique, clear articulation, and excellent projection. He believed in a disciplined vocal instrument and very expressive speech. Simplicity and clarity created precise patterns of speech, rooted in natural movement and emotion. Stanislavski treated *words* as the physical side of action and images in the mind as the psychological side of action. Perhaps the most important contribution Stanislavski made to stage speech was his explanation that there are reasons why characters say words. The actor's task is to make the author's words his own. Thus, dialogue must have purpose if words are to be meaningful and have impact. The actor then uses his craft through intonation, enunciation, and expression to color vocal delivery imaginatively. Stanislavski believed that mechanical memorization ruined believability and created artificial vocal delivery. Stanislavski often said, "Treasure the spoken word." He knew that energetic language and vocal expressiveness stirred emotions. A word becomes a verbal action when the action is motivated by purpose. Therefore, speech influences character and emotion. Stanislavski knew that actors should analyze their speeches in order to deliver them logically and convincingly. He believed that speaking was acting. Stanislavski also knew that verbal action depends upon physical action (which is discussed later).

Exercise 1   Voice

1. Sing the vocal scale repeatedly until it becomes instinctive. You should be capable of using the scale when speaking as well as when singing in a modified manner.

2. Think of the front of your face as a mask with resonators connecting the mouth and nose. Imagine you are in a canyon calling back and forth to your own echo. Call or sing such expressions as *Hellooooooooo, Farewelllllllll,* and *Where are youuuuuu.* With conscious effort you should be able to actually feel vibrations in the resonating areas of your face.

3. Study the speeches by Nora and Tusenbach given at the beginning of this chapter. Determine the purpose or motivation for each idea in the speech and, if possible, for each word. When you have determined purpose, deliver the speech using imaginative, colorful intonation, pauses, and natural expressiveness. Finally, permit natural gestures to accompany your vocal delivery.

Movement

Training the body in movement was an important part of the Stanislavski acting system. His actors worked for complete, graceful control of all physical activity. Stanislavski opposed the artificial mannerisms and mechanical gestures of most of the preceding acting styles. He believed that gestures should relate to inner experience. Stanislavski insisted upon movement that was motivated, honest, and logical. He stressed that actors must practice every day just as must musicians and singers. Both voice and body must be trained to the point at which they instantly express correct, external activity linked to and motivated by inner experience.

The significance of external form and physical detail was directly tied to correct costuming. Stanislavski recognized that costumes and properties were not extraneous or mere support items. They were rather an integral part of character, tied to motivation, action, and emotion.

Onstage, an actor must be physically free, attain muscular control and relaxation, and have limitless concentration.

Stanislavski believed in dance training for actors because he considered it important in increasing physical dexterity of both actors and musical theatre performers. Movement should be simple, vital, and natural. Movement is an actor's most intense means of expression.

An actor's whole physical being represents the character being interpreted. Stanislavski taught that an actor should always be "in character," should not recognize the audience, and should concentrate on producing an ensemble effect in production. Personalization was in effect the foundation for physical activity in the Stanislavski system. That is, after study and practice an actor's person united with the role until they *appeared* to be one and the same. Great art hides art. Stanislavski knew that the organic totality of an actor's personality and physical being was always at work in the art of role creation.

Exercise 2   Movement

1. Relax your body using any of the exercises described in chapters 1, 2, or 3.

2. Select music from Brahms, Debussy, Ravel, or Stravinsky and as the music plays interpret the moods and rhythms of the music through improvised movement. In some instances the movement can become modern dance activity.

3. Sit down before the group. Conversationally and naturally relate an interesting personal experience. Animate your story with instinctive natural gestures, particularly of the face, hands, and upper portions of the body. When you have completed the story, discuss the gestures you have used. Listen carefully to any criticism concerning arbitrary, meaningless, or repetitive gestures. Relate another personal story and attempt

Scene from *The Three Sisters* by Anton Chekhov. Directed by Jerry L. Crawford. Designed by Jody Meswarb. University of Nevada, Las Vegas.

to use more expressive, artistic, disciplined gestures without losing the natural, spontaneous, inner-motivated behavior.

4. Perform the following series of natural, everyday activities using as much total body movement as possible. You need not speak. Concentrate solely upon purposeful activity. Your entire organic being should focus upon your task. When necessary, pantomime the use of objects.

    a. Walk into a room, sit upon a chair, and remove your shoes.

    b. Enter a room, prepare a cold drink, and drink it.

    c. Brush your teeth.

    d. Pick up a newspaper and read it.

    e. Remove your makeup.

    f. Search an entire room for a lost key.

    g. Move furniture from one location to another.

    h. Put a series of things away on a high shelf.

    i. Dance to imaginary kinds of music.

    j. Fly a kite in a strong wind.

    k. Jump rope; play kickball; play an imaginary game of softball, basketball, or touch football; imagine you are roller-skating or ice-skating.

    l. Hold hands and create a chain of movement proceeding all over the room.

Character and Emotion

In his search to discover the inner truth of human feeling and experience, *Stanislavski urged his actors to personalize and display character motivation and emotion simply and naturally.* In addition to this role creation technique, Stanislavski suggested heavy reliance on intuition. In time, Stanislavski discovered that most of his actors were continuing to "act" rather than to behave naturally. The intuitive method, combined with background material from the play, produced only surface character. The actor was executing the appropriate walk, emotional state, and rhythm of speech, but the depth of true inner character was still missing. It remained for the tremendous influence of Anton Chekhov to bring that deep inner truth to the productions of the Moscow Art Theatre. Chekhov's plays required actors to use an extra dimension in character portrayal. The complexity of the writing demanded that actors seek the truth of their inner life and then equalize that reality with their role. In seeking to liberate the deeper individuality of the actor, Stanislavski rose to the task Chekhov presented. Stanislavski helped his actors free their innermost feelings, moods, thoughts, and experiences. As you learned in Part I, one of the best techniques of role creation involves actor personalization. Stanislavski's actors strove to achieve expression of an inner image by awakening the subconscious from which flowed the outer image. The roots of the personalization theory of acting are imbedded in that striving.

    One of the first steps in Stanislavski's process of using the actor's person as the foundation for role creation is the technique known as the "Magic If." Stanislavski thought that actors must believe in the possibility of events in their own life before they could believe in events onstage. He saw the value of transforming a character's aim into an actor's aim. An actor says to himself, "If I were the character in this situation, what would I do?" Providing the answer to the Magic If enables him to react to the unreal life onstage as if it were real.

Stanislavski believed the next step in role creation was to examine the given circumstances of a play including time and place of action, director's interpretation, setting, lighting, and sound effects.

Stanislavski also stressed concentration as the key to dynamic, believable performance onstage (see chapter 2). Concentration leads to truthful, believable, relaxed stage activity, which in turn leads to what Stanislavski called "communion" or interaction with other people. Both physical communion and psychological communion are necessary to accomplish action that is both realistic and naturalistic.

An important aspect of communion involves "adaptation" or adjustment. An actor must overcome many obstacles to achieve his goal, finding ways to adapt or adjust his activity or action to accomplish his goal. He asks himself: What must I do? Why must I do it? and How can I do it? Both personal adaptation and character adaptation are involved in acting. For example, if you are a woman playing a love scene with a man several inches shorter than you, the need for physical adaptation is obvious. The actors and director must find an adjustment to the problem, probably by seating both persons for the love scene. Similar, but more complex, characterization may demand that you sob convulsively. You must find a way to adapt to the demand and accomplish the behavior.

Finally, the actor focuses upon tempo-rhythm in execution of all aspects of a role. Correct speed and varying intensity of activity are identified and rehearsed. The tempo-rhythm is tied to the emotional disposition of both character and actor.

Stanislavski knew that the foremost method of expressing the truthful emotional life of a character was through observation, imagination, and use of the senses. An actor recalls and draws attention to each encountered object to discover its living substance. This method is known as affective memory or emotional memory (see chapter 4), a process by which the actor selects emotions from his living experiences analogous to those of his character and utilizes duplication of emotional sensations within the role (again, see chapter 4). Emotional recall leads to inspiration whereby an actor uses the best within himself and carries it onstage. The use of emotional recall varies according to the necessities of a play. In any event, when emotions are created in this manner onstage, they are usually alive and vital.

Stanislavski believed in thorough role analysis prior to onstage performance. The tenets of role analysis described in chapter 10 correspond closely to Stanislavski's concept of role analysis. Central to Stanislavski's theory was identifying what he called "the Super-Objective" and "the Through Line of Actions." The Super-Objective was the main idea or final goal of each performance. Some theatre artists call the Super-Objective the "spine" of the role. The Through Line of Actions is a logical mental line running through a role which an actor can trace in his mind. The Through Line of Actions guides the actor toward accomplishment of his Super-Objective. For example, all of the Through Lines of Actions by Willy Loman in *Death of a Salesman* lead to the Super-Objective of winning back Biff's love.

Exercise 3   Character and Emotion

The main exercise technique employed by Stanislavski in the practice of his theories focused on improvisation. Define the circumstances before performing actions.

1. You are in a small elevator when it becomes lodged between floors. What do you do?
2. You arrive at the home of a civic leader on the wrong night for a banquet. What do you do?
3. You receive word of the death of a beloved family member. What do you do?
4. You are walking home late at night along a dark street. You think someone is following you. You learn you are in a blind alley. What do you do?
5. You are alone on your first solo flight as a pilot when you learn you have forgotten your maps, your radio is out, and your gas is low. What do you do?
6. You are waiting for a message concerning an operation performed on a beloved family member. What do you do?
7. Listen carefully to all sounds. React to each sound individually.
8. Treat the room as though it were a sunken submarine incapable of surfacing. What do you do?
9. You are in a cell awaiting execution. What do you do?
10. You are a criminal lawyer interrogating a prisoner about a murder. Relate to one another.
11. You are proposing marriage to a girl. Relate to one another.
12. You are meeting a blind date. What do you do?
13. You are in a hurry, but you are at the rear of a supermarket line. What do you do?
14. You are waiting to meet a truant officer after having skipped school for a week. What do you do?
15. An alarm wakes you and you discover you are one hour late for an appointment. Establish the correct tempo-rhythm for what you do.
16. You are alone on the beach at sunset. Establish the correct tempo-rhythm for what you do.

The influence of Stanislavski has been continued through the work of such disciples and pupils as Eugene Vakhtangov, Vsevolod Meyerhold, Richard Boleslavsky, Michael Chekhov, Lee Strasberg, Sonia Moore, and many others, particularly actors who studied in the famous Actor's Studio in New York.

While Realism and Naturalism remain the foundation of most twentieth-century acting style, important new acting styles remain to be examined.

Suggested Characters and Plays for Scene Work

Ibsen, Henrik

Hedda Gabler, Eilert Lovborg, Judge Brack, Miss Tesman
    Hedda Gabler
Bernick, Mrs. Bernick
    Pillars of Society
Nora Helmer, Torvald, Mrs. Linde
    A Doll's House
Dr. Stockman, Mrs. Stockman
    An Enemy of the People
Mrs. Alving, Oswald
    Ghosts
Gregers, Hialmar, Gina, Hedvig, Old Ekdal
    The Wild Duck

Shaw, George Bernard

Gloria, Valentine
    You Never Can Tell
John Tanner, Ann Whitfield
    Man and Superman
Barbara, Undershaft
    Major Barbara
Dick Dudgeon, Reverend Anderson, Mrs. Anderson
    The Devil's Disciple

Synge, John M.

Maurya, Nora, Cathleen, Bartley
    Riders to the Sea
Christopher, Pegeen
    Playboy of the Western World

O'Casey, Sean

Fluther, Mrs. Gogan, Nora
    The Plough and the Stars
Juno, Joxer, Boyle
    Juno and the Paycock

Turgenev, Ivan

Natalya, Vera, Adam, Alexey
    A Month in the Country

Gogol, Nikolai

Khlestakov, Osip, Anton, Anna, Marya
    The Inspector General

Wilde, Oscar

Algernon, Cecily, Gwendelon, John Worthing, Lady Bracknel
    The Importance of Being Earnest

Zola, Emile

Thérèse Raquin, Laurent
Thérèse Raquin

Chekhov, Anton

Masha, Olga, Irina, Natasha, Kulygin, Vershinin, Tusenbach
The Three Sisters
Nina, Trigorin, Treplev, Irina
The Seagull
Madman Renevsky, Lopahin, Anya, Varya, Gaev, Trofimov, Firs
The Cherry Orchard
Yelena, Sonia, Serebryakov, Uncle Vanya, Ostrov
Uncle Vanya

Strindberg, August

Miss Julie, Jean
Miss Julie
Laura, The Captain
The Father

Gorky, Maxim

Luka, The Baron, The Actor, Satin, Vassilisa, Natasha
The Lower Depths

Actor Checklist   *Realism and Naturalism*

Voice	Lifelike, more precise articulation and projection in Realism; more vocal pointing used in Realism; emphasis on dialects; unusual use of silence and pauses; conversational mode, but more heightened in Realism; use of full vocal scale; expressive speech; motivated speech; intonation and imaginative coloring.
Movement	Motivated by thoughts, feelings, and speech; total and controlled body response; considerable physical interaction with others; some selective movement imposed in Realism, seemingly none in Naturalism; all stage areas used; all body positions used; totally representational.
Gestures	Related to inner experience; natural and spontaneous; full use of the entire body; lifelike; more selective in Realism.
Pantomimic Dramatization	Costuming and properties integrally related; extremely inventive; detailed in Naturalism, more selective in Realism; lifelike; motivated; closely tied to environment and scenery, especially in Naturalism.
Character	Rooted in inner psychology and believable human emotion; multidimensional; tied to environment, particularly in Naturalism; subjective, internal use of observation, imagination, senses, and personal experience; highly motivated, particularly in Naturalism; Super-Objective clear; ensemble important.

Emotion	Complex; rooted in human psychology; use of affective or emotional memory; motivated; closely tied to physical action and speech; audience identification and empathy strong.
Ideas	Strong social orientation in Realism; strong human orientation in Naturalism; related to experiences in daily living, problems of environment, and heredity.
Language	Lifelike prose; often rich in symbolism and imagery; more selective in Realism.
Mood and Atmosphere	Closely tied to character, situation, and environment; not superimposed for theatrical purposes; mixed and varied; lifelike.
Pace and Tempo	Unusually varied.
Special Techniques	Full use of Stanislavski system: (1) personalization, (2) Magic If, (3) given circumstances, (4) concentration, (5) tempo-rhythm, (6) observation, (7) imagination, (8) the senses: affective memory or emotional memory, (9) role analysis: Super-Objective and Through Line of Actions.

Suggested Readings

Antoine, André. *Memories of the Théâtre Libre.* Translated by Marvin Carlson. Coral Gables, Fla.: University of Miami Press, 1964.

Arvin, Neil E. *Eugene Scribe and the French Theatre, 1815–60.* Cambridge, Mass.: Harvard University Press, 1924.

Carter, Lawson A. *Zola and the Theatre.* New Haven, Conn.: Yale University Press, 1963.

Clark, Barrett, and Freedley, George. *A History of Modern Drama.* New York: Appleton-Century-Crofts, 1947.

Cole, Toby. *Acting: A Handbook of the Stanislavski Method.* New York: Crown Publishers, 1949.

Edwards, Christine. *The Stanislavsky Heritage.* New York: New York University Press, 1965.

Houghton, Norris. *Moscow Rehearsals: An Account of Methods of Production in the Soviet Theatre.* New York: Harcourt Brace Jovanovich, 1936.

Houghton, Norris. *Return Engagement: A Postscript to "Moscow Rehearsals."* New York: Holt, Rinehart, and Winston, 1962.

Gorchakov, Nikolai. *The Vakhtangov School of Stage Art.* Moscow: 1960. Translated by G. Ivanov-Mumjier.

Lavrin, Janko. *Ibsen, an Approach.* New York: Russell & Russell, 1969.

Lewis, Robert. *Method or Madness?* New York: Samuel French, 1958.

Lucas, F. L. *The Drama of Ibsen and Strindberg.* New York: Macmillan Co., 1962.

Marowitz, Charles. *The Method as Means.* London: Herbert Jenkins, 1961.

Marowitz, Charles. *Stanislavsky and the Method.* New York: Citadel Press, 1964.

Melcher, Edith. *Stage Realism in French Between Diderot and Antoine.* Bryn Mawr, Pa.: Bryn Mawr College, 1928.

Moore, Sonia. *The Stanislavski System.* New York: Viking Press, 1974.

Munk, Erica, ed. *Stanislavski and America.* New York: Hill & Wang, 1966.

Norvell, Lee. "Stanislavsky Revisited." *Educational Theatre Journal,* March 1962, pp. 29–37.

Sondel, Bess S. *Zola's Naturalistic Theory with Particular Reference to the Drama.* Chicago: University of Chicago Libraries, 1939.

Sprigge, Elizabeth. *The Strange Life of August Strindberg.* New York: Macmillan Co., 1949.

Stanislavski, Constantin. *Actor's Handbook,* 1963; *An Actor Prepares,* 1936; *Building a Character,* 1949; *Creating a Role,* 1961; *My Life in Art,* 1952. Translated by Elizabeth R. Hapgood. New York: Theatre Arts Books.

Strindberg, August. *Open Letters to the Intimate Theatre.* Seattle: University of Washington Press, n.d.

Styan, J. L..*Chekhov in Performance: A Commentary on the Major Plays.* London: Cambridge University Press, 1971.

Valency, Maurice. *The Flower and the Castle.* New York: Macmillan Co., 1963. (About Ibsen and Strindberg.)

Waxman, S. M. *Antoine and the Théâtre Libre.* Cambridge, Mass.: Harvard University Press, 1926.

Willis, Ronald. "The American Lab Theatre." *Tulane Drama Review,* Fall 1964, pp. 112–16.

The Wild Duck

by *Henrik Ibsen*

Translated by Frances Archer

from
Act III

Characters

Gregers Werle, friend of Hialmar Ekdal
Hedvig, daughter of Gina, age 14
Hialmar Ekdal, photographer
Gina, wife to Hialmar

Scene

The sitting room next to a garret in the modest home of Hialmar Ekdal; the sitting room serves as Hialmar's photographic studio.

Situation

Hialmar Ekdal, a poor retoucher of photographs, lives a happy life with his wife, Gina, and daughter, Hedvig. However, an old friend, Gregers Werle, enters his life determined to force Hialmar to drop his romantic illusions and live an ideal life based on truth. Gregers knows that Hedvig was probably the daughter of another man (Gregers' own father, in fact). In this scene, Gregers works to gain the confidence and trust of Hedvig.

GREGERS   Did the wild duck sleep well last night?

HEDVIG   Yes, I think so, thanks.

GREGERS   (*turning towards the garret*) It looks quite different by day from what it did last night in the moonlight.

HEDVIG   Yes, it changes ever so much. It looks different in the morning and in the afternoon; and it's different on rainy days from what it is in fine weather.

GREGERS   Have you noticed that?

HEDVIG   Yes, how could I help it?

GREGERS   Are you, too, fond of being in there with the wild duck?

HEDVIG   Yes, when I can manage it——

GREGERS   But I suppose you haven't much spare time; you go to school, no doubt.

HEDVIG   No, not now; father is afraid of my hurting my eyes.

GREGERS   Oh; then he reads with you himself?

HEDVIG   Father has promised to read with me; but he has never had time yet.

GREGERS   Then is there nobody else to give you a little help?

HEDVIG   Yes, there is Mr. Molvik; but he is not always exactly—quite——

GREGERS   Sober?

HEDVIG   Yes, I suppose that's it!

GREGERS   Why, then you must have any amount of time on your hands. And in there I suppose it is a sort of world by itself?

HEDVIG   Oh, yes, quite. And there are such lots of wonderful things.

GREGERS   Indeed?

HEDVIG   Yes, there are big cupboards full of books; and a great many of the books have pictures in them.

GREGERS   Aha!

HEDVIG   And there's an old bureau with drawers and flaps, and a big clock with figures that go out and in. But the clock isn't going now.

GREGERS   So time has come to a standstill in there—in the wild duck's domain.

HEDVIG   Yes. And then there's an old paint-box and things of that sort, and all the books.

GREGERS   And you read the books, I suppose?

HEDVIG   Oh, yes, when I get the chance. Most of them are English though, and I don't understand English. But then I look at the pictures.—There is one great big book called "Harrison's History of London." It must be a hundred years old; and there are such heaps of pictures in it. At the beginning there is Death with an hour-glass and a woman. I think that is horrid. But then there are all the other pictures of churches, and castles, and streets, and great ships sailing on the sea.

GREGERS   But tell me, where did all those wonderful things come from?

HEDVIG   Oh, an old sea captain once lived here, and he brought them home with him. They used to call him "The Flying Dutchman." That was curious, because he wasn't a Dutchman at all.

GREGERS   Was he not?

HEDVIG   No. But at last he was drowned at sea, and so he left all those things behind him.

GREGERS   Tell me now—when you are sitting in there looking at the pictures, don't you wish you could travel and see the real world for yourself?

HEDVIG   Oh, no! I mean always to stay at home and help father and mother.

GREGERS   To retouch photographs?

HEDVIG   No, not only that. I should love above everything to learn to engrave pictures like those in the English books.

GREGERS   H'm. What does your father say to that?

HEDVIG   I don't think father likes it; father is strange about such things. Only think, he talks of my learning basket-making and straw-plaiting! But I don't think that would be much good.

GREGERS   Oh, no, I don't think so either.

HEDVIG   But father was right in saying that if I had learnt basket-making I could have made the new basket for the wild duck.

GREGERS   So you could; and it was you that ought to have done it, wasn't it?

HEDVIG   Yes, for it's my wild duck.

GREGERS   Of course it is.

HEDVIG   Yes, it belongs to me. But I lend it to father and grandfather as often as they please.

GREGERS   Indeed? What do they do with it?

HEDVIG   Oh, they look after it, and build places for it, and so on.

GREGERS   I see; for no doubt the wild duck is by far the most distinguished inhabitant of the garret?

HEDVIG   Yes, indeed she is; for she is a real wild fowl, you know. And then she is so much to be pitied; she has no one to care for, poor thing.

GREGERS   She has no family, as the rabbits have—

HEDVIG   No. The hens, too, many of them, were chickens together; but she has been taken right away from all her friends. And then there is so much that is strange about the wild duck. Nobody knows her, and nobody knows where she came from either.

GREGERS   And she has been down in the depths of the sea.

HEDVIG   (with a quick glance at him, represses a smile and asks) Why do you say "depths of the sea"?

GREGERS   What else should I say?

HEDVIG   You could say "the bottom of the sea."[2]

GREGERS   Oh, mayn't I just as well say the depths of the sea?

HEDVIG   Yes; but it sounds so strange to me when other people speak of the depths of the sea.

GREGERS   Why so? Tell me why?

HEDVIG   No, I won't; it's so stupid.

GREGERS   Oh, no, I am sure it's not. Do tell me why you smiled.

HEDVIG   Well, this is the reason: whenever I come to realize suddenly—in a flash—what is in there, it always seems to me that the whole room and everything in it should be called "the depths of the sea."—But that is so stupid.

GREGERS   You mustn't say that.

HEDVIG   Oh, yes, for you know it is only a garret.

GREGERS *(looks fixedly at her)*   Are you so sure of that?

HEDVIG *(astonished)*   That it's a garret?

GREGERS   Are you quite certain of it?

(HEDVIG *is silent, and looks at him open-mouthed.* GINA *comes in from the kitchen with the table things.*)

GREGERS *(rising)*   I have come in upon you too early.

GINA   Oh, you must be somewhere; and we're nearly ready now, anyway. Clear the table, Hedvig.

(HEDVIG *clears away her things; she and* GINA *lay the cloth during what follows.* GREGERS *seats himself in the armchair and turns over an album.*)

GREGERS   I hear you can retouch, Mrs. Ekdal.

GINA *(with a side glance)*   Yes, I can.

GREGERS   That was exceedingly lucky.

GINA   How—lucky?

GREGERS   Since Ekdal took to photography, I mean.

HEDVIG   Mother can take photographs, too.

GINA   Oh, yes; I was bound to learn that.

GREGERS   So it is really you that carry on the business, I suppose?

GINA   Yes, when Ekdal hasn't time himself——

GREGERS   He is a great deal taken up with his old father, I daresay.

GINA   Yes; and then you can't expect a man like Ekdal to do nothing but take pictures of Dick, Tom, and Harry.

GREGERS   I quite agree with you; but having once gone in for the thing——

GINA   You can surely understand, Mr. Werle, that Ekdal's not like one of your common photographers.

GREGERS   Of course not; but still——

(*A shot is fired within the garret.*)

GREGERS *(starting up)*   What's that?

GINA   Ugh! now they're firing again!

2. Gregers here uses the old-fashioned expression "havsens bund," while Hedvig would have him use the more commonplace "havets bund" or "havbunden." [Translator's note.]

GREGERS   Have they firearms in there?

HEDVIG   They are out shooting.

GREGERS   What! (*at the door of the garret*) Are you shooting, Hialmar?

HIALMAR (*inside the net*)   Are you there? I didn't know; I was so taken up——
(*to* HEDVIG) Why did you not let us know? (*comes into the studio*)

GREGERS   Do you go shooting in the garret?

HIALMAR (*showing a double-barrelled pistol*)   Oh, only with this thing.

GINA   Yes, you and grandfather will do yourselves a mischief some day with that
there pigstol.

HIALMAR (*with irritation*)   I believe I have told you that this kind of firearm is
called a pistol.

GINA   Oh, that doesn't make it much better, that I can see.

GREGERS   So you have become a sportsman, too, Hialmar?

HIALMAR   Only a little rabbit-shooting now and then. Mostly to please father,
you understand.

GINA   Men are strange beings; they must always have something to pervert
theirselves with.

HIALMAR (*snappishly*)   Just so; we must always have something to divert
ourselves with.

GINA   Yes, that's just what I say.

HIALMAR   H'm. (*to* GREGERS) You see the garret is fortunately so situated that no
one can hear us shooting. (*lays the pistol on the top shelf of the bookcase*)
Don't touch the pistol, Hedvig! One of the barrels is loaded; remember that.

GREGERS (*looking through the net*)   You have a fowling-piece, too, I see.

HIALMAR   That is father's old gun. It's no use now; something has gone wrong
with the lock. But it's fun to have it all the same; for we can take it to pieces
now and then, and clean and grease it, and screw it together again.—Of
course, it's mostly father that fiddle-faddles with all that sort of thing.

HEDVIG (*beside* GREGERS)   Now you can see the wild duck properly.

GREGERS   I was just looking at her. One of her wings seems to me to droop a bit.

HEDVIG   Well, no wonder; her wing was broken, you know.

GREGERS   And she trails one foot a little. Isn't that so?

HIALMAR   Perhaps a very little bit.

HEDVIG   Yes, it was by that foot the dog took hold of her.

HIALMAR   But otherwise she hasn't the least thing the matter with her; and that
is simply marvellous for a creature that has a charge of shot in her body and
has been between a dog's teeth——

GREGERS (*with a glance at* HEDVIG)   ——and that has lain in the depths of the
sea—so long.

HEDVIG (*smiling*)   Yes.

GINA (*laying the table*)   That blessed wild duck! What a lot of fuss you do make
over her.

HIALMAR   H'm;—will lunch soon be ready?

GINA   Yes, directly. Hedvig, you must come and help me now. (GINA *and* HEDVIG
go out into the kitchen.)

(*END*)

The Three Sisters

by *Anton Chekhov*

Translated by Constance Garnett

from
Act III

Characters

Irina, the youngest sister, 24
Olga, the eldest sister, a schoolteacher, 28
Masha, the middle sister, married to Kuligin, a schoolmaster, but in love with
    Vershinin, a married army colonel
Andrey, brother to the three sisters
Natasha, domineering wife to Andrey
Ferapont, an old servant

Scene

An upstairs bedroom of Olga and Irina, in the Prozoroff home in the Russian provinces, far from Moscow.

Situation

Over a year after their father's death, three sisters live their days without purpose, longing to return to their childhood home and happiness in Moscow. Weary and alone as a fire rages in the town, the sisters express the tortures of their existence and confess their desires and problems.

IRINA   Yes, how petty our Andrey has grown, how dull and old he has become beside that woman! At one time he was working to get a professorship and yesterday he was boasting of having succeeded at last in becoming a member of the Rural Board. He is a member, and Protopopov is chairman. . . . The whole town is laughing and talking of it and he is the only one who sees and knows nothing. . . . And here everyone has been running to the fire while he sits still in his room and takes no notice. He does nothing but play his violin . . . (*nervously*). Oh, it's awful, awful, awful! (*Weeps*). I can't bear it any more, I can't! I can't, I can't!

(OLGA *comes in and begins tidying up her table.*)

IRINA (*sobs loudly*)   Turn me out, turn me out, I can't bear it any more!
OLGA (*alarmed*)   What is it? What is it, darling?
IRINA (*sobbing*)   Where? Where has it all gone? Where is it? Oh, my God, my God! I have forgotten everything, everything . . . everything is in a tangle in my mind. . . . I don't remember the Italian for window or ceiling . . . I am forgetting everything; every day I forget something more and life is slipping away and will never come back, we shall never, never go to Moscow. . . . I see that we shan't go. . . .
OLGA   Darling, darling. . . .
IRINA (*restraining herself*)   Oh, I am wretched. . . . I can't work, I am not going to work. I have had enough of it, enough of it! I have been a telegraph clerk and now I have a job in the town council and I hate and despise every bit of the work they give me. . . . I am nearly twenty-four, I have been working for years, my brains are drying up, I am getting thin and old and ugly and there is nothing, nothing, not the slightest satisfaction, and time is passing and one feels that one is moving away from a real, fine life, moving farther and farther

away and being drawn into the depths. I am in despair and I don't know how it is I am alive and have not killed myself yet. . . .

OLGA   Don't cry, my child, don't cry. It makes me miserable.

IRINA   I am not crying, I am not crying. . . . It's over. . . . There, I am not crying now. I won't . . . I won't.

OLGA   Darling, I am speaking to you as a sister, as a friend, if you care for my advice, marry the baron!

(IRINA *weeps*.)

OLGA *(softly)*   You know you respect him, you think highly of him. . . . It's true he is ugly, but he is such a thoroughly nice man, so good. . . . One doesn't marry for love, but to do one's duty. . . . That's what I think, anyway, and I would marry without love. Whoever proposed to me I would marry him, if only he were a good man. . . . I would even marry an old man. . . .

IRINA   I kept expecting we should move to Moscow and there I should meet my real one. I've been dreaming of him, loving him. . . . But it seems that was all nonsense, nonsense. . . .

OLGA *(puts her arms round her sister)*   My darling, lovely sister, I understand it all; when the baron left the army and came to us in a plain coat, I thought he looked so ugly that it positively made me cry. . . . He asked me, "Why are you crying?" How could I tell him! But if God brought you together I should be happy. That's a different thing, you know, quite different.

(NATASHA *with a candle in her hand walks across the stage from door on right to door on left without speaking*.)

MASHA *(sits up)*   She walks about as though it were she had set fire to the town.

OLGA   Masha, you are silly. The very silliest of the family, that's you. Please forgive me *(a pause)*.

MASHA   I want to confess my sins, dear sisters. My soul is yearning. I am going to confess to you and never again to anyone. . . . I'll tell you this minute *(softly)*. It's my secret, but you must know everything. . . . I can't be silent . . . *(a pause)*. I am in love, I am in love. . . . I love that man. . . . You have just seen him. . . . Well, I may as well say it straight out. I love Vershinin.

OLGA *(going behind her screen)*   Leave off. I don't hear anyway.

MASHA   But what am I to do? *(Clutches her head.)* At first I thought him queer . . . then I was sorry for him . . . then I came to love him . . . to love him with his voice, his words, his misfortunes, his two little girls. . . .

OLGA *(behind the screen)*   I don't hear you anyway. Whatever silly things you say I shan't hear them.

MASHA   Oh, Olya, you are silly. I love him—so that's my fate. It means that that's my lot. . . . And he loves me. . . . It's all dreadful. Yes? Is it wrong? *(Takes* IRINA *by the hand and draws her to herself.)* Oh, my darling. . . . How are we going to live our lives, what will become of us? . . . When one reads a novel it all seems stale and easy to understand, but when you are in love yourself you see that no one knows anything and we all have to settle things for ourselves. . . . My darling, my sister. . . . I have confessed it to you, now I'll hold my tongue. . . . I'll be like Gogol's madman . . . silence . . . silence. . . .

(Enter ANDREY *and after him* FERAPONT.)

ANDREY *(angrily)*   What do you want? I can't make it out.

FERAPONT (*in the doorway, impatiently*)   I've told you ten times already, Andrey Sergeyevitch.

ANDREY   In the first place I am not Andrey Sergeyevitch, but your honour, to you!

FERAPONT   The firemen ask leave, your honour, to go through the garden on their way to the river. Or else they have to go round and round, an awful nuisance for them.

ANDREY   Very good. Tell them, very good. (FERAPONT *goes out*). I am sick of them. Where is Olga? (OLGA *comes from behind the screen.*) I've come to ask you for the key of the cupboard, I have lost mine. You've got one, it's a little key.

(OLGA *gives him the key in silence;* IRINA *goes behind her screen; a pause.*)

ANDREY   What a tremendous fire! Now it's begun to die down. Hang it all, that Ferapont made me so cross I said something silly to him. Your honour . . . (*a pause*). Why don't you speak, Olya? (*a pause*) It's time to drop this foolishness and sulking all about nothing. . . . You are here, Masha, and you too, Irina—very well, then, let us have things out thoroughly, once for all. What have you against me? What is it?

OLGA   Leave off, Andryusha. Let us talk to-morrow (*nervously*). What an agonising night!

ANDREY (*greatly confused*)   Don't excite yourself. I ask you quite coolly, what have you against me? Tell me straight out.

(VERSHININ's *voice:* "Tram-tam-tam!")

MASHA (*standing up, loudly*)   Tra-ta-ta! (*To* OLGA) Good night, Olya, God bless you . . . (*Goes behind the screen and kisses* IRINA.) Sleep well. . . . Good night, Andrey. You'd better leave them now, they are tired out . . . you can go into things to-morrow (*goes out*).

OLGA   Yes, really, Andryusha, let us put it off till tomorrow . . . (*goes behind her screen*). It's time we were in bed.

(END)

17 Early Twentieth-Century Nonrealism

Distortion—A New Reality

Scene: The steward's box of velodrome during a bicycle race. Jewish gentlemen, stewards, come and go. They are all alike; little animated figures in dinner jackets, with silk hats tilted back and binoculars slung in leather cases. Whistling, catcalls and a restless hum from the crowded tiers of spectators unseen, off right. Music. All the action takes place on the platform.

Stage Direction   Scene Five   *From Morn to Midnight* by Georg Kaiser

If life is a dream, then a drama is a dream of a dream, even though you have employed it as reality.

Instructor   *The Isle of the Dead* by August Strindberg

Because Realism and Naturalism were so entrenched, rebellion by certain playwrights and poets who believed that the theatre should reflect abstract and intangible values finally occurred. These artists rejected science as a valuable life force. The Symbolists and, in particular, the Expressionists lead the nonrealistic movement in theatre. While pure Expressionist plays are rarely performed today, their influence in terms of playwriting, design, and acting has remained strong in the theatre during the twentieth century. It is important for an actor to study the Expressionist acting style as preparation for work in such acting styles as Epic (chapter 18), Absurd (chapter 19), and Eclectic (chapter 20).

Overview of Nonrealism

By 1900, the naturalistic movement had reached its peak and gave way to nonrealistic forms and styles. Many European playwrights turned away from Realism and Naturalism and adopted techniques of symbolic and nonrealistic drama. In his later years, Ibsen wrote symbolic plays such as *The Master Builder, Rosmersholm, John Gabriel Borkman*, and *When We Dead Awaken*. Gerhart Hauptmann, from Germany, turned from Naturalism (*The Weavers*) to Symbolism. Hauptmann's *The Sunken Bell* is a highly successful play in the symbolic style. Strindberg abandoned Realism around the turn of the century. Although his later plays were forerunners of Eclecticism (see chapter 20) in which at least three styles—Realism, Naturalism, and Expressionism— were combined, Strindberg's later dramatic work was overridingly symbolic.

Maurice Maeterlinck, from Belgium, favored an impressionistic-symbolistic technique in all of his plays. *The Intruder, The Blind, The Blue Bird*, and *Pelléas and Melisande* are his best-known works. Maeterlinck espoused the belief that most dramatic moments onstage should be static and silent, with thought, introspection, mystery, and intuition revealing the secrets of existence. His plays are famous for sound interspersed with silence, frequent vocal repetition, and dreamlike color combinations in lighting. The plots and characters in Maeterlinck's plays are not based on realistic circumstances. His characters live on another plane—on a mystical level where they communicate with a "higher world." In a world beyond reality, characters appear to move through a dream in which personification and symbolism take precedence. During the 1890s, Alfred Jarry, from France, wrote *Ubu Roi*, a play that had far-reaching impact on playwrights of the twentieth century. Because of his extreme dependency on Symbolism and caricature distortion, Jarry was in a sense an early Surrealist and Absurdist[1] (absurd drama is discussed in chapter 19).

1. In 1917 a movement known as Dadaism (*dada* means "hobby horse" in French) proposed to free the plastic and graphic arts, as well as the verbal arts, from traditional ways of seeing and feeling. The Dadaists took their lead from the dreamlike writings of Franz Kafka. They formulated a style of writing akin to the formless apparitions of the subconscious mind. Dadaism was followed in the 1920s by a

The Symbolists reacted violently against the popular notion of a writer's scientific duty to propound social problems in political terms. The basic tenet of Symbolism stresses the autonomy of art, measured entirely in terms of aesthetic standards. Authors used symbols to transcend what was normally considered "realistic" in everyday life. They hoped that the symbols would take them beyond the truth which heretofore had been expressed only directly and explicitly (as in Realism). Characters were created in poetic terms. Ideas were expressed in sophisticated form and term, as opposed to the naturalistic simplicity of, for example, Maxim Gorky (*The Lower Depths*). Symbolists firmly believed that literature should not be used as a weapon for social reform.

The Expressionists were even more influential than the Symbolists in the development of nonrealistic theatre forms. The Expressionists delved deeply into the world of the subconscious mind. Existence of the subconscious human mind has been thought probable since ancient times. In explaining the subconscious, ancient men spoke of Pandora's box. According to this legend, the god Mercury left a box in the cave of Pandora with a warning not to open it. Curiosity got the better of Pandora. She opened the box and allowed all the evils and sufferings of the world to escape. According to mythology, if forces of the subconscious mind were given free expression, universal chaos would result.

However, there is another aspect of subconsciousness. Pandora's box also contained the spirit of hope which sustains and uplifts mankind. The subconscious is a reservoir of individual and collective wisdom, just as Pandora's box promised "all gifts" to those who possessed it. It is possible to take all that we have seen and heard from our subconsciousness and bring it into harmony with our consciousness (see discussion of dormant emotion and experience in chapter 5).

The most direct knowledge of subconsciousness comes from the study of dreams. Expressionists and other nonrealists of the twentieth century were particularly influenced by dreams. Although Sigmund Freud provided the definitive modern analysis of dreams in the nineteenth century, the ancients also recognized the power of the subconscious mind. Alexander the Great was always accompanied by men versed in dream interpretation. On the night before he lay siege to the city of Tyre, he dreamed of a satyr dancing in victorious triumph. The sages foretold that Alexander would take the city, and Tyre fell before the Macedonians as was predicted.

Artemidorus lived during the time of Emperor Hadrian (A.D. 76–138).

---

movement called Surrealism. Its leader, Guillaume Apollinaire, coined the term *Surrealism* in the preface to his play *The Breasts of Tiresias* (subtitled "Drama Surrealisti"). Dadaism and Surrealism promised to free the mind of rational control by exposing the dreamlike, subconscious mind of man. The literature and plays provided audiences with vague scenery, fragmentary and unmotivated characters, minimal conscious activity, disjointed events, and in general a chaotic universe. These philosophical forerunners of the Absurd movement preached a new psychology based on combining the dreaming state with the waking state. The goal was to find a new reality, a kind of *sur* ("above") reality.

His theory of dreams was modern in tone. According to Artemidorus, a dream "happens in that instant when the affections are so vehement that they ascend up to the brain during our sleep and meet with the more watchful spirits." Thus, Artemidorus recognized the presence of conflict in dreams, anticipating Freud's modern theories.

Prior to Artemidorus, Plato stated, "In all of us, even in good men, there is a lawless, wild beast nature, which peers out in sleep."

A fourth-century writer, Synesius of Cyrene, emphasized a value in dreaming beyond that of providing a safety value for man's animal nature. He remarked, "We do not sleep merely to live, but to learn to live well."

When we sleep, we escape from the outer world. Dreaming proves that while we sleep our mind is active. Our mind reacts in a specific way while we sleep. It creates strange events from both reality and fantasy. Although we forget most dreams soon after waking, other dreams remain with us for a long time.

Freud's psychological theory of dreams focused on wish fulfillment, that is, a wish appearing in a dream travels from the subconscious mind (i.e., the *id*) to the conscious mind (i.e., the *ego*). Since the id constantly demands satisfaction from the ego in terms of fulfilling its wishes, a dream often presents a conflict situation. Since the subconscious operates differently from the conscious, perception of the subconscious alters perception of the conscious and distortion in the conscious mind arises. Material is condensed and displaced in illogical patterns and structures.

Expressionism was a loosely used term, and confusion often arises as to what exactly the term means. Its definition came from the work of Freud (and precursors) and his interpretation of dreams. Expressionism as a movement began with artists such as Pablo Picasso and Wassily Kandinsky. As early as 1910 these painters turned from painting observed reality and to applying a principle of distortion to art. Their art was not merely an imitation of reality. Well-defined objects, as such, were unimportant as subjects for their artistic work. The Expressionists believed that the universe and all that lived therein could be viewed only through the ego *and* the id—man's consciousness *and* subconsciousness. Hence, their art contained mystical and religious elements. These artists, working in the abstract, combined strange colors and patterns. While subjugating reality to his ego and id, the expressionistic artist distorted the subject of his painting, carefully selecting a subject from his experience—experience which had sifted or filtered through visions and dreams. Their paintings were meant to represent the intrinsic, abstract nature of materials as perceived by a creative mind.

Dramatic artists became increasingly disenchanted with scientific study of man and his environment. Since the material of science must have a cultural base to give it human significance, many German writers perceived man and his value system as a reflection of a mechanical, contrived, stifling, intellectually oppressive society. As noted earlier, Strindberg was one of the first major playwrights to traverse the confines of Naturalism by exploring an expressionistic dramatic form. In the preface to his *Dream Play*, written

Scene from *A Dream Play* by August Strindberg. Directed by Philip Benson. Scenery designed by Thad Torp. Scenic projections by Hal Howe. Lighting design by David Thayer. Costumes by Margaret Hall. The University of Iowa.

in 1911, Strindberg said he wanted to follow the pattern of dreams in which anything seemed possible, in which time and space had no reality. In other words, he began to explore the subconscious mind through the forces of the conscious mind in the Freudian tradition. Strindberg believed that by using imagination in combination with memory, fantasy, absurdity, and improvisation a dramatist could create new patterns of existence. Characterization was not to be based in reality. Instead, characters split, doubled and multiplied, vanished and reappeared in a dramatic structure held together by the consciousness of the Dreamer (i.e., the central character who often represented the author). Strindberg advocated a new dramatic form based on artistic subjectivity as opposed to Naturalism which was based on objectivity. Strindberg's dream world was also created from an imaginative "soul." His characters were never fixed, and changed according to his subjective, introspective whims. Strindberg was devoted to interpreting life using spiritual methods and to discovering the secrets of the subconscious mind. His most famous expressionistic plays are *To Damascus* (a trilogy), *A Dream Play*, and *The Ghost Sonata*—all variations on the mind of a dreamer.

In Expressionism fantasy and symbolism are combined, as well as fragments of Realism and Naturalism (as do the dream sequences of the human mind). A playwright's subjectivity is necessarily affected by his emotional experiences which in turn affect his view of the world. Hence, distortion in experience, thought, and character occur. Characters are more or less representative of states of mind, comparable to dreams or deliriums, in which appearance, time, and space lose continuity. A playwright, then, "objectifies the subjective"—that is, he puts onstage the happenings inside the head, in the mind. Because in expressionistic plays fantasy and reality alternate in remarkable elusiveness, characters *at times* appear to be robots or dream figures and at other times to be real (the appearance of robotlike characters are reflections of a mechanized society). In expressionistic plays, people are usually not bound by traditions of duty, morality, society, or family. Man is not represented as an individual nor classified in a specific role. Characters often have generalized names such as Mother, Worker, and so on. The playwright transcends the individual to reveal all of Mankind, or the playwright emphasizes human values and polarizes an individual at odds with a collective entity (see German Expressionism). Expressionism was consciously primitive and simplified in order to penetrate man's universality.

Expressionism spread throughout central Europe after 1912. In utilizing expressionistic techniques, playwrights aligned themselves with contemporary painters such as Franz Marc, Edvard Munch, Emile Nolde, and Paul Klee. In music, Expressionism was fostered by such composers as Arnold Schoenberg and Alban Berg. Following a war with France (Franco-Prussian War) and facing the probability of another war, artists (of theatre, music, literature, and art) experienced the aftereffects of revolt on social and political values. Several great expressionistic playwrights emerged, such as Walter Hasenclever (*The Son, The Seduction*), Georg Kaiser (*From Morn to Midnight, Gas I, Gas II, The Coral*), Ernst Toller (*Man and the Masses*), Franz Wedekind (*Spring's Awakening*), and the Capek brothers, Josef and Karel (*R.U.R., The World We Live In* or *The Insect Comedy*). By using fluid scenes, condensation of reality, situations and characters abstracted by symbolism, intensified distortion, illogical patterns, and lyricism, these authors wrote Expressionist plays. Generally, language was compressed into a staccato or telegram style. Juxtaposed against these abstractions was occasional interpolation of long monologues. Continuity of action was lost in dream sequences.

Some expressionistic plays have one or two acts with large numbers of scenes, and in other plays acts are missing altogether in favor of many scenes or tableaux. Sometimes physical action in expressionistic plays is so dominant that language becomes unnecessary (when this occurs, the actor must focus on pantomimic dramatization).

In many plays women and men were social equals. A woman served as a comrade or friend to a man. She loved with complete understanding. To the Expressionist, love was absolute, a way to escape the restrictions and compromises of the world. Sexual passion was not usually a major theme. Since Expressionism depicted the worthiness of mankind, characters were drawn with pathos. They also had a definite social point of view which usually represented the view of the author.

Scene from *The Insect Play* by Josef Capek and Karel Capek. Directed by Joan Snyder. Ed W. Clark High School, Las Vegas.

Expressionistic plays require kaleidoscopic outdoor and indoor settings. Scenic units and props are symbolic. For example, in *A Dream Play* note the scenic transformation of the flower bud on the roof which opens into a gigantic chrysanthemum (usually accomplished onstage by lighting or slide projection). Settings are used to support the main thought of the play. For example, in *Gas I* and *Gas II* by Georg Kaiser, spacious concrete domes with massive girders and wire apparatus, fanning out from a central platform, suggest the functional industrial architecture of an age of mass production and mechanization. Little or no naturalistic detail is included. Light and shadow contrast frequently to create spectacle (i.e., to create visual wonder and excitement). Music and sound effects are integrated much like music and sound in a film. A "total theatre" approach is used—that is, balanced integration of all theatrical elements.

As the twentieth century began, Stanislavski's system was the dominate acting style. However, by 1910 he had started to modify and reclarify his system. He became interested in Hindu philosophy, especially the Toga system of abstract meditation and mental concentration. At the end of 1914, Stanislavski explored further the sphere of the subconscious to discover other methods of stimulating activity. He subsequently conceptualized and wrote his theory of emotional memory. Later, Meyerhold modernized Stanislavski's style of acting. Uncomfortable with a theatre designed to mirror life, Meyerhold advocated a presentational theatre experience whereby actors and audiences encountered one another with mutual recognition. Meyerhold labeled his acting theories "biomechanics" (see discussion that follows).

To perform expressionistic drama, approach your interpretation of character with the techniques of Stanislavski in order to provide a human base. However, when the human elements of character give way to nonrealistic and dehumanized elements, Meyerhold's technique of biomechanics may be used to great advantage. The term *biomechanics* referred to a style of acting appropriate to the machine age. In other words, the acting style was kinetic and mechanical, utilizing gymnastics, circus movement, ballet, dance, and acrobatics. All of these mechanics were superimposed upon the actor by a strong director. Meyerhold believed that such activity could best be performed on platforms, ramps, trapezes, cylinders, and scaffolding—a type of scenery and locale called *constructivism*.

The acting style was highly theatrical and for the most part diametrically opposed to the work of his mentor, Stanislavski. Meyerhold rejected psychological Realism in favor of the science of biomechanics. He believed that movement was superior to speech. He also borrowed heavily from Oriental acting style and staging techniques (Oriental acting is discussed in chapter 18). Under Meyerhold, actors studied in three phases: a period of movement, a static period of posing, and a so-called realistic period related to lifelike mimicry. Meyerhold was devoted to grotesque satire. Despite this devotion, he retained some of the influence of Stanislavski in his actor coaching, allowing truthful human feeling to be expressed occasionally.

Voice

Although three major nonrealistic styles are discussed in this chapter (Symbolism, Expressionism, and biomechanics), the major focus is on Expressionism because it was most influential on the work of the twentieth century.

Vocal work in symbolist drama primarily utilizes the tenets of Stanislavski and Realism, with heightened use of silence and static intonation. Also, in some passages in symbolic plays poetic lyricism is necessary.

The dialogue in expressionistic plays modulates between realistic language, nonrealistic, staccato language, and lengthy, at times, poetic monologue (poetic in imagery though usually written in prose).

The key quality of expressionistic language is its clipped repartee mixed with staccato sounds. Generally, linguistic or literary conventions are disregarded and the language is concise and direct. Articles are often omitted, verbs are usually separated and forged into strange union, and nouns are frequently arranged in a series of lines. Alliteration is used abundantly, and continuous repetition of one sound is frequent. Crescendos heighten the impact of theme. As a result, your speaking is rhythmic and intense, rather than natural and fluid. When the script calls for dehumanized behavior, you may chant and intone or shout and bark to produce noise rather than words. Vocal sounds and noise have direct emotional impact on other characters and the audience. You may lapse into spiritual ecstasy; suddenly you may burst into wild screaming. For example, in the plays of the German playwright Hasenclever wild noise in combination with telegram-style language is often used. At times the sound is just short of a yell, other times it is a lyrically ecstatic cry, or it may be simply a wild, piercing yell. Verse is frequently used to increase the emotional intensity of the play and to heighten the mysticism and the imagination of both participant and viewer. The playwright often creates fables in order to transcend the material world and enter the realm of the imagination. For example, people become robots or insects.

To deliver expressionistic language you need wide vocal range, flexible vocal quality, and varied vocal rhythmic patterns. The staccato or vocal telegram segments require exceptional vocal clarity, breath control, and emotional intensity. Rhythmic variety and control are equally important to all your vocal and physical work in this style, especially in the robot and dream segments.

Exercise 1   Voice—Early Twentieth-Century Nonrealism

1. Practice the following speech aloud. In the speech staccato, expressionistic dialogue is emphasized, with articles omitted, words separated by dashes—all in a machine-gun-like manner. The effect should be somewhat mechanical and dehumanized.

> This Lady from Florence—who claims to come from Florence—has a
> vision like that ever visited you in your cage before? Furs—perfume!
> The fragrance lingers—you breathe adventure. Superbly staged. Italy . . .
> enchantment—fairy-tale—Riviera—Mentone—Prodighera—Nice—
> Monte Carlo—where oranges blossom, fraud blooms too.
>
> Scene One   *From Morn to Midnight*   Georg Kaiser

2. Practice the following speech aloud. The speech emphasizes the lyric monologue also found in expressionistic, symbolic, and nonrealistic drama. The effect may be somewhat ethereal, human, but elevated to a dream quality.

> Why did I hesitate? Why take the road? Whither am I bound? From first
> to last you sit there, naked bone. From morn to midnight, I rage in a
> circle . . . and now your beckoning finger points the way . . . whither?
>
> Scene Seven   *From Morn to Midnight*   Georg Kaiser

Movement

Movement serves as the social function and theme of most nonrealistic plays and less frequently as the actor's personal motivation as well as the character's motivation. Movement helps define character relationships; movement also helps clarify emotional and symbolic attitudes. For example, expressionistic plays require you to fill stage space with pantomimic dramatization and curious dances as others speak or during long periods of silence. At times

The two passages on this page are from *From Morn to Midnight* by Georg Kaiser. In *Introduction to Drama* edited by Robert C. Roby and Barry Ulanov, McGraw-Hill Book Company. Reprinted with permission of Robert C. Roby and Barry Ulanov.

The Formless Fears. Scene design for the nonrealistic play *The Emperor Jones* by Eugene O'Neill.

you perform theatrical acrobatics (as called for in Michel de Ghelderode's *Christophe Colomb* and *Pantagleize*). Movement is often enhanced by strange lighting and weird music. Around you the "drift of dream" or the "mechanics of routine" prevails in an essentially naked environment.

The key problem in nonrealistic movement is "to leave much of your real world behind"—that world of logical, organized action relatively free from chaos and surging passion. A nonrealistic play carries you into a world in which reality and dream abstractions mingle. Action is often only symbolic stereotype resulting from the nightmares and mental distortions of the playwright. Actions are fragmentary and disconnected and take place within symbolic forms or open spaces. Characters often wear symbolic masks and makeup in order to generalize the concept of mankind (exemplified in Eugene O'Neill's *The Great God Brown*). Frequently the realistic base of movement is dehumanized and distorted. In the manner of a marionette, movements are either slow and ephemeral (dreamlike) or mechanical and robotlike. Gestures are graceful, free, and fluid or abrupt, studied, and stilted. As you enter the world of distortion, conventional logic disappears. Nonetheless, your movement must retain some semblance of realism because realism is part of a dream, and a dream is in part true to observed, experienced reality. Yet, the overall projection of nonrealistic movement (especially expressionistic movement) must be distorted and incongruous with everyday life.

Meyerhold's biomechanics work extremely well for nonrealistic acting. Gymnastic and acrobatic activity reinforce the mechanical aspects of movement. Ballet and dance are effective for ephemeral dream movement.

Exercise 2   Movement—Twentieth-Century Nonrealism

Following is a list of exercises which will enable you to practice nonrealistic movement.

1. Construct a facial mask which typifies a stereotype attitude, emotion, or character (possibly you can purchase a mask from a party shop). Wear the mask and study it in a mirror. Then practice movement which exemplifies the countenance of the mask. Explore many types of physical action. For example, move in slow motion, move rapidly across the room, move mechanically, move grotesquely, and so on.
2. Imagine you are a puppet. Move according to the strings controlling your arms, legs, head, back, and torso.
3. Imagine you are an insect. Move according to the type of insect you choose to be.
4. Imagine you are a robot. Move according to how a robot behaves.
5. Imagine you are any kind of modern machine (for example, an adding machine, a typewriter, a washing machine, a telephone, and so on). Move according to the actions of the machine.
6. Imagine you are a snowflake, a cloud, rain, lightning, wind, a leaf, a feather, or any similarly lightweight or fragile thing. Move according to the activity of the object in motion.

Character and Emotion

To perform early twentieth-century expressionistic and nonrealistic styles use Stanislavski's character premise that acting is like living, and then counter and balance the style by using Meyerhold's depersonalization role identification theory. At times believability in role creation is needed in expressionistic and other nonrealistic acting styles, while at other times a formalized or mechanical design and shape is needed to accomplish some of the actions and movements of characters. The actor and director have the important task of careful script analysis to determine which factor is operative at any given moment (e.g., is it Stanislavski's realism? is it Meyerhold's biomechanics?). Combined properly, realism and biomechanics define character and emotion in expressionistic and nonrealistic acting styles. This mix produces a range of character and emotion complexity from simplistic to multidimensional. For example, the mix of realism and biomechanics can be applied clearly and effectively in Kaiser's *From Morn to Midnight*. The Teller (or the Cashier as he is sometimes called) is the central character. In part I, scene 1, the Teller is totally immersed in mechanical routine. Kaiser provided over twenty-four stage directions for the Teller without one word of dialogue. Most of the stage directions involve counting money or rapping on the Teller's window ledge. Analysis quickly reveals how dehumanized the Teller's life in the bank is. Finally, at the end of scene 1, the Teller chokes out the words, "Fetch—glass of water!" The Teller is little more than a robot in the assembly line of the banking business. In this scene, highly formalized robot action and speaking dictate the acting style.

However, in scene 3, the Teller is alone in a snow-covered field near a single tree. As the sun casts bluish shadows on the snow, the Teller begins a long monologue in which he explores the change in his life now that he has stolen money and run away. As the scene and speech progress, a storm develops. The Teller is engulfed in a dreamlike trance, his eyes scanning the field. He murmurs, "snow, snow, sun, silence." His words and movements glide into the ethereal formality of slow motion. As the wind and storm increase, the dream becomes a nightmare. The tree takes on the shape of a human skeleton with grinning jaws. In dream and nightmare fashion, the Teller converses with the tree. In this scene, highly formalized dream movement and speaking dictate the acting style, contrasting vividly with the earlier robot or mechanical style. Of course, both of these formalized elements are constantly contrasted with the real or human element at the base of the character, that of a man with a home, a mother, a wife, daughters, a job, and so on. As the play moves toward its conclusion, the Teller becomes increasingly humanized, discarding his robot and dream natures. By the final scene of the play, the Teller has achieved self-understanding as well as understanding of the world he lives in. No longer a robot or a dreamer, he sees himself and the world clearly. In this scene, the Teller must be performed with genuine warmth and naturalness; the best of Stanislavski realism can be applied here to enhance audience identification and empathy with the pathetic, martyred Teller. Realistic acting should prevail throughout his confession speech. Then, as the play concludes with his death, the audience both observes and feels the loss of a sacrificial human being.

The journey of the Teller provides a perfect example of the mixture of styles necessary for successful work with character and emotion in expressionistic acting. Careful role and play analysis determine when to use Realism and when to use biomechanics (either as the unreality of a robot or as a dream).

Exercise 3 Character and Emotion—Early Twentieth-Century Nonrealism

Perform the following brief improvisations, first, as a mechanical robot, second, as a sleepwalker midst a dream or nightmare, third, as any insect of your choice, and fourth, as any modern machine of your choice. Be certain to define the circumstances prior to performing the improvisation. Keep each of the four phases of the improvisation under five minutes.

1. A woman serves breakfast to her husband.
2. A bank teller receives money from a customer.
3. A woman pleads with her dead son to lay down in his grave and be still.
4. A man and a woman hoard food by piling it in a cellar.
5. A man stands lost on a street corner on Madison Avenue, New York City, as people rush by.
6. An accountant adds columns of figures as his boss observes him.
7. A man lost in a thick jungle thinks the trees are horrifying figures of fear.

A clear understanding of nonrealistic acting techniques is vital if you are to make the playwright's philosophic premise clear. The universality of these styles usually rests with the playwright's emphasis on human values, on love, and on spiritual brotherhood. Understanding these styles and the stylistic writing techniques of early twentieth-century nonrealists, the actor applies a mix of realistic and biomechanic acting techniques to fulfill the intentions of the author.

While so-called pure Expressionism and similar nonrealistic movements in theatre disappeared by the mid-1920s, their influence on writing, design, and acting style has continued. When combined with Stanislavski's system of Realism and Naturalism, the styles of the nonrealists led to the unique innovations of Bertolt Brecht and the Absurdists which finally culminated in the contemporary Eclectic theatre.

Suggested Characters and Plays for Scene Work

Stringberg, August

Father Indra, Indra's daughter, Officer, Lawyer
  A Dream Play
Hummel, The Student, The Milkmaid, The Lady in Black, The Mummy
  The Ghost Sonata

Kaiser, Georg

Gentleman in White, The Clerk, The Engineer, The Billionaire's Son
  Gas Part I

Cashier, Salvation Lass, The Lady, The Son
From Morn to Midnight

Shaw, Irwin

Bess, Schelling, Joan, Levy, Julia, Morgan, Katherine, Driscoll, Martha, Webster
Bury the Dead

Rice, Elmer

Mr. Zero, Mrs. Zero, Daisy, Shrdlu
The Adding Machine

O'Neill, Eugene

Brutus Jones, Henry Smithers, The Little Formless Fears
The Emperor Jones
Yank, Mildred Douglas, Paddy
The Hairy Ape
Dion Anthony, Margaret, Lillian Brown, Cybel
The Great God Brown

Capek, Karel

Harry Domin, Sulla, Marius
R.U.R.

Capek, Karel and Josef

Parasite, Chrysalis, Vagrant, Mr. Beetle, Mrs. Beetle, Fly, Larvae
The Insect Play

Maeterlinck, Maurice

Pelléas, Golaud, Melisande
Pelléas and Melisande
Boy, Girl, Fairy, Light, Night
The Blue Bird

Jarry, Alfred

Ubu Roi (King Turd)
Ubu Roi

Wedekind, Frank

Melchoir, Wendla, Moritz
Spring's Awakening

Toller, Ernst

The Woman, Nameless One
Man and the Masses

Connelly, Marc, and Kaufman, George S.

Composer, Girl
Beggar on Horseback

Barrie, Sir James M.

Peter Pan, Wendy, Nana, Captain Hook, John
Peter Pan

Scene from *Peter Pan* by Sir James M. Barrie. Directed by Robert N. Burgan. Scene and costume design by Ellis M. Pryce-Jones. University of Nevada, Las Vegas.

Actor Checklist   *Early Twentieth-Century Nonrealism*

Voice	Extensive range; lyrical when appropriate; staccato when appropriate; extensive use of pause and silence; varied rhythms; when appropriate, extensive use of chant, intonation, yells.
Movement	Motivated by idea, social function, and theme; when appropriate, distortion through robotlike, puppetlike dehumanization; when appropriate, distortion through slow and ephemeral dream quality; mix of presentational and representational mode; varied.
Gestures	Graceful, free, fluid, as appropriate; or abrupt, studied, stilted as appropriate; more selective in dehumanized moments; full use of entire body.
Pantomimic Dramatization	Use of masks; oriental techniques; acrobatics, strange dances; gymnastics; extremely inventive.
Character	Human reality base; distorted through dehumanization when appropriate, for example, mechanical and dreamlike; symbolic, clear social universality; combination of personalization and role identification and biomechanic formalism; when appropriate, analogous to inaminate objects, machines, animals, insects, and so on.
Emotion	Simplistic in dehumanized moments; complex in human moments; closely tied to social, thematic concepts.

Ideas	Strong philosophical and social orientation against machine age and modern technology; antiscientific; oriented to the common masses.
Language	Mix of prose and verse; mix of staccato and telegramlike dialogue and lyrical monologue.
Mood and Atmosphere	Closely tied to idea and social theme; generally serious; mix of reality and fantasy.
Pace and Tempo	Unusually varied.
Special Techniques	Careful analysis necessary to combine Stanislavski realism and Meyerhold biomechanics; unusual flexibility in physical activity.

Suggested Readings

Arnold, Paul. "The Artaud Experiment." *Tulane Drama Review,* Winter 1963.

Artaud, Antonin. *The Theatre and Its Double.* Translated by Mary C. Richards. New York: Grove Press, 1958.

Balakian, Anna E. *Surrealism: The Road to the Absolute.* Rev. ed. New York: E. P. Dutton & Co., 1959.

Benedikt, Michael, and Wellwarth, George, eds. *Modern French Theatre: The Avant-Garde, Dada, and Surrealism.* New York: E. P. Dutton and Co., 1964.

Braun, Edward, ed. *Meyerhold on Theatre.* New York: Hill & Wang, 1969.

Breton, Andre. *What Is Surrealism?* London: Faber & Faber, Ltd., 1936.

Dahlstrom, C. E. W. L. *Strindberg's Dramatic Expressionism.* New York: Benjamin Blom, 1930.

Fowlie, Wallace. *Age of Surrealism.* Bloomington, Ind.: Indiana University Press, 1960.

Kenworthy, B. J. *Georg Kaiser.* London: Oxford University Press, 1957.

Lehman, Andrew G. *The Symbolist Aesthetic in France, 1885–1895.* London: Oxford University Press, 1950.

Lumley, Frederick. *Trends in Twentieth Century Drama: A Survey Since Ibsen and Shaw.* 2nd ed. London: Barrie and Rockliff, 1960.

Samuel, Richard, and Thomas, R. H. *Expressionism in German Life, Literature and the Theatre (1910–1924).* London: Cambridge University Press, 1959.

From Morn to Midnight

by *Georg Kaiser*

Translated by Ashley Dukes

from
scene i

Characters   Manager
Porter
Lady
Serving Maid
Cashier

Scene   Interior of a small bank, Germany.

Situation   An anonymous cashier works in robot fashion in the deadly routine of his job. The soft allure of a beautiful foreign woman prompts him to break his dehumanized state, embezzle funds, and embark on a strange search for happiness and identity.

MANAGER   This lady from Florence—who claims to come from Florence—has a vision like that ever visited you in your cage before? Furs—perfume! The fragrance lingers—you breathe adventure. Superbly staged. Italy . . . enchantment—fairy-tale—Riviera—Mentone—Pordighera—Nice—Monte Carlo—where oranges blossom, fraud blooms too. Swindlers—down there every square foot of earth breeds them. They organize crusades. The gang disperses to the four winds—preferably small towns—off the beaten track. Then—apparitions—billowing silks—furs—women—modern sirens. Refrains from the sunny south—*o bella Napoli!* One glance and you're stripped to your undershirt—to the bare skin—to the naked, naked skin. (*He drums with a pencil on the* CASHIER's *hand.*) Depend upon it, this bank in Florence knows as much about the lady as the man in the moon. The whole affair is a swindle, carefully arranged. And the web was woven not in Florence, but in Monte Carlo. That's the place to keep in mind. Take my word for it, you've just seen one of the gadflies that thrive in the swamp of the Casino. We shall never see her again. The first attempt missed fire; she'll scarcely risk a second! I joke about it but I have a keen eye—when you're a banker—I really should have tipped off the police! Well, it doesn't concern me—besides, banks must be discreet. Keep your eye on the out-of-town papers—the police news. When you find something there about an adventuress, safe under lock and key— then we'll talk about it again. You'll see I was right—then we'll hear more of our Florentine lady than we'll ever see of her and her furs again.

(*Exit.* CASHIER *seals up rolls of bank notes.*)

PORTER (*enters with letters, hands them to* CLERK)   One registered letter. I want the receipt.

(CLERK *stamps receipt form, hands it to* PORTER. PORTER *rearranges glass and waterbottle on the table, and goes out.* CLERK *takes the letters into* MANAGER's *room, and returns.*)

LADY (*reenters; comes quickly to the counter*)   I beg your pardon.

(CASHIER *stretches out his hand, without looking at her. Raps.*)

LADY (*louder*)   If you please! (CASHIER *raps on the counter.*) I don't want to
     trouble the Manager a second time. (CASHIER *raps on the counter.*) Please tell
     me—would it be possible for me to leave you the letter of credit for the whole
     sum, and to receive an advance of three thousand in part payment? (CASHIER
     raps impatiently.) I should be willing to deposit my diamonds as security, if
     required. Any jeweler in the town will appraise them for you. (*She takes off a
     glove and pulls at her bracelet.* SERVING MAID *comes in quickly, plumps down
     on sofa, and begins rummaging in her market-basket.* LADY, *startled by the
     commotion, looks round. As she leans on the counter her hand sinks into the
     * CASHIER'S. CASHIER *bends over the hand which lies in his own. His spectacles
     glitter, his glance travels slowly upward from her wrist.* SERVING MAID, *with a
     sigh of relief, discovers the check she is looking for.* LADY *nods kindly in her
     direction.* SERVING MAID *replaces vegetables, etc., in her basket.* LADY, *turning
     again to the counter, meets the eyes of the* CASHIER. CASHIER *smiles at her.*
     LADY *drawing back her hand*) Of course I shall not ask the bank to do anything
     irregular. (*She puts the bracelet on her wrist; the clasp refuses to catch.
     Stretching out her arm to the* CASHIER) Would you be so kind? I'm clumsy
     with the left hand. (CASHIER *stares at her as if mesmerized. His spectacles,
     bright points of light, seem almost to be swallowed up in the cavity of his
     wide-open eyes. To* SERVING MAID) You can help me, mademoiselle. (SERVING
     MAID *does so.*) Now the safety catch. (*With a little cry*) You're pinching my
     flesh. Ah, that's better. Thank you so much. (*She bows to the* CASHIER *and goes
     out.* SERVING MAID *coming to the counter, planks down her check.* CASHIER
     *takes it in trembling hands, the slip of paper flutters and crackles; he fumbles
     under the counter, then counts out money.*)
SERVING MAID (*looking at the pile of coins*)   That isn't all mine.

(CASHIER *writes.* CLERK *becomes observant.*)

SERVING MAID (*to* CLERK)   But it's too much! (CLERK *looks at* CASHIER. CASHIER
     rakes in part of the money.) Still too much!
(CASHIER *ignores her and continues writing.* SERVING MAID *shaking her head, puts
the money in her basket and goes out.*)
CASHIER (*hoarsely*)   Get me a glass of water! (CLERK *hurries from behind the
     counter; comes to table.*) That's been standing. Fresh water—cold water—
     from the faucet. (CLERK *hurries out with glass.* CASHIER *goes quickly to electric
     bell, and rings.* PORTER *enters from the hall.*) Get me fresh water.
PORTER   I'm not allowed to go so far from the door.
CASHIER (*hoarsely*)   For me. Not that slime. I want water from the faucet.

(PORTER *seizes waterbottle and hurries out.* CASHIER *quickly crams his pockets with
bank notes. Then he takes his coat from a peg, throws it over his arm, and puts on
his hat. He lifts a flap in the counter, passes through, and goes out.*)

MANAGER   (*absorbed in reading a letter, enters from his room*)   Here's the letter
     of advice from Florence, after all!

(CLERK *enters with a glass of water.* PORTER *enters with a full waterbottle.*)

MANAGER (*looking up*)   What the devil . . . ?

(END)

18 Brecht and Epic Style
Didacticism

PHILOSOPHER   The other day I met my
      audience
In a dusty street
He gripped a pneumatic drill in his fists.
For a second
He looked up. Rapidly I set up my theatre
Between the houses. He
Looked expectant.
Today
I brought it off again. Outside the station
With brass bands and rifle butts I saw him
Being herded off to war.
In the midst of the crowd
I set up my theatre. Over his shoulder
He looked back
And nodded.
    "Buying Brass," from *Poems on the Theatre*
                    by Bertolt Brecht

. . . don't show him too much
But show something. And let him observe
That this is not magic but
Work, my friends.
                    Bertolt Brecht
        from Kenneth Tynan, *Curtains.*

Of all works, my favourite
Are those which show usage.
The copper vessels with bumps and
    dented edges,
The knives and forks whose wooden
    handles are
Worn down by many hands: such forms
To me are the noblest.
                    Bertolt Brecht
      from Kenneth Tynan, *Curtains.*

MOTHER COURAGE   I won't have my war
all spoiled for me! It destroys the weak,
does it? Well, what does peace do for
'em? Huh?
(She sings her song)
So cheer up, boys, the rose is fading
When victory comes you may be dead
A war is just the same as trading
But not with cheese—with steel and lead!
    Christians, awake! The winter's
        gone!
The snows depart, the dead sleep on.
And though you may not long survive
Get out of bed and look alive!
      Mother Courage by Bertolt Brecht

Overview of Brecht Epic Theatre—From Illusion to Fact and Social Action

It is told that shortly after the death of Bertolt Brecht in 1956, Lotte Lenya, a principal actress in the Berliner Ensemble, was speaking in Iowa. According to the story of this incident, she related a personal account about Brecht to a group of university students. Lotte was having great difficulty understanding Brecht's acting theories as they applied to a role she was playing in one of his plays. Upon asking Brecht how she was to interpret her role to achieve a performance faithful to his Epic theories, Brecht supposedly patted her reassuringly on the shoulder and said she should simply "follow her instincts" and "go about the business of acting." This was Brecht's way of admitting that his famous theories can be taken only so far, that ultimately traditional acting craft must also be part of the work necessary to present his plays effectively. In other words, there is a vast distinction between Brecht's theories and Brecht's practice.

Since 1956, the ideas of Brecht have revolutionized playwriting, production techniques, and acting methodology. Ironically Brecht's theatre concepts had far-reaching impact only after his death. Brecht wrote his first play (*Baal*) in 1918 and formulated his writing style during the 1920s (*A Man is a Man* and *The Threepenny Opera*). When the Nazis began their rise to power in 1933, Brecht left Germany and settled in Scandinavia. While in exile, he wrote several major works: *The Private Life of the Master Race, Mother Courage, Galileo, The Resistible Rise of Arturo Ui,* and *The Good Woman of Setzuan*. Later, he left the northern countries of Europe for the United States, making his home in Hollywood until the end of World War II. One of Brecht's most famous plays was written during this time, *The Caucasian Chalk Circle*. Although Brecht had become a convert to Marxism, he did not return to the Eastern Sector of Berlin immediately after the war. He spent some time in Switzerland in 1947, finally settling in East Berlin in 1948. After his self-imposed exile, the name and work of Bertolt Brecht found acceptance and acclaim throughout Europe, the United States, and England.

German theatre during the 1920s received its inspiration from the director Erwin Piscator. Upon founding the First Epic Proletarian Theatre, Piscator formed an alliance with Brecht. Both men were interested in treating subjects in strictly intellectual, didactic terms. They opposed the traditional late nineteenth-century and early twentieth-century focus on Realism, Naturalism, and orientation toward "suspension of disbelief" with its emotional element and its escape-into-make-believe quality. Piscator and Brecht favored a social activist theatre in which the audience remained aware that they were in a theatre absorbing messages and ideas. They documented plays by prefacing scenes with electronically or mechanically projected captions explaining themes and exhorting action. The expressionistic technique of constructing a series of disjointed, episodic scenes was used as a desirable method for abolishing suspense, which was an emotional and undesirable characteristic of traditional theatre. Music was used to neutralize emotion rather than to intensify it. Atmospheric lighting was rejected in favor of general illumination. Actors wore everyday dress; property items were used as blatant theatre props to assist in making an idea clear rather than in reinforcing an emotional "reality." Scenery was constructivist in design, using stairs, levels, scaffolding, treadmills, and revolving stages. Films, used as background scenery, projected images of places and people from a variety of historical periods and subjects on screens, all for the purpose of better explaining present social circumstances (this technique, later known as *historification*, is explained in detail later in this chapter). Piscator dominated the Berlin theatre of the 1920s and provided an important function by creating a milieu for Brecht's plays.

Scene from *The Three-penny Opera* by Bertolt Brecht. Directed by Gerard Larson. Designed by Larry Schumate. California State University, Sacramento.

However, before the 1920s ended, Piscator and Brecht ended their collaboration. Although both men sought enlightenment and education of the masses, the means of achieving that end became a source of contention between them. The young Brecht felt the only true means of achieving social action in the theatre was elimination of all emotion from the stage. Piscator did not want to banish emotion completely; instead, he tried to correlate fictional dramatic story and real contemporary world (e.g., surrounding the play with contemporary slide projections and films from real contemporary society). However, the tempo of the times in Germany (i.e., the concentrated rise of Fascism) proved to Brecht that Epic Theatre had to heighten and intensify didacticism in order to change the social, economic, and political conditions of the country. Piscator's desire to combine traditional emotionalism and didacticism was seen by Brecht as a weakening of their work. Brecht began to explore a more pragmatic theatrical concept (i.e., Didactic

Materialism) aimed at unifying the thinking of his audiences. Brecht hoped to provoke viewers into direct, strong social action.

The Epic play presents historical subject matter from the viewpoint of a single storyteller. Sections of dialogue and narration are interspersed throughout the play. Changes in time and place are frequent, and time is bridged by a sentence or a brief passage. In Epic Theatre the sweep of a specific historical period is presented similarly to the manner in which Homer wrote his poetic narration the *Iliad*. Since Epic plays narrate or report many experiences, audiences have little opportunity to identify with the action on-stage. Few Brechtian characters gain audience empathy. (Although the Epic actor consciously demonstrates, suggests, and describes behavior, rather than realistically create the inner truth of a role, Piscator would not have denied that emotion is an integral element of characterization. As Lotte Lenya's story proves, in later years Brecht came to agree!) To counteract emotion onstage, Epic Theatre provides a narrator whose primary function is to *observe* the action and *report* events. The actors, in conjunction with the narrator, attempt to arouse the capacity for social action in an audience. The actors propose arguments, hoping to force decisions involving change in social conditions. To further clarify the didactic elements of the play, Epic staging includes use of general illumination of both the stage and the auditorium, elimination of act curtains, use of blatant scene-shifting with revolves, and use of slide and film projections. The main thesis in Epic Theatre is that human beings can be altered, are capable of change; from moment to moment, man makes many decisions affecting social and economic circumstances.

By the late 1920s, in his theoretical writing Brecht began to explore and expand his concept of Epic Theatre. He also wrote poems, aphorisms, stories, essays, polemics, and novels. However, his greatest achievements were his forty plays and adaptations. In 1948, Brecht published his theoretical writings. Chief among this work was "Small Organum for the Theatre." Thereafter, he turned from the concept of Epic Theatre to theatre oriented more toward didacticism. Although most of Brecht's theories may be categorized under the term *epic*, his plays tend to transcend the limitations of this label. His plays are a rich mixture of Realism and Expressionism embellished by new and special techniques.

The Brechtian era initiated a change in drama and theatrical production. Brecht viewed the old dramatic theatre as a rigid structure that presented fixed, unchangeable events. Historical subjects were treated in historical terms. Past and present remained separated. Audiences were accustomed to watching events which mirrored their own emotional or psychological makeup, and their sensibilities had been lulled into acceptance of and passivity toward the old order of events. Brecht did not intend to pacify audiences; his plays were meant to arouse, shock, and "make strange" (i.e., alienate audiences by making them *think* and, hopefully, *act* to change society).

The subject matter of Brecht's plays is always based on history. He emphasizes the past in order to place the present in perspective. Brecht believed an audience should see the present through the past. In this manner an audience can view both present and past objectively, unemotionally, and with detachment. The present, then, offers a spectator alternatives for positive action. Brecht labeled this philosophy or technique "historification," a concept dependent on psychological behaviorism. Analysis is possible at any given moment by the thrust of a man's action in a particular circumstance. The primary subject of Brecht's plays is the relationship between men. Instead of watching modern man relate to the present, we study his behavior as he reacts to the past. Or the process is reversed and we watch historic figures react to the present (e.g., St. Joan in a Chicago stockyard, Hitler in an American gangster environment, and so on). The didactic lesson of historification can be likened to a Medieval morality play or to the biblical style of writing in parables. In effect, historification is a kind of propaganda made palatable by quality theatricalism.

An integral element of the process of historification is the concept of *verfremdungseffekt* or *alienation*. The literal translation of *alienation* is "to make strange" (to make actions strange). Objectivity is implied in the theory of alienation. An audience does not identify or empathize with strange events that take place in a blatantly theatrical way. Such events take precedence over character and emotional depth. To this end Brecht employed a number of shock-making theatrical devices: visible theatre mechanics; scenery changed in view of the audience; musicians participating in stage events; fragmentary, practical sets designed only *to indicate* the place of the scene. Piscator's theatre set the tone for Brechtian production by using

Set design for Berliner Ensemble production of *The Caucasian Chalk Circle* by Bertolt Brecht.

multiple treadmills rotating in opposite directions, lifts to hoist actors, and screens to project documentary films. (Documentary films usually confirm or contradict what the characters say by showing *reallife* figures in support of or in contrast to *created* characters onstage.) Films show similar events simultaneously in different places, thereby revealing the world in flux. The Epic scenic design can be easily constructed and does not impede the action of the story or the flow of actors onstage. The set is often lighted in flat, white light, and no attempt is made to represent different moods or shades of meaning. Illusion is frequently assaulted by the open use of visual mechanics on the stage.

Brecht also used music as a means to further objectify stage action. He used dissonant music to aid in communicating the text. In Brecht's plays, music helps to eliminate meaning by delineating moral attitude. Songs comment on the action; they become means of arousing social consciousness.

Brecht used comic dance and mime in his plays for both theatrical diversion and didactic purposes. His plays were studded with farcical elements in the tradition of the circus clown—laughter tinged with sadness, pratfalls, and jokes. Brecht deliberately added comedy to his plays to reveal the ludicrous nature of man's helplessness in a corrupt capitalist world. (It was also fun and entertaining!) Shocking and strange devices were used at every turn: for example, long presentational songs with dissonant music (*The Caucasian Chalk Circle*); signs from the ceiling proclaiming War Is Evil (*Mother Courage*); a man standing in a 1930 business suit speaking with a Chicago accent as a motion picture reveals Hitler speaking in the same manner (*The Resistible Rise of Arturo Ui*); an American flier surrounded by Chinese coolies (*The Good Woman of Setzuan*); unmasked peasants surrounded by masked tyrants (*The Caucasian Chalk Circle*); an actor throwing away a moustache and costume to speak as himself rather than as a character (at the final line of *The Resistible Rise of Arturo Ui*).

Oriental Influence on Brecht

The virtuosity of Brecht's Epic Theatre is allied to ancient Asiatic or Oriental theatre (mainly of India, Indonesia, China, and Japan).

Early Indian plays were primarily dance and music set to plays written in Sanskrit. Later Indian plays were very romantic and highly symbolic—for example, Kalidasa's *Shakuntala*.

Indonesia was famous for its shadow puppet plays and its dance drama.

Mainland China produced two types of drama, Southern drama and the Northern drama. Today, the Peking Opera is the center for classical Chinese drama, a highly symbolic combination of dance and music oriented toward civil and military stories.

Japanese drama has been the most influential of the Eastern dramas. Japan has produced three major theatrical forms: Noh plays, puppet theatre, and Kabuki dramas. Noh is essentially dance drama whose plays are brief and deal with gods, warriors, women, spirits, and demons. The actors are all male. Japan's puppet theatre is internationally famous and centers around a group called Bunraku. Kabuki is the most flexible and most popular Japanese drama. The three types of Kabuki drama are historical and domestic plays and dance dramas. Kabuki plays are inordinately long, running as much as five or more hours. The material is both comic and serious. The American occupation of Japan produced a new kind of theatre called Shingeki, in which Western plays are adapted to the Japanese language.

Acting is the key to all Oriental dramatic forms. The performer, be he dancer, singer, or actor, uses highly complex symbolic systematic gestures emanating from every part of the body. Oriental audiences recognize and immediately understand the system. Oriental acting emphasizes body control and discipline, focusing primarily on movement, gesture, pantomimic dramatization, mood, and use of intricate masks, costumes, and makeup. Character and language are subordinate to the theatrical elements just listed. However, speaking, chanting, and singing are nonetheless important. The vocal work combines with the musical accompaniment of the drama and requires unusually clear, precise diction. Character is primarily symbolic and far less complex and psychological than in Western drama. The presentational mode dominates in Oriental acting. The overall effect is colorful and blatantly theatrical. Brecht found this effect appealing because Oriental acting style provided practical models for his acting theories. Of particular importance to Brecht was the disciplined physical prowess of Oriental actors. Movement is graceful, forceful, and rhythmic. Basically the Chinese use three types of walking, each distinguished by prescribed movements:

1. The roll-walk, in which the hips rotate as the feet move carefully from the ball of the foot onto the heel
2. The flat-walk, in which there is no hip movement and the entire foot lands flat at each step
3. The kick-walk, a goose step in which the lower leg is thrust forward at each step

Gestures are fluid, full, mimetic, and descriptive, and their action and attitude are also symbolic. For example, to indicate a door opened forcefully, an actor raises both hands in front of him and then separates them violently. Some other prescribed gestures are these:

1. An action to repulse, in which one arm is thrust forcefully sideways
2. An action of resolution, in which one arm is thrust forcefully high above the head and the other arm is thrust down and backward at the side
3. An action to conceal, in which the back of the hand is placed across the eyes
4. An action for weeping, in which the fingers are moved up and down in the conceal position

All of these and other important gestures used in the Oriental theatre are accentuated by manipulation of *watersleeves* worn at the wrists of most costumes. Watersleeves are long, dangling scarflike draperies that create lovely, flowing images during movement. (The feet are as important as the hands to gesture. In fact, every part of the body is used for precise, meaningful communication.)

In Oriental theatre, action is enhanced by vocalization. Emotion is indicated by symbolic body gestures coupled with either dissonant or lyrical vocal qualities. At times, the voice is clipped, staccato, or monotone. The depth of the emotion is indicated by ascending or descending emphasis on the combined effect of body and vocal elements. Diction is always precise and clear.

Music is an integral part of Oriental theatre. However, it is used for supportive purposes rather than for independent value. Whereas Brecht wanted music to stand as an independent element in the drama, in Oriental theatre it is used to create mood and to reinforce thought.

The total theatrical effect of Oriental theatre is substantially less didactic than Brecht's theatre. In spite of his admiration for it, Brecht found Oriental theatre too hypnotic. However, he enthusiastically favored the transparent power and grace of Chinese acting techniques. Brecht discovered a well of social communication within the mimetic and gestural expression of the Chinese theatre. He soon discovered that his actors could clarify and define social relationships if they performed in a detached manner, as though observing their own actions. Thus, both performer and audience became observers. This is the identifying characteristic of Brecht's theatre.

Voice

One of the most striking features of Brecht's plays is the language. Brecht wrote "colloquial-poetry" which has sensual simplicity. His poetry contains melancholy, tenderness, sadness, malice, wit, lyricism, logic, and paradox. If Brecht is new to an actor, he may continually make the mistake of fighting the theory that "factual statements claiming reason over emotion" must dominate textual analysis. The language of Brecht is filled with poetry and emotion. The songs (generally set to music by Kurt Weill) are the epitome of Brecht's poetic diction.

Vocal work in Brecht's plays is a selective combination of believable human speech and overtly theatrical, detached, or even dehumanized speech. In other words, both Realism and nonrealism are at work in the Epic plays of Brecht. His is not a pure form. Elements of Realism, Naturalism, Symbolism, and Expressionism can be identified in his scripts. As a result, your voice must be pliant, flexible, and lively to achieve subtle variations of meaning, as well as overt variation of style. Constant attention should be paid to vowels and consonants. National and regional dialects are common in Brechtian plays and must be handled perfectly. Class distinctions are also written carefully into the language. The voice must be used economically. When characterization is multidimensional, as for Grusha in *The Caucasian Chalk Circle*, vocal nuances should reflect the best of Stanislavski's realistic vocal training. On the other hand, when the speech is mechanical and theatrical, as for the Iron Soldiers in *The Caucasian Chalk Circle*, vocal work should reflect the best of the nonreal expressionistic techniques discussed in chapter 17. A large vocal range is of aid to an actor in Brecht's Epic plays. When they are appropriate, dissonant singing, chanting, and intonation in the expressionistic and Oriental manners are valuable assets. Occasionally, lyrical passages require harmonious, pleasant vocal delivery. Sometimes, with very little transition, such passages are followed by disconnected, dissonant, strange-sounding segments. A disciplined, fully trained vocal mechanism is essential for effective delivery of Brecht's plays.

Exercise 1   Voice—Brecht Epic Theatre

Practice the speech from *Mother Courage* given at the beginning of this chapter, emphasizing the following techniques.

1. Believable, human, realistic delivery
2. A variety of regional and national dialects (e.g., British, Japanese, Italian, Irish, Swedish, and American Southern)
3. A variety of class distinctions (e.g., British royalty, common Cockney, American Midwestern middle class, Southern hillbilly, and so on
4. Robot or mechanical
5. Dreamlike ephemeral
6. Singing, chanting, and intonation

Note: Both men and women should practice this speech. Actresses may impersonate male roles, and vice versa.

Movement

Movement, gesture, and pantomimic dramatization in Brecht again require combining several kinds of techniques, namely, realistic, biomechanical, expressionistic, and Oriental. Careful script analysis by you and your director will lead you to the correct determination of which to employ, and when. Such variety of movement necessitates a totally trained body, a body whose muscles must remain loose and flexible for maximum control. Acrobatics, dance, mime, and gymnastic training are highly effective in acting Brecht.

Exercise 2   Movement—Brecht Epic Theatre

1. Again using the speech from *Mother Courage* appearing at the beginning of this chapter, invent movement, gestures, and pantomimic dramatization to accommodate each of the vocal deliveries used in all six of the techniques in foregoing Exercise 1.
2. Practice the following Oriental techniques of movement described in this chapter:
   a. The roll-walk
   b. The flat-walk
   c. The kick-walk

    d. The gesture to repulse
    e. The gesture of resolution
    f. The gesture to conceal
    g. The gesture for weeping

If possible, attach makeshift watersleeves to your wrists when performing.

Character and Emotion

Except when creating key three-dimensional roles such as Grusha in *The Caucasian Chalk Circle* and Mother Courage in the play of the same name, you usually will not create complex characterization. A certain objectivity or detachment in performance reveals the *actor* as well as the *character*. In theory, most of Brecht's characters do not grow or develop onstage (in practice, growth sometimes takes place in spite of Brecht and his theory). You often encounter your audience directly and honestly; similarly, you often encounter your fellow actors in the same manner. The play and the acting are not disguised by illusion. Your objective is to provoke examination of social issues and raise questions for the viewers. You must frequently increase the spectator's awareness of being in the theatre by revealing your total consciousness in performing your role. In theory, your audience will then concentrate on ideas and action, rather than on emotion and character. (In practice, audiences still seem to respond best to emotion and character in Brecht, rather than to ideas.)

In his plays, Brecht provides you with devices to enhance the concept of alienation such as overt prologue, epilogue, narration, direct address, reference to the author, episodic scene progress, and didactic trial argument. Brecht also outlined a series of specific acting techniques related to character and emotion which can help you discover how to accomplish some of his theory.

1. Perform with an awareness of being watched.

2. Look at the floor and openly calculate movement.

3. Separate vocalization from gesture (in other words, make vocal and physical timing strange and disconnected).

4. Remain uninvolved with other actors, physically and emotionally.

5. Stand and move in a simple, loosely held together group (removed from your colleagues, you are free to change the course of action and make independent decisions).

6. In order to better instruct your audience, freely acknowledge their diversity by speaking to the various collective units as well as to individuals within the units. For example, isolate a group of businessmen by focusing your eyes on the group, and then focus on each member in turn within the group. Similarly, recognize other groups and then each individual within a group until you have contacted the entire audience.

7. Address the audience directly from center stage in full-front presentational fashion.

8. Speak your lines as if they were a quotation and in the manner of delivering a speech in the third person.

9. Occasionally speak stage directions aloud to intensify unemotional acting.

10. Be critical of your character, as though all of your actions had occurred in the past.

11. Change roles with other actors during rehearsals and even during performances to purify and conceptualize ideas and to remain unattached to any role.

12. Stand in front of a mirror and meticulously study your movements and gestures.

Scene from *The Good Woman of Setzuan* by Bertolt Brecht. Directed by Paul C. Harris, Jr. University of Nevada, Las Vegas.

Total attention to the concept of alienation can produce theatre generally free from emotional, empathic response from viewers. Do not strive for feeling and passion. Express excitement in terms of symbolism or ritual. Emotional portrayal is decorously exemplified and economically projected (for example, to indicate disdain or aloofness, simply turn your back on other actors). The emotional response of your audience need not correspond to the economic emotions of the character portrayed (for example, a spectator may laugh when you are angry). One of the most effective means of heightening alienation in Brecht Epic Theatre is to follow the Oriental example of using white makeup on your face. For example, a curtain opens to reveal you sitting on the stage. Your body is completely still; you rest your head in your hands. Slowly, with much ceremony, your head comes up, revealing a stark white face and traces of the makeup on your hands. No one in the audience misses the point. You are an actor in a theatre! All subsequent action should be tied to that theatrical beginning, even if you later remove the makeup.

In Brecht Epic Theatre, emotional power over an audience is frequently muted, leaving the actors and characters free to perform thought-provoking action. To protect the intellectual content of his plays, Brecht also uses some expressionistic techniques involving robot or mechanical and dreamlike action. Characters frequently and suddenly burst into song or formal commentary. Characters often become grotesque and unreal (e.g., Hitler as a marionette in *The Resistible Rise of Arturo Ui*). With practice and experience, you can adjust to these unusual techniques and provide the appropriate response—such as "dropping character" and singing a song that has nothing to do with the emotion of action and everything to do with the intellectual message or performing in a dehumanized, robot manner as for The Iron Soldiers in *The Caucasian Chalk Circle*.

Exercise 3   Character and Emotion—Brecht Epic Theatre

1. Using the scene at the end of this chapter from *The Caucasian Chalk Circle*, practice the twelve techniques for character and emotion just described.
2. Practice the scene again with only selected items from the twelve techniques, appropriately combining realistic, biomechanical, expressionistic, and Oriental techniques.

In concluding the discussion of Brecht's acting theories, we must caution that, paradoxically, any totally faithful application of Brecht's theories to his or other Epic plays (see the work of Peter Weiss, Rolf Hochhuth, and Max Frisch, for example) is doomed to almost certain failure. Audiences have generally rejected rigid use of alienating and didactic techniques.

The problem is how to reconcile Brecht's theory with Epic plays and sustain audience interest. Edward Payson Call, an American director, provided one of the keys to solving this problem. His analysis and directing of highly successful productions of Brecht plays have captivated audiences. Call uses Brechtian acting theory with discretion and pinpoint selectivity. Apart from Brecht's Epic theories and some use of expressionistic, biomechanical, and Oriental techniques, Call permits certain actors in key roles to perform in a traditional, realistic style, creating emotion and empathy (again, Grusha in *The Caucasian Chalk Circle* and Mother Courage must be played this way). As a result, the eclectic *mix* of the Epic, the nonreal, and the real creates palatable Brecht onstage and also imparts the appropriate didacticism. Perhaps Brecht's advice to Lotte Lenya (given at the beginning of this chapter) best guides your acting: *Once aware of and rehearsed in the Epic techniques, follow your instincts and play the role.* You cannot worry continually whether the audience is being properly instructed and activated. Brecht's plays probably present adequate opportunity to achieve his intention without inordinate application of all his acting theories.

Suggested Characters and Plays for Scene Work

Brecht, Bertolt

Azdak, Grusha, The Ironshirt, Ludovica, The Governor's Wife
    The Caucasian Chalk Circle
Shen Te/Shui Ta, Mr. Shu Fu
    The Good Woman of Setzuan
Arturo Ui, Givola, Roma, Dogsborough, Docdaisy
    The Resistible Rise of Arturo Ui
Galileo
    Galileo
Mother Courage, Swiss Cheese, Catherine, Eilif, Yvette
    Mother Courage
Polly, Macheath, Peachum, Lucy
    The Threepenny Opera
Joan
    St. Joan of the Stockyards
Any role
    A Man's a Man

See also the list of characters and plays at the end of chapter 20 for playwrights influenced by Brecht Epic Theatre, Weiss, Hochhuth, and Frisch.

Actor Checklist   *Brecht Epic Theatre*

Voice	Selective combination of human and dehumanized; pliant, flexible; lively; unusual attention to vowels and consonants; national and regional dialects; class distinction; dissonant singing, chanting, intonation, and lyrical, as appropriate.
Movement	Appropriate mix of realistic, biomechanical, expressionistic, Oriental; loose and flexible muscle control; some use of acrobatics, dance, mime, and gymnastics; ranges from graceful to forceful; mix of presentational and representational mode.

Gestures	Varied; at times full use of entire body; highly inventive; at times use of specific Oriental techniques; descriptive; fluid; isolated body gestures.
Pantomimic Dramatization	Unusual use of mask, makeup, music, costume, particularly for Oriental; highly inventive; theatrical; rhythmic.
Character	Combination of real and nonreal; combination of historical and fictional; ranges from simple to complex; oriented toward social issues and themes; clear; controlled; realized with a mix of alienation devices and human behavior; diversified and theatrical.
Ideas	Unusually important; clear; didactic; socially, politically, and philosophically oriented; directed to the masses.
Emotion	Ranges from simple to complex; ranges from human to nonhuman; ranges from full empathy to no empathy.
Language	Colloquial-poetic; sensual simplicity; diversified; unusual use of songs.
Mood and Atmosphere	Clear; controlled; tied to idea, social, and political purpose; combination of real and nonreal; combination of serious and comic.
Pace and Tempo	Unusually varied.
Special Technique	Selective use of alienation devices and Oriental techniques; unusual vocal and physical flexibility; unique character and emotional analysis and execution.

Suggested Readings

Brecht, Bertolt. *Brecht on Theatre*. Translated by John Willett. New York: Hill & Wang, 1964.

Brockett, O. G. *History of the Theatre*. 2nd ed. Rockleigh, N. J.: Allyn & Bacon, 1968.

Brockett, O. G. *The Theatre: An Introduction*. 3rd ed. New York: Holt, Rinehart, and Winston, 1974.

Esslin, Martin. *Brecht: The Man and His Work*. Rev. ed. New York: Doubleday & Co., 1971.

Gray, Ronald. *Brecht*. New York: Grove Press, 1961.

Willet, John. *Brecht on Theatre*. New York: Hill & Wang, 1959.

Weideli, Walter. *The Art of Bertolt Brecht*. New York: New York University Press, 1963.

The Caucasian Chalk Circle

by *Bertolt Brecht*

from
Part Two, 1   *English version by Eric Bentley and Maja Apelman*

Characters

The Story Teller	Shauwa
Chorus	The Blackmailer
Azdak	The Innkeeper
The Invalid	Ludovica
The Limping Man	The Stableman
The Doctor	An Ironshirt

Scene   A makeshift Court of Justice in a Caucasian city.

Situation   The civil war in a country turns a drunken rascal into a powerful judge who is asked to decide on the custody of a governor's son. Should the child go to his actual mother, who abandoned him, or to his adopted mother, who cared for him? Prior to the crucial decision, Azdak, the judge, engages in comic trials and decisions with a variety of cases.

THE STORY TELLER

> And there was civil war in the land.
> The ruler was unsafe.
> And Azdak was made a judge by the Ironshirts.
> And Azdak remained a judge for two years.

THE STORY TELLER AND CHORUS

> Conflagration's heat, and blood in every street,
>> And cockroach and bug in every town.
> In the castle, fànatics. At the altar, heretics.
>> And Azdak wearing a judge's gown.

(AZDAK *sits in the judge's chair, peeling an apple.* SHAUWA *is sweeping out the hall. On one side an invalid in a wheelchair. Opposite, a young man accused of blackmail. An* IRONSHIRT *stands on guard, holding the Ironshirt's banner.*)

AZDAK   In consideration of the large number of cases, the Court today will hear two cases at a time. Before I open the proceedings, a short announcement—I accept—(*He stretches out his hand. The* BLACKMAILER *is the only one to produce any money. He hands it to* AZDAK.)—I reserve for myself the right to punish one of the parties here for contempt of court. (*He glances at the* INVALID.) You (*To the* DOCTOR) are a doctor, and you (*To the* INVALID) are bringing a complaint against him. Is the doctor responsible for your condition?

THE INVALID   Yes. I had a stroke because of him.

AZDAK   That would be professional negligence.

THE INVALID   More than negligence. I gave this man money for his studies. So far, he hasn't paid me back a cent. And when I heard he was treating a patient free, I had a stroke.

AZDAK   Rightly. (*To a* LIMPING MAN) And you, what do you want here?

THE LIMPING MAN   I'm the patient, your honor.

AZDAK   He treated your leg for nothing?

THE LIMPING MAN   The wrong leg! My rheumatism was in the left leg, and he operated on the right. That's why I limp now.

AZDAK   And you got it free?

THE INVALID   A five-hundred-piaster operation free! For nothing! For a God-bless-you! And I paid for this man's studies! (To the DOCTOR) Did they teach you to operate free?

THE DOCTOR   Your Honor, it is actually the custom to demand the fee before the operation, as the patient is more willing to pay before an operation than after. Which is only human. In the case in question I was convinced, when I started the operation, that my servant had already received the fee. In this I was mistaken.

THE INVALID   He was mistaken! A good doctor doesn't make mistakes! He examines before he operates.

AZDAK   That's right. (To SHAUWA) Public Prosecutor, what's the other case about?

SHAUWA (busily sweeping)   Blackmail.

THE BLACKMAILER   High Court of Justice, I'm innocent. I only wanted to find out from the landowner concerned if he really had raped his niece. He informed me very politely that this was not the case, and gave me the money only so I could pay for my uncle's studies.

AZDAK   Hm. (To the DOCTOR) You, on the other hand, can cite no extenuating circumstances for your offense, huh?

THE DOCTOR   Except that to err is human.

AZDAK   And you are perfectly well aware that in money matters a good doctor is conscious of his responsibility? I once heard of a doctor who made a thousand piasters out of one sprained finger: he discovered it had something to do with blood circulation, which a less good doctor might have overlooked. On another occasion he made a real gold mine out of the careful treatment of a somewhat disordered gall bladder. You have no excuse, Doctor. The corn merchant, Uxu, had his son study medicine to get some knowledge of trade, our medical schools are so good. (To the BLACKMAILER) What's the name of the landowner?

SHAUWA   He doesn't want it known.

AZDAK   In that case I will pass judgment. The Court considers the blackmail proved. And you (to the INVALID) are sentenced to a fine of one thousand piasters. If you get a second stroke, the doctor will have to treat you free. Eventually he will have to amputate. (To the LIMPING MAN) As compensation, you will receive a bottle of rubbing alcohol. (To the BLACKMAILER) You are sentenced to hand over half the proceeds of your deal to the Public Prosecutor to keep the landowner's name secret. You are advised, moreover, to study medicine—you seem well suited to that calling. (To the DOCTOR) You are acquitted in consideration of an unpardonable error in the practice of your profession! Next cases!

THE STORY TELLER AND CHORUS

With a pound you're on firm ground (no one is willing for a shilling)
   And the law is a cat in a sack.
But one whelp brings help to the many for a penny.
   The name of this rascal? Azdak.

(Enter AZDAK *from the caravansary on the highroad, followed by an old bearded innkeeper. The judge's chair is carried by a stableman and* SHAUWA. *An* IRONSHIRT, *with a banner, takes up his position.)*

AZDAK   Put it here. Then we'll get some air and maybe a good breeze from the lemon grove over there. It does justice good to be administered in the open: the wind blows her skirts up and you can see what she's got underneath. Shauwa, we've eaten too much. These official journeys are very exhausting. *(To the* INNKEEPER*)* Where's your daughter-in-law?

THE INNKEEPER   Your Worship, it's a question of the family honor. I wish to bring an action on behalf of my son, who's on business on the other side of the mountain. This is the offending stableman, and here's my daughter-in-law.

(Enter the Daughter-in-law, a voluptuous wench. She is veiled.)

AZDAK *(sitting down)*   I accept . . . *(Sighing, the* INNKEEPER *hands him some money.)* Good. Now the formalities are disposed of. This is a case of rape?

THE INNKEEPER   Your Honor, I caught the fellow in the act. Ludovica was already in the straw on the stable floor.

AZDAK   Quite right, the stable. Beautiful horses! I particularly liked the little roan.

THE INNKEEPER   The first thing I did, of course, was question Ludovica. On my son's behalf.

AZDAK *(seriously)*   I said I particularly liked it.

THE INNKEEPER *(coldly)*   Really? Ludovica confessed the stableman took her against her will.

AZDAK   Take your veil off, Ludovica. *(She does so.)* Ludovica, you please the Court. Tell us how it happened.

LUDOVICA *(well-schooled)*   When I entered the stable to see the new foal the stableman said to me on his own accord: "It's hot today!" and laid his hand on my left breast. I said to him: "Don't do that!" But he continued to handle me indecently, which provoked my anger. Before I realized his sinful intentions, he had got much closer. It had already taken place when my father-in-law entered and accidentally trod on me.

THE INNKEEPER *(explaining)*   On my son's behalf.

AZDAK *(to the* STABLEMAN*)*   Do you admit you started it?

THE STABLEMAN   Yes.

AZDAK   Ludovica, do you like to eat sweet things?

LUDOVICA   Yes, sunflower seeds!

AZDAK   Do you like to lie a long time in the bathtub?

LUDOVICA   Half an hour or so.

AZDAK   Public Prosecutor, drop your knife—there—on the floor. *(*SHAUWA *does so.)* Ludovica, go and pick up the knife. *(*LUDOVICA, *swaying her hips, does so.)* See that? *(He points at her.)* The way it moves? The rape is now proven. By eating too much—sweet things, especially—by lying too long in warm water, by laziness and too soft a skin, you have raped that unfortunate man. Do you imagine you can run around with a behind like that and get away with it in court? This is a case of intentional assault with a dangerous weapon! You are sentenced to hand over to the Court the little roan which your father liked to ride "on his son's behalf." And now, come with me to the stables, so the Court may inspect the scene of the crime, Ludovica.

When visiting your neighbor sharpen up your ax,
For Bible texts and sermons are trivial knickknacks.
What miracles past believing the ax's edge can do!
Sometimes Azdak believed in miracles too.

(*END*)

19 Absurd

Beyond Reason

. . . We are here as on a darkling plain,
Swept with confused alarms of struggle
    and flight
Where ignorant armies clash by night.
                    Matthew Arnold
    from James H. Clancy, "Beyond Despair:
        A New Drama of Ideas," in Morris
    Freedman, *Essays in Modern Drama.*

ORATOR   He faces the rows of empty
chairs; he makes the invisible crowd
understand that he is deaf and dumb; he
makes the signs of a deaf-mute; desperate
efforts to make himself understood; then
he coughs, groans, and utters the gutteral
sounds of a mute: He, mme, mm, mn.
Je, gou, hou, hou. Heu, heu, go, fou,
gueue.

        The Chairs by Eugene Ionesco

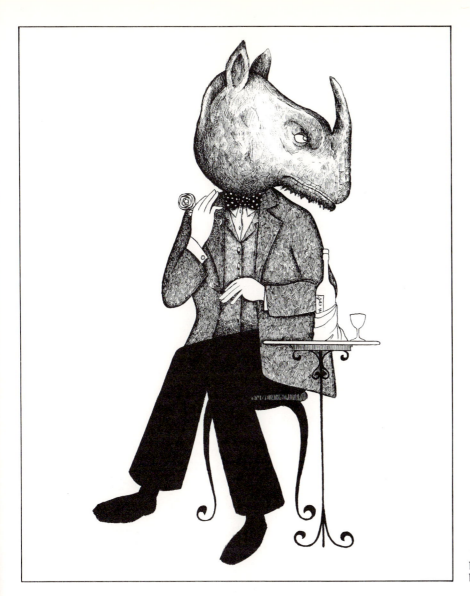

Bérenger in *Rhinoceros*
by Eugene Ionesco.

As Arnold so poetically notes, man frequently finds himself immersed in a
dark and confusing struggle. A case in point was World War II. It was in
many ways an unreasonable and devastating war in which innocent people,
ranging from the victims of the atrocities of Nazi concentration camps to
those of atomic bombs dropped on densely populated cities, were slaughtered. Such devastation renders humanity insensitive; the meaning of life
deteriorates; communication fails. As with Ionesco's Orator, the confusion
leads to meaningless sounds and groans. After this war, man needed to rediscover himself and his world and the universe in which he lived. Philosophers, poets, and playwrights were once again the leaders in the search.

Overview of the Existential, the Absurd

The actor playing the role of Vladimir (Didi) in Samuel Beckett's play *Waiting for Godot* came despondently into the Little Theatre at the University of Nevada, Las Vegas, and approached the director. "I can't go on with this. You'll have to let me out. This character—this play—I'm really depressed. The way Didi thinks, his habits—they're getting to me. I feel worthless—a bum. Eating a radish—putting on my boots—everything's debilitating. I feel like Didi—I need a belt strong enough to hang myself!" At that moment the director removed his own belt, handed it to the actor, and grinned. A general burst of laughter relaxed the very honest and serious actor. The laughter was important for more than one reason. To act Absurd drama, you must find the humor "relief valve" in the script and in the role, or audiences may find the negative, existential philosophy of these plays totally unpalatable. Similarly, you must retain and utilize a sense of humor in rehearsal to relieve the inevitable tension. Such is the power of the strange but effective contemporary dramatic genre labeled Theatre of the Absurd.

Originating in the philosophical ideas of Existentialism as expounded by the great French philosopher-authors Albert Camus (1913–1960) and Jean-Paul Sartre (1905–) this genre burst impressively upon the theatre world in the early 1950s in the work of such playwrights as Beckett, Eugene Ionesco, and Jean Genet. The genre made a steady, pure contribution to world theatre for more than ten years, and its influence continues to the present day.

How considered Absurd? In what way, Absurd? What does the word mean in the context of drama and acting?

The answers to these questions begin with examination of *Existentialism* as employed by the main precursors of Absurd drama, Jean-Paul Sartre and Albert Camus. Other forerunners of the Absurd include Alfred Jarry (discussed in chapter 17) and Luigi Pirandello (1867–1936). Pirandello was an Italian dramatist who emphasized that truth was a matter of personal viewpoint. Pirandello's plays, such as *Six Characters in Search of an Author*, *Right Your Are*, and *Masks*, depict grotesque conflict between illusion and reality.

Existentialism refers to a particular view of the nature of man's existence. The existentialist believes that man starts life with nothing. His life is made up of acts; through the process of acting man becomes conscious of his original nothingness. By choosing to act, man passes into the arena of human responsibility which makes him the creator of his own existence. However, the existence inevitably ends with death. Man returns to his original state of nothingness. This existential notion eliminates the Western concept of man's exalted nature. Life becomes meaningless and useless—a condition which is in essence "absurd." Man's only freedom in this condition is the exercise of his conscious mind. However, consciousness means conflict—between man's awareness of the absurdity of his existence and his need for justification of his human action.

The Sartrian existentialist sees man as adrift in the world. There is no God or religion; man is a quirk of environmental accident and development, "absurdly" (meaning unreasonably) thrust into special consciousness beyond his animal relatives due to the persecuting factors of mind and voice (e.g., thinking and speaking). What man is left with is the tedious condition of waiting to die, whereby he evaporates into nothingness in an empty or meaningless universe. However, if man can recognize and accept the simultaneous existence of his absurdity and his responsibility to give himself definition through choice and action, *there is hope.*

The chief twentieth-century exponents of existential philosophy are Jean-Paul Sartre and the late Albert Camus. Sartre, a playwright as well as a novelist, dramatizes existential man struggling to cope with a meaningless world. Orestes, in *The Flies,* acts as a free man devoid of emotional attachments in a corrupt world. Although Orestes takes full and, in his view, courageous responsibility for his actions, freedom serves only to isolate him. Absurdity again triumphs. Meaningful existence is only as valuable as man views it to be in light of the demands he places on himself. Since God does not exist (if He did exist, the world would not be in chaos), values are created on the basis of individual decision alone. Most of Sartre's plays focus on a character faced with moral choices or struggles (e.g., *The Flies* and *No Exit*).

Camus' characters are usually repulsed by their existence and violently attack their world (e.g., *Caligula*). The importance of Camus as an existential playwright rests on his rejection of a didactic premise for his plays in favor of presenting the world as a chasm of frantic, aimless activity. Camus was the first playwright to use the term *absurd* in describing the senselessness of the human condition. By abandoning the rational approach to life, the existential man must attempt to find values in a world devoid of values; he must attempt to find order in a world gone mad (as opposed to Brecht, whose characters do not accept absurdity, but rather look to social change for a more purposeful, rational world).

The nonrealistic theatre movements discussed in chapter 17 and the work of Brecht were well known by Sartre and Camus. These movements had considerable influence upon their theatrical thinking.

Another important influence on the Theatre of the Absurd came from Antonin Artaud (1895–1948), a French theatrical genius whose work began in the 1930s. His theatre experimentations proposed to cure the ills of the traditional Western theatre which he believed was deadening the lives of its members as well as of its audiences. Artaud described theatre in terms of ritual and myth, expecting the audience to experience trance and inspiration. His work attempted psychologically to remove the audience from the present to a primitive past by eliminating words and reliance upon script. Influenced by the Balinese dances and Eastern theatre, Artaud bore witness to a theatre of mystifying spectacle where words had no power and language became incantation. Artaud felt that the Western theatre was a slave to words, to text, and to realistic imitation. Instead, he wanted the Western theatre to be the "double" of the Eastern theatre and create a shock force which would jar audiences from the complacent conditions of everyday life. Artaud used mechanical devices to create visible and audible frenzy. Light, sound, and physical movement and dance were used to tyrannize or assault the sense of the audience. The overall effect was similar to the impact of Oriental theatre wherein gestures, signs, postures, and sounds were compressed and symbolized.

Artaud called his dramatic theory the Theatre of Cruelty. In this concept of *cruelty* a bloodless state was implied. Artaud defined cruelty as a psychological purging of man's soul, freeing him from the bondage of logical and verbal experience. To effect a reevaluation of our lives, Artaud used shocking, violent, and often pornographic techniques to stimulate a vision that reached beyond ordinary reality. He wanted the subconscious mind to probe the mysteries of existence. The idea of cruelty was comparable to the high priest (actor) disrupting the logical response of the congregation (audience) to subject them ruthlessly to emotional and primitive response.

Absurd plays depict man tyrannized by nonman, by the intractable universe. Life is a "waiting period" which is at best painful and monotonous. For escape, man is left routine and fantasy. In the concept of good and evil each cancels the other out—nothing is absolute—everything is relative. The Absurdists obliterate the distinction between human and nonhuman (for example, men and animals are interchangeable, speech is disconnected and noncommunicative). References to God's abandoning man to isolation and alienation are frequent. There are no more Western myths or illusions about an Omnipresent Being holding sway over man. Without hope, time and space are meaningless references. Within the concept of time, everything has happened before. Man can only perpetuate the art of game-playing to pass the insidious factor of time. Idle songs may be sung, dances danced, jokes exchanged—violence, sex, and simple hygiene may take on hedonistic excess—inanimate objects may take on life and inordinate significance. If man is strong enough to face reality, he is left to the only certain escape, namely, death, via what may be man's only possibility for a heroic act—suicide—through willful choice.

The Absurdists force us to look over the precipice into the abyss defined by the existentialists. We reach that precipice through our subconsciousness and our dreams. We doubt our reality, our traditional and usually abstract values such as love, family, art, science, occupation, religion, education, and so on. These are narrow confines and are rendered meaningless and beyond communicative possibility. An occasional laugh is the most convenient relief from living in such fantasy (and perhaps more meaningful than any of the traditional values). Pain comes with the knowledge that a vast difference separates what we are from what we might be.

How do the existential Absurdists justify the creation of art (plays) if they philosophically view all activity as ultimately meaningless? The playwright invariably justifies the writing as being merely *his* particular fantasy, *his* escape, and thereby *validates* the philosophy. Ask him to explain his philosophy and he may reply, "The forceps of birth lead directly to the shovel of death." To the Absurdist, the surgeon becomes the gravedigger merely by exchanging instruments. In between birth and death is only an absurd or unreasonable existence, voided forever by the only certain end of any living existence: death in an eternal anonymity. Paradoxically, while the Absurdist view of life seems negative (chaotic, disintegrated, and despairing), he finds hope in man's effort to abandon his illusions and confront the truth of his existence. Recognizing his limitations gives man strength to go beyond reality and confront the intangible—a test of ultimate reality. In 1968 the challenging intellectual and emotional impact of these plays reached its zenith when the Nobel Prize was awarded to Samuel Beckett. His "forcept-gravedigger" image stands as one of the clearest symbols of the entire Absurdist movement in theatre.

Now that the viewpoint of existential Absurd drama has been briefly clarified, it is easy to sympathize with the plight of the actor playing the role of Didi. To perform a role in one of these plays, you should retain a sense of humor and adhere to your life values. It is distracting and pointless (possibly even dangerous) to become overinvolved in existential philosophy, especially if you find yourself agreeing with that philosophy. Your task is to understand the point of view and then, as always, turn to the vital work of creating your role honestly, truthfully, and in the appropriate style.

In *The Theatre of the Absurd*, Martin Esslin, the acknowledged leading critic of Absurd Theatre, discusses the leading playwrights of the Absurdist movement. Chief among them are Eugene Ionesco (1912–), Samuel Beckett (1906–), and Jean Genet (1910–). While Harold Pinter (1930–), Edward Albee (1928–), Tom Stoppard (1938–), and others have also been considered Absurdists by some critics, they are perhaps better classified as contemporary Eclectics. As such, they are discussed in chapter 20.

Scene from *Rosencrantz and Guilderstern Are Dead* by Tom Stoppard. Directed by Robert N. Burgan. Designed by Fredrick L. Olson. University of Nevada, Las Vegas.

Ionesco called his plays "antiplays"—plays lacking traditional action, characters, and dialogue. His plays are emersed in fantastic hallucination, secret desires, and pulverizing fears. On the surface, Ionesco's plays resemble light comedies; further examination reveals serious social implication aligned with existential thought. Ionesco usually uses a conventional middle-class drawing room for his setting and conventional clichés for his dialogue (taken from a language primer). The result is a put-on with serious intent. Characters are carried away by words, changing identity, and farcial activity (such as having no head, as in *The Leader*, or laying eggs, as in *The Future Is in Eggs*). In *The Bald Soprano*, the banalities of their clichéd dialogue serve to make two middle-class British families appear mad. In *Rhinoceros*, a man changes into a rhinoceros. The images created by Ionesco are immediate and strange, comparable to those experienced in a dream or by primitive man. Images evolve with the irrational but compulsive logic of a dream. A corpse grows in a bedroom and Ionesco makes it seem perfectly normal (e.g., *Amedée*). Human beings are displaced by the proliferation of objects (e.g., furniture in *The Tenants*; chairs in *The Chairs*). Displacement such as this is a common occurrence in our lives. Do not material possessions often govern our thoughts and actions? In these plays everything appears to make sense, yet paradoxically is beyond reason. Nightmares are staged in the most unpredictable, irrational, abrupt manner. Dialogue is rendered meaningless by use of countless puns, speech inversions, sonic associations, non sequitors, purposeless nouns, and so on.

Yet, beneath the structure of the game-playing, the automatized language, the mimetic action, and the farcical antics smolders a curious disenchantment. Ionesco sees the individual consciousness isolated in an absurd universe. His characters are generally clowns and marionettes who ape man. The mechanical forces inhibiting man only provoke our laughter, making us nostalgic for the human element.

Early in the 1950s, Samuel Beckett, who is Irish, began to publish frequently in Paris. *Malloy, Malone Dies, The Unnamable,* and *Waiting for Godot,* all originally written in French, were published between 1950 and 1952. Fifteen remarkable years later Beckett was awarded the Nobel Prize for Literature—a prize which recognized the man as a renowned playwright and the Absurd movement as a major force in the world of literature. Early in the Absurd movement, Beckett was usually associated with Ionesco, a fact which severely limited the importance of Beckett. For Ionesco, absurdity meant uproarious farce; for Beckett, absurdity meant a life lived in isolation and despair. Hence, Beckett's vision of the world is not as irrational and unpredictable as is the world depicted by Ionesco. Beckett's unique contribution to the Absurd movement is his view that man's absurdity is simply an outgrowth of his self-conscious condition. As man approaches the end of the game (i.e., life), he remains, above all, rational and precise. The best man can do is pass the waiting time as painlessly as possible. He can plot his life and calculate his actions, making himself "sane" by repetitious patter and vaudeville calamities (e.g., pratfalls and collapsing trousers). This is both the worst and the best that can befall man. The best that man can hope for!

Scene from *Waiting for Godot* by Samuel Beckett. Directed by Jerry L. Crawford. University of Nevada, Las Vegas.

The comic and tragic merge in Beckett's plays. (*Endgame, Happy Days, Krapp's Last Tape, Play.*) Any line spoken in a Beckett play can provoke either reaction. Actions, characters, dialogue, and business are a tragicomic commentary on the infinite complexities of our daily lives.

Jean Genet is primarily interested in exploring the spatial and optical possibilities of the theatre. His plays are renderings of ceremonies and rituals created to depict a universe in the throes of annihilation. For Genet, the theatre is the ultimate exorcist of man's fantasies. Characters are reflections of something other than themselves, prisoners of their own imagination (e.g., *The Balcony* and *The Maids*). What appears to be truth is simply an illusion. The real meaning of life lies in the opposite of what is expected: black is white, white is black; evil is good, good is evil; the criminal is virtuous, the virtuous is criminal (*The Blacks*). Ritual is the means devised to perpetuate some semblance of order in a chaotic universe. In keeping with the Absurdist concept of purposeless existence, Genet heightens and grotesquely shapes his so-called order and puts it on display. As members of the audience, we are confronted by our own image in shattered glass—an image distorted and horrifying. According to Genet, we wear black suits, yellow shoes, excessive makeup, clashing and gaudy colors; we wear patched garments and incorrect masks (we are black, not white; we are white, not black—what is *color?*). We use highly artificial language, often eloquent and poetic; yet we steal from the language of the gutter. We curse and scream. No action onstage justifies our outcast existence. We are all alienated, although we pretend not to be. Agree with it or not, Genet presents a highly effective treatise on the decadence of the individual isolated in society doomed to a meaningless death.

Voice

It is interesting that words and language in Absurd plays are frequently considered part of the spectacle. That is, words are frequently used as sound and noise (therefore, spectacle) rather than for purposes of logical communication. In a way, words are transparent, revealing only immediate meaning. Language seems to "participate" in the theatrical activity, similarly to properties and scenery. On the surface, speech is frequently confusing and nonsensical. However, you should play against the emptiness of the stereotyped language. In other words, you must speak the words with energy, variety, and certainty, even when they seem to be meaningless. Silences and pauses are vital in handling language in Absurd plays. Your vocal tools must function exceptionally well to vary your speech patterns, vocal rhythms, and speaking-singing range. Language is often redundant and monotonous. As a result, many audience members reject the material if actors are not especially effective at providing vocal variety to alleviate the monotony. (Of course, you must be selective in providing variety because if it is overdone, you may violate the philosophical intention of the playwright who has deliberately established the tedium of the language.) When the characters and action involve nonreal, dehumanized activity, you should apply the vocal techniques for such behavior discussed in chapters 17 and 18. However, since most Absurd characters are based on reality, you begin with the tenets of vocal delivery for Realism (see chapter 16). Careful script analysis by you and your director will clarify whether to apply realistic or nonrealistic vocal techniques.

Exercise 1   Voice—Absurd

Select one of the longer speeches by Estragon or Vladimir in the scene from *Waiting for Godot* at the end of this chapter (the speeches work effectively for both men and women). Practice the speech applying the following techniques:

1. As realistic prose
2. As nonsense gibberish through use of strange pauses, inflections, intonations, and so on
3. As an ephemeral dream
4. As a mechanical robot
5. As a didactic message
6. As primitive, ruthless rage
7. As philosophic reflection

Finally, practice the speech with an appropriate mix of any or all of the above foregoing techniques. (Ionesco's *The Bald Soprano* or any of his other plays are also particularly well suited to this exercise.)

Movement

Absurd plays are unusually antiliterary and frequently nonverbal because they are linked to ritualistic ceremony, circus activity, and routines and techniques used by commedia dell'arte, itinerant jugglers, mime troupes, music hall burlesques, acrobatics, and silent films (including those of Buster Keaton, Charlie Chaplin, the Keystone Cops, Laurel and Hardy, and the Marx Brothers). In all of these activities complex physical dexterity and precise timing are stressed (the timing is even more important when coordinated with dialogue and sounds). These activities are closely tied to what we think of as popular entertainment, that is, visual escape entertainment which is often used as a time-passer. Hence, these activities relate closely to the philosophical premise of the material (e.g., meaningless routine and passing of time). Your body should be relaxed, disciplined, and nimble. You should be as agile as the old-time vaudeville burlesque comedians. Recall the deft fingers of these comedians as they toss several hats into the air with ease and precision. The entertainment style of the Irish pub humorists, the English dance-hall performers, and the American burlesque entertainers provide a unique ingredient required for mastery of movement in the Absurd style of acting. Again, a combination of the techniques of movement discussed in chapters 16, 17, and 18 are effectively employed.

Exercise 2   Movement—Absurd

1. Everyone become involved in silently arranging twenty chairs in the room. Once arranged, completely rearrange them. Continue rearranging them for a full five minutes.
2. After five minutes of Exercise 1, relieve the monotony by performing a variety of the following activities. Interchange activities at will, always being certain that between each activity you return to some rearrangement of the chairs.
   a. Remove your shoes, shake them out, put them on again.
   b. Practice a soft-shoe shuffle.
   c. Practice juggling two or more objects.
   d. Practice a series of gymnastic or acrobatic exercises.
   e. Rearrange the chairs in the speeded-up tempo of a silent film being run at fast speed.
   f. Vary your tempo in all of these activities by using mechanical robot movement, ephemeral dreamlike movement, Epic alienation techniques, and primitive assault techniques.

Character and Emotion

Character and emotion in Absurd plays range from one-dimensional and lack of feeling to multidimensional and sensitive feeling. For example, Berenger in Ionesco's *Rhinoceros* is a full-dimensional, human characterization which permits the use of Stanislavski's techniques. On the other hand, the characters in Ionesco's *The Bald Soprano* are fundamentally one-dimensional stereotypes. Berenger passes through a gamut of emotion, whereas *Soprano's* characters seem relatively free of feeling. In view of the fact that Absurd characters frequently seem involved in pointless activity devoid of traditional plot action, it is best not to ask, What comes next? but rather, What is happening *now?* Neither the actor nor the audience can rely on cause and effect and logical sequence of action. We can only be amused or shocked by the often grotesque nature of the moment.

Most characters in Absurd plays are based on realism. However, at some point in the play the authors usually distort reality by dehumanization or by having inanimate objects take on life. Absurdist playwrights utilize many of the alienating techniques of Epic Theatre. In fact, some critics believe Absurdist playwrights are more effective alienists than was Brecht (such as the proliferation of objects, changes in identity, and repetition of language and action).

Absurd material also lends itself well to the primitive assault techniques of Artaud. For example, Absurd characters assault the sensibilities of an audience by such activity as "urinating" onstage and crudely masticating food (see Beckett's *Krapp's Last Tape*). An actor can perform these activities alternately as realistic behavior or as ritualistic behavior. The latter is germane to Artaud's intentions. For example, peeling and eating a piece of fruit can be performed as primitive man's discovery of nourishment.

At times, the nonrealistic distortion of robot and ephemeral dreamlike behavior can also be used effectively in Absurd theatre. For example, Lucky and Pozzo in *Waiting for Godot* seem almost to be dehumanzied robots of power and slavery. In the same play, Didi and Gogo (Vladimir and Estragon) speak of living in a dream. In these moments the actors can permit the characters to react as in a dream state.

Line-by-line textual analysis will help you find the correct style and mood and provide the appropriate interpretation. Absurdist playwrights have a tendency to carry poetry, farce, dialogue, and cabaret activity to excess. When a conflict exists between realistic and nonrealistic characterization and emotion, you are usually well advised to play the humor arising from the incongruity. It is this safety valve of humor which makes the Absurd character palatable to most audiences. At such moments you generally need not rely upon the realistic techniques of Stanislavski for motivation or probe for deep emotion. Simply perform the immediate action. An appropriate combination of laughter and despair will usually follow naturally. If you follow the principle that emotion and empathy are used during realistic moments and restricted during nonrealistic or ritualistic moments, you will usually find the appropriate performance level.

Creating Absurd characters and emotion requires acute awareness of your own personality and physical and mental resources. The Absurd acting style is a sensitive combination of several preceding styles (e.g., Realism, Naturalism, Expressionism, and Epic, plus vaudeville humor). Its execution necessitates using an inordinate amount of your own personality traits and your own behavioral habits and routines. Once again, personalization is

Scene from *Oh Dad, Poor Dad, Mamma's Hung You in the Closet and I'm Feelin' So Sad* by Arthur Kopit. Directed by Charles Whittman. Designed by Larry Schumate. California State University, Sacramento.

the key to success—ability to skillfully observe your world, sensitive and active perception of your own sensory equipment, vivid imagination, and active knowledge of how your body rhythms fluxuate as you pass the time or engage in routine life activities.

Above all, understand the intentions of the playwright. Do not lose yourself in the interchangeable nature of his vision of the universe. The next moment onstage is unimportant in light of the question, What is happening *now?* Your task is to penetrate both the internal and external realities of action moment by moment.

Exercise 3   Character and Emotion

Select a monologue from a character of your choice from one of the Absurd plays given in the list at the end of this chapter. Perform the monologue after analysis, incorporating the types of character and emotion just discussed (e.g., realistic, expressionistic, Epic, and cabaret or vaudeville). Your character and emotion should range from multidimensional and real to simplistic and nonreal. For the purpose of the exercise, do not hesitate to superimpose some of these stylistic techniques for the sake of practice. However, you should note that an effective mix of styles cannot usually be accomplished in a single monologue (an exception might be Lucky's unique monologue from *Waiting for Godot*).

In the 1960s the Absurd movement splintered. The final style for our examination is the natural extension of the combination of techniques used in Absurd drama. Playwrights ranging from Eugene O'Neill at the beginning of the twentieth century to such contemporary artists as Harold Pinter intermingle the stylistic considerations prevalent in the last seventy-five or more years. Our remaining study is of the proliferation of eclectic, stylistic acting techniques of the last three decades. Also, contemporary innovative theatrical groups and movements must be examined (see Appendix B).

Suggested Characters and Plays for Scene Work

Camus, Albert

Caligula, Caesonia, Scipio
  Caligula

Sartre, Jean-Paul

Goetz, Heinrich, Nasti, Tetzel, Hilda, Cathrine
  The Devil and the Good Lord
Kean, Soloman, Anna, Amy, Eleana
  Kean
Estelle, Inez, Garcin
  No Exit
Orestes, Electra, Aegistheus, Clytemnestra
  The Flies

Jarry, Alfred

Ubu Roi
  Ubu Roi

Pirandello, Luigi

Mother, Father, Stepdaughter, Son
  Six Characters in Search of an Author

Beckett, Samuel

Vladamir, Estragon, Lucky, Pozzo
  Waiting for Godot
Krapp
  Krapp's Last Tape
Winnie, Willy
  Happy Days
Nagg, Nell, Hamm, Clove
  Endgame

Ionesco, Eugene

Mr. Smith, Mrs. Smith, Mr. Martin, Mrs. Martin, The Firechief
  The Bald Soprano
Old Man, Old Woman
  The Chairs
Pupil, Professor
  The Lesson
Berenger, Daisy, Jean
  Rhinoceros

Genet, Jean

Claire, Solange
  The Maids
Green Eyes, Maurice, Lafranc
  Deathwatch

The Bishop, Irma, The Chief of Police, The Judge
> *The Balcony*

Archibald, Deodatus, Adelaide, Newport News, Augusta, Felicity, Diouf
> *The Blacks*

The playwrights included in this list were early leaders of Absurd drama. Later and related dramatists are discussed in chapter 20.

Actor Checklist   *Absurd*

Voice	Words, sound, and noise as spectacle; energy; variety; certainty; unusual use of silence and pause; rhythmic; monotone; wide range; combination of real and nonreal techniques.
Movement	Mix of realistic, nonrealistic, ritualistic, circus, commedia, acrobatics, silent film; dexterity and precise timing; muscles relaxed; disciplined and nimble; vaudeville and dance activity; balance of presentational and representational mode.
Gestures	Inventive; disciplined; fluid; considerably oriented to hands and feet.
Pantomimic Dramatization	Inventive as appropriate to routine behavior of life, combined with theatrical and entertainment techniques; see Movement, above.
Character	Combination of multidimensional and complex with stereotype and simplistic; heavily oriented to action of the moment; real to nonreal.
Emotion	Same combination as described for Character, above; special use of primitive, ritualistic Artaud techniques.
Ideas	Clear and usually relevant to Existentialism.
Language	Part of theatrical spectacle; often illogical; often immediate meaning only; often stereotyped and clichéd; combination ranging from prose to lyric poetry; philosophical—usually existential.
Mood and Atmosphere	Extremely varied; at times, moment-to-moment combination of serious and comic.
Pace and Tempo	Generally used in consistently fast or consistently slow tempo.
Special Techniques	Cabaret or vaudeville activity; soft-shoe and tap dancing, pratfalls, tumbling, juggling, magic, balancing, sight gags, and slapstick.

Suggested Readings

Barnard, G. C. *Samuel Beckett: A New Approach.* New York: Dodd, Mead & Co., 1960.

Chiari, Joseph. *The Contemporary French Theatre: The Flight from Naturalism.* London: Barrie and Rockliff, 1958.

Cohn, Ruby, ed. *Cookbook on Waiting for Godot.* New York: Grove Press, 1967.

Esslin, Martin. *Absurd Drama.* London: Penguin Books, 1965.

Esslin, Martin. *The Theatre of the Absurd.* Rev. ed. Garden City, N. J.: Doubleday & Co., 1969.

Grossvogel, David. *Brecht, Ionesco, Beckett, Genet: Four Playwrights and a Postscript.* Ithaca: Cornell University Press, 1962.

Guicharnaud, Jacques. *Modern French Theatre from Giraudoux to Beckett.* New Haven, Conn.: Yale University Press, 1961.

Killinger, John. *World in Collapse: The Vision of Absurd Drama.* New York: Dell Publishing Co., 1971.

Waiting for Godot
by Samuel Beckett

Estragon (Gogo)
Vladimir (Didi)

An unidentified country road, by a tree.

Two tramplike men wait wearily for an unknown figure known as Godot to come to them. They pass their time in idle routine and fanciful games and activities. A man named Pozzo drives a slave named Lucky past them and later the two return and the master-slave roles are reversed. Finally, alone as they began, Estragon and Vladimir continue consideration of their dilemma.

ESTRAGON   Why don't we hang ourselves?
VLADIMIR   With what?
ESTRAGON   You haven't got a bit of rope?
VLADIMIR   No.
ESTRAGON   Then we can't.

(silence)

VLADIMIR   Let's go.
ESTRAGON   Wait, there's my belt.
VLADIMIR   It's too short.
ESTRAGON   You could hang on to my legs.
VLADIMIR   And who'd hang on to mine?
ESTRAGON   True.
VLADIMIR   Show all the same. (ESTRAGON *loosens the cord that holds up his
  trousers which, much too big for him, fall about his ankles. They look at the
  cord.*) It might do at a pinch. But is it strong enough?
ESTRAGON   We'll soon see. Here.

(They each take an end of the cord and pull. It breaks. They almost fall.)

VLADIMIR   Not worth a curse.

(silence)

ESTRAGON   You say we have to come back to-morrow?
VLADIMIR   Yes.
ESTRAGON   Then we can bring a good bit of rope.
VLADIMIR   Yes.

(silence)

ESTRAGON   Didi.
VLADIMIR   Yes.
ESTRAGON   I can't go on like this.

VLADIMIR   That's what you think.
ESTRAGON   If we parted? That might be better for us.
VLADIMIR   We'll hang ourselves to-morrow. *(Pause)* Unless Godot comes.
ESTRAGON   And if he comes?
VLADIMIR   We'll be saved.

(VLADIMIR takes off his hat [LUCKY's], peers inside it, feels about inside it, shakes it, knocks on the crown, puts it on again.)

ESTRAGON   Well? Shall we go?
VLADIMIR   Pull on your trousers.
ESTRAGON   What?
VLADIMIR   Pull on your trousers.
ESTRAGON   You want me to pull off my trousers?
VLADIMIR   Pull ON your trousers.
ESTRAGON   *(realizing his trousers are down)*. True.

(He pulls up his trousers.)

VLADIMIR   Well? Shall we go?
ESTRAGON   Yes, let's go.

(They do not move.)

(END)

Oh Dad, Poor Dad, Mamma's Hung You in the Closet and I'm Feelin' So Sad

by *Arthur Kopit*

from
scene iii

Jonathan Rosepettle, a 17-year-old boy who dresses like a child of 10
Rosalie, a 19-year-old girl, very sensual, but dressed in sweet girlish pink
Two Venus'-Flytraps,* enormous carnivorous plants
Rosalinda the Fish,* a silver piranha fish in a bowl

Characters

A hotel room in Havana, Cuba.

Scene

Emerging from his hiding place, after listening to strange stories told by his mother, Jonathan begins to rebel against her suffocating and strange domination by killing her man-eating plants and killer-fish. In this comic but frightening play, Jonathan travels with his bizarre mother who keeps his dead father's body hanging in the closet wherever they travel. A seductive girl named Rosalie returns to see Jonathan, bent on seducing him in his journey toward manhood, freedom, madness, murder, sanity, or insanity. This is a philosophically perplexing, self-mocking theatre piece in the Absurd style.

Situation

JOHNATHAN *emerges from behind the* VENUS'-FLYTRAPS. *He runs to the door, puts his ear to it, then races back to the balcony and stares down at the street below. Carnival lights flash weirdly against the night sky and laughter drifts up. The* VENUS'-FLYTRAPS *reach out to grab him, but somehow he senses their presence and leaps away in time.*

VENUS'-FLYTRAPS (*gruffly*)   Grrrrrr! (*He walks dazedly into the living room.*)

ROSALINDA THE FISH   (*Snarlingly.*) Snarrrrrrl! (*The* VENUS'-FLYTRAPS *have grown enormous. Their monstrous petals wave hungrily in the air while they growl.* JONATHAN *stares at them fearfully, the laughter below growing stronger all the while. Suddenly he runs to the wall and smashes the glass case that covers the fire axe. He takes out the axe. He advances cautiously toward the* FLYTRAPS. *He feints an attack, they follow his movements. He bobs, they weave. It is a cat-and-mouse game of death. Suddenly* JONATHAN *leaps upon them and hacks them apart till they fall to the floor, writhing, then dead.* JONATHAN *stands above them, victorious, panting, but somehow seeming to breathe easier. Slowly he turns and looks at the fish bowl. His eyes seem glazed, his expression insanely determined. He walks slowly toward the fish bowl. . . . There are three knocks on the door. He does not hear them. He raises his axe.*) *The door opens.* ROSALIE *enters. She is dressed in an absurdly childish pink dress with crinolines and frills—the picture of innocence, the picture of a girl ten years old. Her shoes are black leather pumps and she wears short girlish-pink socks. Her cheeks have round circles of rouge on them—like a young girl might have who had never put on makeup before.*

* Typically cast with either actors or actresses.

ROSALIE   Jonathan! Jonathan! What *have* you done? [JONATHAN *stops. He does not look at her but stares at the fish bowl.*] Jonathan! Put down that silly axe. You might hurt yourself. [*He still does not answer but stares at the bowl. He does not lower the axe.*] Jonathan! [*Slowly he turns and faces her.*]

JONATHAN   I killed it.

ROSALIE   Ssh. Not so loudly. Where'd you put her body?

JONATHAN   (*pointing to the* PLANTS)   There.

ROSALIE   Where? I don't see a body. Where is she?

JONATHAN   Who?

ROSALIE   Your mother.

JONATHAN   I haven't killed my mother. I've killed her plants. The ones I used to feed. I've chopped their hearts out.

ROSALIE   (*with an apologetic laugh*)   I thought you'd . . . killed your mother. (*The* PIRANHA FISH *giggles.* JONATHAN *turns and stares at it again. He starts to move toward it, slowly.*)

ROSALIE   Jonathan, stop. (*He hesitates, as if he is uncertain what to do. Slowly he raises the axe.*) Jonathan! (*He smashes the axe against the fish bowl. It breaks. The fish screams.*)

ROSALINDA THE FISH   (*fearfully*)   AAIEEEEEEEEEEEEEEEE!

ROSALIE   Now look at the mess you've made.

JONATHAN   Do you think it can live without water?

ROSALIE   What will your mother say when she gets back?

JONATHAN   Maybe I should hit it again. Just in case. (*He strikes it again.*)

ROSALINDA THE FISH   (*mournfully*)   UGHHHHHHH! (JONATHAN *stares in horror at the dead* FISH. *He drops the axe and turns away, sickened and weak.* ROSALIE *walks over and touches him gently, consolingly, on the arm.*)

ROSALIE   There's something bothering you, isn't there? (*pause—coyly.*) What's-a matter, Jonathan? (JONATHAN *does not answer at first but stares off into space frightened, bewildered.*)

JONATHAN   (*weakly*)   I never thought I'd see you again. I never thought I'd talk to you again. I never thought you'd come.

ROSALIE   Did you really think that?

JONATHAN   She told me she'd never let you visit me again. She said no one would *ever* visit me again. She told me I had seen enough.

ROSALIE   But I had a key made.

JONATHAN   She . . . she hates me.

ROSALIE   What?

JONATHAN   She doesn't let me do anything. She doesn't let me listen to the radio. She took the tube out of the television set. She doesn't let me use her phone. She makes me show her all my letters before I seal them. She doesn't—

ROSALIE   Letters? What letters are you talking about?

JONATHAN   Just . . . letters I write.

ROSALIE   To *whom?*

JONATHAN   To people.

ROSALIE   *What* people?

JONATHAN   Oh . . . various people.

ROSALIE   Other girls? Could they be to other girls, by any chance?

JONATHAN   No. They're just to people. No people in particular. Just people in the phone book. Just names. I do it alphabetically. That way, someday, I'll be able to cover everyone. So far I've covered all the "A's" and "B's" up to Barrera.

ROSALIE   What is it you say to them? Can you tell me what you say to them . . . or
is it private? Jonathan, just what do you say to them!?

JONATHAN   Mostly I just ask them what they look like. (*Pause. Suddenly he starts
to sob in a curious combination of laughter and tears.*) But I don't think she
ever mails them. She reads them, then takes them out to mail. But I don't think
she ever does. I'll bet she just throws them away. Well if she's not going to
mail them, why does she say she will? I . . . I could save the stamps. Why must
she lie to me? Why doesn't she just say she's not going to mail them? Then I
wouldn't have to wait for letters every day.

ROSALIE   Guess why I had this key made.

JONATHAN   I'll bet she's never even mailed one. From Abandono to Barrera, not
one.

ROSALIE   Do you know why I had this key made? Do you know why I'm wearing
this new dress?

JONATHAN   She doesn't let me stand in the window at noon because the sun is too
strong. She doesn't let me stand in the window at night when the wind is
blowing because the air is too cold. And today she told me she's going to nail
shutters over the windows so I'll never have to worry about being bothered by
the sun or the wind again.

ROSALIE   Try and guess why I'm all dressed up.

JONATHAN   She tells me I'm brilliant. She makes me read and reread books no
one's ever read. She smothers me with blankets at night in case of a storm.
She tucks me in so tight I can't even get out till she comes and takes my
blankets off.

ROSALIE   Stop talking about that and pay attention to me!

JONATHAN   She says she loves me. Every morning, before I even have a chance to
open my eyes, there she is, leaning over my bed, breathing in my face and
saying, "I love you, I love you."

ROSALIE   Jonathan, isn't my dress pretty?

JONATHAN   But I heard everything tonight. I heard it all when she didn't know I
was here. (*He stares off into space, bewildered.*)

ROSALIE   What's the matter? (*He does not answer.*) Jonathan, what's the matter?

JONATHAN   But she must have known I was here. She *must* have known! I mean
. . . where could I have gone? (*Pause.*) But . . . if that's the case . . . *why did
she let me hear?*

ROSALIE   Jonathan, I do wish you'd pay more attention to me. Here, look at my
dress. You can even touch it if you like. Guess how many crinolines I have on.
Guess why I'm wearing such a pretty, new dress. *Jonathan!*

JONATHAN (*distantly*)   Maybe . . . it didn't make any difference to her . . . whether
I heard it or not.

(*END*)

20 Eclectic

Intermingling

. . . conglomerations of past and present
stages of civilizations, bits from books
and newspapers, scraps of humanity,
rags and tatters of fine clothing, patched
together. . . .

August Strindberg discussing plays and
characters in *Preface to Miss Julie*

I can sum up none of my plays. I can
describe none of them, except to say:
That is what happened. That is what
they said. That is what they did.

Harold Pinter
from a speech by Harold Pinter
at The University of Hamburg,
June 4, 1970.

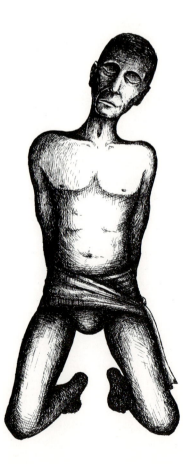

Overview of Eclectic

Theatre in the Western hemisphere in the 1960s and 1970s has been somewhat diffused. The mixing of styles that followed the nonrealistic movements were embellished by new contributions from Brecht and the Absurdists. However, in the past decade and one-half, playwrights have generally written in various styles to produce an extremely Eclectic drama and, as a result, an extremely Eclectic style of acting. *Eclectic* refers to material drawn from several sources, much as just described by Strindberg. The result is plays that are difficult to categorize or label. As Pinter noted at the beginning of this chapter, the plays cannot be summed up nor described. They merely happen.

What are the results of the eclectic intermix of Realism, nonrealism, Brecht Epic Theatre, and Absurd drama?

The most important playwrights influenced by Brecht Epic Theatre include Max Frisch, Rolf Hochhuth, and Peter Weiss. Each of these authors used history as the basis for interpretation of the present. Also, dramatic structure, use of music, and other staging techniques in their plays clearly illustrate Epic influence. However, each author modifies that influence and creates fresh theatrical experience which is best categorized as Eclectic. Also, they tend to use less Oriental material, although Frisch does use the technique in *The Chinese Wall*. Also their plays have more emotional content and less focus on Didacticism. *The Firebugs* is one of the most important plays by Frisch. *The Deputy* by Hochhuth is a modern landmark of controversy because of its attack on the Catholic church and Pope Pius XII. Hochhuth's *Soldiers* is similarly controversial because of its attack on Winston Churchill. Weiss's *Investigation* and *Marat/Sade* are exciting theatrical pieces in the Epic tradition. Again, Weiss differs from Brecht, particularly in his premises which elicit emotional rather than intellectual response from an audience.

The most important contemporary playwrights influenced by the Absurd drama of the 1940s and 1950s included Harold Pinter, Edward Albee, Tom Stoppard, Arthur Kopit, David Storey, Boris Vian, Jack Gelber, Fernando Arrabal, Jack Richardson, and Francois Billetdoux, among others. Of these, Pinter, Albee, Stoppard, Kopit, and Storey are the most produced in the United States. Each of these playwrights has written plays directly in the Absurd vein, but perhaps with an even greater sense of humor than the early European leaders of the movement. Some of these authors have also written plays that are distinctly entrenched in other forms and styles such as Realism, Symbolism, and Epic. For example, Albee's *Zoo Story*, *The American Dream*, and *Tiny Alice* are Absurdist, but *Who's Afraid of Virginia Woolf?* is closely related to Realism and Symbolism. Kopit's *Oh, Dad, Poor Dad* is Absurdist, but *Indians* is in the Epic manner. Stoppard's plays are the most consistently Absurdist, but have fresh, contemporary humor. Storey's plays are considerably more realistic than Absurd.

Pinter's plays are especially unique in use of character, environment, language, and silence. In Pinter's plays, characters handle the menace of

Scene from *The Birthday Party* by Harold Pinter. Directed by Fredrick L. Olson. Chabot College, California.

the unknown and unspoken with comic fright. Unable to come to grips with reality, they dwell miserably in a room which becomes their entire world. Settings have only realistic overtones; conversations begin with comic realism. With varying rhythm, comedy reveals the hidden menace that threatens the characters. The colloquial pattern of London speech degenerates into repetition, staccato rhythm, and, finally, silence. Minds wander through vague recollection with no certainty about what happened or what is happening (*Old Times*). In his early plays, the menacing quality climaxes in violent action (such as when Bert Hudd attacks a blind Negro in *The Room*). After *The Caretaker* and *The Birthday Party*, Pinter used sex as the prime force in the breakdown of an individual (e.g., *The Homecoming* and *Old Times*).

In contrast to Pinter, Albee uses vicious comic dialogue to reveal the serious-tragic aspect of human experience. Albee's serious drama does not grow out of the comedy (as does Pinter's). The serious intent of Albee's characters, their motivation, and their underlying justification force action to be immediately serious, although often sentimental. Albee's biting, satirical, highly intense dialogue leaps at an audience (e.g., *Who's Afraid of Virginia Woolf?*). Recently, he has written plays in the manner of the Eclectic playwrights (e.g., *A Delicate Balance*, *All Over*, and *Seascape*).

Both Pinter and Albee reject the Absurd label. They consider their plays to be highly personal forms of symbolic Realism and basically comic.

Other leading authors of Eclectic drama in recent years include Arthur Miller, Tennessee Williams, Robert Bolt, Jean Anouilh, Jules Feiffer, Peter Ustinov, John Guare, and Friedrich Dürrenmatt, among others. Still other contemporary authors are more inclined toward straight dramatic realism including such playwrights as Clifford Odets, Lillian Hellman, William Inge, Neil Simon, Jason Miller, Paul Zindel, Leonard Gershe, Frank Gilroy, Robert Anderson, Jean Kerr, Lanford Wilson, William Gibson, and others. Earlier in the century, Eugene O'Neill, James Thurber, George S. Kaufman, Moss Hart, and Thornton Wilder wrote plays in such a variety of styles that in an overall view of their work they may best be called Eclectic. American authors such as Sherwood Anderson, Elmer Rice, Paul Green, Carson McCullers, Mary Chase, William Saroyan, and others have contributed a generally Eclectic drama whose roots are in realism with branches in nonrealism. In France, Jean Cocteau and Jean Giraudoux did much the same thing, with some effort at a return to Classicism. Maxwell Anderson, T. S. Eliot, Christopher Fry, Federico García Lorca, Archibald MacLeish, and others led the way into modern poetic verse drama.

Scene from *Cat on a Hot Tin Roof* by Tennessee Williams. Directed by Fredrick L. Olson. Designed by Timothy Tunks. University of Nevada, Las Vegas.

Scene from *Thurber Carnival* by James Thurber. Directed by Jerry L. Crawford. Designed by Fredrick L. Olson. Costumes by Pat Crawford. University of Nevada, Las Vegas.

Perhaps O'Neill, Williams, and Miller can be considered the most successful and popular American dramatists of this century. Their plays combine many styles which draw material from many sources. Because of this, it is difficult to place their work in an overall category. For example, Miller's *Death of a Salesman* and Williams' *The Glass Menagerie* exemplify detailed Naturalism mixed with Expressionism. At times, pure stylistic form was used principally by O'Neill. For example, O'Neill's *Lazarus Laughed* is Epic in nature; *The Hairy Ape, The Great God Brown*, and *Emperor Jones* are all Expressionism; *Beyond the Horizon* is Realism; *Long Day's Journey into Night* is Naturalism; *Mourning Becomes Electra* is based on the classical Greek *Oresteia*; and *Strange Interlude* is an intermix of several styles. O'Neill's canon of plays envelops a mixture of forms and styles probably unparalleled in dramatic history. Most of the plays of O'Neill, Williams, and Miller permit the Naturalism approach to character creation as determined by role analysis (see chapter 10), personalization, and Stanislavski techniques (see chapter 16). Nonetheless, the varied Eclectic influence of the nonrealists on these authors at times obligates an actor to draw from other style sources ranging from Absurd techniques to Epic and Expressionism techniques. For example, such plays as Miller's *The Creation of The World and Other Business* and *After the Fall* and Williams' *Camino Real* and *The Milk Train Doesn't Stop Here Anymore* all require a combination of acting styles dependent upon careful analysis. Accordingly, an actor is best trained to handle the Eclectic body of work offered by these three great American authors *after* training in all the other major twentieth-century acting styles.

During the 1960s, there was a tremendous upsurge in Eclectic theatrical innovation in an attempt to explore new dramatic expressions in which the written word was reexamined and reshaped. The innovation also produced a new kind of actor, playwright, director, and scene designer, as well as a new kind of audience. The world of the sixties was in flux, changing and adapting to a new society whose ethics and values produced a new liberalism in social, political, and cultural patterns. The new dramatists rejected many of the concepts of Realism and Naturalism, particularly in stage scenery and environment. Since Realism and Naturalism perpetuated the traditional social order in which humanity was emphasized and man's quest for freedom repressed, they were not harmonious with the political atmosphere of the times. Theatre innovators of the sixties shared the Absurdist playwrights' distrust of the written word, of language, of dialogue. They limited the meaning and structure of words, and they communicated ideas with imprecision and inaccuracy.

The motivation of the new Eclectic theatre artists was primarily nonverbal. They created basically out of improvisational techniques and modern dance under the direction of an artist-leader rather than of a director. The artist-leader differed from a director in that he was often a creative performer onstage with the actors, rather than a backstage re-creative interpreter who assists actors. Much of the Eclectic theatrical expression centered on group efforts. The groups were closely united by common goals and strong social and political commitments. Their goal was a total theatre activity aimed at bringing the masses into the theatre again.

As discussed in chapter 19, Artaud championed the concept of total theatre, which correlates with Eclectic theatre. This concept became highly influential in theatre movements of the 1960s. Artaud believed that theatre should be an interplay and synthesis of music, movement, voice, scenery, and lighting—a convergence of the arts as sensory modalities, transmitting information through integrated effects. The controlling factor in this theatre was the emotional ordering of what is often called "multimedia scenography." Artaud's theatre was nonliterary and emphasized dance, sound, and light as the primary expressions of language. Movement became highly stylized similar to ancient hieroglyphic writings in which one sign (e.g., gesture or movement) combined many different meanings in a single prealphabetical symbol or emblem. Ideally, the space where a performer worked was unlimited and thereby no restrictions were placed. Marshall McLuhan, modern media theorist, saw this theatre as a "retribalization" of culture that focused on participation, tactility, and sculptural values. Artaud wanted a return to an archaic, primitive, ceremonial mode of expression. He wished to rediscover the "other" or intangible meaning of our existence, the deeper perceptions of the sensory and abstract. Artaud was too far ahead of his time to have significant impact. His was a theatre of the future—a theatre of dynamic forms and colors, filled with chaotic but expressive movement (e.g., jugglers, dancers, and gymnasts). Thirty years early, Artaud established the foundation for the Eclectic theatre of the 1960s.

The artist-leader of the 1960s attempted to elicit a group expression with didactic purposes (social, political, and religious) in the Brechtian tradition. As a result, the improvisational actor of the sixties became a performer of tasks rather than a creator of roles. The performer's own personality provided some characterization—but impersonation in much of this theatre activity was a dead issue. The goal was a compatible group effort in a highly charged theatrical presentation. Actual audience participation in the theatrical event was encouraged by some groups (see Appendix B). Note that Brecht did not desire audience participation in the theatre event itself. He and Artaud wanted audiences to think and proceed to social action after the event.

Leading contemporary experimental theatre groups, companies, and artists are discussed in Appendix B.

Voice

It is obvious that vocal training for the Eclectic drama of the twentieth century requires a totally trained mechanism. The intermingling of styles requires extensive range, effortless articulation and projection, and flexible variation. However, it is unsettling to note the fact that many contemporary American actors are generally regarded to be deficient in vocal execution. According to the critics involved in the American College Theatre Festival competition, voice and diction are glaringly deficient areas of ability. Perhaps this is the result of the great emphasis in the 1960s upon nonverbal, physical, improvisational activity. Nonetheless, in the 1970s there is new concern for emphasis upon vocal training for both collegiate and professional actors. With the emphasis on production of musical theatre it is necessary that an aspiring actor put concerted effort into vocal training. Most theatre departments in American colleges and universities are adding specialized courses in stage voice to their curriculums.

Exercise 1 Voice—Eclectic

Create an improvisation based on a job interview. Define your circumstances clearly. Perform the improvisation in three different ways.
  a. With no human speech, relying solely on sounds and noises
  b. With no human speech, relying solely on gibberish which, unlike sounds and noises, includes use of consonants and vowels
  c. Using human speech with good range, articulation, projection, and variety

Movement

Eclectic drama in the twentieth century has been unusually oriented toward movement and physical, nonverbal activity. The experimental groups of the 1960s were particularly outstanding for their focus on movement. These troupes went so far as to eliminate standard theatrical environment, frequently leaving the performer with only his body as the means of communication. It follows that the contemporary actor working in Eclectic drama must possess a totally trained physical apparatus. Dance training is almost

Scene from *The House of Bernarda Alba* by Federico García Lorca. National Finalist production, Center for the Performing Arts, Washington, D. C., American College Theatre Festival, 1975. Directed by Jerry L. Crawford. Designed by Fredrick L. Olson. Costumes by Ellis M. Pryce-Jones. University of Nevada, Las Vegas.

a necessity. Academic and professional training centers also stress fencing, weight training, gymnastics, acrobatics, mime, Oriental techniques (such as those found in the Tai Chi Chuan system of movement), the Laban theory of movement (a system of spatial movement), and improvisational games.

Exercise 2   Movement—Eclectic

1. Imagine that you are encased in a transparent ice cube. Explore the confines of your rigidly defined space. Perform this exploration with every part of your body. Be aware that the area is extremely cold. Eventually permit your body heat to melt the cube and free you.

2. Select several interesting photographs of people in unusual physical positions. Practice moving from an aligned standing position into the physical positions shown in the photographs. From each position, move into another unusual physical position which evolves naturally from your sense of the space you occupy.

3. Position your body in an unusual way, for example, in a squatting position. Explore kinesthetic movement patterns emanating from particular parts of your body. Begin with extensive arm activity, varying movement in direction and tempo. Continue the kinesthetic experience with movement of the head. Continue the exercise by altering the position while using movement from other parts of the body; for example, recline upon your back, lift your legs in the air, and explore space with them.

4. Create an improvisation related to the Garden of Eden. Define your circumstances. Perform the improvisation without language, using movement and sound as the sole means of telling the story.

Ice Cube exercise

Scene from *Marat/Sade* by Peter Weiss. Directed by Fredrick L. Olson. Designed by Fredrick L. Olson. Costumes by Ellis M. Pryce-Jones. University of Nevada, Las Vegas.

Character and Emotion

In acting the contemporary Eclectic style of drama careful textual analysis is necessary. Actors must play the realistic elements when character demands it, perform Brechtian techniques in Epic and intellectual segments, utilize Absurd stand-up cabaret or vaudeville humor at moments, use Artaud assault techniques when appropriate, use improvisation when required, combine nonrealistic and realistic techniques, and generally work with the fundamental of effective personalization. In other words, character and emotion in Eclectic drama range from simplistic to multidimensional, from stereotype to uniquely individual.

As Joseph Chaikin has noted, "When working on character, it isn't enough just to imitate. What a person says is not as important as where he sees from."

The contemporary actor should be familiar with and capable of using techniques ranging from Stanislavski to Brecht to Artaud to Grotowski. He should understand human emotion and know when and how to use it or restrict it. The contemporary actor is often called upon to be playwright, director, and performer. In other words, full personalization is at work. It is probably to the credit of contemporary theatre with its Eclectic base that the art of the actor in terms of character, emotion, movement, and voice seems to be moving to the forefront of dramatic activity. Also, much of the drama of the late 1960s requires skill in audience participation techniques, use of partial or full nudity, use of abusive, profane language, and heightened sexual activity. The so-called Power Plays are examples of such drama (see *The Drama Review,* vol. 14, no. 4 [September 1970]). Some of this activity has carried into film acting in the 1970s.

Exercise 3   Character and Emotion—Eclectic

1. Review the character and emotion exercises given in chapters 11 through 19.

2. Create an improvisation whose setting is a cocktail party. Define your circumstances clearly. Begin the cocktail party in a human form. Slowly, begin to change from being human to being nonhuman. Continue the improvisation until the last nonhuman has left the party.

3. Two people perform an improvisation in which there are two clearly defined characters (e.g., an impolite salesman and an irate customer). At various points throughout the improvisation, your instructor or director will call for reversal of roles. Attempt to change roles easily and smoothly in the improvisation.

4. Four people perform an improvisation in which there are four clearly defined characters involved in a specific activity (e.g., four neighborhood women getting ready for a Fourth of July party). When the director so indicates, change acting styles in the following sequence:

    a. Realism

    b. Expressionism

    c. Epic

    d. Absurd

The contemporary theatre offers a continually expanding experience for actors. The demands imposed upon the actor are astonishing. He should not only study his role (à la Stanislavski), but also relate his own psychical and physical beings to those of a character. Further, he should learn how to work "detached," as in Brecht, often combining all these techniques in one Eclectic, complex performance. The excitement generated by contemporary acting evolves around the attempt to extend a character into life in an organic structure. It is an ongoing experiment. The search to discover an ultimate medium for playing the impulses of a character and yet make that character functional for the stage takes an extraordinary degree of intelligence, discipline, and concentration.

At this point, it may be justifiably asked: What does the contemporary dramatic scene mean in terms of the growth and development of an actor? Where is the training to take place? What is the specific training? And how does the actor train for a theatre in which audience participation is sometimes an integral part of the action onstage?

If university theatre departments, studio schools, and repertory workshops do not provide the necessary courses in textual analysis, dance, movement, voice, and improvisational techniques, if actors must still fight the concept of the master director who demands complete control in all areas of production and training, we can then only direct actors toward a new

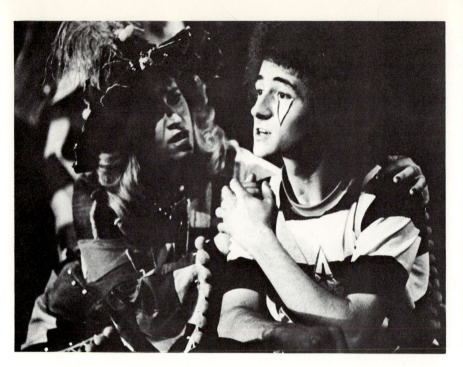

Scene from *Godspell* by
Stephen Schwartz. Di-
rected by Fredrick L.
Olson. Designed by
Timothy Tunks. Cos-
tumes by Ellis M. Pryce-
Jones. University of
Nevada, Las Vegas.

way of *thinking* about contemporary acting. Perhaps traditional *conceptions*
(too often stereotyped) can be altered to encompass what acting in the theatre *should* be—*an important and respected art.*

Suggested Characters and Plays for Scene Work

O'Neill, Eugene

Jamie, Edmund, Mary, Tyrone
>   *Long Day's Journey Into Night*
Melody, Sarah
>   *A Touch of the Poet*
Nina, Dr. Darrell, Sam, Charlie
>   *Strange Interlude*
Christine, Lavinia, Ezra, Adam, Orin
>   *Mourning Becomes Electra*
Nat, Essie, Richard, Muriel, Lilly, Sid
>   *Ah, Wilderness!*
Hickey, Harry, Larry, Don, Pearl, Margie, Lora
>   *The Iceman Cometh*
Anna, Chris, Mat
>   *Anna Christie*

Miller, Arthur

Chris, Ann, Keller
>   *All My Sons*
Willy, Biff, Happy, Linda
>   *Death of a Salesman*

Eddie, Catherine, Rudolfo, Beatrice
A View From the Bridge
Proctor, Abigail, Elizabeth, Reverend Hale, Danforth
The Crucible
Quentin, Maggie
After the Fall
All characters
The Price

Williams, Tennessee

Amanda, Laura, Tom, The Gentleman Caller
The Glass Menagerie
Blanche, Stella, Stanley, Mitch
A Streetcar Named Desire
Alma, John
Summer and Smoke
Reverend Shannon, Maxine, Hannah
The Night of the Iguana

Pinter, Harold

Bert, Rose, Mr. Kidd, Mr. Sands, Mrs. Sands
The Room
Max, Sam, Lenny, Joey, Teddy, Ruth
The Homecoming
Sarah, Richard
The Lover
Anna, Kate, Deeley
Old Times
Mich, Aston, Davies
The Caretaker
Meg, Stanley, Petey, Lulu, Goldberg, McCann
The Birthday Party

Kopit, Arthur

Jonathan, Rosalie, Madam Rosepettle, Commodore
Oh, Dad, Poor Dad, Mamma's
Hung You in the Closet and
I'm Feelin' So Sad
Buffalo Bill, Sitting Bull, Wild Bill Hickok
Indians

Stoppard, Tom

Rosencrantz, Guildenstern, The Player
Rosencrantz and Guildenstern Are Dead
Moon, Birdboot, Felicity, Cynthia, Hound
The Real Inspector Hound
George, Dorothy, Archie, Bones, Crouch
Jumpers
Henry Carr
Travesties

Albee, Edward

Jerry, Peter
The Zoo Story

Martha, George, Nick, Honey
Who's Afraid of Virginia Woolf?
Mommie, Daddy, Grandma, Mrs. Barker, Young Man
The American Dream
Nancy, Charlie, Leslie, Sarah
Seascape

Gagliano, Frank

All characters
Father Uxbridge Wants to Marry
Tobias, Agnes, Claire, Julia
A Delicate Balance
Miss Alice, Julian, Lawyer, Cardinal
Tiny Alice
The Wife, The Mistress, The Son, The Daughter
All Over

Simon, Neil

Barney, Elaine, Bobbi, Jeanette
The Last of the Red Hot Lovers
Felix, Oscar
The Odd Couple
Mel, Edna
Prisoner of Second Avenue
Willy, Al
The Sunshine Boys
Evy, Polly
The Gingerbread Lady
Corrie, Paul
Barefoot in the Park
All characters
Plaza Suite
All characters
The Good Doctor
All characters
God's Favorite

Inge, William

Alma, Grace, Bo, Cherie
Bus Stop
Doc, Lola
Come Back, Little Sheba
Howard, Rosemary, Hal, Madge
Picnic

Bolt, Robert

Sir Thomas More, Henry VIII
A Man for All Seasons
Mary, Elizabeth
Vivat! Vivat! Regina!

Wilder, Thornton

Sabina, Mr. Antrobus, Mrs. Antrobus
The Skin of Our Teeth

314   Acting: In Style

Emily, George, Stage Manager
  Our Town
Dolly, Barnaby, Cornelius, Minnie, Vandergelder
  The Matchmaker

Anouilh, Jean

Becket, Henry
  Becket
Antigone, Creon
  Antigone

Rabe, David

Harriet, Ozzie, David, Ricky
  Sticks and Bones
Ardell, Pavlo
  The Basic Training of Pavlo Hummel
Chrissy, Eric, Susan, Al
  In the Boom Boom Room

Feiffer, Jules

Patsy, Marjorie, Carol, Alfred, Reverend Dupas
  Little Murders

Storey, David

Harry, Jack, Marjorie, Cathleen
  Home
The Athletes
  The Changing Room
Ewbank, Claire, Maurice, Kay, Marshall
  The Contractor

Miller, Jason

Tom, George, James, Phil, Coach
  That Championship Season

Guare, John

Artie, Bunny, Ronnie, Bananas
  The House of Blue Leaves

Weller, Michael

The Students
  Moonchildren

Zindel, Paul

Beatrice, Tillie, Ruth, Nanny
  The Effect of Gamma Rays
  on Man-In-The-Moon Marigolds
Cathrine, Anna, Ceil
  And Miss Reardon Drinks a Little
All characters
  The Private Affairs of Mildred Wild

Gershe, Leonard

Don, Jill, Mrs. Baker, Ralph
  Butterflies Are Free

Barry, Julian

Lenny
  Lenny

Gilroy, Frank

John, Timmy, Nettie
  The Subject Was Roses

Frisch, Max

Biedermann, Babette, Sepp, Will
  The Firebugs
The Contemporary, The Maskers
  The Chinese Wall

Durrenmatt, Friedrich

Claire, Anton, Teacher
  The Visit
Newton, Einstein, Mobiles
  The Physicists

Hochhuth, Rolf

Father Riccardo, Gerstein, Pope Pius XII
  The Deputy
Churchill, Dorland, Bell, Helen
  Soldiers

Weiss, Peter

DeSade, Marat, Charlotte
  Marat/Sade

Wasserman, Dale

MacMurphy, Nurse, Ratched
  One Flew Over the Cuckoo's Nest
Don Quixote, Sancho, Aldonza
  Man of La Mancha

Ayckbourn, Alan

Jane, Sidney, Ronald, Marion, Eva, Geoffrey
  Absurd Person Singular

Stein, Joseph

Tevye, Motel, Golde
  Fiddler on the Roof

Macleish, Archibald

Zuss, Nickles, J. B., Sarah
  J. B.

Wilson, Lanford

The People, The Residents
  The Hot L Baltimore

Hopkins, John

Julian, David, Alan, Jacqueline
  Find Your Way Home

Shaffer, Peter

All characters
  Equus

Anderson, Robert

Gene, Margaret, Alice, Tom
  I Never Sang for My Father
Muriel, Herbert
  I'm Herbert
Tom, Laura
  Tea and Sympathy

van Itallie, Jean-Claude

Applicants, Interviewers
  Interview
Hal, Susan, George
  T. V.
Motel-Keeper, Man, Woman
  Motel
The Group
  The Serpent

Terry, Megan

The Group
  Viet Rock
He, She
  Comings and Goings

May, Elaine

All characters
  Adaptation

McNally, Terrence

Two Soldiers
  Botticelli
All characters
  Tour
  Next
  The Ritz
Otto, April, Roy, Dr. Pepper, Hiram, Dolly
  Bad Habits
Tommy, Greta, Nedda, Bunny, Ben, Arnold the Dog
  Where Has Tommy Flowers Gone?

Shepard, Sam

All characters
> *Operation Side-Winder*

Hoss, Crow, Cheyenne, Becky Lou
> *The Tooth of Crime*

Jones, LeRoi (Imamu Amiri Baraka)

Clay, Lula
> *Dutchman*

Grace, Walker, Easley
> *The Slave*

Hanley, William

Glas, Randell, Rosie
> *Slow Dance on the Killing Ground*

Baldwin, James

Richard, Meridian, Lyle, Parnell, Juanita
> *Blues for Mister Charlie*

Hansberry, Lorraine

Ruth, Walter, Beneatha, Mamma, George, Bobo
> *A Raisin in the Sun*

Gordone, Charles

Johnny, Gabe, Cora, Shanty, Sweets
> *No Place to Be Somebody*

Bullins, Ed

All characters
> *The Electronic Nigger*

All characters
> *Goin' A Buffalo*

Sherwood, Robert

Abe, Ann
> *Abe Lincoln in Illinois*

Gibson, William

Jerry, Gittle
> *Two for the Seesaw*

Will, Anne, Meg, Kemp
> *A Cry of Players*

Odets, Clifford

Joe, Mr. Bonaparte
> *Golden Boy*

All characters
> *Awake and Sing!*

Osborne, John

Jimmie Porter, Alison, Helena, Cliff
> *Look Back in Anger*

McCullers, Carson

Bernice, Frankie
  Member of the Wedding

Kaufman, George S., and Hart, Moss

Penelope, Essie, Grandpa, Mr. DiPina
  You Can't Take It With You

Saroyan, William

Tom, Joe, Kitty, Kit Carson
  The Time of Your Life

Hellman, Lillian

Martha, Karen
  The Children's Hour
Regina, Oscar, Ben, Birdie
  The Little Foxes

Anderson, Maxwell

Mio, Miriamne
  Winterset

Behan, Brendan

Meg, Pat, Monsewer, Miss Gilchrist, Leslie, Terresa
  The Hostage

Ustinov, Peter

The Unknown Soldier, Wife, Archbishop, General
  The Unknown Soldier and His Wife

Solzhenitsyn, Alexander

Nemor, Kostya, Lyuba
  The Love-Girl and the Innocent

Actor Checklist   *Eclectic*

Voice	Extensive range; effortless articulation and projection; flexible variation; intermix of many stylistic techniques.
Movement	Total body as communicator; dance, mime, gymnastic, acrobatic, Oriental, Tai Chi Chuan, Laban, spatial activity, improvisational; mix of presentational and representational mode; combination of many stylistic techniques.
Gesture	Inventive; varied; flexible.
Pantomimic Dramatization	Inventive; varied; flexible; improvisational theatre; limited use of objects, properties, and costumes.
Character	Ranges from stereotype to uniquely individual and multidimensional; intermingling of many stylistic techniques; at times includes audience contact, nudity, and profanity.

Emotion	Ranges from simplistic to complex; ranges from human to void.
Ideas	Usually complex; oriented heavily to social and political activity; at times extremely Freudian and sexual base.
Language	Usually de-emphasized in most plays; intermingling of many stylistic forms.
Mood and Atmosphere	Varied; experimental theatre oriented to the serious and grotesquely humorous; commercial theatre oriented to comedy and music.
Pace and Tempo	Varied; experimental theatre unusually slow; commercial theatre unusually rapid.
Special Techniques	Analysis and application of intermix of characteristics; diversified grasp of contemporary experimental theatre.

Note: Because of the wide scope of contemporary Eclectic acting styles, the suggestions given in this list must be adapted individually according to the particular author, play, and role being acted.

Suggested Readings

Baxandall, Lee. "Spectacles and Scenarios: A Dramaturgy of Radical Activity." *TDR The Drama Review,* Summer 1969.

Bentley, Eric. *The Playwright as Thinker: A Study of Drama in Modern Times.* New York: Harcourt Brace Jovanovich, 1946.

Bentley, Eric. *In Search of Theatre.* New York: Alfred A. Knopf, 1953.

Brecht, Stefan. "Family of the f.p. Notes on the Theatre of the Ridiculous." *TDR The Drama Review* 13 (1969):117–41.

Brockett, Oscar G. *Perspectives on Contemporary Theatre.* Baton Rouge, La.: Louisiana State University Press, 1971.

Brook, Peter. *The Empty Space.* New York: Atheneum Publishers, 1968.

Brustein, Robert. *The Theatre of Revolt.* Boston, Mass.: Atlantic Monthly Press, 1964.

Brustein, Robert. *The Third Theatre.* New York: Alfred A. Knopf, 1969.

Chaikin, Joseph. "The Open Theatre." *Tulane Drama Review,* Winter 1964, pp. 191–97.

Cheney, Sheldon. *The New Movement in the Theatre.* New York: Benjamin Blom, 1914.

Cohn, Ruby. *Currents in Contemporary Drama.* Bloomington, Ind.: Indiana University Press, 1969.

Corrigan, Robert W. *The Theatre in Search of a Fix.* New York: Dell Publishing Co., Delta Books, 1974.

Esslin, Martin. *Reflections: Essays in the Modern Theatre.* New York: Doubleday & Co., 1969.

Fowlie, Wallace. *Dionysus in Paris.* Gloucester, Mass.: Peter Smith, 1960.

Freedman, Morris. *Essays in the Modern Drama.* Boston: D. C. Heath, 1964.

Fuchs, Georg. *Revolution in the Theatre.* Translated by C. C. Kuhn. Ithaca, N. Y.: Cornell University Press, 1959.

Gardner, R. H. *The Splintered Stage.* New York: Macmillan Co., 1965.

Gassner, John. *Directions in Modern Theatre and Drama.* New York: Holt, Rinehart and Winston, 1965.

Gassner, John. *Form and Idea in the Modern Theatre*. New York: Holt, Rinehart, and Winston, 1956.

Gassner, John. *Theatre at the Crossroads: Plays and Playwrights of Mid-Century American Stage*. New York: Holt, Rinehart, and Winston, 1960.

Gassner, John. *The Theatre in Our Times: A Survey of the Men, Materials and Movements in the Modern Theatre*. New York: Crown Publishers, 1954.

Grossvogel, David I. *Twentieth Century French Drama*. New York: Columbia University Press, 1961.

Grotowski, Jerzy. *Towards a Poor Theatre*. New York: Simon & Schuster, 1968.

Grotowski, Jerzy. "Holiday." *TDR The Drama Review*, June 1973.

Grotowski, Jerzy. "Interview" by Richard Schechner. *TDR The Drama Review*, Fall 1968.

Hayman, Ronald. *Contemporary Playwrights: Harold Pinter*. London: Heinemann Educational Books, 1968. In same series: Samuel Beckett and John Osborne.

Hinchcliffe, Arnold P. *Harold Pinter*. New York: Twayne Publishers, 1967.

Houghton, Norris. *The Exploding Stage: An Introduction to Twentieth Century Drama*. New York: Weybright & Talley, 1971.

Kerr, Walter. *God on the Gymnasium Floor and Other Theatrical Adventures*. New York: Dell Publishing Co., Delta Books, 1974.

Kirby, Michael. *Happenings*. New York: E. P. Dutton & Co., 1965.

Kirby, Michael. "The New Theatre." *Tulane Drama Review*, Winter 1965, pp. 30–34.

Kirby, Michael. *The New Theatre: Performance Documentation*. New York: New York University Press, 1974.

Kitchin, Laurence. *Drama in the Sixties: Form and Interpretation*. London: Humanities Press, 1966.

Little, Stuart W. *Off-Broadway: The Prophetic Theatre*. New York: Dell Publishing Co., Delta Books, 1974.

Mann, Paul. "Theory and Practice." *Tulane Drama Review*, Winter 1964, pp. 84–96.

Marowitz, Charles. "Notes on the Theatre of Cruelty." *TDR The Drama Review* 1 (1966):152–72.

Neff, Renfreu. *The Living Theatre: USA*. New York: Bobbs-Merrill Co., 1970.

Orzel, Nick, and Smith, Michael, eds. *Eight Plays from Off-Off Broadway*. New York: Bobbs-Merrill Co., 1966.

Pasolli, Robert. *A Book on the Open Theatre*. New York: Bobbs-Merrill Co., 1970.

Price, Julia. *The Off-Broadway Theatre*, Metuchen, N. J.: Scarecrow Press, Inc., 1962.

Roberts, Vera Mowry. *The Nature of Theatre*. New York: Harper & Row, Publishers, 1971.

Roose-Evans, James. *Experimental Theatre*. New York: Universe Books, 1970.

Rostagno, Aldo; Beck, Julian; and Malina, Judith. *We, the Living Theatre*. New York: Ballantine Books, 1970.

Schechner, Richard. *Public Domain: Essays on the Theatre*. Indianapolis: Bobbs-Merrill Co., 1969.

Schechner, Richard. "Audience Participation." *TDR The Drama Review*, Summer 1971, pp. 73–89.

Schechner, Richard. "Guerrila Theatre: May 1970." *TDR The Drama Review*, May 1970, pp. 163–68.

Smith, Michael. "The Good Scene." *Tulane Drama Review*, Summer 1966, pp. 159–76.

Styan, J. L. *The Dark Comedy*. London: Cambridge University Press, 1962.

Van Itallie, Jean-Claude. "Playwright at Work: Off-Off Broadway." *Tulane Drama Review,* Summer 1966, pp. 154–58.

Weales, Gerald. *American Drama Since World War II.* New York: Harcourt Brace Jovanovich, 1962.

Wellworth, George, and Benedickt, Michael. *Theatre of Protest and Paradox.* 2nd ed. New York: New York University Press, 1968.

Wilson, Edwin. *The Theatre Experience.* New York: McGraw-Hill Book Co., 1976.

Strange Interlude
by Eugene O'Neill

from
Part I, Act IV

Nina, age 22 years
Darrell, age 28 years

Characters

The study in the home of Professor Henry Leeds; evening; New England, a
small university town; autumn.

Scene

Nina Leeds loved a man who was killed in the war. She marries a professor,
becomes pregnant, but has an abortion, fearing that an insanity streak in the
family might affect the child. She decides to strike a bargain with Dr. Darrell
to father a child with her. (Indented dialogue represents the inner thoughts of
each character which when spoken cannot be heard by the other character.)

Situation

NINA (*enters silently. She has fixed herself up, put on her best dress, arranged her
hair, rouged, etc.—but it is principally her mood that has changed her,
making her appear a younger, prettier person for the moment.* DARRELL
*immediately senses her presence, and, looking up, gets to his feet with a smile
of affectionate admiration. She comes quickly over to him saying with frank
pleasure*)   Hello, Ned. I'm certainly glad to see you again—after all these
years!

DARRELL (*as they shake hands—smiling*)   Not as long as all that, is it? (*thinking
admiringly*)
> Wonderful-looking as ever . . . Sam is a lucky devil! . . .

NINA (*thinking*)
> Strong hands like Gordon's . . . take hold of you . . . not like Sam's . . .
> yielding fingers that let you fall back into yourself . . .

(*teasingly*) I ought to cut you dead after the shameful way you've ignored us!

DARRELL (*a bit embarrassedly*)   I've really meant to write. (*his eyes examining
her keenly*)
> Been through a lot since I saw her . . . face shows it . . . nervous tension
> pronounced . . . hiding behind her smile . . .

NINA (*uneasy under his glance*)
> I hate that professional look in his eyes . . . watching symptoms . . .
> without seeing me . . .

(*with resentful mockery*)   Well, what do you suspect is wrong with the
patient now, Doctor? (*She laughs nervously.*) Sit down, Ned. I suppose you
can't help your diagnosing stare. (*She turns from him and sits down in the
rocker at center.*)

DARRELL (*quickly averting his eyes—sits down—jokingly*)   Same old unjust
accusation! You were always reading diagnosis into me, when what I was
really thinking was what fine eyes you had, or what a becoming gown, or—

NINA (*smiling*)   Or what a becoming alibi you could cook up! Oh, I know you!
(*With a sudden change of mood she laughs gaily and naturally.*) But you're
forgiven—that is, if you can explain why you've never been to see us.

DARRELL   Honestly, Nina, I've been so rushed with work I haven't had a chance to go anywhere.

NINA   Or an inclination!

DARRELL *(smiling)*   Well—maybe.

NINA   Do you like the Institute so much? *(He nods gravely.)* Is it the big opportunity you wanted?

DARRELL *(simply)*   I think it is.

NINA *(with a smile)*   Well, you're the taking kind for whom opportunities are made!.

DARRELL *(smiling)*   I hope so.

NINA *(sighing)*   I wish that could be said of more of us—*(then quickly)*—meaning myself.

DARRELL *(thinking with a certain satisfaction)*
     Meaning Sam . . . that doesn't look hopeful for future wedded bliss! . . .
(teasingly) But I heard you were "taking an opportunity" to go in for literature —collaborating with Marsden.

NINA   No, Charlie is only going to advise. He'd never deign to appear as co-author. And besides, he never appreciated the real Gordon. No one did except me.

DARRELL *(thinking caustically)*
     Gordon myth strong as ever . . . root of her trouble still . . .
(keenly inquisitive) Sam certainly appreciated him, didn't he?

NINA *(not remembering to hide her contempt)*   Sam? Why, he's the exact opposite in every way!

DARRELL *(caustically thinking)*
     These heroes die hard . . . but perhaps she can write him out of her system. . . .
(persuasively) Well, you're going ahead with the biography, aren't you? I think you ought to.

NINA *(dryly)*   For my soul, Doctor? *(listlessly)* I suppose I will. I don't know. I haven't much time. The duties of a wife—*(teasingly)* By the way, if it isn't too rude to inquire, aren't you getting yourself engaged to some fair lady or other?

DARRELL *(smiling—but emphatically)*   Not on your life! Not until after I'm thirty-five, at least!

NINA *(sarcastically)*   Then you don't believe in taking your own medicine? Why, Doctor! Think of how much good it would do you!—*(excitedly with a hectic sarcasm)*—if you had a nice girl to love—or was it learn to love?—and take care of—whose character you could shape and whose life you could guide and make what you pleased, in whose unselfish devotion you could find peace! *(more and more bitterly sarcastic)* And you ought to have a baby, Doctor! You will never know what life is, you'll never be really happy until you've had a baby, Doctor—a fine, healthy baby! *(She laughs a bitter, sneering laugh.)*

DARRELL *(after a quick, keen glance, thinking)*
     Good! . . . she's going to tell . . .
(meekly) I recognize my arguments. Was I really wrong on every point, Nina?

NINA *(harshly)*   On every single point, Doctor!

DARRELL *(glancing at her keenly)*   But how? You haven't given the baby end of it a chance yet, have you?

NINA *(bitterly)*   Oh, haven't I? *(then bursts out with intense bitterness)* I'll have you know I'm not destined to bear babies, Doctor!

DARRELL (*startledly*)

What's that? . . . why not? . . .

(*again with a certain satisfaction*)

Can she mean Sam? . . . that he . . .

(*soothingly—but plainly disturbed*) Why don't you begin at the beginning and tell me all about it? I feel responsible.

NINA (*fiercely*)   You are! (*then wearily*) And you're not. No one is. You didn't know. No one could know.

DARRELL (*in same tone*)   Know what? (*thinking with the same eagerness to believe something he hopes*)

She must mean no one could know that Sam wasn't . . . but I might have guessed it . . . from his general weakness . . . poor unlucky devil . . .

(*then as she remains silent—urgingly*) Tell me. I want to help you, Nina.

NINA (*touched*)   It's too late, Ned. (*then suddenly*) I've just thought—Sam said he happened to run into you. That isn't so, is it? He went to see you and told you how worried he was about me and asked you out to see me, didn't he? (*as* DARRELL *nods*) Oh, I don't mind! It's even rather touching. (*then mockingly*) Well, since you're out here professionally, and my husband wants me to consult you, I might as well give you the whole case history! (*wearily*) I warn you it isn't pretty, Doctor! But then life doesn't seem to be pretty, does it? And, after all, you aided and abetted God the Father in making this mess. I hope it'll teach you not to be so cocksure in future. (*more and more bitterly*) I must say you proceeded very unscientifically, Doctor! (*then suddenly starts her story in a dull monotonous tone recalling that of* EVANS' *mother in the previous act*) When we went to visit Sam's mother I'd known for two months that I was going to have a baby.

DARRELL (*startled—unable to hide a trace of disappointment*)   Oh, then you actually were? (*thinking disappointedly and ashamed of himself for being disappointed*)

All wrong, what I thought . . . she was going to . . . then why didn't she? . . .

NINA (*with a strange happy intensity*)   Oh, Ned, I loved it more than I've ever loved anything in my life—even Gordon! I loved it so it seemed at times that Gordon must be its real father, that Gordon must have come to me in a dream while I was lying asleep beside Sam! And I was happy! I almost loved Sam then! I felt he was a good husband!

DARRELL (*instantly repelled—thinking with scornful jealousy*)

Ha! . . . the hero again! . . . comes to her bed! . . . puts horns on poor Sam! . . . becomes the father of his child! . . . I'll be damned if hers isn't the most idiotic obsession I ever . . .

NINA (*her voice suddenly becoming flat and lifeless*)   And then Sam's mother told me I couldn't have my baby. You see, Doctor, Sam's great-grandfather was insane, and Sam's grandmother died in an asylum, and Sam's father had lost his mind for years before he died, and an aunt who is still alive is crazy. So of course I had to agree it would be wrong—and I had an operation.

DARRELL (*who has listened with amazed horror—profoundly shocked and stunned*)
Good God! Are you crazy, Nina? I simply can't believe! It would be too hellish! Poor Sam, of all people! (*bewilderedly*) Nina! Are you absolutely sure?

NINA (*immediately defensive and mocking*)   Absolutely, Doctor! Why? Do you think it's I who am crazy? Sam looks so healthy and sane, doesn't he? He fooled you completely, didn't he? You thought he'd be an ideal husband for me! And poor Sam's fooling himself too because he doesn't know anything about all this—so you can't blame him, Doctor!

DARRELL (*thinking in a real panic of horror—and a flood of protective affection for her*)

God, this is too awful! . . . on top of all the rest! . . . how did she ever stand it! . . . she'll lose her mind too! . . . and it's my fault! . . .

(*Getting up, comes to her and puts his hands on her shoulders, standing behind her—tenderly.*) Nina I'm so damn sorry! There's only one possible thing to do now. You'll have to make Sam give you a divorce.

NINA (*bitterly*)   Yes? Then what do you suppose would be his finish? No, I've enough guilt in my memory now, thank you! I've got to stick to Sam! (*then with a strange monotonous insistence*) I've promised Sam's mother I'd make him happy! He's unhappy now because he thinks he isn't able to give me a child. And I'm unhappy because I've lost my child. So I must have another baby—somehow—don't you think, Doctor?—to make us both happy? (*She looks up at him pleadingly. For a moment they stare into each other's eyes—then both turn away in guilty confusion.*)

DARRELL (*bewilderedly thinking*)

That look in her eyes . . . what does she want me to think? . . . why does she talk so much about being happy? . . . am I happy? . . . I don't know . . . what is happiness? . . .

(*confusedly*) Nina, I don't know what to think.

(*END*)

The Glass Menagerie
by Tennessee Williams

from
scene i

Tom Wingfield
Amanda, his mother
Laura, Tom's sister

Characters

An alley and the Wingfield apartment, St. Louis.

Scene

Tom, narrator of the play and a character in it, introduces this play from his
memory involving the fantasy and real worlds of his crippled sister, Laura, and
his mother, Amanda.

Situation

TOM   Yes, I have tricks in my pocket, I have things up my sleeve. But I am the
opposite of a stage magician. He gives you illusion that has the appearance of
truth. I give you truth in the pleasant disguise of illusion.

To begin with, I turn back time. I reverse it to that quaint period, the
thirties, when the huge middle class of America was matriculating in a school
for the blind. Their eyes had failed them, or they had failed their eyes, and so
they were having their fingers pressed forcibly down on the fiery Braille
alphabet of a dissolving economy.

In Spain there was revolution. Here there was only shouting and
confusion.

In Spain there was Guernica. Here there were disturbances of labor,
sometimes pretty violent, in otherwise peaceful cities such as Chicago,
Cleveland, Saint Louis . . .

This is the social background of the play.
(music)

The play is memory.

Being a memory play, it is dimly lighted, it is sentimental, it is not
realistic.

In memory everything seems to happen to music. That explains the fiddle
in the wings.

I am the narrator of the play, and also a character in it.

The other characters are my mother, Amanda, my sister, Laura, and a
gentleman caller who appears in the final scenes.

He is the most realistic character in the play, being an emissary from a
world of reality that we were somehow set apart from.

But since I have a poet's weakness for symbols, I am using this character
also as a symbol; he is the long delayed but always expected something that we
live for.

There is a fifth character in the play who doesn't appear except in this
larger-than-life-size photograph over the mantel.

This is our father who left us a long time ago.

He was a telephone man who fell in love with long distances; he gave up his job with the telephone company and skipped the light fantastic out of town . . .

The last we heard of him was a picture post-card from Mazatlan, on the Pacific coast of Mexico, containing a message of two words—

"Hello—Good-bye!" and no address.

I think the rest of the play will explain itself. . . .

(AMANDA's *voice becomes audible through the portieres*)

(LEGEND ON SCREEN: "OÙ SONT LES NEIGES")

He divides the portieres and enters the upstage area. AMANDA and LAURA are seated at a drop-leaf table. Eating is indicated by gestures without food or utensils. AMANDA faces the audience. TOM and LAURA are seated in profile. The interior has lit up softly and through the scrim we see AMANDA and LAURA seated at the table in the upstage area.

AMANDA (*calling*)   Tom?

TOM   Yes, Mother.

AMANDA   We can't say grace until you come to the table!

TOM   Coming, Mother. (*He bows slightly and withdraws, reappearing a few moments later in his place at the table*)

AMANDA (*to her son*)   Honey, don't *push* with your *fingers*. If you have to push with something the thing to push with is a crust of bread. And chew—chew! Animals have sections in their stomachs which enable them to digest food without mastication, but human beings are supposed to chew their food before they swallow it down. Eat food leisurely, son, and really enjoy it. A well-cooked meal has lots of delicate flavors that have to be held in the mouth for appreciation. So chew your food and give your salivary glands a chance to function!

(TOM *deliberately lays his imaginary fork down and pushes his chair back from the table.*)

TOM   I haven't enjoyed one bite of this dinner because of your constant directions on how to eat it. It's you that make me rush through meals with your hawk-like attention to every bite I take. Sickening—spoils my appetite—all this discussion of—animals' secretion—salivary glands—mastication!

AMANDA (*lightly*)   Temperament like a Metropolitan star! (*He rises and crosses downstage*) You're not excused from the table.

TOM   I'm getting a cigarette.

AMANDA   You smoke too much. (LAURA *rises*)

LAURA   I'll bring in the blanc mange. (*He remains standing with his cigarette by the portieres during the following*)

AMANDA (*rising*)   No, sister, no, sister—you be the lady this time and I'll be the darky.

LAURA   I'm already up.

AMANDA   Resume your seat, little sister—I want you to stay fresh and pretty—for gentlemen callers!

LAURA   I'm not expecting any gentlemen callers.

AMANDA (*crossing out to kitchenette. Airily*)   Sometimes they come when they

are least expected! Why, I remember one Sunday afternoon in Blue Mountain—
(enters kitchenette).

TOM   I know what's coming!

LAURA   Yes. But let her tell it.

TOM   Again?

LAURA   She loves to tell it.

(AMANDA *returns with bowl of dessert.*)

AMANDA   One Sunday afternoon in Blue Mountain—your mother received—
seventeen—gentlemen callers! Why, sometimes there weren't chairs enough
to accommodate them all. We had to send the nigger over to bring in folding
chairs from the parish house.

TOM *(remaining at portieres)*   How did you entertain those gentlemen callers?

AMANDA   I understood the art of conversation!

TOM   I bet you could talk.

AMANDA   Girls in those days *knew* how to talk, I can tell you.

TOM   Yes?

(IMAGE: Amanda AS A GIRL ON A PORCH, GREETING CALLERS)

AMANDA   They knew how to entertain their gentlemen callers. It wasn't enough
for a girl to be possessed of a pretty face and a graceful figure—although I
wasn't slighted in either respect. She also needed to have a nimble wit and a
tongue to meet all occasions.

TOM   What did you talk about?

AMANDA   Things of importance going on in the world! Never anything coarse or
common or vulgar. *(She addresses* TOM *as though he were seated in the vacant
chair at the table though he remains by portieres. He plays this scene as though
he held the book.)* My callers were gentlemen—all! Among my callers were
some of the most prominent young planters of the Mississippi Delta—planters
and sons of planters!

(TOM *motions for music and a spot of light on* AMANDA. *Her eyes lift, her face
glows, her voice becomes rich and elegiac.*)

(SCREEN LEGEND: "OÙ SONT LES NEIGES")
There was young Champ Laughlin who later became vice-president of the
Delta Planters Bank.
Hadley Stevenson who was drowned in Moon Lake and left his widow
one hundred and fifty thousand in Government bonds.
There were the Cutrere brothers, Wesley and Bates. Bates was one of my
bright particular beaux! He got in a quarrel with that wild Wainwright boy.
They shot it out on the floor of Moon Lake Casino. Bates was shot through
the stomach. Died in the ambulance on his way to Memphis. His widow was
also well-provided for, came into eight or ten thousand acres, that's all. She
married him on the rebound—never loved her—carried my picture on him
the night he died!
And there was that boy that every girl in the Delta had set her cap for!
That beautiful, brilliant young Fitzhugh boy from Greene County!

TOM   What did he leave his widow?

AMANDA   He never married! Gracious, you talk as though all of my old admirers
had turned up their toes to the daisies!

TOM   Isn't this the first you've mentioned that still survives?

AMANDA   That Fitzhugh boy went North and made a fortune—came to be known as the Wolf of Wall Street! He had the Midas touch, whatever he touched turned to gold!

And I could have been Mrs. Duncan J. Fitzhugh, mind you! But—I picked your *father!*

LAURA *(rising)*   Mother, let me clear the table.

AMANDA   No, dear, you go in front and study your typewriter chart. Or practice your shorthand a little. Stay fresh and pretty!—It's almost time for our gentlemen callers to start arriving. *(She flounces girlishly toward the kitchenette.)* How many do you suppose we're going to entertain this afternoon?

(TOM throws down the paper and jumps up with a groan.)

LAURA *(alone in the dining room)*   I don't believe we're going to receive any, Mother.

AMANDA *(reappearing, airily)*   What? No one—not one? You must be joking! *(*LAURA *nervously echoes her laugh. She slips in a fugitive manner through the half-open portieres and draws them gently behind her. A shaft of very clear light is thrown on her face against the faded tapestry of the curtains.* MUSIC: "THE GLASS MENAGERIE" UNDER FAINTLY. *Lightly)* Not one gentleman caller? It can't be true! There must be a flood, there must have been a tornado!

LAURA   It isn't a flood, it's not a tornado, Mother. I'm just not popular like you were in Blue Mountain. . . . *(*TOM *utters another groan.* LAURA *glances at him with a faint, apologetic smile. Her voice catching a little.)* Mother's afraid I'm going to be an old maid.

THE SCENE DIMS OUT WITH "GLASS MENAGERIE"

MUSIC

(END)

Death of a Salesman
by *Arthur Miller*

from
Act I

Characters

Willy Loman, a salesman, past 60 years
Charley, his friend and neighbor, in his 60s
Ben, Willy's dead brother returning to inhabit his fantasies, in his 60s
Biff, Willy's oldest son, age 34 years
Hap, Willy's other son, 32 years
Linda, Willy's wife, in her 50s

Scene

The kitchen of the Loman home in Brooklyn.

Situation

An exhausted Willy has returned from his sales job on the road in New England. Confused over the loss of love from his oldest son, his economic problems, and the decline of his effectiveness, Willy's mind wanders in and out of the past and the present. His neighbor Charley joins him for a late-night game of cards to sooth and quiet him.

WILLY   I'm awfully tired, Ben.

(BEN's *music is heard.* BEN *looks around at everything.*)

CHARLEY   Good, keep playing; you'll sleep better. Did you call me Ben?

(BEN *looks at his watch.*)

WILLY   That's funny. For a second there you reminded me of my brother Ben.
BEN   I only have a few minutes. (*He strolls, inspecting the place.* WILLY *and* CHARLEY *continue playing.*)
CHARLEY   You never heard from him again, heh? Since that time?
WILLY   Didn't Linda tell you? Couple of weeks ago we got a letter from his wife in Africa. He died.
CHARLEY   That so.
BEN (*chuckling*)   So this is Brooklyn, eh?
CHARLEY   Maybe you're in for some of his money.
WILLY   Naa, he had seven sons. There's just one opportunity I had with that man . . .
BEN   I must make a train, William. There are several properties I'm looking at in Alaska.
WILLY   Sure, sure! If I'd gone with him to Alaska that time, everything would've been totally different.
CHARLEY   Go on, you'd froze to death up there.
WILLY   What're you talking about?
BEN   Opportunity is tremendous in Alaska, William. Surprised you're not up there.
WILLY   Sure, tremendous.
CHARLEY   Heh?

WILLY   There was the only man I ever met who knew the answers.

CHARLEY   Who?

BEN   How are you all?

WILLY *(taking a pot, smiling)*   Fine, fine.

CHARLEY   Pretty sharp tonight.

BEN   Is Mother living with you?

WILLY   No, she died a long time ago.

CHARLEY   Who?

BEN   That's too bad. Fine specimen of a lady, Mother.

WILLY *(to CHARLEY)*   Heh?

BEN   I'd hoped to see the old girl.

CHARLEY   Who died?

BEN   Heard anything from Father, have you?

WILLY *(unnerved)*   What do you mean, who died?

CHARLEY *(taking a pot)*   What're you talkin' about?

BEN *(looking at his watch)*   William, it's half-past eight!

WILLY *(as though to dispel his confusion he angrily stops CHARLEY's hand)*   That's my build!

CHARLEY   I put the ace—

WILLY   If you don't know how to play the game I'm not gonna throw my money away on you!

CHARLEY *(rising)*   It was my ace, for God's sake!

WILLY   I'm through, I'm through!

BEN   When did Mother die?

WILLY   Long ago. Since the beginning you never knew how to play cards.

CHARLEY *(picks up the cards and goes to the door)*   All right! Next time I'll bring a deck with five aces.

WILLY   I don't play that kind of game!

CHARLEY *(turning on him)*   You ought to be ashamed of yourself!

WILLY   Yeah?

CHARLEY   Yeah! *(He goes out.)*

WILLY *(slamming the door after him)*   Ignoramus!

BEN *(as WILLY comes toward him through the wall-line of the kitchen)*   So you're William.

WILLY *(shaking BEN's hand)*   Ben! I've been waiting for you so long! What's the answer? How did you do it?

BEN   Oh, there's a story in that.

(LINDA enters the forestage, as of old, carrying the wash basket.)

LINDA   Is this Ben?

BEN *(gallantly)*   How do you do, my dear.

LINDA   Where've you been all these years? Willy's always wondered why you—

WILLY *(pulling BEN away from her impatiently)*   Where is Dad? Didn't you follow him? How did you get started?

BEN   Well, I don't know how much you remember.

WILLY   Well, I was just a baby, of course, only three or four years old—

BEN   Three years and eleven months.

WILLY   What a memory, Ben!

BEN   I have many enterprises, William, and I have never kept books.

WILLY   I remember I was sitting under the wagon in—was it Nebraska?

BEN   It was South Dakota, and I gave you a bunch of wild flowers.

WILLY   I remember you walking away down some open road.

BEN *(laughing)*   I was going to find Father in Alaska.

WILLY   Where is he?

BEN   At that age I had a very faulty view of geography, William. I discovered after a few days that I was heading due south, so instead of Alaska, I ended up in Africa.

LINDA   Africa!

WILLY   The Gold Coast!

BEN   Principally diamond mines.

LINDA   Diamond mines!

BEN   Yes, my dear. But I've only a few minutes—

WILLY   No! Boys! Boys! *(Young* BIFF *and* HAPPY *appear.)* Listen to this. This is your Uncle Ben, a great man! Tell my boys, Ben!

BEN   Why, boys, when I was seventeen I walked into the jungle, and when I was twenty-one I walked out. *(He laughs.)* And by God I was rich.

WILLY *(to the boys)*   You see what I been talking about? The greatest things can happen!

BEN *(glancing at his watch)*   I have an appointment in Ketchikan Tuesday week.

WILLY   No, Ben! Please tell about Dad. I want my boys to hear. I want them to know the kind of stock they spring from. All I remember is a man with a big beard, and I was in Mamma's lap, sitting around a fire, and some kind of high music.

BEN   His flute. He played the flute.

WILLY   Sure, the flute, that's right!

(New music is heard, a high, rollicking tune.)

BEN   Father was a very great and a very wild-hearted man. We would start in Boston, and he'd toss the whole family into the wagon, and then he'd drive the team right across the country; through Ohio, and Indiana, Michigan, Illinois, and all the Western states. And we'd stop in the towns and sell the flutes that he'd made on the way. Great inventor, Father. With one gadget he made more in a week than a man like you could make in a lifetime.

WILLY   That's just the way I'm bringing them up, Ben—rugged, well liked, all-around.

BEN   Yeah? *(to* BIFF*)* Hit that, boy—hard as you can. *(He pounds his stomach.)*

BIFF   Oh, no, sir!

BEN *(taking boxing stance)*   Come on, get to me! *(He laughs.)*

WILLY   Go to it, Biff! Go ahead, show him!

BIFF   Okay! *(He cocks his fists and starts in.)*

LINDA *(to* WILLY*)*   Why must he fight, dear?

BEN *(sparring with* BIFF*)*   Good boy! Good boy!

WILLY   How's that, Ben, heh?

HAPPY   Give him the left, Biff!

LINDA   Why are you fighting?

BEN   Good boy! *(Suddenly comes in, trips* BIFF*, and stands over him, the point of his umbrella poised over* BIFF'S *eye.)*

LINDA   Look out, Biff!

BIFF Gee!

BEN *(patting* BIFF's *knee)* Never fight fair with a stranger, boy. You'll never get out of the jungle that way.

(*END*)

The Homecoming

by *Harold Pinter*

from
Act II

Characters

Ruth, wife of Teddy, in her early 30s
Teddy, a professor in an American college, middle 30s
Max, father of Teddy and Lenny, 70
Lenny, a pimp and hustler, early 30s

Scene

The old home of Max, in North London; a large living room.

Situation

Teddy is ending the uncomfortable homecoming with his male family to return to
America to teach. However, his father and brothers have asked Teddy's wife,
Ruth, to remain with them as a mother-prostitute figure. Ruth encounters Max
and Lenny who make the proposition.

(RUTH *comes down the stairs, dressed. She comes into the room. She smiles at the
gathering, and sits. Silence.*)

TEDDY   Ruth . . . the family have invited you to stay, for a little while longer. As
  a . . . as a kind of guest. If you like the idea I don't mind. We can manage
  very easily at home . . . until you come back.
RUTH   How very nice of them.

(*pause*)

MAX   It's an offer from our heart.
RUTH   It's very sweet of you.
MAX   Listen . . . it would be our pleasure.

(*pause*)

RUTH   I think I'd be too much trouble.
MAX   Trouble? What are you talking about? What trouble? Listen, I'll tell you
  something. Since poor Jessie died, eh, Sam? we haven't had a woman in the
  house. Not one. Inside this house. And I'll tell you why. Because their mother's
  image was so dear any other woman would have . . . tarnished it. But you . . .
  Ruth . . . you're not only lovely and beautiful, but you're kin. You're kith.
  You belong here.

(*pause*)

RUTH   I'm very touched.
MAX   Of course you're touched. I'm touched.

(*pause*)

TEDDY   But Ruth, I should tell you . . . that you'll have to pull your weight a little,
  if you stay. Financially. My father isn't very well off.
RUTH (*to* MAX)   Oh, I'm sorry.

MAX No, you'd just have to bring in a little, that's all. A few pennies. Nothing much. It's just that we're waiting for Joey to hit the top as a boxer. When Joey hits the top . . . well . . .

(*pause*)

TEDDY Or you can come home with me.
LENNY We'd get you a flat.

(*pause*)

RUTH A flat?
LENNY Yes.
RUTH Where?
LENNY In town.

(*pause*)

But you'd live here, with us.
MAX Of course you would. This would be your home. In the bosom of the family.
LENNY You'd just pop up to the flat a couple of hours a night, that's all.
MAX Just a couple of hours, that's all. That's all.
LENNY And you make enough money to keep you going here.

(*END*)

The Deputy

by *Rolf Hochhuth*

Translated by *Richard and Clara Winston*

from
Act IV

Characters

Father Riccardo, a priest
Cardinal
Pope Pius XII
Fontana, Riccardo's father

Scene

A throne room in the Papal Palace, the Vatican, Rome.

Situation

Father Riccardo, a young and conscious-stricken priest, can no longer tolerate the silence from the Pope concerning the European slaughter of the Jews. He confronts the Pope to appeal for a public, specific statement against the genocide.

RICCARDO   Holy Father . . .

(*He bows to the* CARDINAL, *who coldly refers him to the* POPE.)

POPE   We are delighted with you, Riccardo, and contemplate your zeal with affection. He who defends the persecuted, always speaks as We would wish. But—We have just heard with dismay that you or Bishop Hudal in Our name has protested the arrest of the Jews. Is that so? Eminence—please send for the Father General.

(CARDINAL, *at the door, gives a command to the* SWISS GUARD.)

RICCARDO (*still not understanding, very politely*)   I? No, Your Holiness, I heard from my liaison man in the SS that Your Holiness through Bishop Hudal has threatened to protest.

POPE (*angered*)   What have you arrogated to yourself—to conspire with the SS?

CARDINAL (*malignantly*)   The Holy Father, you know, has just heard the first word of his alleged statement.

POPE   I am speaking to him, Eminence!

RICCARDO (*crushed, turns to his father, but does not lower his voice*)   So—after all—nothing whatsoever has been done! (*He still cannot believe it.*) But Your Holiness did threaten a protest. I do not understand . . . (*However, he has understood; he says passionately, almost crying out.*) Your Holiness, the Jews are being shipped out, murdered.

CARDINAL   Be still!

POPE (*smiling*)   Why, no, Your Eminence . . . God bless you, Riccardo. Speak, your heart is good. Only you must not negotiate with the SS. The Father General will tell us what has happened. Hold yourself back! At your age modesty alone honors one.

RICCARDO   I am not concerned about my honor, Your Holiness. I am concerned for the honor of the Holy See, for that is dear to me . . .

FONTANA   Riccardo!

(*The* POPE *remains silent; the* CARDINAL *answers swiftly for him.*)

CARDINAL   Aha, he is concerned for the honor of the Curia! And have you never heard that we have set up whole bureaus, offices and committees, solely in order to help, to rescue—why, you know, it seems to me that we have several times discussed that very matter, haven't we?

RICCARDO *(more and more losing his self-control)*   Such assistance reaches only some Jews in Italy, Your Eminence. That too has been discussed often enough. *(He now turns to the* POPE.)But the terror rages in the other countries! In Poland alone one million eight hundred thousand Jews have already been slaughtered! Since that figure, Your Holiness, was confirmed last July, and officially communicated by the Polish ambassador in Washington to the Papal Legate there—God cannot wish Your Holiness to ignore it!

CARDINAL *(indignantly)*   Leave at once! What language in the Holy Father's presence! Count, say something to your son . . .

(During RICCARDO's *last words the* POPE *had risen, but he sits down again. A moment passes before he is able to speak, with utmost effort.)*

POPE   "Ignore!" We do not intend to account for Our actions to Riccardo Fontana—does his father make no comment? Nevertheless, We would be pleased if We might also be permitted to speak a word on the matter. *(with mounting bitterness, attempting to change the subject)* Do you know, for example, my young man, that weeks ago we were already prepared to help the Jews of Rome, who were threatened with arrest, out of their predicament with gold, considerable gold. Hitler's bandits offered the Jews freedom for a ransom. They attempted to extort from Us a sum that was no longer realistic. *Nevertheless* we would have paid it!

RICCARDO *(has turned, aghast, to his father; now speaks softly to the* POPE)   Then Your Holiness has already known—for weeks—what the SS here intended to do to the Jews?

POPE *(agitated, evasively)*   What are you saying! Father General can bear witness to all that has already been accomplished. The monasteries stand open . . .

(END)

No Place to Be Somebody
by Charles Gordone

from
scene i

Characters

Gabe, young black narrator-author of the "play"
Johnny, young black owner of the bar
Shanty, young Caucasian musician-drummer-worker
Dee, a young Caucasian woman
Evie, a young black woman

Scene

Johnny's Bar, New York City.

Situation

Gabe introduces life in a run-down New York bar where the pain and struggle
of black life in white America unfolds.

GABE   Excuse me. Forgot you were out there. My name is Gabe. Gabe Gabriel,
to be exact. I'm a writer. Didn't mean to lose my temper. Something I've been
working on all my life. Not losing my temper. (*Takes out marihuana
cigarette. Lights it. Inhales it. Holds smoke in.*) Right now I'm working on a
play. They say if you wanna be a writer you gotta go out an' live. I don't
believe that no more. Take my play for instance. Might not believe it but I'm
gonna make it all up in my head as I go along. Before I prove it to you, wanna
warn you not to be thinkin' I'm tellin' you a bunch'a barefaced lies. An' no
matter how far out I git, don't want you goin' out'a here with the idea what
you see happenin' is all a figment of my grassy imagination. 'Cause it ain't!
(*He picks up Bible from table. Raises it above his head. Without looking turns
pages.*) "And I heard a Voice between the banks of the U'Lai. And it called,
Gabriel! Gabriel! Make this man understand the vision! So He came near
where I stood! And when He came, I was frightened and fell upon my face!"

(*He closes Bible. As he exits, lights dim out, then come up on* SHANTY, *at jukebox.
Jazz is playing.* SHANTY *takes out his drumsticks. Begins to rap on bar.* JOHNNY
enters. Hangs up raincoat and umbrella.)

JOHNNY   Cool it, Shanty.
SHANTY   Man, I'm practicing.
JOHNNY   Damned if that bar's anyplace for it. Git on that floor there.
SHANTY (*Puts drumsticks away. Takes broom.*)   Ever tell you 'bout the time I
went to this jam session? Max Roach was there. Lemme sit in for him.
JOHNNY   Said you played jus' like a spade.
SHANTY   What's wrong with that? Ol' Red Taylor said wasn't nobody could hold
a beat an' steady cook it like me. Said I had "the thing"! Member one time we
played "Saints." For three hours, we played it.
JOHNNY   Had to git a bucket'a col' water an' throw it on you to git you to quit,
huh?
SHANTY   One these days I'm gonna have me a boss set'a skins for my comeback.
Me an' Cora was diggin' a set up on "Four-Six Street." Sump'm else ag'in.
Bass drum, dis'pearin' spurs, snares, tom-toms. . . .

JOHNNY   Gon' steal 'em?

SHANTY   I been savin' up. Gonna git me them drums. Know what I'm gonna do then? I'm gonna quit you flat. Go for that. Sheee! I ain't no lifetime apron. That's for damned sure.

JOHNNY   Yeah, well meantime how 'bout finishin' up on that floor? Time to open the store. (DEE *and* EVIE *enter. Hang coats up.*) You broads let them two ripe apples git away from you, huh?

DEE   Don't look at me.

EVIE   Aw, later for you an' your rich Texas trade.

DEE   Just gettin' too damned sensitive.

EVIE   Sensitive my black behin'! Excuse me, I mean black ass. (*Goes to jukebox. Punches up number.*)

DEE   Last night we bring those two johns up to her pad. An' like, Jack? One with the cowboy hat? Stoned? Like out of his skull. And like out of nowhere he starts cryin'.

EVIE   All weekend it was "Nigger this an' Nigger that."

DEE   Never bothered you before. I didn't like it when he started sayin' things like "The black sons a'bitches are gettin' to be untouchables! Takin' over the country!"

EVIE   Bet he'll think twice before he says sump'm like that ag'in.

DEE   That lamp I gave her? One the senator brought me back from Russia? Evie goes an' breaks it over his head.

JOHNNY   What the hell'd you do that for?

EVIE   Sure hated to lose that lamp.

JOHNNY   Wouldn't care if they b'longed to the Ku Klux Klan long's they gimme the bread. (*He goes into* DEE's *purse.*)

SHANTY   Sure had plenty of it too! When they was in here, they kept buyin' me drinks. Thought I was the boss.

JOHNNY   Crackers cain't 'magine Niggers runnin' nothin' but elevators an' toilets.

DEE   Leave me somethin', please.

EVIE   Ain't gon' do nothin' with it nohow.

JOHNNY   (*Finds pair of baby shoes in* DEE's *purse*)   Thought I tole you to git rid'a these?

DEE   I forgot.

JOHNNY   Save you the trouble. (*He starts to throw them away.*)

DEE   Don't you do that, you black bastard. So help me, Johnny.

EVIE   Aw, let 'er have them things, Nigger! Wha's the big deal?

JOHNNY   'Tend to your own business, bitch. Ain't a minute off your ass for messin' it up las' night.

EVIE   Excuse me. Didn't know you was starvin' to death.

JOHNNY   (*Goes for* EVIE *but quickly checks himself when she reaches for her purse. He turns back to* DEE.)   Look'a here, girl. I ain't gon' have no harness bulls knockin' down yo' door.

DEE   All of a sudden you worried about me.

JOHNNY   Jus' git rid'a that crap. Worrin' over sump'm pass, over an' done with.

(*END*)

Interview

From America Hurrah

by Jean-Claude van Itallie

*from
beginning of play*

First Interviewer
First Applicant
Second Applicant
Third Applicant
Fourth Applicant (a Lady's Maid)

Characters

A basically empty stage with a few blocks to sit on; two subway stairs at the back. *Scene*

A group of job applicants come before an interviewer for questioning in this improvisationally created script. *Situation*

FIRST INTERVIEWER *(standing)*   How do you do?
FIRST APPLICANT *(sitting)*   Thank you, I said, not knowing where to sit.

(The characters will often include the audience in what they say, as if they were being interviewed by the audience.)

FIRST INTERVIEWER *(pointedly)*   Won't you sit down?
FIRST APPLICANT *(standing again quickly, afraid to displease)*   I'm sorry.
FIRST INTERVIEWER *(busy with imaginary papers, pointing to a particular seat)*
    There. Name, please?
FIRST APPLICANT   Jack Smith.
FIRST INTERVIEWER   Jack what Smith?
FIRST APPLICANT   Beg pardon?
FIRST INTERVIEWER   Fill in the blank space, please. Jack blank space Smith.
FIRST APPLICANT   I don't have any.
FIRST INTERVIEWER   I asked you to sit down. *(pointing)* There.
FIRST APPLICANT *(sitting)*   I'm sorry.
FIRST INTERVIEWER   Name, please?
FIRST APPLICANT   Jack Smith.
FIRST INTERVIEWER   You haven't told me your MIDDLE name.
FIRST APPLICANT   I haven't got one.
FIRST INTERVIEWER *(suspicious but writing it down)*   No middle name.

(SECOND APPLICANT, *a woman, a Floorwasher, enters.*)

FIRST INTERVEWER   How do you do?
SECOND APPLICANT *(sitting)*   Thank you, I said, not knowing what.
FIRST INTERVIEWER   Won't you sit down?
SECOND APPLICANT *(standing)*   I'm sorry.
FIRST APPLICANT   I am sitting.

FIRST INTERVIEWER *(pointing)*   There. Name, please?

SECOND APPLICANT *(sitting)*   Jane Smith.

FIRST APPLICANT   Jack Smith.

FIRST INTERVIEWER   What blank space Smith?

SECOND APPLICANT   Ellen.

FIRST APPLICANT   Haven't got one.

FIRST INTERVIEWER   What job are you applying for?

FIRST APPLICANT   Housepainter.

SECOND APPLICANT   Floorwasher.

FIRST INTERVIEWER   We haven't many vacancies in that. What experience have you had?

FIRST APPLICANT   A lot.

SECOND APPLICANT   Who needs experience for floorwashing?

FIRST INTERVIEWER   You will help me by making your answers clear.

FIRST APPLICANT   Eight years.

SECOND APPLICANT   Twenty years.

(THIRD APPLICANT, a Banker, enters.)

FIRST INTERVIEWER   How do you do?

SECOND APPLICANT   I'm good at it.

FIRST APPLICANT   Very well.

THIRD APPLICANT *(sitting)*   Thank you, I said, as casually as I could.

FIRST INTERVIEWER   Won't you sit down?

THIRD APPLICANT *(standing again)*   I'm sorry.

SECOND APPLICANT   I am sitting.

FIRST APPLICANT *(standing again)*   I'm sorry.

FIRST INTERVIEWER *(pointing to a particular seat)*   There. Name, please?

FIRST APPLICANT   Jack Smith.

SECOND APPLICANT   Jane Smith.

THIRD APPLICANT   Richard Smith.

FIRST INTERVIEWER   What EXACTLY Smith, please?

THIRD APPLICANT   Richard F.

SECOND APPLICANT   Jane Ellen.

FIRST APPLICANT   Jack None.

FIRST INTERVIEWER   What are you applying for?

FIRST APPLICANT   Housepainter.

SECOND APPLICANT   I need money.

THIRD APPLICANT   Bank president.

FIRST INTERVIEWER   How many years have you been in your present job?

THIRD APPLICANT   Three.

SECOND APPLICANT   Twenty.

FIRST APPLICANT   Eight.

(FOURTH APPLICANT, a Lady's Maid, enters.)

FIRST INTERVIEWER   How do you do?

FOURTH APPLICANT   I said thank you, not knowing where to sit.

THIRD APPLICANT   I'm fine.

SECOND APPLICANT   Do I have to tell you?

FIRST APPLICANT   Very well.

FIRST INTERVIEWER   Won't you sit down?

FOURTH APPLICANT   I'm sorry.
THIRD APPLICANT (*sitting again*)   Thank you.
SECOND APPLICANT (*standing again*)   I'm sorry.
FIRST APPLICANT (*sitting*)   Thanks.
FIRST INTERVIEWER (*pointing to a particular seat*)   There. Name, please?

(FOURTH APPLICANT *sits.*)

ALL APPLICANTS   Smith.
FIRST INTERVIEWER   What Smith?
FOURTH APPLICANT   Mary Victoria.
THIRD APPLICANT   Richard F.
SECOND APPLICANT   Jane Ellen
FIRST APPLICANT   Jack None.
FIRST INTERVIEWER   How many years' experience have you had?
FOURTH APPLICANT   Eight years.
SECOND APPLICANT   Twenty years.
FIRST APPLICANT   Eight years.
THIRD APPLICANT   Three years four months and nine days not counting
   vacations and sick leave and the time both my daughters and my wife had the
   whooping cough.
FIRST INTERVIEWER   Just answer the questions, please.
FOURTH APPLICANT   Yes, sir.
THIRD APPLICANT   Sure.
SECOND APPLICANT   I'm sorry.
FIRST APPLICANT   That's what I'm doing.

(SECOND INTERVIEWER, *a young man, enters and goes to inspect* APPLICANTS. *With the entrance of each* INTERVIEWER, *the speed of the action accelerates.*)

SECOND INTERVIEWER   How do you do?
FIRST APPLICANT (*standing*)   I'm sorry.
SECOND APPLICANT (*sitting*)   Thank you.
THIRD APPLICANT (*standing*)   I'm sorry.
FOURTH APPLICANT (*sitting*)   Thank you.

(*END*)

Last of the Red Hot Lovers
by *Neil Simon*

*from
beginning of Act II*

Characters   Barney, runs a fish and seafood restaurant, age 47 years
Bobbi, a young, attractive woman, about 27 years

Scene   The apartment of Barney's mother, New York City, in the East Thirties; late afternoon, August.

Situation   Suffering from middle-age insecurity, Barney has decided to have an extramarital affair. Having failed in his first attempt, he now encounters a young woman he had met the day before. A pleasant but nervous man, Barney hopes to seduce the girl who *appears* to be innocent and uncomplicated.

BARNEY   Well, hello.

BOBBI   Oh, thank God, air conditioning. Do you know it's a hundred and forty degrees outside? I swear. I mean it gets hot in California but nothing like this. Hi. Bobbi Michele?

BARNEY   Yes, yes. Come in, I'll close the door. It's cooler. (*She comes in; he closes the door*)

BOBBI   I was wandering up and down the hall. All these apartments look alike. (*looks quickly*) Oh, this is nice. I like this. I'm not disturbing you now, am I? I mean you're not busy or anything?

BARNEY   No, no. I was expecting you. Remember I said—

BOBBI   I wasn't sure I'd be here on time. I just got through with my audition.

BARNEY   No, you're fine. Remember I said three o'clock—

BOBBI   It's got to be a hundred and ten, right? (*crosses to the air conditioner*) I mean forget about breathing, it's over. (*stands with her back to the air conditioner*) You sure I'm not disturbing you? I could come back later.

BARNEY   No, I'm positive. I'm clear till five. (*He smells his fingers.*) Can I get you a cool drink?

BOBBI   I love this neighborhood. I knew this street looked familiar. I once had a girl friend who lived on this block. Forty-seventh between First and York.

BARNEY   This is Thirty-seventh.

BOBBI   Thirty-seventh. Of course. Then she couldn't have lived on this block. Ohh, that's better. The Shubert Theatre was a sauna bath. Oh, listen, my accompanist *did* show up, which I have you to thank for because you were so sweet in the park yesterday and I want you to know I have not forgotten it, but here I am talking and talking and I really haven't said hello yet. Hello.

BARNEY   Hello.

BOBBI   Hello. Here I am.

BARNEY   So I see.

BOBBI   Oh, God, I talk a lot when I get nervous. Have you noticed that? I'll try
     and stop it if I can. You'll have to forgive me.
BARNEY   Are you nervous?
BOBBI   Well, I'm not nervous now. I was nervous before. I just had a terrible
     experience with a cab driver. Well, I don't want to go into it. Ohh, God, I just
     wilt in the heat. If I pass out on the floor, I'm just going to have to trust you.
BARNEY   *(smiles)*   You don't have to worry.
BOBBI   Well, you're not a cab driver. You wouldn't try something like that.
BARNEY   Like what?
BOBBI   He wanted to make it with me under the Manhattan Bridge during his
     lunch hour. Listen, can we forget about it, it's over now. I must look awful.
BARNEY   Not at all. You look lovely.
BOBBI   Oh, poof, I don't.
BARNEY   You do. You do.
BOBBI   Give me three minutes, I'll dazzle you. Did you get shorter?
BARNEY   Shorter? Since yesterday?
BOBBI   Why do you look shorter?
BARNEY   I can't imagine why I should look shorter. *(He sits next to her.)*
BOBBI   Oh, flats.
BARNEY   Flats?
BOBBI   I was wearing flats yesterday. I put on heels for the audition today. I got
     taller. Actually, you're not really short. Well, you know that.
BARNEY   Yes, well, sometimes when a person has large bones—
BOBBI   You know, I couldn't make out your handwriting. I thought I had the
     wrong address. 432 East Thirty-seventh?
BARNEY   No, that's the right address.
BOBBI   Well, I should hope so. Otherwise where am I and who are you? *(She
     laughs; he tries to.)* Oh, that's silly. If I'm goofy today, it's the heat.
BARNEY   You're not goofy at all.
BOBBI   I am. I'm goofy, let's face it.
BARNEY   I think you're charming.
BOBBI   Oh, I know I'm charming but I'm also goofy which I think is part of my
     charm. That's a terrible thing to say, isn't it?
BARNEY   Not at all. Sometimes frankness can be—
BOBBI   It's terrible, I can't help it. I'm so open about things. That's why I'm
     always getting myself into trouble, you know what I mean?
BARNEY   What kind of trouble do you get—
BOBBI   My God, I didn't even notice it. You shaved your moustache.
BARNEY   What moustache?
BOBBI   Didn't you have a moustache yesterday?
BARNEY   Me? No.
BOBBI   You *never* had a moustache?
BARNEY   Never. I don't look good in a moustache. It doesn't grow in thick on the
     left side.
BOBBI   Who am I thinking of? Who did I meet yesterday with a moustache?
BARNEY   That I couldn't tell you.
BOBBI   Well, I can't think straight. I'm still a nervous wreck over that cab incident.
     I've been back in New York three days and look what happens. I just want to
     forget about it.

BARNEY   Certainly. How about a drink? I have J&B Scotch, Wolfschmidt
          vodka . . .

BOBBI   I wrote the cabbie's name down. Max Schoenstein. I was going to report
         him to the police but he started to cry. Tears pouring down his face, I thought
         his cigar would go out. Then he pleaded with me he's married twenty-seven
         years with one son in Vietnam and another son in medical school and that he
         didn't mean any harm and I felt sorry for him and I said all right, I wouldn't
         report him, so he thanked me and asked me to reconsider going under the
         Manhattan Bridge. *(brushes her hair and poses)* How do I look? Better?

BARNEY   Marvelous. Gee, that's terrible.

BOBBI   Oh, it happens to me all the time. Coming in on the plane from California.
         The man sitting next to me kept feeling me up all during the movie. Well, I
         don't want to go into that. *(looks around)* This is the kind of place I'm looking
         for. Does it have a terrace?

BARNEY   No, no terrace. He was *feeling* you?

BOBBI   Well, he said he was looking for the dial to turn up the volume but he
         didn't even have the headset plugged in his ears . . . Nice view.

BARNEY   Why didn't you say something to him?

BOBBI   Well, he was Chinese, I didn't want to seem bigoted. Then he has the
         nerve to call me, in the middle of the night. Some strange Chinaman.

BARNEY   How'd he get your number?

BOBBI   I don't know. I must have given it to him or something. What's the
         difference? Look, it's over, let's forget it. Am I talking too much? I haven't
         given you a chance to say anything.

BARNEY   I'm fascinated. Those are incredible stories.

BOBBI   How do you mean incredible? You don't believe them?

BARNEY   I do. I do believe them.

BOBBI   Because they're true.

BARNEY   That's the fascinating part.

BOBBI   Maybe to you. They were terrifying to me.

BARNEY   To me too.

BOBBI   Could I have a drink?

BARNEY   What a good idea. J&B? Vodka?

BOBBI   I don't provoke these things. They just happen.

BARNEY   I'm not surprised. You're such a pretty girl.

BOBBI   I don't know why they single me out. I'm always getting these obscene
         telephone calls.

BARNEY   Well, there's an awful lot of that going on.

BOBBI   I get them wherever I go. Once I wasn't home, he left an obscene message.

BARNEY   My goodness.

BOBBI *(looking at the photos on the table)*   And the language. I never heard such
         filth. I once got a call where this psycho actually described vile and indecent
         acts for over fifteen minutes.

BARNEY   FIFTEEN MINUTES!

BOBBI   Listen, if you don't shut me up I'll never stop talking. What time is it?

BARNEY   A quarter after three.

BOBBI   Oh, God, I've got to make a call. May I? I don't have one on me.

BARNEY   Yes, certainly.

BOBBI   Is this where you write those sea stories you were telling me about?

BARNEY   Yes, I work here during the day. Actually it's my mother's apartment.

BOBBI   I knew this writer in California. A registered weirdo. He used to write these underground movies you see on Eighth Avenue. You know, *Sex Family Robinson, Tom Swift and His Incredible Thing* . . . I thought I was in love with him until I found out he was deranged. I mean the things he wanted me to do.

BARNEY   Like what?

BOBBI   Oh, God, I couldn't repeat them.

BARNEY   That's all right. You can repeat them.

BOBBI   *(dials the phone and listens)*   She hears the phone. She's just a lazy bitch.

BARNEY   But like what? What kind of things did he want you to do?

BOBBI   I couldn't tell you. I told my analyst, he went into cardiac arrest . . . Can you believe this? I could wait here twenty minutes.

BARNEY   You mean things together or alone? What kind of things?

BOBBI   If I tell you this man had his teeth sharpened, can you fill in the rest?

(She inspects the photos on the table)

BARNEY   His teeth? My God!

BOBBI   The man was psychotically inclined. *(smiles at a photo)* This is adorable. Your mother?

BARNEY *(shakes his head)*   No, it's me. But did you ever do any of them? These things he wanted?

BOBBI   Me? No! Never! Of course not . . . Some. I had to do some otherwise I was afraid he would kill me. Is this you and your father?

BARNEY   Yes . . . He actually forced you to do these things?

BOBBI   You don't play it cool with a man who had his teeth sharpened.

(END)

That Championship Season

by *Jason Miller*

from
Act I

Characters   Coach, retired high school basketball coach
George, the local Mayor
James, brother of Tom, in local politics and a junior high school principal
Phil, a local businessman
Tom, an alcoholic
All the men are in their forties except the coach, who is past sixty.

Scene   The living room of the coach, somewhere in the Lackawanna Valley, Pennsylvania.

Situation   Members of a former state championship basketball team meet for a reunion in the home of their old coach. Generally disappointed and frustrated men, their charismatic coach enters to meet them and begin the reunion.

COACH   All right. Line it up. Shape it. Twenty laps around the room. Too much fat in the ass around here. I want my boys lean and mean. *(great laughter)* A voice from the past boys, the old gunner can still bray with the best. *(pouring whiskey)* Hit those boards hard, Romano . . . And you, Sikowski, don't just stand there with your finger up you know where, move! . . . And you, Daley, have a drink. . . . *(laughs)* And you big Daley [JAMES], hustle some of this whiskey into you. Imported. Jamison. Boil your brains, this stuff!

GEORGE   You haven't changed in twenty years.

COACH   I haven't changed in sixty years. I can take the four of you around the court till you drop, run you into the ground. *(proudly)* Even one eighty-five. Weighed that in 1940. *(gets down and does ten quick push-ups)* And that's after having my belly cut open, twenty stitches. *(opens shirt)* Look at that sonofabitch. Belly looks like a baseball.

JAMES   What's the secret?

COACH   "Walk softly and carry a big stick." *(Pause. Great joy, shy almost)* Oh, Christ, boys, Christ, it's so good . . . the joy in my heart to feel you around me again, *(he pats, feels, whacks them all)* together again, can't find words to say it. . . . Magnificent! My boys standing around me again! A toast to the 1952 Pennsylvania State High School Basketball Champions! *(they drink)* You were a legend in your time, boys, a legend. Never forget that, never.

GEORGE   We owe it all to you, Coach.

(MEN *ad lib agreement.*)

COACH   I used to tell people you boys were like a fine watch. My very expensive and fine watch that kept perfect time. You froze the ball against Tech for three minutes. Fantastic. Stay in shape. Lean and mean. You're in your thirties and that's the heart-attack season, boys. Most important muscle in your body, boys . . . the heart . . . keep it in shape, work it out!

GEORGE   Bought one of those exercise bikes. Keeps the stomach flat.

PHIL   But your ass is still down around your knees.

GEORGE   That's it, start on me, the old scapegoat.

TOM   You love it.

GEORGE   Yeah.

COACH   Drink up, boys, put it away, night's young. Take off your jackets, relax.

GEORGE   Chicken is in the stove.

COACH   You're working on your third chin yourself, Phil.

PHIL   I'm an executive.

COACH   James, you're starting to sag a little too, you look tired.

JAMES   I haven't been sleeping well, Coach.

COACH   Why?

JAMES   My teeth.

COACH   What's the matter?

JAMES   They're gone.

COACH   Gone.

JAMES *(embarrassed)*   They took them out last month.

COACH   You got plates?

JAMES   Yeah.

COACH   Let's see. Open your mouth. Uh-uh. Good job. They look almost real.

PHIL *(laughs)*   Never had enough Vitamin C in your diet!

JAMES *(half-smile)*   Try feeding five kids.

COACH   You didn't feed them your teeth, did you? You need iron in your blood. . . . *(opens mouth)* I got twenty-seven originals.

(MEN *laugh*)

JAMES   Actually they've recently completed studies proving that nerves can cause severe damage to teeth.

COACH   Really! Maybe you should have gotten your nerves out! *(laugh)* Have another shot and relax, James.

COACH   Better put that chicken on low, George. Tom, . . . *(Hugs him; they touch glasses and drink.)* I'm so goddam happy, so grateful you're back with us again. Doesn't he look wonderful, boys?

TOM *(pouring)*   Nothing keeps the old gunner down, either.

COACH   You were a thing of rare . . . beauty, boys. Life is a game and I'm proud to say I played it with the best. We were one flesh twenty years ago; never forget that as long as you live! *(pause)* Ten seconds left on the clock . . . we were down by one point . . . remember . . . unbelievable!

GEORGE *(quiet intensity)*   I passed inbounds to Tom.

TOM   I brought the ball up.

PHIL   Passed to me in the corner.

COACH *(urgent)*   Six seconds left!

PHIL   I hit James coming . . .

JAMES   Across the court and I saw . . .

COACH   Three seconds left!

JAMES   Martin at the foul line . . .

GEORGE   Martin caught the ball in mid-air . . . he went up . . .

JAMES   Up...

COACH   One second...

GEORGE *(jumping up)*   Yes!

COACH   State Champions! They said we couldn't do it, boys. We beat a school three times our size. We beat them in Philadelphia. We performed the impossible, boys, never forget that, never. Jesus, remember they had an eight-foot nigger, jumped like a kangaroo. *(proudly)* There's the trophy, boys. Fast, Jesus, fast, you were a flash of legs ... gone, like lightning!

GEORGE   Martin was a pressure ballplayer.

COACH   He thrived on it ... loved it.

JAMES   He had a great eye.

COACH   Priceless.

GEORGE   The perfect ballplayer.

COACH   Not a flaw. He made it all go ... magnificent talent! *(pause. quietly)* Yeah. Not a word in twenty years. Let's say a little prayer for him, boys, a prayer that he's safe and happy and still a champion. *(They lay their hands together. Moment of silence)* We never had a losing season, boys; there's not many that can say that....

(END)

The contemporary approach to acting as described by Brecht, Artaud, Grotowski, Beck, Chaikin, and others does not ask the actor to avoid illusion on the stage. Actors must recognize that *everything* in the theatre is illusion. They should be guided, provoked, stimulated, and occasionally even yielded to in order for them to realize a personalized performance. Actors must run the risk of penetrating the inner self. By using improvisation, actors must move away from lifelessness onstage and open themselves to creative impulses and thereby respond to truth instantly. Perhaps for the first time actors must realize that they have the vital responsibility to economize when creating a character. Actors must be capable of self-detachment and personal objectivity to discover the clichés and hollowness lurking in preconceived value systems. The concern of an actor should be to live fully in mind and body, giving himself over completely to really personalizing, not merely performing, through his dexterity and expertness. Sincere, honest, dedicated art comes also from the unconscious state of the artist. Surface description makes for imitation and destroys spontaneity. Once he is in complete control of his mental, emotional, and physical faculties, an actor should be able to personalize onstage with confidence and with discipline. Having discovered the ability to unmask himself, an actor has found the means to interest an audience, lower its defenses, and provide it with awareness of the complex levels inherent in both existence and in art.

> The mask which an actor wears
> is apt to become his face.
> Plato

Epilogue

Quo Vadis?

Curtain Call and Farewell. From *Company* by George Furth and Stephen Sondheim. Directed by Robert N. Burgan. Designed by Fredrick L. Olson. University of Nevada, Las Vegas.

Appendix A

Instructions for Play Analysis

Separate your analysis into four major sections as follows. Effective play analysis must be written out. It is not merely mental activity. The acronymn PASTO, used throughout these instructions, stands for preparation, attack, struggle, turn, and outcome.

Section One

In this section list the following important facts about the author of the play and its production.

1. Brief author information.
2. Brief information on the initial production of the play if known.
3. Brief information on any *vital* or *unusual* subsequent production if known.

Section Two

This is a specific discussion encompassing your overall analysis of the *form* of the play and its structural components which you are to accomplish by completing twenty-three separate paragraphs, numbered 1 through 23, in the following sequence.

1. Identify and clarify the *Preparation* section of the play by specifying the pages and page numbers of your script used for this aspect of the PASTO.

2. Identify and clarify the *Point of Attack* in terms of the earliest incident in the play that exposes the basic conflict of the play. State the nature of the basic conflict—who is it between or what is it between, what it is, and page number of *Attack*.

3. Identify and clarify the *Major Dramatic Question*—MDQ—of the play.

4. Identify the *protagonist* of the play and give a brief justification for your identification.

5. Identify the chief *antagonist* of the play and state a brief justification for your identification.

6. Identify who or what resolves the conflict (i.e., the *Deciding Agent*) and state briefly how and where in the play the resolution occurs (give page number of the conflict resolution).

7. Identify and clarify the *Struggle* section of the play by specifying the pages and page numbers of your script used for this aspect of the PASTO. NOTE: You need to identify the *key Complications* of the play in paragraph 7 after you have clarified the pages and page numbers used for the *Struggle*. Simply list them in the order they occur: for example, p. 16, the protagonist's brother suddenly arrives from California; p. 27, the brother is discovered murdered in the library; and so forth. These complications should be numbered Complication No. 1, and so on.

8. Identify and clarify the major crisis or *Turn* of the play. Where and how does it take place? Give the page number of your script on which it occurs.

9. If a *Climax* can be distinguished from the major crisis, identify and clarify it. Where and how does it take place? Give the page number of your script on which it occurs.

10. Identify and clarify the denouement or *Outcome* section of the play by specifying the pages used for this aspect of the PASTO and by briefly clarifying what gets wrapped up in this section.

11. Identify and clarify the subject *Issues* of the play. List them as one-word subjects or as subject-and-issue questions or as both, as you prefer. List them in priority of importance (e.g., justice, revenge, and so on).

12. Identify and clarify the *key Drives* (nervosity) or character desires for all the characters in the play. List these in priority of importance for each character. Also list the characters in order of importance in the action of the play. Thus,

Hamlet's *Drives* would be listed in order of their importance first; then Claudius' Drives would be listed in order of their importance; and so on.

13. Clearly state the *major Theme* or central idea of the play in one complete sentence. Then list any important subordinate themes in order of importance.

14. In one succinct paragraph comment on the quality of the author's skill with the *Plot* in the play (for example, is it strong with Suffering and Discovery, but weak with Reversal? How well is the story organized? Etc.).

15. Repeat number 14 relative to *Character*. For example, are the personalities clear and well distinguished from one another? Are they believable? Are they of full dimension? Do they possess emotion and thought?

16. Repeat number 14 relative to *Thought*. For example, comment on the overall intellectual content of the play: Is it shallow? Is it philosophical? Does it have a theme or themes?

17. Repeat number 14 relative to *Language, Diction,* and *Discourse*. For example, does the play employ iambic pentameter verse? How good is it? Is it naturalistic American dialogue? How good is it? Is it good "heard" language?

18. Repeat number 14 relative to *Melody* and *Music*. For example, are the lines conducive to musical effect? Is there use of actual instrumentation? of singing? How good are all these effects?

19. Repeat number 14 relative to *Spectacle*. For example, are all the visual and audible effects theatrical? Are they handled well? evocative? static? What are their outstanding qualities? Do certain technical effects of spectacle tend to dominate the play? For example, is there constant use of drum sounds? Is lighting particularly vital to the play? If so, how? What do the costumes contribute? the scenery? etc.

20. Clarify the meaning of the title of the play.

21. Categorize the *overall Rhythm* of the play. For example, are the rhythmic surges of the play similar to a gathering thunderstorm? If so, explain how. Relate your brief discussion directly to major action incidents of the play that clarify your discussion of the rhythm. Categorize the overall tempo of the play (*speed*-of-movement factor).

22. Categorize the *overall Mood* of the play. For example, does the overall mood of the play express the emotion and feeling of sexual heat or frustration? What are the dominate emotions and feelings that make up the overall mood of the play? Relate your discussion of mood to a few key specifics from the actual play.

23. As a categorizing label, state precisely what the *Form* of the play is, based on the foregoing twenty-two points of analysis (e.g., Classic Greek Tragedy; farce; melodrama; Expressionist serious drama, etc.). As needed for further clarification, elaborate upon the succinct label: for example, an expressionistic farce in the French tradition, an Elizabethan tragedy in the Aristotelian sense influenced by Seneca, and the like.

Section Three

In this section you are to record the following important information on the script itself, in this manner.

1. Cut out the actual script and paste or mock it up on large sheets of paper with openings cut so that both sides of the script can be read. Standard-size acting scripts pasted on 8½-by-11-inch paper is the usual procedure.

2. Include on the script, written in the margins, both your *Literal* and *Metaphorical* analyses. Use separate Comment Sheets for lengthy comments and insert the sheets in proper order among the script pages.

3. On the script designate all *French Scenes* as they occur. Include both your *Literal* and *Metaphorical* titles for each French Scene.

4. On the script designate all major *Complications* as set down earlier in number 6, section 2.

5. On the script categorize the *Tempo* (rate of beat) for each French Scene (e.g., rapid to slow, etc.).

6. On the script identify the *Mood* of each French Scene (e.g., violence, anger, gentle love, etc.).

Note: In section 3, analysis of some items covered previously in section 2 (e.g., complications, major crisis, attack, MDQ, etc.) are usually repeated.

Section Four

Make the conclusion of your play analysis succinct. The conclusion should explicate the play's *Commanding Image* and should be stated in a clear, complete sentence which begins: The play is like . . . Base your conclusion on the *Metaphorical Analysis* noted in the script margins as directed in section 3. For example: The play is like the eye of a hurricane.

Note: Your analysis should be the result of your *own* thinking. If you include the views of critics or scholars in any way, they must be properly acknowledged or footnoted. However, play analysis is *not* research. It should be individual creative play analysis in preparation for acting or directing the play, and it should originate with you.

Seventeen specific steps in role analysis are given in chapter 10.

The Happening

One of the first adventures into new theatrical expression in the 1960s was the Happening. A Happening consisted of creating and projecting visual or aural images into a large open space (such as a field) through open-ended, task-oriented activities. The image projected had no preset meaning; performers improvised in a number of artistic mediums such as painting, sculpture, dance, and music. Each individual addressed himself to the task at hand and participated in an activity focused on a theme, a chance combination, a game, or a trip. Happenings were sometimes staged performances (e.g., dance or multimedia) and sometimes work activities (e.g., building a fence with blocks of ice). Sometimes, Happenings had ceremonial significance (e.g., Allan Kaprow's *Overtime*, 1968). The general aim of a Happening was to consume energy and talent. Happenings were literally exercises in mass consumption. The individual role diminished significantly due to the communal aspect of the task-oriented project. Often, actors were not needed at all when Happenings were strictly technological or work oriented. By the 1970s the Happening was no longer a viable theatrical form. The ultraliberalism of both the theatre and society of the 1960s was joined in a return to structure and conservatism in the 1970s.

The Happening disappeared, leaving a considerable contribution. The Happening explored possibilities for new relationships between participants and spectators, reevaluated and infused life into habitual routines and habits, and made us more aware of the process of creating art. The Happening was powerfully antiliterary, antiactor, antidirector, and antidesigner. The concept was literally divorced from all traditional types of theatre experience. It existed somewhere between the theatricalism of Artaud and the alienation of Brecht and gave little recognition to the theatre of Stanislavski. However, the Happening did open the door to concrete experimentation in communication, body movement, concentration, emotion, and audience participation. Because of the importance of Stanislavski's methodology in twentieth-century theatre, it was very difficult for modern critics and artists to ignore his influence. The Happening helped to break that influence. Surface truth was revealed to be as important as inner truth in view of the fact that it was not always possible for the spectator to experience the same feelings as the actor. However, it was possible for the actor to affect an audience, sometimes involuntarily. The test for truthfulness was not always possible in the realm of intense and authentic personal feeling. The Artaudian actor, on the other hand, could shape feeling into a communicative image by gesture, movement, and a sequence of actions.

Polish Laboratory Theatre

In 1959, Jerzy Grotowski began his unusual study of acting. Grotowski was influenced by Stanislavski (particularly his work on physical actions), Meyerhold (his work on biomechanical training), Vakhtangov (his concept of the actor's central position in a theatre company), Artaud (his Theatre of Cruelty), and Delsarte (his investigations of centrifugal reactions). In addition, Grotowski was sensitive to Oriental theatre (particularly the Peking Opera, the Kathakali, and the Noh theatre of Japan). Grotowski probed the spiritual nature of the actor by penetrating the psychic and physical faculties of man. To enter Grotowski's training program, actors must be willing to devote several years of selfless service. All training is precise, disciplined, and intensely physical. The central effort of Grotowski's work is exploration of the confrontation which takes place between the performer's mask (i.e., his role) and his self and how the two relate to the written text. Grotowski sees the performer's mask (or role) as a system of signs designed to reveal the man behind the mask. If the actor is in a spiritual state (i.e., disciplined

Appendix B

Experimental
Theatre Groups
and Activities

psyche and body), the signs will be rhythmically articulated and artistically formed through acting, dancing, and singing.

How does the actor reveal the man behind the mask? behind the role?

In the Polish Laboratory Theatre, Grotowski's actors embark on a concentrated training program of self-exploration. They work first within the context of personalization. The core of their studies include exercises in concentration and psychophysical body movement. The initial step involves unblocking the conscious and subconscious processes by evoking silence. Silence turns attention inward toward complete concentration. (Incidentally, Grotowski rejects Yoga exercises for concentration because the Yoga aspect of breath control becomes too excessive, thereby blocking expressiveness. However, Yoga exercises are helpful for relaxation and confidence to facilitate natural adaptation to space.) Once the mind and body are at rest and unified, senses can be put to creative use. Grotowski urges reliance upon free personal impulses instead of upon manipulated and calculated moves, looks and thoughts. Actors become "resigned to doing" what they do not want to do. Thoughts and associations flow evenly and freely. They are disarmed and defenseless and have no need to hide behind clothes, ideas, signs, or intellectual concepts.

After the discovery of inner freedom, Grotowski turns to externals. Again personalization is used to project impulses and associations; the character evolves and comes to the actor through his psyche. In this step, the actor finds his "secure self" by learning how to create while being controlled by others and how to create without the security of awareness. The goal is an authentic creation of role through actor (i.e., the role comes to him in the context of his own experiences). Grotowski also trains a well-developed vocal apparatus. During this process, Grotowski cautions actors to remain private by eliminating external friendliness among actors, a social activity which only reintroduces the mask behind which an actor can hide (recall Dustin Hoffman's point on actor relationships in chapter 8). Grotowski actors use no makeup or regular theatre costumes. Lighting and sound effects are not provided (except illumination of both actors and spectators). Few properties if any, are used. Grotowski prefers that actors "transform" objects through action and gesture such as treating a plain table as though it were an ornate religious confessional. The stripping away of all theatrical "luxuries" (i.e., lighting, costumes, and so on) explains the term *poor theatre*. Grotowski's productions are inexpensive to produce and to attend—are truly a poor theatre.

Grotowski's theatre environment is shaped by the confrontation between actors and their subsequent transformation of space (which implicates the audience physically). Hence, the audience shares all space with the actors. Movement is free, but not random. The cubic space is designed to provide easy and free movement through the audience. Grotowski's early experimentation with audience participation failed. His actors forced audiences into a false position by applying pressure on them to perform with the actors. His rejection of this approach led to the idea of having spectators perform the "role of spectators" naturally and freely within the context of the play's action. Grotowski designed his theatre to include flexible seating arrangements adjusted to the needs of the play (e.g., seats were partially eliminated, or spectators viewed the action from above, or seating changed during a performance, depending on the action). Thus, space, time, and events are unified by the ability of both actors and audience to negotiate with the environment.

Grotowski prefers to have his actors perform classical works (for example, Shakespeare, Sophocles, Calderón) because he believes that the classics allow actors to confront "great actions" by exchanging personal actions with those of great characters. It is precisely this kind of exchange between the actor as human being and the role as art which produces theatre. The transformation between actor and role sometimes makes textual alteration necessary. If certain actions do not conform to personal impulses or are not harmonious with the group, then text may be rearranged or sections omitted. However, Grotowski keeps such changes to a minimum. The literary work remains substantially intact.

In effect, the poor theatre of Grotowski is a way of life (see his book *Towards a Poor Theatre*). It is mostly a training program; few productions reach an audience. When they do, less than one hundred spectators are permitted to watch. Clearly, this is the antithesis of commercial theatre. The discipline of Grotowski's theatre is designed to initiate the process of revealing the actor. The actor "sacrifices" himself as a gift to the art and to the spectators. In this sense, Grotowski calls his theatre a "holy theatre" that relinquishes all but its humanity.

The Living Theatre

An exciting and noteworthy group of performers calling themselves The Living Theatre also had an important influence on the theatre of the 1960s. The impetus for The Living Theatre (organized in 1959 by Julian Beck and Judith Malina) is their commitment to political revolution as a means of destroying capitalism. The group is a nomadic community of continually travelling social-political artists. Their philosophical intent is similar to that of Artaud. Acting is living in the moment; it is a magical, vigorous creation dedicated to a lucid consciousness and to the joy and pain of creation. The theatre is the ultimate experience, a rebirth. The Living Theatre became famous for its insistence upon audience participation. During the transformation of spectator to participant, the actors give the audience a transfusion by assaulting them with sound, nudity, sexuality, mechanical and programmed gestures, incantation, and frenetic activity.

The Living Theatre is influenced by the stylized movements of the Oriental theatre. Artaud's concept of the theatrically spectacular integration of the arts is also an influence. For example, in plays such as *Mysteries, The Chord, Frankenstein,* and *The Bacchae* a mixture of Pop Art, mythology, science fiction, and the "Late Late Show" creates a strange type of total theatre experience. Plays are relatively unstructured (sometimes only a synopsis is used). All action is directed toward reinforcing political dogma and moral polemics. The plays are kinetically executed with animal energy. They frequently verge on political anarchy in their quest for communal freedom.

In 1964, The Living Theatre left the United States for Europe, exiled because they refused to pay "back" taxes to the federal government. As their art, ideology, and collective existence gained importance in Europe, their popularity increased in the United States. The Becks were instrumental in introducing Eastern religious and philosophical ideas into the theatre. The establishment of the community and communal experience was essential to the fulfillment of their spiritual essence. Yoga was used to help the actors accelerate breathing patterns in order to create different levels of energy. The discovery that breathing can control organic function including blood circulation had far-reaching effect on the emotional status of Beck's company. They learned that sound is a manifestation of certain vibratory energy and that different audience moods can be created by effecting chemical changes in the bodies of the spectators. Tangential to all of their work is the belief that every man is a universe unto himself, that once bodily truth is known universal truth is known. Physical contact between actors and between actors and spectators is central to the theatrical technique of The Living Theatre. Beck's actors use space, a scenario, themselves, and the audience to create a theatre experience in which the actor or performer is the controlling agent.

All plays produced by The Living Theatre are created collectively. In an effort to make theatre a living experience, theatrical speech is rejected because of its artificial nuances and regality. Instead, they use natural or impromptu speech projected by a total vocal effort. More important, they attempt to communicate without words through physical and sensory experiences.

In 1968, The Living Theatre returned to the United States to perform their most important work, *Paradise Now*. Since returning, their energies have dissipated somewhat due to ever-increasing emphasis on political ideology at the expense of good theatre technique. At the August 1972 American Theatre Association Convention in San Francisco, Beck stated that theatre is only a means to their political ends. The Living Theatre's contribution to the new theatre movement has been extensive.

Off-Off Broadway

During the 1960s experimental theatre was produced in coffee houses away from both the Broadway theatrical center and the original Off-Broadway theatres. This endeavor, which was called Off-Off Broadway, produced a conglomeration of plays written by new playwrights performed by actors trained in improvisation and directed by both directors and artist-leaders.

The objective of the original Off-Broadway movement was to enable new playwrights to have their plays produced with less financial risk.

The watchwords of the Off-Off Broadway café theatres were freedom, economy, and intimacy. The general attitude was that professional theatre procedures were inadequate to foster theatrical experimentation, give new playwrights ample opportunity to have their plays produced, and elevate the political consciousness of the public. The most well-known and important theatres were Cafe Cino, under the direction of the late Joe Cino; Café La Mamma, operated by Ellen Stewart (who sponsored such directors as Jacques Levy); The Judson Memorial Theatre, under the direction of playwright Al Carmines; the Genesis Theatre, under the direction of Ralph Cook; and the Theatre of the Ridiculous under the direction of John Vaccaro (see p. 362).

Most of the café theatres operate workshops for actors and playwrights. The artists-in-residence rediscover the premise that theatre can be an effective collaborative art experience. Plays take shape from exploratory improvisation, focusing on social and political conditions of the day. Acting exercises are shaped into spontaneous audience events. Dream, myth, and poetry are explored and funneled into spiritual and political commitments. Most of the plays rely on Artaud, Brecht, and Absurdist techniques to make their political or social comment. Each café acting company researches and reexamines the role of every type of person in our culture. Great effort is made to explore the unlimited potential for expression of human sensibility. Disciplined movement training is stressed, but voice becomes a matter of untrained individual expression for the actor. The workshop setting provides actors with the opportunity to work on dance and improvisational techniques. Here the work of the actor and director overlap. The actor finds he must have a director's knowledge of how to elicit specific responses from an audience, and the director realizes that he needs an actor's knowledge of how to create a performance.

The café Off-Off Broadway Theatre stresses nonillusionistic techniques and audience interaction with the theatrical event. Few of the plays are conventional expressions of Realism or Naturalism. They are usually ironic, self-mocking, and unsentimental. Costumes, sets, lighting effects, and casts are kept at a minimum because of the low production budget. The list of playwrights and plays from these small theatres is indeed impressive: Sam Shepard's *Chicago* and *Operation Side-Winder*; Jean-Claude van Itallie's *America Hurrah* and *The Serpent*; Joel Oppenheimer's *The Great American Desert*; Rochelle Owen's *Futz*; Le Roi Jones' *The Dutchman*; Paul Foster's *Tom Paine* and *Balls*; Megan Terry's *Viet Rock* and *Calm Down Mother*; Terrence McNally's *Apple Pie* and *Next*; Maria Irene Fornes's *The Successful Life of 3*; Frank O'Hara's *The General Returns from One Place to Another*; Kenneth Brown's *The Brig*; Al Carmines's *Promanade*; and many others.

The Open Theatre

Perhaps the most well-received and well-known experimental theatre in America was Joseph Chaikin's The Open Theatre. Established in the first half of 1963, Chaikin's theatre was organized to help actors deal with nonrealistic material. Influenced by Nola Chilton and Stanislavski's method, Chaikin constructed his studies around a "sound-and-movement" procedure. Chilton evolved acting exercises based on physical adjustment as a means of helping actors create characters in the plays of the Absurd. For example, she used an exercise called Weapons in which actors assumed sound and body movement analogous to a particular weapon (such as lurching into the air with a shout in the manner of a shot fired from a bazooka). This type of exercise provides the entry to nonpsychological characterization required by many nonrealistic plays.

Chilton's physical adjustment exercises lead Chaikin to new sound-and-movement techniques—use of impulsive, spontaneous sounds and movements to transmit energy kinetically between actors and, subsequently, to an audience. These impulsive actions had a snowball effect on Chaikin's actors which lead them to expressive extension of the sound-and-movement concept. Chaikin's innovations in the area of kinetic responses were instrumental in breaking traditional ties between artistic forms and fixed doctrines of naturalistic representation and emotional expressiveness.

Early in his career when he was concerned with his own acting, Chaikin turned to Brecht and the Absurd playwrights. However, during the middle sixties, he moved into exploratory areas of avant-garde literature which subsequently demanded new acting techniques. The central thrust of most avant-garde plays is the paradoxical use of simplicity and clarity to dramatize complexity and confusion. How can the actor-performer make the complex and chaotic visibly simple and clear to an audience and thereby give it the necessary impetus to participate in developing similar perceptions? Chaikin's answer was to develop new deeply penetrating techniques of improvisation. He led his actors to the discovery of their own intuition, their own inner dimension. Chaikin's actors explored their inner lives (somewhat similar to the creating of subtext, except without verbalization). Chaikin learned that inner emotions are rarely externalized. He knew, in fact, that external behavior often contradicts inner feeling. (In the play *Interview* by Jean-Claude van Itallie, the Politician speaks realistically to the people while they speak to him in sounds and movements reflecting the inner feelings of the earlier external action.) Chaikin also borrowed many of the techniques of Viola Spolin's theatre games. The easy structure of games helps actors free themselves from over-reliance on Stanislavski techniques. Games help actors use their bodies, their inventiveness, and their sensory experience in task-oriented exercises (e.g., walking in space, molding objects, mirroring images, exploring the interrelated parts of a machine; exploration of machines is an important aid in examination of social roles in society—since machines are analogous to society, the various machine parts are analogous to the people who make up society). In his search for a "communal dynamic," Chaikin was also influenced by his work with The Living Theatre and, above all, by Grotowski and the Polish Laboratory Theatre. Chaikin conducted exercises in breathing and talking together, in starting and stopping in unison, in trusting one another (by creating, for example, a trust circle; see chapter 2), in orchestration and musical conducting, and in chord harmony (all actors inhale breath and hum in unison to affirm the collective identity). Improvisational investigation led to the study of "perfect people" whose social behavior is predictable and deadening. Chaikin's actors were sensitized to the idea of being alive in the world and to the possibilities of communication through nonverbal behavior. Chaikin's work attacked social taboos and social conflicts. Improvisations developed into short nonstructured scenes based on political and social satire.

In 1964–1965, The Open Theatre began to perfect performance techniques. The start-and-stop exercises and the transformation concept tightened discipline (e.g., improvising reversal of roles or places; changing from human to nonhuman form; changing styles, lines of texts, or brief dialogue). A collaborative play between Megan Terry and The Open Theatre actors called *Comings and Goings* evolved. The most important single collaborative effort was Terry's *Viet Rock*.

Further gains were made by Chaikin's company when Grotowski visited the United States. Grotowski provided new artistic control through exercises in seeking spiritual privacy, in experiencing emotion physically, and in sharing space with an imaginary "partner-in-security." (See Grotowski's *Towards a Poor Theatre* for exercises on the Cat, Big Tower, Small Tower, headstands, somersaults, and so on.) Under the direction of Lee Worley, The Open Theatre pursued further innovation through unusual work with masks. The result was the company's final collaborative effort of director Jacques Levy and playwright Jean-Claude van Itallie—a striking play called *The Serpent*.

Later, the effectiveness of Chaikin's company diminished. The November 1973 dissolution of The Open Theatre came, probably from the inability of the troupe to incorporate a harmonious blend of the inner theatre of Artaud's vision of transcendental ceremonial theatre and the external theatre of Brecht's alienation concept—a problem common to all forms of experimental theatre in recent years. The Open Theatre gave its final performance in Santa Barbara, California. Chaikin stated at the conclusion of the last tour: "Intuitively we feel that it's time to disband. We can no longer be transitional and in progress without becoming an institution . . ." The legacy that Chaikin and his company willed to the American theatre scene has proved invaluable in expanding the concept of what theatre should be and in re-establishing a broader, deeper inner experience (linked with the mysterious and sacred). The Open Theatre's major contribution was probably in providing the playwright with a new role, that of functioning as a member of an acting company collectively involved in creating a play. Playwrights such as van Itallie and Terry helped devise a new concept of playwriting by fitting words to actor impulses (as opposed to dictating those impulses). Actors became interpreters of the collective vision of a particular company.

Chaikin's group was not the only ensemble unit doing radical or ritual theatre in the 1960s. However, it was the most effective instrument for demonstrating that an American ensemble company *could* be a *poor theatre* (in the Grotowski sense) and a *holy theatre* (in the sense of the contemporary British experimental director Peter Brook). Recently Chaikin has fostered a new group called The Working Theatre, revitalizing his earlier work.

Other revolutionary and socially articulate theatre companies appeared in full force on the American scene during the sixties. Perhaps the most outstanding examples were the Guerrilla Theatre, the Bread and Puppet Theatre, the Free Southern Theatre, the ethnic theatre groups, the Theatre of the Ridiculous, and the Theatre of Fact.

Guerrilla Theatre

Guerrilla Theatre began with people who generally lacked training. A number of companies composed of dedicated amateurs sprang up throughout the United States. Anyone with a burning desire to teach and demonstrate social and political doctrines could join this theatre. It had no home but the streets. Performances were usually conducted outdoors on grassy areas, in public parks, in clean middle-class residential suburbs, in dilapidated ghettos, and in urban renewal projects. Guerrilla Theatre was established on the principles of guerrilla warfare and its action was symbolic of guerrilla tactics. The how-to manuals and handbooks on the procedures necessary to conduct Guerrilla Theatre state that tactics should be simple and that mobility is imperative, that groups should be small, that social weakness should be pressured from all sides, and that the element of surprise must be utilized. Guerrilla Theatre reveals a problem and urges the audience to solve it (the Viet Nam War was a prime target for Guerrilla Theatre troupes). Actors perform in Guerrilla Theatre much like a commedia dell'arte troupe, complete with colorful masks, music, and mime. A backdrop and platform are set up for a performance and removed as the company changes location. Guerrilla plays are usually simple in design, utilizing the general format of morality play, burlesque, rock show, modern dance, vaudeville, and circus. The longevity of Guerrilla Theatre/action theatre is minimal and sporadic. Such theatre activity quickly dissipates when the revolutionary spirit subsides. However, the San Francisco Mime Troup continues to work successfully in sociopolitical Guerrilla Theatre activities. The Provisional Theatre Group is another successful organization specializing in sociopolitical themes.

Bread and Puppet Theatre

Peter Schumann and his Bread and Puppet Theatre use the theatre as a pulpit to preach, sermonize, and ritualize life on a level of purity and ecstasy. Performances in which puppets and/or masked figures dramatize social and political expressions are given in the streets (much like Guerrilla Theatre). These inanimate figures scream and dance, displaying life in highly stylized, ritualized stories. The action is simple and dancelike and requires specialized gestures. Ten-foot rod-puppets (each puppet having a different construction) are used as replacements for live actors. The puppet show uses imaginary characters—gods, monsters, legendary animals, magicians, and the like—to enlarge the basic theme of the play. Individual characterization and motivation are not used. A number of dramatic sequences are performed using noise, music, narration, speech, and modern dance. Emotions, meanings, and attitudes are expressed entirely through strong movements and gestures. The effect is an enlarged, almost grotesque picture of parading puppets and puppeteers who have taken to the streets to celebrate a ceremony called *Life*.

Bread and Puppet Theatre.

Ethnic Theatre

In the late 1950s and early 1960s, the Southern American black began to agitate for liberation. The Free Southern Theatre was established by Len Holt, Gilbert Moses, and John O'Neal. These and many other artists joined in a collective movement aimed at influencing the shape of black folklore and black psychology, ultimately cutting through the fear of white aggression. Organized in a church basement, the Free Southern Theatre preached the gospel and sang spirituals as freedom songs. Political rhetoric was used to energize black people. Unfortunately, the Free Southern Theatre was unable to establish a continuity of meaningful Black Theatre. Neither did it communicate the needs of blacks. The overall program failed to sustain a unified understanding concerning problems of black people, nor did the program propose solid solutions to the problem of identifying the cultural dynamic. Beset by arguments over the black-white composition of the group, the members of the Free Southern Theatre saw their work as merely another extension of white Western drama. They disbanded. The black movement desperately needed to discover a black heritage rooted solely in black people.

This alternative to Western dramatic tradition appeared on the American theatre scene in the late 1960s and early 1970s. The soul and spirit of the black experience surfaced in the writings of Ed Bullins (*In the Wine Time*), Le Roi Jones (Imamu Amiri Baraka) (*Dutchman* and *The Slave*), Jimmy Garett (*And We Own the Night*), Ben Caldwell (*The King of Soul*), N. R. Davidson (*Eli Haji Malik*), James Baldwin (*Blues for Mister Charlie*), Lorraine Hansberry (*A Raisin in the Sun*), Lonnie Elder III (*Ceremonies in Dark Old Men*), Charles Gordone (*No Place to Be Somebody*), Joseph A. Walker (*The River Niger*), and Douglas Turner Ward (*The Reckoning*). Ossie Davis (*Purlie Victorious*) and Ted Shine (*Contribution*) are also active black playwrights of note, as are Carlton and Barbara Molette (*Rosalee Pritchett*) and Judi Mason (*Livin' Fat*). Plays reveal the world as it is—a world seeking to transcend reality into a world as it can be or should be. The major characteristics of modern black plays are their allegorical character, melodramatic action, and simple language. The most important work being done in the area of Black Theatre is that of the Negro Ensemble Company in New York, a group devoted to producing the work of black playwrights and providing a training ground for black actors.

The Chicano theatre groups, particularly the groups in California, represent another movement in Ethnic Theatre. For example, Luis Valdez has developed the Téatro Camposina into a viable, exciting company that champions the cause of Chicanos.

Theatre of the Ridiculous and the Liquid Theatre

A unique alternative to the revolutionary and social experimental theatre groups was the Theatre of the Ridiculous led by John Vacarro. By erotic, self-assertive, playful, imaginative means, the Theatre of the Ridiculous held public authority up to ridicule. The main purpose of this highly bizarre theatre was to dramatize the fictitious nature of our illusions. The plays attempted to prevent escape into those illusions by forcing us to look at our ridiculous reality. The Happenings influenced the direction of the Theatre of the Ridiculous, as did Spolin's improvisational games and Grotowski's confrontation and disarming techniques. This theatre was a format for task-oriented activities. Lacking characters and logical plot organization, actors simply displayed their own personalities or created clichéd stereotypes.

Using the format of the Theatre of the Ridiculous, the Liquid Theatre sought to present a similar barrage of theatricality, utilizing active audience participation. It now appears to have been a short-lived experiment.

Theatre of Fact

A more stimulating and seemingly lasting experience known as the Theatre of Fact evolved in the late 1960s. Originating in Germany from the Brecht influence and led by Rolf Hochhuth and Peter Weiss (see chapter 20), the movement developed drama based on factual history. Later, Heiner Kipphard in his play *In the Matter of J. Robert Oppenheimer* raised ethical questions concerning the conflict between science and humanity. The actor in the Theatre of Fact operates in an environment similar to Brecht's Epic Theatre. He has full intellectual knowledge of the subject matter being presented and a heightened consciousness of all action. In effect, he is "standing in" for a particular person who cannot be there to speak for himself. The actor's task is to create a believable, historic human being and yet to keep the didactic polemic operative (see the plays *Pueblo*, *The Trail of the Cantonsville Nine*, and *Are You Now or Have You Ever Been*, the latter by Eric Bentley).

Performance Group

In 1968 Richard Schechner organized an experimental theatre group in a converted New York garage devoted to what he termed *environmental theatre*. He called the troupe the Performance Group. Schechner believed that his concept of theatre was placed somewhere between a Happening and traditional theatre presentation. The actors used all the space in the theatre including audience area and stage. The total environment was involved. Any space could be converted into a production area. Schechner's group at times used a text, but generally worked improvisationally. His most important productions were *Dionysus 69*, *Makbeth*, and *Commune*.

The Public Theatre

Joseph Papp has introduced more new American playwrights than any other producer in recent years through his efforts for a free public theatre in New York City, particularly in Central Park. *Hair*—a landmark rock musical presentation—was produced by Papp. Later, plays by such promising playwrights as Charles Gordone and Jason Miller were produced under the auspices of Papp.

Other Groups

Other experimental theatre companies included Andre Gregory's Manhattan Project, Robert Wilson's Byrd Hoffman School, Ernie McClintock's Afro-American Studio Theatre in Harlem, and Herbert Blau's Oberlin Group.

Experimental theatre reached its apex during the civil rights and antiwar movements of the middle 1960s. The early efforts of most of these groups have faded, but their influence remains in some Off-Off Broadway activity. The character of this theatre changes almost weekly. Recently, Off-Off Broadway entered a period of consolidation. The "company" idea has given stability to Off-Off Broadway and has enabled small groups of actors and directors to control their artistic destiny. The emphasis on Off-Off Broadway has shifted from the script and the playwright to the artistic cohesiveness of the company. Experimental theatre is no longer identified strictly with youth and rebellion.

Glossary

Above. To be or go behind something or someone. The general area farther away from the audience.

Acoustics. The qualities that govern the transmission of sound.

Action. Any change of form or condition on the stage which forcibly affects the mind or senses of the spectator; physical movement; a lively series of stimulations causing a feeling of suspense; a rapid progression of arresting ideas. Action when conceived as the movement of sensory stimuli may be expressed by the voice of the actor as well as by his body.

Ad lib (from Latin *ad libitum*, "at pleasure"). To add, especially to improvise, words or gestures.

Affective memory (Emotion memory or recall; Sensory memory or recall). Recollection of details and situations that have deeply moved an actor to assist him in achieving an inner justification that lets him enter into the character's experiences. Important to the Stanislavski system of acting (popularly called the Method in the United States).

Alarum. An offstage sound effect of trumpets, drums, and guns in Elizabethan drama.

Alienation effect (German, ver Fremdungseffekt). Theatrical devices in Brecht's Epic plays designed to estrange the audience from excessive emotional response; to "make strange" action in order to respond to it intellectually.

Antagonist. The person, group, or force in opposition to the central character (hero or protagonist).

Antecedent events. Part of *exposition* in a play; the important actions which have occurred *before* the play begins.

Apron. The part of the stage extending beyond the proscenium curtain line toward the audience.

Arena. A playing space for actors which is surrounded by spectators; in England, a playing space with audience on three sides and a wall at the back of the players. In the United States, the latter is usually called *horseshoe* or even *thrust* staging.

Arras. A curtain. A common term in Elizabethan drama.

Aside. Dialogue intended for the audience with the accepted convention that other characters cannot hear it.

Attack. *See* **Point of attack.**

Audience. The viewers and hearers of a theatre performance.

Audition. A demonstration of performance ability, usually competitive, usually prepared. Many directors distinguish an audition from a *tryout* by designating the latter as a reading without memorization or preparation.

Auditorium. The theatre area usually designated for the audience; often called the *house*.

Awareness. A state of sensory alertness; a preparedness to respond to sight, sound, taste, touch, and odor. A sensitive recognition of other stage presences.

Backdrop or Back cloth. A flat, screen, curtain, canvas, or scrim hanging behind the performers, usually painted with a sky or scene.

Backstage. All of the theatre back of the stage proper including the wings, shop, dressing rooms, and so forth.

Balance. The equilization of attention onstage (as between actors, between stage set properties, etc.).

Barnstorm. To tour in a play performing in makeshift theatres.

Baroque. Usually associated with art and architecture, in theatre the term may be associated loosely with eighteenth-century drama, with its elaborate and ornate patterns of language. For example, the work of some of the English sentimentalists and even the work of Sir Richard B. Sheridan.

Batten. A wooden or metal stiffener used behind stage cloth or canvas or as a mount for lighting instruments.

Beats. A term employed by actors of the Stanislavski system meaning the distance from the beginning to the end of a character's intention, whether explicitly stated in the dialogue or not.

Below. To be or go in front of something or someone. The stage area closest to the audience in a proscenium theatre.

Blackout. A sudden extinguishing of all stage lighting; usually used for a theatrical effect at the end of a scene.

Blocking. To work out all movement of actors.

Bombast. Ranting, loud, ornate dramatic speech.

Book. The nonmusical segments of musical plays.

Borderlights. *See* **Striplights.**

Bourgeois drama. Serious plays with middle-class characters, particularly popular in the eighteenth and nineteenth centuries, as in George Lillo's *The London Merchant*, 1731.

Box. In some theatres an isolated seating area for four to six persons.

Box office. A place usually at the front of a theatre where tickets are sold.

Box set. Scenery representing an interior, usually realistic, with three walls, ceiling, doors, and windows.

Broadway. A famous avenue in the theatre district of New York City. By popular concept, the heart of commercial theatre.

> **Off-Broadway.** The more artistic, less commercial *avant-garde* theatre performed in improvised theatres in New York City.

> **Off-Off Broadway.** Usually considered the true standard-bearer of Off-Broadway drama since Off-Broadway has become very commercialized.

Build. The increase of emotion, tension, or energy directed toward a peak or climax.

Business. Minor physical action, often with the hands, by a performer (includes facial expression).

Cadence. The measure or beat of any rhythmic motion, as in verse, dance, and music.

Call. (1) An announcement listing cast, rehearsals, and performances. (2) Readiness to do anything in the theatre.

Cast. (1) Performers in a play. (2) To assign roles to actors.

Catharsis (Katharis). The purging of emotion and suspense which occurs at the end of a tragedy; experienced by the audience and, at times, by the characters as well.

Center stage or stage center. A position approximately in the middle of the acting area.

Character. One of the dramatis personae; the personality of such a figure. The agent(s) of the plot. One of the six key elements of a drama according to Aristotle.

Character role. Normally an elderly or an eccentric character.

Cheat. To move or turn slightly to provide more space for other actors or to improve the compositional stage picture. To pretend you can see someone onstage as you speak to him when in reality you cannot. To project the voice more to the audience than to the character you are addressing.

Chorus. In Greek drama, a group of performers who play a role (in modern drama, the chorus is often supplanted by a narrator). In musical theatre, a group of dancers and/or singers.

Classical. In ancient times, used to designate an author of the "first class." Today, term commonly means an author or work whose greatness is universally recognized.

Clean up. (1) To polish, work, or rehearse a scene to perfect it. (2) To move slightly to afford other actors space and provide a better compositional picture onstage.

Climax. The moment of highest interest in a play which leads to the answer to the MDQ and resolution of the conflict. The climax can be the *major crisis* or *turn*, or it can occur later. In *Hamlet* the *turn* occurs at the end of the play-within-a-play scene in act 3, and the *climax* occurs in the duel scene in act 5. In *Death of a Salesman* the *turn* and *climax* occur together after Biff cries in Willy's arms and Willy exits to commit suicide.

Close. To turn away from the audience.

Clown. A comic figure present in much drama. At times the clown merges with the *Fool*, a *jester* having unique wisdom.

Comedy. One of the two central forms of drama (tragedy is the other). Broadly, comedy is anything that amuses, movement from unhappiness to happiness, or action that excites mirth.

Community Theatre. A theatre operated by and for the entertainment and edification of local people of a town or city.

Company. A group of actors who perform together. Also called a troupe.

Complication. An incident which alters the direction of a play's action line (turns the action in a new direction). For example, Hamlet's killing Polonius is a major complication.

Concentration. Complete attention to something as concentration on a task. A key element in effective acting.

Confidant. A character in whom a principal character confides (as Horatio to Hamlet).

Conflict. Forces of opposition, central to the action of most plays.

Constructivism. A scenic and staging movement associated with Meyerhold and Tairov in Russia in which painted realistic scenery was rejected in favor of ladders, platforms, and other constructed items.

Convention. An unrealistic device that the public agrees to tolerate or accept. (For example, it is a convention that one actor cannot hear another speak an aside.)

Counter. To shift position to compensate for the movement of another actor to maintain an effective compositional picture.

Cover. To hide from view of the audience, often deliberately, so as not to make obvious some necessary action of artifice.

Crisis (Major crisis). *See* **Turn.**

Cross. A movement onstage from one area to another.

Cue. A signal, usually a word or a gesture, to which an actor or member of the crew must respond.

Curtain. A drapery used to conceal part of the stage. Sometimes the term is used to denote the end of a scene or an act.

Curtain call. The appearance by the cast at the end of a play to receive applause. Generally considered a professional courtesy, it also provides the cast with the opportunity of acknowledging the audience. It is usually self-indulgent rudeness to forgo a curtain call.

Cyclorama, or Cyc. A shell-shaped structure at the rear of the stage, curved at the sides, usually made of cloth. Properly lighted, it gives the illusion of depth and of sky.

Deciding agent. The person or event in a play that resovles the conflict between the forces (between protagonist and antagonist). Often the deciding agent is a third person (such as a girl choosing between male rivals for her hand in marriage), or it is the will and decision of the protagonist (e.g., Hamlet is the deciding agent as well as the protagonist).

Denouement. Unknotting or resolution of the main plot. The end of a play; usually follows the climax.

Designer. One who makes the plans from which scenery, costumes, and the like are constructed.

Deus ex machina.   In classical Greek plays a god lowered in a machine or basket to provide an ending for the play. Today, any improbable device used to conclude a work.

Dialogue.   Speech between characters; speech of a single character.

Diction.   Choice of words or wording in a play. Language. Today, a performer's manner of speaking including pronunciation and phrasing. One of the six key elements of a drama according to Aristotle.

Director (Régisseur).   The coordinator of all artists and technicians working on a theatre production.

Double.   To play more than one role in a single production. In films, to stand in place of another performer, as for dangerous stunts.

Downstage.   Toward the audience on a proscenium stage.

Dramatis personae (Latin, "masks of the play").   The characters in a play.

Drame.   A solemn but not tragic play; associated with eighteenth-century bourgeois drama.

Dress the stage.   (1) To move slightly to provide more space for other actors and to improve the compositional stage picture. (2) To furnish props and items to hang on the scenery to improve the appearance of the stage.

Drive (Nervosity).   The dramatic thrust of character desires in a play. The emotional hungers or nervosity of each character.

Dumb show.   A scene having action without words; used frequently in Elizabethan drama.

Emotion.   Feelings; impulses manifested outward from within (as grief, joy, anger, etc.).

Emotion memory or recall.   *See* **Affective memory.**

Empathy.   The projection of one's feelings into a perceived object. Distinguished from *sympathy:* we empathize if we feel *with* a character; we sympathize if we feel *for* a character.

Emphasis.   Accent or special focus on an action, line, person, or word.

Ensemble acting.   Presentation in which the performance of the group, rather than the individual, is stressed.

Entrance.   (1) Act of entering the stage in view of the audience. (2) An opening in a set through which actors may enter.

Epic.   The label given to Bertolt Brecht's plays whose aim was to arouse an audience's detached thought. Usually instructive episodic drama in the structural mode of Homer's Epic poems or narratives.

Epilogue.   An appendix or concluding address in a play.

Exit.   (1) Departure from a stage area. (2) An opening in a set through which actors may leave.

Exposition.   The essential information provided the audience to begin the action of a play, or given later to clarify action.

Extra (Supernumerary).   One with so small a role in a play that he need have no training or talent (as a court guard who merely stands by the door in a trial scene).

Flat.   A light wooden or metal frame covered by canvas and used for scenery.

Flies.   The area above the stage used for hanging scenery, lighting equipment, and so on.

Floodlight.   A lensless lamp that provides broad illumination.

Floor plan (Ground plan).   An outline drawing of a stage setting as it would look from above.

Fluff.   A blunder or error onstage.

Focal point.   The point of greatest interest onstage at any given moment.

Foil.   (1) A character who sets off another, as Laertes and Fortinbras set off Hamlet. (2) A piece of fencing equipment.

Folio. A book made of sheets folded once, each sheet providing two leaves or four pages. Shakespeare's plays were first published as a folio in 1623.

Fool. *See* **Clown.**

Footlights. *See* **Striplights.**

Form. *See* **Play form.**

French Scene. That stage action contained between the entrance and exit of any character in a play.

Gallery. An area above and at the rear of theatres; called a balcony today.

Gestalt. The synthesis of separate elements of emotion, experience, and the like to constitute an organic whole.

Give. To move a bit to provide space for another actor. To respond or offer emotion, energy, or activity onstage. To provide greater emphasis to someone else onstage.

Given circumstance. A Stanislavski term referring to any dramatic occurrence which affects an actor's playing of a scene.

Greasepaint. Stage makeup. Coloring-matter mixed with grease in sticks or tubes used as a base to help the features look natural under artificial illumination.

Greenroom. The traditional name for a theatre lounging room for performers and their guests.

Grid. The framework of beams above the stage area in the flies.

Ground plan. *See* **Floor plan.**

Ground row. A flat or scenic piece with an irregular profile, usually used as a wall, mountain, hedge, or the like, often used to mask lighting instruments.

Groundlings. The patrons who stand in front of a stage to see a play, particularly in an Elizabethan theatre.

Ham. An incompetent performer who overacts.

Hamartia. A Greek-based word referring to the tragic flaw or error in judgment of the hero in tragedy.

Heads up! A warning that something (usually scenery) is being lowered (or falling) onstage.

Heavens (Shadow). The canopy area over the stage in Elizabethan drama where an actor could hide from view from other characters or where musicians resided.

Heavy. A solemn major character, especially a villain.

Hero, or Heroine. The central character or protagonist; the leading romantic character.

Hold. To stop or delay action onstage (usually because of laughter or applause.)

Hubris. A Greek-based word for excess pride, the most common form of hamartia (flaw in tragic characters).

Humor. The quality of being amusing.

Humour. In ancient physiology, one of the four principal bodily fluids—blood, phlegm, choler (yellow bile), and melancholy (black bile). These humours were believed to influence health and temperament.

Iambia trimeter. A verse composed of three measures, consisting of three dipodies (six feet) in ancient or classical Greek dramatic poetry.

Imagination. The process of forming mental images. The reproduction of images from memory. The mental ability to create original and striking images and concepts. A key element in effective acting.

Imitation (Greek, *mimesis*, "to imitate or imitative"). Not a pejorative term in the theatre. It implies "making" or "re-creating" or "representing" in the theatre.

Impersonate. To invest with personality; to personify; to assume or act the person or character.

Improvisation. Invention of lines and stage business by performers.

In. To the center of the stage.

Ingenue. (1) The role of an innocent young woman. (2) The actress who plays such a role.

Intention. A Stanislavski term for an actor's real reason for being in a scene, regardless of the actor's dialogue. *See* **Subtext.**

Interlude. Light entertainment, usually musical, while scenery is being shifted. In sixteenth-century England, a short farce play.

Intermission. A period between scenes or acts permitting audiences to go to the theatre lobby.

Intuition. Immediate comprehension or knowledge of something without the conscious use of reasoning.

Irony. A condition in plays in which the truth is the reverse of what the participants think. Irony is usually more fully understood by the audience than by the characters.

Jester. *See* **Clown.**

Jig. A short farce, sung and danced at the end of some Elizabethan plays.

Kill. To spoil by accident or deliberately cease any activity onstage.

Kinesics. The study of body motions as related to the nonverbal aspects of interpersonal communication.

Lead. A principal role.

Legitimate drama. In eighteenth-century England, a play performed in a *licensed* theatre. Today, a play, in contrast to a musical, vaudeville, film, and the like.

Lighting. Illumination of the theatre, especially of the stage. Today, the province of artistic designers and technicians.

Limelight. (1) A stage lighting device of the nineteenth century which produced illumination by directing an oxyhydrogen flame against a piece of lime. (2) Today, to give special focus or attention.

Line. (1) A rope or wire used to hang scenery. (2) Dialogue in a play.

Living Newspaper. A cinematic dramatic form in the United States in the 1930s in which factual data and dramatic vignette were integrated. Part of the brief Federal Theatre Project headed by Hallie Flanagan Davis (1890–1969), the Living Newspaper produced such works as *Triple A Plowed Under* in 1936.

Lobby. The lounge area for spectators in a theatre, usually at the front of the building.

Major crisis. *See* **Turn.**

Major Dramatic Question (MDQ). The question upon which the action of a play focuses. Usually the MDQ is not presented as a direct question in the script, but is recognized to be the key action factor by the audience. For example, the audience ponders whether Hamlet will revenge his father's murder and restore order to the Kingdom.

Make up. To disguise one's face by using cosmetics, false hair, nose putty, and the like.

Makeup. Materials applied to disguise the face.

Marionette. A doll controlled from above or below by rods, wires, or strings.

Mask. A face-covering worn by many actors, especially in Greek drama and commedia dell'arte.

Masque. An entertainment of the Renaissance using lavish scenery and costumes.

Matinee. (from French, *matin*, "morning"). An afternoon (and, rarely, a morning) performance.

MDQ. *See* **Major dramatic question.**

Melody, or Music. (1) Actual music in a play. (2) Any melodic element such as an arrangement of words. One of the six key elements of a drama according to Aristotle.

Method. An American adaptation of the Stanislavski system that focuses on inner motivation, whose chief exponent is an American school of acting, the New York Actors' Studio.

Mezzanine. The front or first balcony in a theatre.

Mime. An ancient dramatic entertainment in which acrobats, jugglers, singers, dancers, actors, and actresses perform. *See also* **Pantomime.**

Mise-en-scène. The stage setting including the scenery, lighting, and arrangement of actors.

Mono-Drama (Mono-Acting). (1) A piece for one actor. (2) One performer doing several roles.

Monologue. (1) A long speech delivered by one character. (2) A performance by a single actor.

Mood. The dominant atmosphere created by a production—usually a combination of tempo, imagery, rhythm, sound, lighting, scenery, costuming, acting, and so forth.

Motivating Force (MF; Spine; Super-Objective). The central emotional hunger or drive of a character; what the character wants above all, usually expressed relative to other characters. For example, the MF or spine of Willy Loman is that he wants to regain the love of his son, Biff; that is Willy's Super-Objective.

Motivation. Grounds in character and situation that make behavior plausible.

Multiple setting (Simultaneous setting). A stage that displays at one time several locales.

Musical comedy (Musical theatre). A piece in which songs and dances are integrated to form a story.

Neon acting. Overacting; performing everything with great emphasis. Usually a very ineffective kind of performance unless varied.

Nervosity. *See* **Drive.**

Obligatory scene (Scène à faire). (1) A scene in a play which an audience foresees and desires and whose absence it may, with reason, resent. (2) The necessary and most dramatic confrontation between two characters.

Observation. (1) The act of studying something closely. (2) The act of learning by observing (in acting, for the purpose of imitation). A key element in effective acting.

Off-Broadway. *See* **Broadway.**

Off-Off Broadway. *See* **Broadway.**

Offstage. The part of the stage out of view of the audience.

Onstage. The acting area of a stage in view of the audience.

Open. To turn more toward the audience.

Out. A direction away from the center of the stage, often toward the audience.

Out Front. Refers to the auditorium, house, or audience.

Overlap. To move or speak slightly ahead of cue.

Overplay. To act with more exaggeration than is needed.

Pace (Pacing; Tempo). The speed with which a play or actor moves.

Pantomime. An ancient dramatic performance featuring a solo performer who gestures and dances without using dialogue. *See also* **Mime.**

Parallel movement. When two or more actors move in the same direction at the same time.

Pathos. A quality that evokes pity.

Peripeteia (from Greek for "reversal"). A plot term indicating a sudden change in conditions, usually in tragedy.

Pickup. To increase the playing pace or to shorten the interval between cues.

Pin. *See* **Rail.**

Pit. An area at the front of the stage where the orchestra sits.

Places! A command for actors to get in position to begin a rehearsal or performance.

Plant. A device to call attention to something which will have special significance later in a play.

Play. (1) A story communicated by impersonators. (2) To act.

Play doctor. One called in to patch up a play's weaknesses by rewriting, cutting, and adding.

Play form. The characteristic kind of play such as tragedy, comedy, farce, melo-drama, and the like (as opposed to play type, which refers to the stylistic mode of the play, e.g., Realism, Expressionism, etc.).

Play type. The stylistic mode of a play such as, realistic, expressionistic, and the like (as opposed to play form such as tragedy, comedy, farce, melodrama, etc.).

Play up (Plug). To emphasize a key moment.

Playhouse. A theatre.

Play-Within-A-Play. A representation of a drama within the drama itself (as in *Hamlet*, act 3, scene 2).

Plot. Story organization. The most important ingredient in a play according to Aristotle—*the* key element in the six elements of a play.

Plug. *See* **Play up.**

Poetic drama. A play whose language is metrical.

Poetic justice. A term denoting reward of the virtuous and punishment of the vicious, coined by Thomas Rymer in 1678.

Point of attack. The earliest incident in a play that arouses strong audience interest and exposes the basic conflict of the play; the point at which an author chooses to begin the story.

Practical. A functioning prop or piece of scenery which can actually be *used* by the actor and which is not merely decorative or ornamental (as a window that can actually be opened).

Precast. To select actors for roles prior to auditions or tryouts. A very unpopular and infrequent practice, particularly in educational and amateur theatre.

Premiere. The first public performance of a work.

Preview. A tryout before an audience of a play previous to the performance considered "the opening."

Producer. In England and Ireland, the director, but in the United States, the entrepreneur chiefly concerned with raising money. The person who often hires the artistic staff.

Production. (1) A dramatic entertainment onstage. (2) The process of getting the work onstage.

Project. To accentuate or intensify vocal delivery, volume, or articulation; to accentuate or intensify movement and emotion as well.

Prologue. A preface or introduction.

Prompter. One who reminds forgetful actors of their lines. Often the assistant director–assistant stage manager.

Property, or Prop. An object or article used in a play and called for in the script.

    Hand props. Props used by the characters in a play.

    Set props. Furniture and other standing props; often unused by the characters in a play.

    Trim or Dress props. Objects hanging on the walls of a set.

Proscenium arch stage. A playing area framed in the front and thus separated from the audience.

Protagonist (from Greek for "first contender"). The chief figure in a play.

Puppet. A doll that can be manipulated. The operator places his hand into the body of a puppet to manipulate it.

Quarto. A book made of sheets folded twice, each sheet supplying four leaves or eight pages. (Shakespeare's plays were issued in quartos before they were collected in a folio.)

Rail (Pin; Tie-Off; Trim). Part of the flies and grid system used to hang scenery in a theatre; related to sandbag and counterweight flying systems.

Raisonneur. A character in a chorus.

Raked stage. A playing area that slopes upward toward the rear wall. In present-day theatre, the rake is usually under the spectator area, rather than under the acting area.

Ramp. A sloping platform used in the manner of a step unit.

Régisseur. In Germany and Russia, the director of a play.

Rehearsal. A practice performance of a dramatic work or part of the work. Rehearsals: reading, line-check, blocking, working, polishing, technical, run-through, dress and costume.

Relaxation. An unstrained but prepared state of readiness. A key element in effective acting.

Repartee. Witty remarks and clever, unexpected answers, usually in rapid delivery.

Repertory (Repertoire). The body of dramatic works a company is trained to perform in turn or frequently. A *Repertory Company* performs a number of plays daily, weekly, or monthly rather than a single play for an extended run.

Response (Respond). A player's manifest reaction to another presence on the stage. Especially, a particular reaction called forth by a particular act.

Return. A flat set parallel to the audience at the downstage edge of the set jutting into the wings just above the tormentor. Any similar flat attached to a larger piece of scenery.

Revival. A production of a play usually long unperformed.

Revue. A loose collection of musical numbers, skits, comic bits, and the like.

Rhythm. The combination of tempo, imagery, stress, beat, sound, accent, motion, and so forth, that creates a pattern of activity. A play has a rhythm; a production has a rhythm; an actor and his role have a rhythm.

Ritual. A ceremonial act.

Routine. Specially rehearsed stage actions, lines, songs, and dances.

Run. (1) The period during which a company performs a play. (2) To run through a scene or act without interruption from the director.

Satire. A work ridiculing aspects of human behavior, usually socially corrective in nature and intended to provoke both laughter and thought.

Scenario. A detailed outline of a dramatic entertainment.

Scene. A subunit of an act or a play.

Score. To determine character activity, business, and pantomimic dramatization. To score a role.

Scrim. (1) A loosely woven gauzelike fabric. (2) A theatre drop. When lighted from the front, a scrim becomes visible, almost opaque, and when lighted from the back it becomes semitransparent, nearly disappearing. A scrim with a scene painted on it is called a *transparency*.

Script. The text of a dramatic work.

Sensory memory or recall. *See* **Affective memory.**

Shadow. *See* **Heavens.**

Share. Equal attention for two or more actors.

Show. A theatrical entertainment.

Side. A sheet containing an actors lines, cues, stage directions, and so forth.

Sight line. The line of vision from any seat in the spectators' area to the stage.

Simultaneous setting. *See* **Multiple setting.**

Sketch (Skit). A short comic entertainment.

Soliloquy. A speech wherein a character utters thoughts aloud while alone; usually delivered directly to an audience and less frequently as self-meditation given aloud.

Soubrette. (1) A minor young female role, usually a maid. (2) An actress who plays such a role.

Sound effect. An imitative sound, often performed offstage. Can be produced "live," on record, on tape, and by machinery.

Spectacle. *All* that is seen or heard onstage, including the actors. Today, that which appeals to the eye, such as lavish scenery. One of the six key elements of drama according to Aristotle.

Spine (Super-Objective). *See* **Motivating force (MF).**

Stage business. *See* **Business.**

Stage center. *See* **Center stage.**

Stage left. Left of stage center; on the actor's left facing the audience.

Stage manager. The person who coordinates the efforts of the producer, director, playwright, actors, technicians, and the like. He "runs" the production during performances.

Stage right. Right of stage center; on the actor's right facing the audience.

Star. A leading performer whose appeal is so great that his name may precede the title of the play.

Static. Little or no movement; a slow pace.

Steal. When one actor draws attention to himself at the expense of other actors (a practice greatly frowned upon when not called for in the script).

Stock company. A repertory group attached to a theatre which commonly changes plays weekly, as in summer stock (the straw-hat circuit).

Straight role. A role without marked characterization; not very particularized or eccentric (normally a young man or young woman).

Straw-Hat circuit. *See* **Stock company.**

Striplights. A lighting unit consisting of a row of lamps. When on the floor at the front of the stage called *footlights*. When suspended on iron pipes overhead called *borderlights*.

Strong. High attention value.

Struggle. The major action line of complication in a play. The longest segment of a play (its body).

Style. (1) The mode of expression. (2) The essence or truth of a particular reality. (3) The total work of art: its material, its language, its historical era, its customs, and the like.

Subject issues. The basic subject matter and questions raised by a play, usually expressed by a single word such as incest, murder, or justice.

Subordinate. To restrict focus or emphasis.

Subtext (Intention). A term common to both the Stanislavski system and the Method. Refers to the meaning underlying dialogue and stage directions. Subtext may include invented autobiographical material about a character provided that it is clearly related to the text and not merely arbitrary.

Supernumerary. *See* **Extra.**

Tableau. A picture presented on stage by motionless actors.

Tag line. The final line before an exit, before the end of a scene, act, or play, or at the end of a joke.

Take stage. To achieve prominent emphasis or to command a scene or situation.

Teaser. Scenic mask (a drop) at the top of the stage.

Telescope. To overlap the reading of lines or execution of business.

Tempo. *See* **Pace.**

Text. The dialogue and stage directions of a play without reference to the underlying meaning.

Theatre or Theater. (1) A seeing place; a hearing place. (2) A playhouse. (3) A body of plays.

Theme. The intellectual content in a play. Generally considered to be that idea basic to the thought of the play; the author's central idea. Usually the theme is expressed in one full sentence using an active verb: Pride taken to excess causes destruction. *See also* **Thought, or Idea.**

Thesis play. A play in which the dramatist argues a point of view, such as Ibsen's, *A Doll's House.*

Thought, or Idea. The intellectual content of a play including its theme or central idea. One of the six key elements of a drama according to Aristotle.

Throw away. To deliberately underplay a line or business. Often used to place greater emphasis elsewhere.

Thrust stage. *See* **Arena.**

Tie-off. *See* **Rail.**

Timing. The art of delivering words or performing movement at the effective instant.

Tirade. A long declamatory speech.

Top. To emphasize a line or an action to make it more emphatic than the preceding dialogue.

Tormentor. Scenic mask at the sides of the stage.

Tragedy. One of the two major forms of drama (the other is comedy). It involves suffering and frequently death and contains universal truths. For Aristotle, a tragedy was a dramatic imitation of action of high and serious importance.

Transparency. A gauze theatre drop with a scene painted on it. *See also* **Scrim.**

Trap. Door or opening cut into the floor of the stage for access to the cellar or area below.

Trilogy. A unit of three works. For example, *Oresteia* by Aeschylus.

Trim. *See* **Rail.**

Tryout. *See* **Audition.**

Turn (Crisis, or Major crisis). The high point of suspense when a decision or action occurs which turns the rising action of a play toward an immediate or eventual climax and denouement (ending). The key turning point of a play.

Type. *See* **Play type.**

Type casting. A theatre practice in which performers are cast according to their age and physical and personality characteristics.

Underplay. To deliberately restrict or de-emphasize emotion when acting. To de-emphasize delivery and stage action.

Understudy. One who prepares a role normally performed by another in order to substitute in the role when necessary.

Upstage. Away from the audience in a proscenium theatre.

Vaudeville. (1) A stage entertainment of song, dance, acrobatics, skits, trained animal acts, and the like. (2) A series of speciality acts. (3) A short comic play or skit.

Vehicle. A play especially suited to exhibit the acting skills of a performer or company.

Walk-on. A small role without lines. *See* **Extra.**

Wardrobe mistress. The person who collects, cares for, and stores costumes.

Weak. Low attention value or weak position onstage.

Well-made play. A play with suspense that relies on a tight, cleverly constructed plot, as in the plays of Scribe, Sardou, and Ibsen.

Wing. The space offstage right or left of the acting area.

Wit. (1) Knowledge, sagacity, good sense. (2) The sudden ingenious association of ideas and words, often amusing.

Altman, George, et al. *Theatre Pictorial: A History of World Theatre as Recorded in Drawings, Paintings, Engravings, and Photographs.* Berkeley: University of California Press, 1953.

Archer, William. *Masks or Faces.* New York: Hill & Wang, 1957.

Barton, Lucy. *Historic Costume for the Stage.* Boston: Walter H. Baker Co., 1940.

Blunt, Jerry. *The Composite of Acting.* New York: Macmillan Co., 1966.

Bowman, Walter P., and Ball, Robert H. *Theatre Language: A Dictionary of the English of the Drama and Stage from Medieval to Modern Times.* New York: Theatre Arts Books, 1961.

Brockett, Oscar G., and Findlay, Robert. *Century of Innovation: A History of European and American Drama Since 1870.* Englewood Cliffs, N. J.: Prentice-Hall, 1973.

Brockett, Oscar G.; Becker, Samuel; and Bryant, Donald. *A Bibliographical Guide to Research in Speech and Dramatic Art.* Chicago: Scott, Foresman and Company, 1963.

Clark, Barrett H., ed. *European Theories of the Drama.* New. rev. Henry Popkin. New York: Crown Publishers, 1965.

Clay, James H., and Krempel, Daniel. *The Theatrical Image.* New York: McGraw-Hill Book Co., 1967.

Clurman, Harold. "Actors in Style—and Style in Actors." *New York Times Magazine,* 7 December 1952, pp. 26–38.

Corey, Irene. *The Mask of Reality: An Approach to Design for the Theatre.* Anchorage, Ky.: Anchorage Press, 1968.

Corson, Richard. *Stage Makeup.* 5th ed. New York: Appleton-Century-Crofts, 1975.

Coquelin, Constant. *The Art of the Actor.* New York: Crown Publishers, 1953.

Diderot, Denis. *The Paradox of Acting.* New York: Hill & Wang, 1957.

Dramatic Index (1909–1949). Boston: F. W. Faxon, Inc. 1910–1950.

Duerr, Edwin. *The Length and Depth of Acting.* New York: Holt, Rinehart and Winston, 1962.

Gassner, John. *Masters of the Drama.* 3rd ed. New York: Dover Publications, 1954.

Geisinger, Marion. *Plays, Players, and Playwrights.* New York: Hart Publishing Co., 1971.

Guthrie, Tyrone. *Tyrone Guthrie on Acting.* New York: Viking Press, 1971.

Hansen, Henry Harold. *Costumes and Styles.* New York: E. P. Dutton & Co., 1956.

Hartnoll, Phyllis, ed. *The Oxford Companion to the Theatre.* 2nd ed. London: Oxford University Press, 1957.

Jones, Margo. *Theatre-in-the-Round,* New York: Harper & Row, 1951.

Kernodle, George R. "Style, Stylization, and Styles of Acting." *Educational Theatre Journal,* December 1960, pp. 251–61.

Murry, J. Middleton. *The Problem of Style.* London: Oxford University Press, 1968.

Nagler, Alois M. *Source Book of Theatrical History.* Orig. title: *Sources of Theatrical History.* New York: Dover Publications, 1952.

Nicoll, Allardyce. *The Development of the Theatre.* 5th ed. New York: Harcourt Brace Jovanovich, 1966.

Nicoll, Allardyce. *World Drama from Aeschylus to Anouilh.* New York: Harcourt Brace Jovanovich, 1949.

Oxenford, Lyn. *Design for Movement.* New York: Theatre Arts Books, 1951.

Prisk, Berneice, and Byers, Jack A. *The Theatre Student: Costuming.* New York: Richards Rosen Press, 1970.

Redgrave, Michael. *Mask or Face.* New York: Theatre Arts Books, 1958.

Reinhardt, Paul D. "Movement in Period Plays." *Educational Theatre Journal,* March 1962, pp. 50–55.

Roberts, Vera Mowry. *On Stage: A History of Theatre.* Rev. ed. New York: Harper & Row, 1974.

Saint-Denis, Michel. *Theatre: The Rediscovery of Style.* New York: Theatre Arts Books, 1969.

Stuart, Donald C. *The Development of Dramatic Art.* New York: Dover Publications, 1928. Paperback reprint.

Wilson, Garff B. "What Is Style in Acting?" *Quarterly Journal of Speech,* April 1955, pp. 127–32.

Index

Freshman: Vocal Analysis of 1 Act —

        Live:
        Radio:
        TV:
        Stage:

Soph: Scarlet Moment Presentation.
Berg

Sr.

Literature: Trialogue   : Scripted
                                    (2-3 People)

Senior: 3 min q 3 Period